THE STONES
OF BRITAIN

A History of Britain through its Geology

Jon Cannon

CONSTABLE

CONSTABLE

First published in Great Britain in 2025 by Constable

1 3 5 7 9 10 8 6 4 2

Copyright © Jon Cannon, 2025

Maps by Jon Cannon and Simon Pascoe

The moral right of the author has been asserted.

A CIP catalogue record for this book is
available from the British Library.

ISBN: 978-1-47211-683-3

Typeset in Minion Pro by SX Composing DTP, Rayleigh, Essex
Printed and bound in Great Britain by Clays Ltd, Elcograf S.p.A.

Papers used by Constable are from well-managed forests
and other responsible sources.

Constable
An imprint of
Little, Brown Book Group
Carmelite House
50 Victoria Embankment
London EC4Y 0DZ

The authorised representative
in the EEA is
Hachette Ireland
8 Castlecourt Centre, Dublin 15,
D15 XTP3, Ireland
(email: info@hbgi.ie)

An Hachette UK Company

www.hachette.co.uk

www.littlebrown.co.uk

To my rocks
Isidore Cyril Cannon (1928–2016)
and Charmian Cannon (1923–2017)
and my greatest loves
Liu Hong, Ann, May and Lily

A map of Britain made of stones collected by Jon during his travels and mounted on the wall in his home.

'The landscape flowed away, back to its source.'
Geoffrey Hill, *Mercian Hymns*, VI (1971)

A Note to the Reader

Stones of Britain is published posthumously. It may be Jon's last book, but his beautifully researched and compelling writing on geology, history and architecture lives on.

While Jon finished the manuscript before his passing, the final touches and illustrations were added at a later date with the help of his beloved wife, Liu Hong Cannon, and good friend, Simon Pascoe. I hope we have done Jon's vision justice.

Contents

PART I

Legend:

Tertiary & Quaternary
Cretaceous
Jurassic

Triassic
Permian

Carboniferous
Devonian

Silurian
Ordovician
Cambrian

Metamorphic
Lewisian
Igneous

Moine Thrust

Great Glen Fault

Highland Boundary Fault

Southern Uplands Fault

Iapetus Suture

The Caledonian Grain

0   50   100
                   miles

Chapter 1

Shaping the scene

We moved from inner London to west Devon in 1974, when I was eleven. One day not long after that we went out for a drive, rounded a corner, and there it was – a dramatic hill of dark, shattered rock; perched at the top was a tiny church: Brentor.

I will never forget that moment. It was as though someone had inserted an enormous key into a keyhole in my heart and turned it. I was at once emotionally overwhelmed and visually thrilled. I wanted to sit and look at it: I also wanted to inhabit it; to climb it. And I wanted to understand it; to know how it came to be there, and to get to grips with my own reaction to it. I've been trying to do so ever since.

So, what did I discover about Brentor? That this turning point in the life of one human being ultimately owes a debt to dramatic tectonic events that took place about 340 million years ago. That Brentor was once a volcano, erupting beneath a shallow sea, and later became a kind of fossil of itself; a dead, hard volcano-shaped lump, buried deep beneath other, younger rocks. That it has only been revealed on the surface again, something of its basic form just about intact, in what are relatively recent times, geologically speaking. That landscapes have come and gone on an unimaginable scale, and that the hard reality of the rocks is as fluid, contingent and dramatic as human history.

I was by no means the first person to have found this landform impressive. The church served a parish, yet it is in the most inconvenient location for miles around; there must have been a very good reason for its founders to put it there. Well over a millennium before that twelfth-century event, other people ringed the foot of the tor with a mighty earthwork. The tor rises through this, a rocky conical finger poking through a rough earthen ring. Both the church and the earthwork are built from the tor itself: the latter by digging and mounding its thin skin of earth (and reinforcing it with local stones), the former by excavating, shaping and transporting its rock (and other rocks that lie nearby).

Each rock had its own long and complex story of assembly, destruction and reassembly before it became part of a building that had itself been reconfigured many times over the centuries. Many less obvious aspects of the tor are man-made, too; despite having an edge of wildness about it, Brentor has been stripped of tree cover by people, and it is our grazing sheep that maintain its rough-cropped grassland. There is an abandoned manganese mine at the base of the tor, and a small quarry on one of its flanks; to make the graveyard, earth had to be carried to the tor-top; within it, human bones are even now adding calcium to the shallow soil.

The categories 'human' and 'natural' are unhelpful here. The power of this place is dependent on the combination of rocky hill, earthwork and church; the latter are made out of the former, enhancements to the landscape made from the landscape itself. There is something architectonic about the tor; there is something crag-like about the church. Architecture is a kind of human place-making; buildings are places made out of other places. People are place-makers.

Such statements can be applied to almost everywhere on the island of Britain, and much of the rest of the world besides. Everywhere, place matters. Landscape, the natural form of the surface of the Earth, cannot be separated from the activities of people throughout history. Landscape and culture are interdependent, and both are laced with the traces of their own pasts. Geology, landscape and history triangulate: geology + people = place.

This book is not simply about geology, or about history; it is about the interaction between the two, and the landscapes that result. My focus is on the island of Britain and the islands immediately offshore (Orkney, the Hebrides and the Scillies are in; Shetland, Ireland, the Isle of Man and the Channel Isles are out). The rocks, of course, continue unheeding below the sea and onto neighbouring land-masses; but the encircling water makes our island a single natural entity; and the story of how the sea has ended up surrounding this particular patch of the Earth's surface is largely a geological one.

As the result of this emphasis, there's also not much in this book about (say) chemicals or fossils; and there is a lot about architecture, and about human events. Such biases might partly be explained by my background: I am an art historian, interested in why material things look the way they do, and how people have marked and manipulated them, and what that tells us about culture, and history, and creativity. I approach the landscape as I would a work of art, one in which nature and humanity both play a crucial role. In doing so, I have tried to guard against determinism, but have been openly subjective: I'm interested as much in exploring character – in how a place feels, and in revealing the associations and themes suggested by the patterns of human life in a place with a given geology – as I am in whether one literally caused the other. But I have tried to seek out stories in which historical events or monuments have clearly been driven or shaped by a pre-existing geological reality, and I call this connection 'geohistorical'. Often the rocks contain potentialities that lie in wait, ever patient, until some concatenation of human events lights upon them and transforms history.

Ultimately, I'd like to help re-enchant our perception of the land beneath us, and to celebrate the human contribution to a grand and elemental story. I want to explain: this is how this island fits together, and what makes Humberside so different to Argyll; Dorset to Ceredigion. I want to help people see their physical environment as something to be entered and surrounded by, to inhabit and be part of, rather than a set of views to be looked at, or driven through blindly following the sat-nav. For this reason I have woven aspects of my own life experience into the narrative: just as nations have geohistories, so do individuals, comprised of the places in which they have lived or which have made the strongest impression on them. If I can help give anyone who lives in or visits this island a sense of the particularity, individuality and personality of landscapes, I will have done my job.

This book is also, against a backdrop of environmental crisis, a plea to see the beauty and greatness that sits alongside destruction in our relationship with the natural world. Our current travails are partly the result of our forgetting that we are a part of the natural environment, not simply an alterer or exploiter of it; an important part, because we are unique among animals in the extent to which we shape its appearance. The beauty of prehistoric stone circles, or of the great hollow mounds of quarried and shaped stone that are the cathedrals, is also the ugliness of the steelworks, the mine and the nuclear power station. That this beauty is flawed only adds to its richness and depth.

This is not a book about wild/natural and human/tamed, of ecology versus destruction; it is a paean to humanity's essential unity with nature, and our contribution to its beauty; an attempt to show how the landscape itself is a compact between humanity and geology, inscribed with visible testaments to past events.

Stone is the oddest thing. We live on a great lump of it hurtling through space. Without it we would have no soil, nor paths for water to make rivers and seas, no life. Yet to us it seems lifeless: dead, solid matter. Think of those strange worlds, the asteroids – barren lumps of pure thing, tiny hurtling landscapes unseen. Yet stone is also endlessly specific, exhaustingly varied, and as intricate, intimate and full of character as a human face. And every living thing on the planet is derived from such raw matter. It's easy to forget it as we move around the landscape, but we would be floppy messes without our calcium-dominated mineraline framework. I said I'd avoid determinism – but it's also true that the stones are really in charge.

Chapter 2

About Britain

About the Earth

I have a piece of Brentor, my life-changing hill in Devon, on my bookshelf. At first glance, this lump of stone just looks rockish: grey, hard, cold. But as the eye focuses in, it's not that simple. The greyness has a blue-green tinge; a reddish shade suffuses part of it. The surface is smooth, almost texture-free, giving it a gnomic, impenetrable quality.

All this is a testament to its origin. Brentor was born as magma poured from a rift in the surface of the Earth into the cooling waters of an ocean. These rapidly fixed it into stone, and they left their traces in the distinctive qualities of this particular rock. The reddish blush tells us that a source of oxygen was nearby, in turn meaning that the water was relatively shallow. So this particular rock comes from the upper part of a small volcanic cone that developed on the sea floor.

The skin of our planet is a shallow thing, a shell of hardened magma. We human beings inhabit it: brief bursts of carbon-based energy all of us. From our perspective the rocks are stable and solid; indeed, we conjure a host of guiding metaphors on that basis. Rock of ages, you are my rock, etc.

But in fact they are constantly, dynamically in motion. It's just that we are too fast, too brief to notice; except when their grand timescale suddenly and briefly keeps pace with our own short and volatile one, usually in the form of violent events: lava flows, landslides, earthquakes.

The rocks – like everything in the universe, it sometimes seems – are in fact caught up in a stately cycle. The stony crust is split into giant plates, on average about 20 miles thick, moving at an average of 8cm a year – that is, about a third faster than your fingernail grows – as convection shifts in the hotter, more mobile world that lies beneath it. Where these tectonic plates are moving apart, magma moves into the gap between them, forming young rocks, a new portion of crust that spreads outwards from its point of origin. This is known as 'seafloor spreading', and it is going on at this moment in the middle of the Atlantic: Iceland sits on a zip-line in the crust, and the island is made of hardened magma that has flowed out of this gap. Volcanoes and lava flows often line such opening scar-lines.

Where the plates come together, portions of crust can collide: an impact that is at once slow and stately and of awesome power. Ultimately, one side will be forced to plunge under the other – 'subduction', this is called – and the two will be conjoined. As they compress, the crust is ruckled like a carpet: enormous mountain ranges are built, basins develop – and, again, strings of volcanoes erupt. The volcanoes of the Mediterranean – Mount Etna, Vesuvius – are caused by this process: in this case, the African tectonic plate is being subducted under the European one. The material that is forced below will eventually be recycled. Some of it may even return to the surface somewhere as the plates move apart. The surface is constantly renewing itself.

The crust has a profound relationship with the upper parts of the earth's interior (indeed the tectonic plates comprise both the crust and the uppermost layer beneath it, the mantle). It likewise interacts with the other entities which stop our planet from being a dead and rocky desert: the life-giving water and the air which shifts across its surface. Each of these elements conducts a kind of dance with the others.

For example, the water and the air erode those rocks which are exposed to them, and this can change their character and appearance. A portion of crust might carry both rocks that are solidified magma – effusions resulting from the shifting of the plates – and rocks that are the compacted detritus of erosion.

The latter, which are called sedimentary rocks, dominate the surface of Earth, and generate the most fertile soils. As a result, although 95 per cent of the crust is made of one kind of hardened magma or another, the landscape we experience is mostly sedimentary.

As these processes go through their cycles of destruction and creation, the surface of our planet changes. Seen from space, Earth is an intense marble of blue, white and green: the white moves hourly, but the balance of blue and green only changes over thousands of years. It reflects the distribution of the two main types of crust.

The water of the oceans mostly covers the areas where the crust is thin (from 4.5 miles deep): this is relatively young material, made from magma that welled up as a result of seafloor spreading, and is known as oceanic crust. Dry land is mostly where the crust is thicker, older, more complex (up to 50 miles thick): this is continental crust.

Precisely where the water sits in relation to these thickenings of the rocky skin will be subject to constant change. Much of the comparatively shallow sea that surrounds most continents sits on top of continental crust; while under the right circumstances – Iceland and Hawaii are prominent examples – oceanic crust can appear above the waters.

In spite of this, from the perspective of human beings, what is dry and what is wet, what is sea and what is land, can seem immutable. It is also crucial to how we live our lives. The sea is at once a barrier and a mode of communication; the land is where we live, and its rocks supply many of the materials on which we depend, from metals to the soil itself, and guide the locations where we grow our food, keep our animals, build our cities and make our roads. Many of the identities we adopt – which nation we are part of, for example, and how cultures form and interact with one another – will be conditioned by the lie of the land, and that in turn is dependent on the arrangement of those rocks exposed at the surface.

About Britain

This is the situation in which all human beings have found themselves: on dry land, trying to work with the environment around us, using it to make food, shelter, tools, culture, and on a particular patch of planet Earth: Britain.

This is a complex chunk of continental crust, much of it very ancient, which emerges above the water at about 54° north and 2° west, and is about 700 miles long north to south as the crow flies, and much narrower east to west. The length of this island is one of its most characteristic properties: it can be balmy in Brighton when it is sub-arctic on Birsay; it is as far from John O'Groats to Southampton as it is from there to Bilbao.

Britain is the largest island in an archipelago that sits on the edge of things: just off the north-western corner of a continental mass which extends as far as China, and only 100 miles from the submerged edge of the continental crust. We are thus placed in relation to our nearest continental land-mass rather as the Solar System is situated vis-à-vis the Milky Way: an outer arm of something vast.

On this island, the higher ground tends to lie in the north and the west, where it is also furthest from the continent, and nearest to the Atlantic Ocean – and also closest to Ireland, the other large island in our archipelago. The rocks here tend to be older, too. Most of the younger, softer, lower ground is to the south and the east, facing the continent. The coast is more complex and indented to the west, simpler to the east. Only three rivers are more than 150 miles long: the Severn flows west to where its mouth opens towards Ireland and the great ocean beyond; the Thames and the Trent (via the Humber), flow east, into the shallower North Sea, from which the continent can be reached relatively easily.

This distinction of highland and lowland is a fundamental one. A series of associations riff from it: geologically ancient and complex and geologically young and simple; hard and soft; fertile and infertile; rich in metals and rich in farmland; empty and populated; 'wild' and 'civilised'; north and south. The two categories are truly the geohistorical *yin* and *yang* of the island as a whole.

After all, we are utterly dependent on the materials of the Earth; our resources ultimately derive from what is in the crust; and the story of the rocks gives meaning to what we see about us. Yet the gap between geological time and human time is profound. We will be exploring the results of a very recent flourishing of activity, on land that is very old. Both are complex stories, and they interact and cross-fertilise in sometimes unexpected ways.

To explore this and other patterns we will move through Britain rock-type by rock-type in the order that they were created, explaining the origin of each group of rocks, exploring the human world that inhabits them, and painting a picture of the characteristics that result: as if human and geological activity were two aspects of a single personality. The result will be a composite portrait of man and the rocks, in which each constituent part has a voice of its own.

Chapter 3

About time

About geological time

Brentor is a short, stiff ascent of perhaps fifteen minutes. Breath and heartbeat alike quicken as you make your way over rocky, sheep-cropped grass, passing the abandoned workings of a nineteenth-century manganese mine, and a few seconds later, a massive series of Iron Age earthworks. Then the hill steepens and obvious signs of human activity fall away – until one approaches the hill's highest point, atop which sits St Michael's church, a building of the mid-twelfth century.

Inside, the air stills. A quiet power seems to fill the space. Sit in a pew; let your mind, and the rhythms of your body, slow. Gradually, time itself seems to thicken. Everything feels as permanent and unchanging as the rock on which it is built. Yet the walls bear the traces of over 800 years of alteration – new windows, small additions – and the hillfort at the foot of the tor is perhaps a millennium older than the church. That seems a long time – until you consider that the stones of which this church is made were formed over 330 million years ago.

Start to count your way backwards through time. It takes ten minutes or so to reach 800, the age of the church; perhaps another ten to reach the Iron Age.

Carrying on to 300 million is no small task. Going at eight hours a day, because you also need to eat and sleep, you would be sitting in that pew for well over thirty-five years. Perhaps the still power inside this building is the bottled essence of time itself.

The rocks of Brentor are not themselves especially old. This planet coalesced out of the dust of space about 4,600 million years ago (Ma). Though there are surviving rocks from as early as 4,000 million years ago, these are very rare. The most ancient British rocks are in the far north-west of Scotland; they are about 2,800 million years old, and are themselves among the oldest in the world. But almost everything else on our island was formed in the last 500–550 million years. Perhaps, then, we can think of Brentor's rocks as middle-aged.

Thirty-five-plus years is a very long time to sit in a pew. Let's try reducing geological time to fit twelve hours of a day. The first four–five hours cover the Precambrian period, during which the oldest rocks were formed. The ensuing seven–eight hours are divided into eleven further periods of various lengths: the first of these, the Cambrian, is when life starts to become obvious in the rock-record: a signal development, because many of the rocks that have been most useful to human beings are themselves formed from the detritus of living creatures. The fifth, the 59-million-year Carboniferous, is notable for an explosion of plant life, which is the source of fossil fuels. This is when the rocks of Brentor came into being.

Each of these periods has its own geohistorical story. But much of what we'll explore together only becomes visible right at the end of our twelve-hour sit-in. It is less than ten minutes ago that the landforms of today begin to develop. With less than a minute to go, the Homo genus evolves, and we start to measure time not by the changing geology but by the materials people use, themselves usually derived from the Earth. These time-periods start with the Palaeolithic, or Old Stone Age – during which, in the last 0.003 of a minute of our day, Homo sapiens becomes a permanent inhabitant of Britain.

Compared to the rest of time, the human presence on this planet is little more than a carbon blink. Yet we have done much to change the landscape. We have to bear both geological and human time in mind as we explore the relationship between our species and the rocks.

We jumped around in history as we climbed Brentor. This is true everywhere in Britain: its multi-layered, historically rich landscape is one of this island's great treasures. As we move through our island's geological story, the historical jumps we make will be many and varied. So let's start with a historical framework of humanity-and-the-rocks: an overall narrative of human history, of people and geology as it has played out on this island.

About human time

The stone ages

Human history, like that of the rocks, begins with a great gulf of time in which much remains unknown: a kind of human Precambrian. The Homo genus has existed for 2.5–3 million years; Homo sapiens for over 300,000 of these. For almost all this time, stone tools were our central technological achievement, making them the longest-lasting technology in our entire story. Crucial discoveries such as how to ignite fire were also partly dependent on geology (flint rapped against iron pyrites nodules being an early technique). In Britain this Palaeolithic begins with our first known (and pre Homo sapiens) human inhabitants, around 500,000 years ago. Thanks to waves of glaciation, our island was empty of people for long periods thereafter.

The ice thawed about 14–15,000 years ago, only to briefly return; so it is a few thousand years later that habitation of Britain becomes continuous to the present. From this period we start to see a palpable improvement in the sophistication of stone tools; and the baking of clay to make objects. Development is divided into two stages: the Mesolithic, or Middle Stone Age, from about 11,600 years ago; and the Neolithic, or New Stone Age. That, from about 6,000 years ago (or 4000 BC), is when the pace of change increases: agriculture is spreading into Britain, and at roughly the same time, people start to make a permanent and visual impact on the landscape.

But people had always had an intimate understanding of the lie of the land. The hills and plains offered clues as to where sources of sustenance and shelter might be found. And earth materials had become more than merely tools. Neanderthal people had used ochre – the oldest and most ubiquitous source of colour in human culture – to colour things. Earth pigments were also used by Homo sapiens when, about 40,000 years ago, we started producing fully fledged works of art.

About 26,000 years ago, a man's body was placed in a limestone cave called Paviland, on the South Wales coast: an opening in a cliff with a view of the game-filled plain that is now the Severn Estuary. His remains were accompanied by artefacts of limestone, flint, chert and volcanic rhyolite, and coloured using ochre.

This is the oldest ritualised burial site in Europe, and it displays an interest both in its setting in the landscape, and in the materials of the Earth. Perhaps, even, an awareness of the power of features like mountains and caves formed a model for architecture when it came along. Although the first true works of monumental stone architecture are in eastern Turkey, and date to 11–12,000 years ago, the story really takes off in the fourth millennium BC, when we start to see ambitious buildings in various places: Peru, Mesopotamia – and the Atlantic fringe of north-west Europe, Britain included.

Neolithic lithophilia

It is in the Neolithic that humans become creatures that build monuments – by which I mean permanent structures of stone – and reconfigure landscapes on a grand scale. In Britain it's a story that starts with places of gathering and of burial. The former come in the arrangement of rough discontinuous circlets of earthen ditches, arranged to enclose hilltops; these are known as causewayed enclosures, and remains of feasting have been found in them. They mark the start of a long tradition in which people select prominent hills for the location of monuments.

The burial places are dominated by communal burial mounds, often longer than they are wide, and of drystone (that is, the pieces of stone are not cemented together) or earthen construction, but containing elaborate drystone structures – tunnels, groups of rooms in which bones were deposited. These structures have various names: long barrows, chambered cairns, long mounds, and more. They are the first true architecture in

Britain, and among the oldest ambitious, permanent buildings in the world. With their hill-like exteriors and cave-like interiors, they remind us that death is where people have always been most inevitably and profoundly connected to geology, reduced to dust, interred within the bones of the Earth, becoming a part of place.

In order to bury a body, after all, you have to remove earth from the ground. Pile this material over the burial and you leave behind a mound. Such a mound is also immediately a monument, its very presence fixing into the landscape the memory of those who have passed.

Alongside partying and mourning, there was also work, and industrial monuments are another landscape-changing development of this period. We see the first quarries and mines, created in a thirst to find specific stones. Such early extraction sites are rare, partly because many have been returned to over the centuries since, destroying the evidence of their own origins.

It can be hard to work out why one buried layer of Cretaceous flint (for example) was chosen over another for tool-making. Clearly, Neolithic people had an intense engagement with the subtly varying qualities of differing rocks. Some of the resulting tools are exquisitely crafted, and very beautiful. The most highly valued tool-making stones were traded over hundreds of miles, making them the first significant 'man-made erratics': rocks moved by people far from their point of geological origin. Most remarkable are the rare and exquisite jadeite axes sourced near the Alps and transported to Britain. Specific stones – quartz in particular – had strong cultural or religious associations, and are found in many ritual contexts.

Quartz is a good examples of the way geology can translate itself into human history. It is made of silica: one of the most common of the minerals from which all rocks are made. It can be very hard, but fractures along clean, sharp-edge lines: hence the popularity of flint, which is also made from silica, for making tools. Such qualities are also cause of the steep, high rubble-covered peaks of quartzite mountains, a related material. In the form of quartz, it is silica's translucent shininess that has attracted people, for both its beauty, and its symbolic implications: perhaps it was thought to be connected to light itself. Distracting-looking rocks have generated disproportionate attention ever since.

All in all, Neolithic culture displays a richness of response to the materials of the Earth, a quality I call 'lithophilia'. As the Neolithic draws to a close, this tendency starts to spread out across entire landscapes. Having been in use for 400 years or so, long barrows and their ilk are sealed up or abandoned. New monuments appear, with a new level of ambition, as areas several square miles across are reconfigured into open-air settings for ritual events.

Everything is subject to erosion, be it a mountain or a monument. The more permanent the material, the longer it will last. Because of this, mountains and hills are often made of rock's harder layers, and such rocks also often happen to be relatively old. In a comparable way, we have lost the large numbers of prehistoric monuments that were made of timber, and many of those of earth, leaving us with larger numbers of those made of stone. These stone monuments are most common in places where geology has delivered quantities of loose, or nearly loose, rocks that required little or no quarrying. It aids their preservation that such places are often also relatively infertile, so there has been less motivation to destroy them. Stone circles, stone rows, cairns, standing stones and henges (circular earthen banks with a ditch inside them) survive in numbers in such landscapes.

Some such structures boil the relationship of human and rock down to their profoundest, most elemental core. Standing stones are at once human-like presences and visual connections between land and sky; cairns, like long barrows, are basically mounds: that most proto-geological of architectonic forms. Both are still being created: gravestones are a kind of standing stone, and mark the presence of an absent human being; cairns, which inevitably cross-fertilise with burial mounds as a monument-type, are ubiquitous as markers of upland routes and peaks: 'a crowd-sourced communication system', the climber Will Gadd calls them. Figures such as Captain James Cook built them in various parts of the globe, early markers of the reach of industrial-era British power.

Other Neolithic innovations were particularly prescient. In Orkney, drystone walling was used to make ambitious domestic dwellings. At Stonehenge, Wiltshire, rocks were hammered into roughly rectilinear blocks. In many places, rocks were carved, sometimes with enigmatic abstract patterns, but more often with 'cup and ring marks', turning flattish exposed rocks into what look like arcane maps. To do this required tools harder than the rock itself, such as quartz. People are at once making sense of the places they find themselves in, and making their mark upon them.

Though the Bluestones there are more famous, the moving of the 25-ton blocks of sarsen stone which dominate Stonehenge from their source 18 miles to the north, and the effort involved in shaping them, is a particularly vivid reminder of the danger and sheer brute physical effort that is integral to humanity's relationship with the rocks. Every great stone building has had to have its site cleared, foundations dug, and blocks of stone laboriously shaped.

The arrangement of Neolithic early monuments displays an intimate sense of the lie of the land. Henges often sit in broad valleys, near to the heads of rivers; long barrows in locations where they sit on the skyline when approached from certain angles. These are open-air architectures, enhancing and enriching the landscape, whether to create a setting for ritual or to help forge relationships with unseen forces: the ancestors, the gods, the elements, the skies. From Orkney to Bodmin Moor, Neolithic and early Bronze Age people reconfigured entire landscapes.

The metal ages

Towards the end of this period, as the term 'Bronze Age' implies, people make another 'Earth-shattering' discovery. Again originating in the Middle East, this is the revelation that certain oddly coloured rocks with a distinctive consistency, when subjected to extraordinary heat, will melt; and that they can then be shaped, and as they cool will become hard, retaining their new form.

Copper was found first, but copper and tin ore smelted together and became metal at a lower temperature than copper alone – one that was also harder, and less prone to corrosion: bronze. Tools made of such materials were more effective than those made of stone; they had a lustre that could compete even with quartz.

It is hard to overstate the practical and cultural implications of the discovery of metal. From this point until written records begin we mark time by its key stages: the Bronze (from c.2600 BC) and Iron (from c.800 BC) ages. Trade in ore becomes a generator of wealth and social change. Sources of ore, which in the Bronze Age included the English south-west, North Wales, Ireland and the Rhineland, became important new industrial sites.

As the metal becomes increasingly significant, achievements in stone take a back seat. It's not that its potential is forgotten: though long mounds are replaced by smaller (mostly) circular cairns and barrows made of earth, each usually containing an individual burial, stones might be placed decoratively or symbolically around them, or the body placed in a small stone coffin-like chamber known as a cist. Stones were still used for tools and hearths; hard, rough-textured ones were selected for the querns needed to grind grain, an important stone tool since the Palaeolithic era.

But the technological cutting edge was bronze, and to make it, ores of copper and tin had to be brought together, as well as the sandstones, clays and limestones that could protect furnace sites from heat or help regulate their temperature. The supply lines required have been credited with driving the notable cosmopolitanism of Bronze Age society, including the major migration into Britain that brought with it the 'Beaker' culture, known for its distinctive and impressive clay pots. These people may have brought with them the Celtic languages, descendants of which are still spoken. They may have been attracted by the ores of Britain: Cornwall has some of the richest deposits of tin in Europe.

Unlike bronze, iron was ubiquitous (if varied in quality and accessibility), and society initially became more insular when, in the Iron Age, this metal started to dominate. The workmanship of some of the resulting objects is extraordinary.

This is also the era of the hillfort: deep-banked earthen (and sometimes mounded stone) enclosures on prominent hills, especially in southern Britain; there is one at Brentor. These were major monuments in the landscape, and emphatic statements of political power, often capable of being used defensively. Their dramatic, highly visible hilltop sites are a premier example of what Nicholas Crane, a geographer and explorer, calls 'stone thrones', a coining I have adopted in this book. Promontory forts, their function obscure, cut off the tips of headlands. Mounded stones were used to build crannogs, artificial islands, in lochs and other watery sites, especially in the far north. In some areas whole drystone villages of roundhouses were created. And towards the end of the period we see signs of new architectural ambition.

These include structures in which some stones have been shaped and corbelled (in the underground fogous of the far south-west, for example); and proto-towns, ringed by earthworks, known as oppida. These are most common in the south-east, a region where we also see metal used to make coins – an innovation that came from the Roman world.

Drystone architecture is particularly impressive in the far north, where there are 'duns' – circular drystone fortifications, often on hilltops; and, centered around Caithness and Orkney, a true stone architecture: the 'broch', a tower-like defensive building – that at Mousa, Shetland, is still over 13m/43ft high. These unique and ambitious works suggest all kinds of future architectural possibilities, but were to be rapidly upstaged by something new.

One only has to glance at a broch to see that drystone architecture can be powerful and impressive. Yet ultimately, the technique had limits and was to become a second-best, a way of building restricted to low-grade structures and boundary walls. It's thus easy to underestimate: yet in those parts of rural Britain where smallish pieces of stone are easy to source (which usually means uplands), the landscape is still largely divided, often on a heroic scale, by drystone walls. They stand alongside cairns and standing stones as one of the most longstanding of building-types: prehistoric techniques that are still with us. There are said to be 12,000 miles of them in the United Kingdom, and though most date to the early modern Enclosure movement, a few – such as those on West Penwith, Cornwall – are truly ancient.

Roman lithophilia

The downgrading of drystone building techniques begins with a culture which, once again, brings innovations with it that originated in the Middle East. The use of metal tools to carve stone to a fine level of detail had begun there; also came the use of dried clay to make bricks, and the knowledge that a kind of stone glue could be made by mixing rubble or sand with a binder (often quicklime, made by burning limestone).

The Romans also brought with them the use of concrete, effectively a stone-hard mortar; the firing of clay to make strong, waterproof bricks; and the use of the arch to span wide spaces. Buildings that used these techniques could be stronger and more elaborate than anything before. Such structures will now dominate our architectural story; it is a story that matters, because stone architecture is the glue between geology and history, people and landscape.

The Roman invasion began in AD 43. It was probably partly driven by a desire for the island's metal ores. With it come our first written accounts of events, bringing prehistory to an end, and creating a much more refined calibration of time: centuries, years, decades, even individual days. We see other step-changes, too.

The Romans founded our first true cities and towns; settlements which were laid out to the same rules across the Empire. Roman cities were less responsive to the specifics of place and geology than earlier monuments had been. They were a new kind of place, configured in grids and lines; in Britain, no culture since has been as relentlessly orthogonal in its planning.

Even the blocks of stone from which the better buildings are made are shaped into perfect, regular cubes and oblongs. An idea arguably nascent at Stonehenge now becomes a whole craft: masonry. A sophisticated language of delicately carved forms helps give these buildings their expressive power. Stone art works, from mosaics to sculptures, develop: statues turn the standing stone into a vividly realised image of a human; stone inscriptions make words permanent. A whole range of new or previously barely existent occupations – masons, architects, quarry workers – develop. Construction of the Roman road network alone might have consumed almost 40 million tons of aggregate, which is crucial to road construction.

The Romans, then, were the source of many aspects of the man-made landscape that remain familiar. Though standing Roman structures are quite rare (no single building survives complete, unless one includes high, battered stretches of town wall) substantial Roman ruins must have been very visible in earlier times, and the Roman achievement shapes the modern landscape in all kinds of ways. This is less marked in the far west, but only completely absent in the northern two-thirds of Scotland – indeed, in the far north hillforts, abandoned in the south, remained in use well into the medieval era – and it reaches a peak on the lowlands that dominate the south-east third of our island. Here a whole series of surviving routes and settlements, from London to the A1, have Roman origins.

Other historical patterns will recur over the centuries to come: a major concentration of wealth in the south-east; cultural differences between highland and lowland; the emergence of important boundaries in the west and north, often coinciding with deep-seated geological divides. Hadrian's Wall, the Scottish border and the ancient and profound geological join known as the Iapetus Suture lie remarkably close together.

The Romans also imported some particularly exotic man-made erratics: marble from Italy and elsewhere, porphyry (for mosaics) from Egypt; querns of Rhineland lava. Equally remarkable was their systematic identification of native resources. Roman surveyors scoured the landscape, finding – or hugely increasing the exploitation of – materials such as salt, lead, iron, copper, silver and gold. They identified almost every decent carvable stone south of the Scottish Highlands. They must have had an amazing rough-and-ready grasp of what we would call geology.

Post-Roman changes

Roman achievements go into a period of occlusion from the fourth century AD, when Britain is abandoned to its fate, settlements fall into ruin, and tribal groups from northern Europe colonise the lowland parts of the island. For a few hundred years, stone quarrying and mineral extraction cease. These Anglo-Saxon immigrants carve out a series of kingdoms whose boundaries can be very geo-sensitive: East Anglia occupies a great hip of young land in the far east; Mercia, in the Midlands, is largely on Permian-Triassic rocks.

The indigenous Britons hung on, albeit increasingly pushed to upland areas, where their Romanised culture survived. Throughout the island, kingdoms competed and coalesced. The Irish Sea was – not for the first time, as something similar happened in the Neolithic – a central cultural circulation point, competing for significance as a focus with the gentler country of the far south-east, where European ideas have generally found their *entrepôts*. In the north, people from Ireland established a kingdom which played a fundamental role in the development of the Scottish nation; they brought with them the Gaelic language, even as English was emerging further south.

The achievements of this 'early medieval' period are considerable. In the sixth and seventh centuries, Christianity, left behind by the Romans, became visible in major monuments and structures, stimulated in Briton-dominated upland areas by missions from Ireland, especially to the north; and in the Anglo-Saxon lowlands, starting with Kent, by missions from Rome. As these developments spread, the cultural traditions of British and Anglo-Saxon areas cross-fertilised and an 'insular' culture developed, politically loyal to local kings, but – after a period of adjustment – spiritually loyal to Rome.

The landscapes created by Christian culture were profoundly influenced by European example. In the wake of the Roman mission (596–7), the Anglo-Saxons rediscovered stone architecture and the idea of the town, locating their first churches in former Roman settlements and building them with stone 'quarried' from Roman ruins. Metals were recycled from Iron Age, Roman and imported objects; the artefacts that result are exquisite. The garnets on the sixth/seventh-century Sutton Hoo helmet, product of the then-pagan East Angles, had originally come from somewhere in Asia.

Though surviving buildings of the Anglo-Saxon era are rare, there are churches with Anglo-Saxon elements in most counties, and a handful survive almost complete. As a shaper of the landscape we inhabit, this period is hugely significant. As urban life and stone architecture were reborn in earnest, the site – and often the detailed footprint – of the centre of many of our cities, towns and villages, as well as the boundaries that define parishes and counties, was defined. All this was given a distinctive twist in eastern England and northern and western Scotland, where there were major Viking colonies (parts of Scotland remained under Norse control until the fifteenth century). The cultural variety of this period is most obvious in place names, for most of these were coined at this period, too.

The landscape is constantly describing itself to us. It mostly does so in Anglo-Saxon/old English, old British/Brythonic, old Norse/Norn, or Gaelic, with a few, usually younger, French, Latin and modern English additions. Gaelic alone has at least ten different words for hill-shapes; including types of slope and ridge, and twenty-eight have been identified in Anglo-Saxon. Sometimes they have a stratigraphy of their own: Pendle Hill in Lancashire means 'hill hill hill' if you deconstruct its layers of Brythonic, Norse and Old English.

Britain at this time developed a unique art form of carved standing stones: the 'Celtic crosses'. Once everywhere, these are particularly well preserved and artistically impressive in the northern part of the island. The cross is of course an anthropomorphic symbol, representing as it does the crucified Christ (and often erected as a monument to the dead); an image also often evoked in the plans of churches. As demand for buildable and carvable stone increases, we see (from the seventh century) the first post-Roman stone-quarrying, ultimately leading not only to the rediscovery of many high-quality stone sources, but also to the identification for the first time of carvable stones in Highland Scotland. Sources of metal ore were also rediscovered: mostly iron, but by the Norman Conquest lead, too.

In the course of this period, Britain gradually became a Christian island. Other gradual changes were equally significant: pushed by Anglo-Saxon migration into the less fertile western uplands, settlement in areas inhabited by Britons remained largely non-urban and scattered, with small, isolated churches and strongholds, and many visible prehistoric sites. These characteristics have many causes, not least the simple fact that this is mostly tough geology to turn into productive land; its rocks are often difficult to shape, but can easily be found littering hillsides and shores in usable pieces.

Picture a tiny church, far from any village and sitting close to the ocean edge, overlooked by a rocky hill draped in prehistoric remains. It's a scene one might find anywhere from the isle of Lewis to Penwith: a landscape we quickly think of as 'Celtic'. The power of such places may be an accident of geology-as-history, but that does not dim their impact: it is a power that has done much to shape the distinctive ethnic identities of western and northern Britain.

Medieval lithophilia

As we move past the Norman conquest of 1066 and enter the medieval period, Wales is a patchwork of kingdoms, while both Scotland and England are united under single kings. England is the largest, wealthiest and most powerful of these entities. People everywhere are building ambitious stone structures (especially churches) and their culture is intimately connected both to Ireland and to the European mainland. London, former capital of Roman Britannia, in Britain's south-east is well on its way to becoming the capital of England, and the largest settlement on the island.

By this time, too, an elaborate network of extractive industries has developed. In areas with reasonable building stone, every village has a small local quarry. Building stone and metal ore were sourced mainly on escarpments and valley-sides with access to navigable waterways, a rule that holds true until the advent of powered transport. Such sites were good places to look for resources, as changes in slope often signal changes in the underlying rocks. They were also of little use for farming, and their angled sides made them relatively easy to dig in to.

The cost of moving stone could be significantly greater than that of excavating it (the Salcombe stone used at fourteenth-century Exeter cathedral cost 2d a ton to quarry and 14d a ton to transport). The use of high-quality stones far from their source became an indicator of wealth. Buildings whose walls are made of imported limestone, for example, have a conspicuous grandeur in areas such as East Anglia, where the local building stone is mostly rough flint. Brick – lost since the Roman era – reappears in the twelfth century; by the end of the medieval period it has become a serious alternative to cut stone. Roof- and floor-tiles are known from this era, too, the latter often covered in decorative designs. As for metal, by about 1300, 1,000 tons of iron ore were being extracted annually in England, and more imported; though England's chief 'industry' was wool production: a product dependent on the grazing potential of its heaths and grasslands, which often relate to calcareous, limestone geologies.

All this is a context for the remarkable lithophiliac achievements of the period, which reaches its apogee in religious monuments. Thousands of churches survive. An astonishing rebuilding of the greater cathedrals and monasteries took place in the forty–fifty years after the Norman Conquest, which at Winchester included a cathedral that was also one of the largest buildings on the planet. Within a century, as an 'Anglo-Norman' culture developed, smaller churches – including that at Brentor – and monastic houses were being built and rebuilt in their thousands, as architecture morphed from round-arched Romanesque into gravity-defying Gothic, and then continued a process of ceaseless, restless stylistic change over the centuries to come. Almost all this was done in mortared cut stone, aided and abetted by quantities of strengthening iron and illuminating glass, both dependent on the materials of the earth.

High-status secular buildings were impressive, too; castles, which survive in their hundreds, were partly designed for defence, but also to impress and visually embody the chivalric values of the day. Many stone-built houses also once existed, though most were constructed of timber – vast quantities of which were also used in the construction of the stone buildings. Again, many survive, especially from towards the end of the period. There is a geological dimension to this material: woodland was thickest in areas that had little agricultural use, whether because the soils were dominated by heavy clay, or were too sandy to retain moisture well.

Medieval people built on Classical achievements by theorising about stone. For the first time – though there are hints in the cults of ancient Rome, and much educated guesswork around Neolithic ideas – we can say detailed, locally specific things about the resulting 'noosphere' (Teilhard to Chardin) or 'mythosphere' (David Miles). This refers to the ideas, myths and reactions to the landscape that we carry around in our heads. I often imagine it as an invisible stratigraphic layer, lying on top of the rocks and earth.

Rocks were deemed to be alive and, like all Creation, riven with messages from God. The cathedrals are partly inspired by Biblical descriptions of Heaven as a city built of shining, precious jewels (Revelation, 19:1–21), creating a new demand for carvable stones that looked precious, such as the polishable limestones of the Isle of Purbeck, Dorset. Alabaster, with its lustrous, flesh-like quality, became popular for monuments to the dead. Gems – blood-red ruby, blue sapphire – from India and Burma made their way into prized items of gold or silver, prized both for their lustre and their symbolic colouring. The colour of sapphires symbolised heaven; rubies were associated with passion, protection, and love. The white and rose-pink stones conspicuous in the east end of Canterbury cathedral, it has been argued, are intended to evoke the symbolic red blood and white brains spilled at the martyrdom of St Thomas Becket.

Locally, the mythosphere filled with stories about the landscape. Often these intimately reflect, and seek to explain, the qualities of stones and landforms. These are hard to date, but are dominated by medieval figures such as Arthur, Robin Hood, and the saints, making it likely that many took form in this period.

In the fifteenth, sixteenth and seventeenth centuries, culture was recognisably heading somewhere new: more questioning, more entrepreneurial; we are passing from the 'late medieval' to the early modern periods. Metal was in ever-increasing demand: lead, for example, was needed for everything from bullets to printing presses. Much of the wealth of church and aristocracy alike remained derived from the control of such mineral resources. Architecturally, Gothic was replaced by a series of Renaissance-inspired styles – Jacobethan, Palladian, Baroque – and with these came a demand for crisp, white stones: marble from Italy, limestone from Portland, Dorset.

In religion, upheaval known as the Reformation led to the rejection of papal authority in England and Wales in 1534, and Scotland in 1560; the island became officially Protestant and Catholics were often persecuted. The English dissolution of the monasteries, from 1536, left in its wake a wave of monumental ruins second only to that left behind by the Romans; the resulting redistribution of wealth from the Church to the aristocracy stimulated the construction of newly ambitious country houses.

In Scotland the monasteries died more gradually, but from 1688 cathedrals joined them as an institution that was no longer required, and many of both types of church fell into ruin. Surviving medieval churches were more completely remodelled or replaced to suit new forms of worship than in England.

In both nations, building stone and lead were robbed from abandoned churches and used in new buildings. There is nothing new about this recycling of stone; another sense in which architecture is like geology. Buildings can be made of other buildings, just as stones can be made of other stones.

From now on, secular buildings rather than religious ones are the main focus of architectural effort and innovation. But changes in religious architecture continued to be significant. Nonconformist chapels proliferated, especially in the nineteenth century, when as a result of Catholic emancipation they were belatedly joined by new Catholic churches. New places of worship were also built, and old ones rebuilt, by the established Protestant churches; especially in Scotland, where the split known as the Great Disruption (1843) was a major event. Synagogues, and more recently mosques, temples and gurdwaras, are architectural embodiment of the waves of inward migration of the industrial and modern eras.

Industrial-era lithophilia

The eighteenth and nineteenth centuries outdo even the Neolithic and Roman eras as the greatest turning point in the story of humanity and the stones in Britain. Indeed – though structures such as Stonehenge are justifiably world-famous – this is when the events on this island would be an indispensable element to any history of humanity, thanks to the industrial revolution, which reconfigured the landscape.

At this time, factories, textile mills and mines proliferated, their location intimately tied to sources of power – especially coal – and metal ore, and thus to geology. Coal became so important that areas of industrial production far from its deposits – the textile mills of the Cotswolds, the ironworks of the Weald – withered on the vine.

Large tracts of the landscape – especially in Lancashire and Yorkshire, South Wales and the Black Country, central Scotland and Cornwall – developed a near-apocalyptic appearance as people extracted the innards of the Earth, with little regard for either her well-being or that of the environment. Deep mines developed: artificial caves on a scale previously unimaginable, their vertical shafts dependent on mechanically assisted drainage, ventilation and extraction. In the eighteenth century, the coal pit at Whitehaven in Cumbria extended around 300m down; a century later, three mines, over 1,000m deep, were among the 1,000-plus known to have existed around Wigan, Lancashire. Though we have been tunnelling in pursuit of rocks since the Neolithic, we humans had now truly become a burrowing species.

By one estimate, over 25 billion tons of British coal has been removed from the Earth since 1760; by another, that's enough of the material to cover our island to a depth of 4.25m (I've not converted tons to tonnes in this book as the ratio is almost 1:1). Almost all this comes from rocks of the Carboniferous period, which are also host to many metal ores, giving that period a particularly powerful geohistorical story.

The ease with which coal and other heavy materials could be transported was also transformed. The Earth was further excavated and reshaped in the form of tunnels and embankments. The resulting turnpike roads, canals and railways carved a new series of linear networks across the island. From the eighteenth century, 4,000 miles of canals were built; having flowed almost entirely along natural routes (freshwater conduits and river straightenings were the main exceptions), water was artificially redirected in the interests of the economy. In the first flush of railway-building, between 1834 and 1841, 54 million cubic metres of earth and rock were excavated. The economic impact was staggering: a single horse-drawn barge could pull ten times the weight of coal that could be hauled by road, reducing its price by half.

At the same time, people migrated in vast numbers from the countryside to rapidly expanding towns and cities – in 1750, only 15 per cent of people lived in urban environments; 150 years later this had grown to 85 per cent. Cities were built that were unlike any that had gone before, again guided by proximity to coal and other resources. Glasgow,

Manchester and Birmingham replaced Bristol, Norwich and York as the major urban areas outside London. New architectures – railway stations, factories, mills – proliferated in these places.

New building materials included ambitious structures of iron and later, concrete and steel, which were dependent on new technologies, from modern 'hydraulic' concrete (from the 1820s) to mass-produced steel (from mid-century). This alloy of iron and carbon can take compressive pressure in a way that iron alone cannot, opening up vast new architectural possibilities. Industrial-era buildings became cathedral-like in ambition. By the nineteenth century a variety of architectural styles was being employed to decorate such buildings.

Housing, too was transformed. Serried rows of terraced houses dominated the new settlements. A forest of chimneys rose from their roofs. Once, a chimney had been a marker of wealth, now it became an essential way to lift coal smoke away from human beings. No home or industrial site was complete without one. In mid-nineteenth-century Glasgow, the chimneys of the St Rollox and J. Townsend chemical works were, at 133m and 138m high respectively, the tallest in the world. The owners of such businesses used their profits to build new country houses. Of the ten richest nineteenth-century aristocrats, four derived much of their wealth from minerals.

A substantial amount of human misery accompanied these developments, and not only in the mines, factories and mills. The near-free labour provided by slavery created much of the wealth that funded early industry. In Liverpool, as the Rev. William Bagshaw Stevens put it in 1797, 'every Brick is cemented to its fellow Brick by the blood and sweat of Negroes [the then-normal term for Black people]'; he could have been talking about Bristol, or Glasgow, or many other places. British emigrants seeking a better life included miners and masons, whose skills left their traces in quarries, mines and buildings everywhere from Australia to Argentina. The British Empire became the largest political entity on Earth. Meanwhile, the nations of Britain – Wales as early as 1283, Scotland from 1702, Ireland (or most of it) until 1922 – coalesced under one Crown, based in Westminster.

Movements of people were echoed by those of stone, resulting in a new and bewildering range of man-made erratics. Some of this flowed inwards: the table-tops of Chatsworth House, Derbyshire, are a veritable museum of the world's prettier rocks. But this is dwarfed by the volume of subterranean Britain that ended up in other parts of the world. By 1900, 85 per cent of the coal consumed on the planet came from Britain, which dominated the market for other earth materials, too. British coal fuelled the rail networks which carved up continents, and which in turn facilitated the exploitation of earth resources in other parts of the planet.

An agricultural revolution took place alongside this. New fertilisers were developed, often dependent on earth materials such as lime. Some of these developments had originated several centuries earlier, but took on a new urgency. In much of lowland England, fields previously held in common were enclosed and divided into farms; in Scotland, entire communities were swept away, their land given over to game and sheepwalk, in the Clearances – a process that could be traumatic and violent. The landscape of that nation was also changed by a wave of foundations of towns or burghs, which peaked in the fifteenth to seventeenth centuries.

The key technological developments of the period often have a geohistorical dimension: the use of coke to smelt iron (by 1709–10) and the commercial steam engine (1712) both ultimately depended on coal as their source of energy. The first machine-dominated textile mills (1720s), were dependent on swift-running water – itself a result of the lie of the land – but ultimately moved to steam, too. The first commercial applications of electricity came in the mid-nineteenth century – generation depended on coal, transmission on copper and other metals. From the 1840s, we see the development of the chemical and oil industries, with the discovery of Benzine and shale-oil; a decade or so later, the transformation of steel-making using the Bessemer and Siemens techniques, from 1856 and 1861 respectively. The (oil-fuelled) car was born with the invention of the four-stroke engine in 1879; by the twentieth century, oil was becoming the fuel of choice, and its sources – then chiefly in America and Iran – were transforming global politics.

Underlying this whole story is a spiralling demand for the materials of the earth: the more steam required to power machines, the more the demand for coal increased; the more metal used to make them, the more

ore was mined. Much the same goes for oil. From the later seventeenth century certain building stones became nationally and international important. 'Superstar stones', I have called them. These include Jurassic limestone, especially from around Bath and the Isle of Portland; and various Carboniferous sandstones, in northern Britain; joined during the nineteenth century by brick-clays, especially from Jurassic Bedfordshire; and by more ancient Scottish granite and Welsh and Scottish slate.

There are manifold ramifications to all this. Oil and coal were used to make the rubber tyres and road surfaces on which transport increasingly depended. The manganese mined at Brentor was one of many minerals whose usefulness was discovered or developed. Major chemical industries, driven by such discoveries, had a particular focus in north Cheshire and south Lancashire, with their proximity to the limestone, salt and coal used in many new processes. All in all, this is a new lithophiliac age (though there is a sense in which the 'stone age' has never finished; it is merely that the full potential of the rocks is being revealed).

The places where such stones were extracted became quarries of jaw-dropping scale; the materials they produced came to drape the island in a kind of architectural monoculture. The character of British buildings no longer moved in step with the warp and weft of local geology. A typical Victorian terraced house in the south might be made of bricks of Bedfordshire clay, topped with slates from Gwynedd. The ability of a given stone to resist the impact of pollution began to affect fashions in building materials, such as terracotta and artificial stone for example.

This period also sees an underlying philosophical or cultural change. Science, for all its manifest power as an intellectual discipline, reduced nature from something created, perhaps potentially alive, to something dead, a happenstance of physical laws, waiting to be enslaved and exploited without concern for the consequences. It is hard to resist the conclusion that the treating of people as objects or possessions is a related condition.

The industrial-era mythosphere also includes new kinds of aesthetic response to the landscape, and these had a physical manifestation in everything from paintings to gardens. The folly-filled Picturesque-designed landscapes of the eighteenth century are one expression of this; the Romantic-era discovery that wild, high places can be thrilling as well as terrifying is another. People began to explore Britain, and to write about what they saw with a fresh-eyed eloquence; some such reports, from Leland in the sixteenth century to Cobbett in the nineteenth, are quoted in this book. Art and literature alike, from John Constable to Thomas Hardy, became intensely responsive to the particularities of place. Many other aspects of our culture that we take for granted, from universal suffrage to religious Nonconformism, are products of a broadly defined industrial era.

Geology itself is a creation of this period, not least because the sinking of mines, the building of canals and the construction of railways revealed more of what lay below the ground than ever before – and here, once again, Britain was in the vanguard. Like art and literature, this is largely a development of the mythosphere, and like them, it affects our reactions to the rocks; just as we explore Wessex or the Lakes with Hardy and Wordsworth in our heads, so we look at granite afresh when we know it originated as magma that has cooled slowly deep underground.

On occasion, geology delivers a 'feedback loop' into the landscape itself, affecting its appearance through the design of monuments, as at Rochdale cemetery (1855), which contains a display of twenty-seven rock-types, a miniature history of the Earth as it was then understood.

These developments are fascinating, and two founding figures stand out. One, the Scot James Hutton, made the fundamental theoretical deduction that unimaginable gulfs of time must separate different phases of rock. The other, Englishman William Smith, made the more practical discovery that specific fossils recurred in comparable layers across the country, and used this insight both to create the science of stratigraphy and to make the first proper map of the rocks of an entire country. Many of the rock names still being used were coined by him, sometimes from local usages.

Fittingly, Hutton's contribution to the landscape includes some of the more abstract 'sacred places' of geological science. The junction of Silurian and Devonian rocks at Siccar Point in Berwickshire was used by him to demonstrate that the cycle of rock-creation had 'no vestige of a beginning, – no prospect of an end'. But it is Smith who left physical monuments behind, whether they be the traces of the canals and quarries whose sites he helped determine (and in some cases invested in himself), or Scarborough's Rotunda Museum, built to his design, to display his geological collections.

The new profession of geology developed rapidly: the Geological Society was founded in 1807; the British Geological Survey, the first such in the world, was set up in 1835. Such organisations helped bring science to bear on working out where useful materials might be found, and finding new uses for them. Today professional geologists are involved in everything from military strategy, to the management of water, to the finding of fuel.

The modern world

We can only sketch out the developments of the last century or so. The collapse of British mining and heavy industry in the second half of the twentieth century has traumatised the communities that depended on it, with huge implications for domestic politics. Yet the global picture is one of expansion; the period since the end of the Second World War is called the 'Great Acceleration' for its near-exponential increases in the consumption of the Earth's resources.

Building techniques such as the ability to make enormous pieces of plate glass and huge structures of steel and reinforced concrete have made for entirely new architectures, stimulating new kinds of style: Modernism and its successors.

Many of the gargantuan distribution sheds on which the modern economy depends are enriched with superstar stones that have a global reach: polished Scandinavian granite gives an upmarket sheen to financial buildings and shopping centres alike. Sandstone from Agra, India, is used on the Bradford Grand Mosque, reflecting the Asian origin of many worshippers. Our energy needs continue to sit at the heart of our relationship with Earth materials, only now oil has replaced coal, and Britain is only one player in a story that distorts global politics. Our use of fossil fuels (and their derivative, plastic) is transforming the environment to an extent that may make it difficult for us to survive in it, even as new sources of energy, such as uranium, have been developed.

Ultimately, the planet itself will shrug off such challenges; it is life that will suffer. Meanwhile, rare earths such as lithium are fundamental to the digital devices we carry in our pockets and on which we increasingly depend, and the internet is an enormous consumer of fossil fuels. As the major sources of such materials are overseas, the impact of this on the landscape is often hidden to us.

We are increasingly distanced from the simple fact that nothing solid exists on this planet that does not ultimately originate in its geology. Yet in 2014, 68.6 million tons of limestone and chalk were extracted from Britain (for use in cement, in the chemical, iron and steel industries, and in agriculture); 37.1 million tons of igneous rock, most of it for roadstone; and 11.2 million tons of coal (with over 40 million more tons imported); quarrying of sandstone, salt and clay was also significant.

At the same time, our digital technologies are reconfiguring our relationship with Place itself: everything from maps, because of our dependence on GPS; to film locations (think of CGI); to gaming (Minecraft) involves new ways of visioning our environment. This is a new kind of mythosphere, at once rendered more visible – because we can all explore it, and create it, online – and less dependent on attention to the actual landscape. Pseudo-geology has joined pseudo-science as a growth area: online crystal shops make all kinds of claims for the qualities of the rocks.

Yet the arts have seen a rebirth of interest in place, and in geology in particular, as intense as any that has gone before: the art of figures such as Antony Gormley and Andy Goldsworthy are among the better-known signs that a new and inspiring kind of lithophilia has developed.

As one indicator of the significance of current changes, a new term, the Anthropocene, has been coined to reflect the way human activity has impacted on the geological record. I will use the term for those landscapes in which the human aspect drowns out all others. We will visit some particularly vivid landscapes of this 'cultural Anthropocene' – but my entire theme is the extent to which people have reacted to the rocks, shaping the landscape as a result. Sometime the resulting places are very special indeed: in particular those where many phases of human history are visible at once, and all are shaped by the underlying geology. Such 'dense places' can have the power to transform lives. As this Anthropocene boy discovered on Brentor.

PART TWO

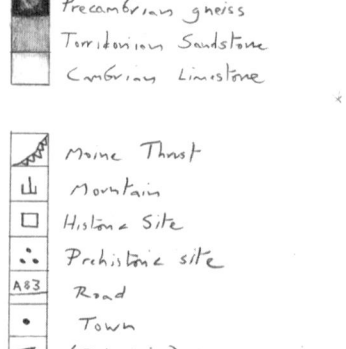

Precambrian gneiss
Torridonian Sandstone
Cambrian Limestone

Moine Thrust
Mountain
Historic Site
Prehistoric site
A83 Road
• Town
(Prehistoric) Quarry or mine

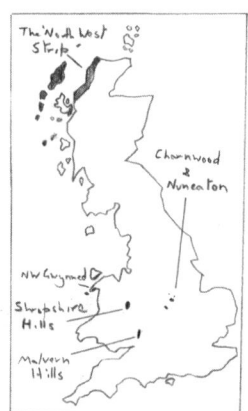

The 'North West
Strip'

Charnwood
&
Nuneaton

NW Gwynedd
Shropshire
Hills

Malvern
Hills

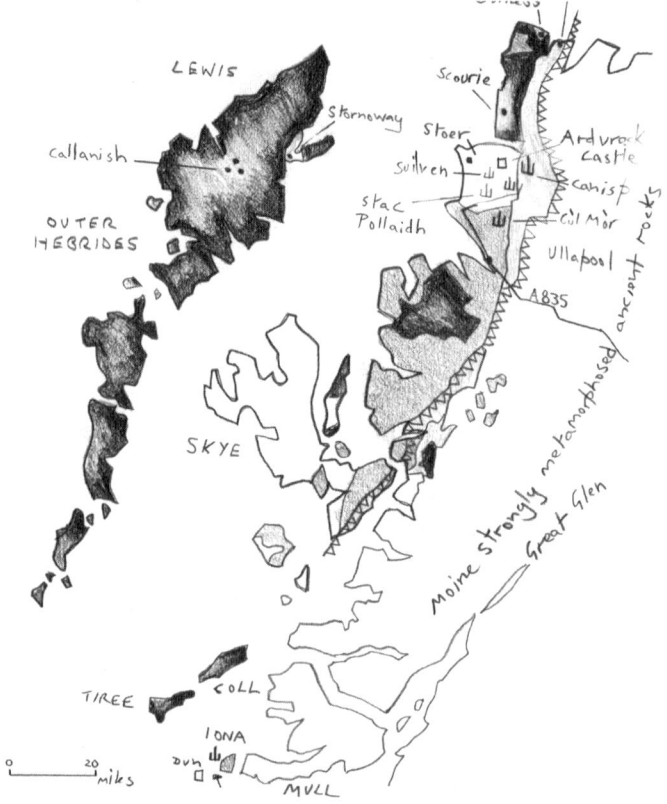

LEWIS

Scourie

Callanish

Stornoway Stoer

Arduvack
Castle

Sullven Canisp

OUTER
HEBRIDES

Stac
Pollaidh Cùl Mòr

Ullapool

A835

SKYE

Moine strongly metamorphosed ancient rocks

Great Glen

TIREE COLL

IONA

DUN

MULL

0 20
miles

Chapter 4

The ancient Precambrian
4,600 million–541 million years ago

Human history sits relatively thinly on the landscape of north-west Scotland: but the geology is raw in tooth and claw. Look north from the spiny ridge of Stac Pollaidh – and one of the great views in the world stretches out.

A plateau extends from the base of this mountain, filled with innumerable small, rocky hills. The gaps between them are filled with dark pools, making for a labyrinthine and alluring sequence of tiny placelets. This country hummocks its way north for fully 6 miles until, quite suddenly, Suilven rises up. This is one of Scotland's great peaks: a 2,398ft-high beast, hunkered on its haunches. Other such isolated mountains are visible. Some, in the right light, have glistening, crystalline peaks. Over to the left, the ocean shines: one can pick out a complex coastline, punctuated by tiny islets.

This landscape is comprised of three elements: hillock-studded plateau; sudden, isolated mountain; and distant sea. Within this underlying pattern, each mountain, each hillock, each island is different. Nature allows a basic template to work its way into an infinite variety of variants: a statement true of everything from a pebble to a planet, an insect to a human being.

But this landscape is particularly special. Its constituent parts have names: the plateau is *cnoc-and-lochan* (Gaelic: 'hillock-and-lakelet'); the isolated mountain, an *inselberg* (German: 'island-mountain').

Signs of human intervention are barely visible from up here. But it is people that cleared the landscape of trees; scattered crofts can be made out lining the coast; and there are small settlements further inland, too. The deserted *cnoc-and-lochan* in front of us once supported two farms and a hamlet-sized township: their disappearance is a historical event in its own right.

The most obvious signs of human intervention today are the footpaths and cairns on Stac Pollaidh itself: the whole ambitious footprint of humanity-and-the-rocks – paths and mounds, roads and buildings, routes and shelters – boiled down to a primeval essence. It is pure natural form, then that makes this landscape as compelling as a work of art: a quality profoundly enriched by what we know about its geology.

Mythospheric mountains

This landscape may be relatively empty of ambitious buildings: but its mythosphere is a full one. Artists and writers have been inspired by it. ('Who possesses this landscape? – / The man who bought it or / I who am possessed by it?' the poet Norman MacCaig asked of Assynt). Many local place-names are Gaelic and Norse evocations of geology and landform: Suilven is *Sula Bheinn* ('pillar mountain'); lochside Stac Pollaidh perhaps 'the pinnacle by the pool' (I will be giving local as well as English names at first use in areas where the majority language is Gaelic or Welsh). But its geological story is what makes the landscape crackle with significance; a creation myth supplied by science, only elucidated from the late nineteenth century onwards.

To explore this geology is to encounter one extraordinary quality after another – and at the same time, to discover the essential building blocks of geology itself. It is odd to talk about this landscape as the product of a single 'period', given that – and here is the first extraordinary thing – it bears the traces of more time than has passed since.

The rocks that dominate this view are Precambrian in date, but that is a catch-all rather like 'prehistoric'. Precambrian rocks lack fossils – life was either non-existent or (later on), too soft-bodied to leave many traces. It is a vast period of time, covering 88 per cent of the age of the Earth – a period over which many lost landscapes came and went.

This was a world of surpassing strangeness. There was no complex life: no plants, no animals. Continents themselves were young, and more dynamic than they are now. Remnants of the era are rarely visible on the surface today. When they do appear, they are a glimpse into the 'basement' of old, hard rocks which lies below everything in this book, like a kind of geological unconscious.

Landscapes underlain by Precambrian rocks are rare in Britain. Like the most respected of elders, their presence is at once appealing and daunting. Outside Scotland, none would take more than a day to walk across, and all date from relatively late in the period.

The area around Stac Pollaidh is different. It is part of a long, narrow strip of territory with a unique geological history; a strip that runs a full 170-or-so miles north to south, along Scotland's north-western coast: from Durness in the far north to Iona, off Mull – while being at its widest barely 15 miles across east to west. This entire coastal strip has a unique geological history – but its spiritual epicentre is here, in an area centred on the large parish of Assynt.

It was very wet when I was last in Assynt; in spite of that, I wanted to get more intimate with the rocks. I chose a spot where a short hike across *cnoc-and-lochan* led to where an *inselberg* reared up. The plateau was surprisingly slow going: the hills a peaty sponge, the gaps between them brackish pools. There were grey boulders everywhere. Then, quite suddenly, the flanks of the mountain rose up so vertically that I could almost stand on the plateau and touch their sides. The rocks here had a ribbed, almost corrugated texture, and were brown in shade.

These are two different rock-types: one hard and grey, the other textured and reddish. Both were once elements of a hazily understood supercontinent called Rodinia by geologists, which sat, mostly in the southern hemisphere, about a billion years ago. And they represent the first two of the three great groups into which all the rocks on the planet can be divided: metamorphic, sedimentary, igneous. The differing qualities of these rocks are the key to the thrilling contrast between the *cnoc-and-lochan* and the *inselbergs* of Assynt.

For Assynt is a 'mixed landscape': a place where contrasting rock-types sit in close proximity. Though here the contrast is especially thrilling, such places often lead to sudden changes in landform – and also in the resources, from metals to soils, which influence human activity. This can make mixed landscapes both visually arresting and historically rich. And here in Assnyt, they also form a lesson in geology.

A metamorphic plateau

The rocks of the *cnoc-and-lochan* plateau are indomitably hard, impervious and acidic. Few things will grow on them, water gathers in their dips and plant material is slow to break down, hence the peat and the pools. They are a variety of the first of the first of our rock-types: metamorphic.

Metamorphic rocks have, in effect, been cooked. They started out as one type of rock, and were transformed at some later period by a powerful combination of pressure, heat and other forces. Their character owes much to both the qualities of the originating rock and the specific balance of the forces they have been put through. This makes them very varied, but in Britain, almost all form hard, infertile country. The process of cooking can cause chemical reactions, creating deposits of minerals and metals. As a result, from Redruth to Tyndrum, metamorphic landscapes have been useful to human beings as a source of everything from copper to gold.

The metamorphic rocks of our north-west strip originated as magma, which then hardened into granite – and later metamorphosed into a rock-type known as gneiss: very hard, and often densely banded with melted blacks and greys, and even soft oranges. It was formed – and here is another extraordinary thing – from rocks already ancient, 2,800 Ma, and 20–30 miles below the Earth's surface, at temperatures of up to 1,000 degrees centigrade; and they were transformed again at a later period and at slightly less extreme depths.

These 'Lewisian gneisses' are among the oldest rocks in the world. Though there are other gneisses in Britain, none is present on a landscape-forming scale, nor are any other rocks remotely this old. This makes them a dense concatenation of strangenesses: material from the deep underworld of the planet, created over profound amounts of time, subjected to extraordinary pressures at extreme depths – and then exposed on the surface for us to see.

1,800 million years separate these rocks from those of the *inselbergs*. That is considerably more time than is covered by the whole of the rest of this book. What geographies came and went in this time we barely know. We are in the presence of an enormous 'unconformity', a place where rocks of one age sit upon rocks of quite another. And yet the rocks of the *inselbergs* are still older than almost any other rocks we will encounter. And they introduce our second type of rock: sedimentary.

Sedimentary peaks

About 1,040 million years ago, a long-vanished Rodinian mountain-range stood somewhere to the west of Assynt. Great wide rivers, their path unimpeded by soil or plants, flowed off these heights, wearing them down, and carrying fragments of them across a Lewisian plain. As the waters flowed, the sediments of the mountains drifted to the river floor. Eventually the gneiss was covered by no less than 2–3 miles of sandy sediment. Under ever-increasing pressure, the silica in the sand glued these grains together – a process known as cementation – and sandstone was formed.

These sediments are thus tiny fragments of lost mountains. They remind us that every mote of dust we breath has been recycled from some previous environment, passed no doubt through other bodies, scuffed from some forgotten wall or washed from some mountaintop. Some dust motes may be tiny, visible only with a microscope; others will be quite substantial. Grain size is one way sedimentary rocks are distinguished from each other: another is material-of-origin.

Sandstone is one of the two main types of sedimentary rock (the other is limestone). It has finer-grained siblings in the form of mudstone, siltstone, shale and clay. The sandstone of the *inselbergs* is called Torridonian, after a part of the north-west strip about 35 miles to the south of Stac Pollaidh, where it dominates the landscape almost to the exclusion of the Lewisian beneath.

Sedimentary rocks are like metamorphic rocks in that the material from which they were made was originally something else. But in this case the conditions that created them were comparatively benign, and what that something else was is evident in their current form. Through them we get a glimpse of a distant past.

The intimacy of this glimpse is one of their great attractions. At Stoer, 13 miles to the north of Stac Pollaidh, I ran over to a rocky inlet. Here, bashed by the cold waters of the sea, the Torridonian rocks preserve the muddy sun-cracks of a single hot day a billion years ago: features formed in a matter of hours, long before anything with eyes was around to witness them.

I watched the lap and crash of the water eating at this hard sandstone. It was being washed away with infinite slowness, and as it was worn down, so the surface of the rock moved backwards in time, uncovering specific moments in forgotten days on another Earth. Likewise, as I cast my eyes down the sides of Suilven, I was moving, second by second, back in time, as over millions of years, one piece of sand falls upon another, stratigraphic. Each grain has been eroded from a lost mountain, carried on a lost river, fallen into place beside its brethren in a split second of a lost age; a moment in time from the dawn of time.

Sedimentary rocks are also of unmatched geohistorical significance. Almost all the fertile, densely settled land in Britain is on such rocks, which also include almost all the best building stones, and our chief repositories of coal, oil and salt. And they create landscapes in which subtle variations between one sedimentary layer and another can deliver striking changes of character.

Yet all are also time-machines, vividly tipping us back into the environments of the past. Visibly freighted with their own histories, they have a kind of clarity: they tell their own story. They are often physically bright, too: some sandstones are pink or scarlet or even green; some limestones honey-yellow or bone-white. The layers of any specific sedimentary rock might vary in quality, texture and usefulness, depending on the shifting vagaries of the environment that created them: freshwater and saltwater create very different rocks; some were dropped by the wind. Such environments can vary from hour to hour, let alone year to year.

These rocks are also testaments to the great cycle in which, under tectonic pressure, the very crust of the Earth shifts, bends and breaks. They tend to gather in features known as basins, where such processes have caused the crust to dip: such structures also often fill with water. Left to themselves, the layers from which such rocks are formed will lie horizontally, and often be clearly visible. But tectonic pressure can push and bend them out of shape, so that these once-flat lines follow great curves and swooping arcs.

The Torridonian sandstones are only one of many sedimentary rocks in our story, yet we will twice again (in the Devonian period, and then in the Permian/Triassic) witness the specific sequence of events that created them: sand washed from young mountains, eroding rapidly in desert conditions, and coloured red. (The redness comes from the oxidisation of iron in the rocks, a process that often creates this colour, as it also does in blood, and in metal, as rust. Red ochre, that ancient geological source of pigment, is formed in this way).

So this great depth of Torridonian sandstone lay on top of the Lewisian gneiss like a great mantle, as lost continents came and went. By the Cambrian era, about 500 Ma – when we begin to approach a story that can, in several parts of Britain, be told more-or-less continuously to the present – much of it had been eroded away. But some great chunks were left behind. These are the *inselbergs*: mountains made of the detritus of other mountains.

The power of erosion

Landscapes are monuments to removal. Over millions of years, erosion can quietly eat away miles of depth of material. And as erosion works, so it shapes. Whether a hill has a soft slope or a steep one, is broken by a crag or cut by a valley, these are the result of erosion.

Compared to the depths of rock that lie below the surface, such landscape features are but wrinkles, small side effects of the way climate and liquid have rubbed at and removed rocks; yet they mean everything to us. The difference between hulking *inselbergs* and low-slung *cnoc-and-lochan* is a difference of erosion; as it is between the grassy plateau of the Cotswolds and the dark, flat expanses of the Fens. We call exposed rocks 'outcrops', but that is the reverse of the truth: something like 'rub-downs' would be more appropriate.

This process can have a counter-intuitive aspect, leaving rocks that are old but soft low-lying beside hills made of rocks that are younger but harder. Each rock formation varies subtly from place to place, and the forces that work on it over time will have varied too: so a single formation can become a wide variety of landforms.

It is erosion, in concert with the qualities of the rocks themselves, that orchestrates the lie of the land. As rocks of different types are eroded at different rates, landforms become as complex and subtle as a piece of music. If that is the case, then Assynt is the geological match for Bach's *Mass in B-Minor*.

Here, the story again has an extraordinary twist. For the sandstones of the Torridonian mountains to have been laid down on top of the gneiss of the plateau, the gneiss must at that point have been on the surface – itself a remarkable thought, given how far below ground it was formed. For a long time, the sandstones must have covered this ancient plateau, only for most of them to be removed, revealing the primeval surface on top of which they formed. The *cnoc-and-lochan* plateau *is* that surface, albeit scoured relatively recently by glacial erosion, covered thinly with peaty earth, and scattered with a few settlements and winding strips of tarmac. It is a landscape from the dawn of time.

One further extraordinary thing. The layers of the Torridonian sandstones, originally laid down flat, dip slightly to the west. This may not seem particularly remarkable – but that's the point. Since the Precambrian era, this sliver of the Earth has moved across at least three-quarters of the planet. It has participated in the formation and dissolution of several continents, during which, in other parts of Britain, entire mountain ranges formed and disappeared. Yet this slight camber is all that seems to have affected it (in fact, the Torridonian rocks have been tilted twice, only later to be moved back close to horizontal).

Nevertheless, though so much material has been removed, these ancient rocks have never been metamorphosed, twisted or upended. The more of the ensuing story you read, the more remarkable this will become.

Igneous rocks

There is one more rock-type, but its role in the appearance of Assynt, while of huge interest to geologists, has little visible impact on the landscape. It can be seen around Scourie, 13 miles north of Stac Pollaidh, where sudden surprising black bands sheet their way across and through the gneiss: the Scourie dykes.

These are made of magma that has been forced through the gneiss by enormous tectonic pressure, before it cooled into rock. This makes it an igneous rock.

Igneous rocks are made of magma that has cooled and hardened. They are of two broad types. The first cooled gradually below the surface of the Earth; the most common and easily recognised is granite, roughly textured and studded with lumps of slow-growing minerals: mica, feldspar and the indestructible, crystallised silica that is quartz. Granite often forms high ground relative to the rocks around it; it erodes into smooth-sided hills, sometimes punctuated by sudden tors. Normatively grey, it can veer from greenish to pinkish depending on how much feldspar it contains.

The second kind of igneous rock has been erupted onto the surface of the Earth as volcanoes or lava flows. Basalt is the most common variety: dense, sharp rocks that snapped into solid form as they flowed into the sea or hit the open air: Brentor is made of basalt. Such rocks can be very tough indeed, and make many of Britain's highest mountains; they also shatter with brittle sharpness under conditions of extreme cold, making for dramatic landscapes.

Igneous rocks of comparable type have much in common, and do very similar things in the landscape. They embody something primeval, a kind of geological id or subconscious: essential to our existence, yet superficially inscrutable. They are also another glimpse of the Earth's interior; indeed, they make its processes visible to us. This gives them a special kind of historic eloquence.

The power of tectonics

Magma does not work its way up into the crust on a whim. It moves because the crust is being compressed or stretched by tectonic forces. The resulting rocks are symptoms of the unceasing grinding and shifting of the plates of crust that cover the planet.

This process is the key to the grand narrative that created all places: a story of slow, but shatteringly dramatic character, as continental masses assemble and disassemble; a story of simultaneous creation and destruction. It explains the underlying structure of our island, and shapes the histories that have played out on it. It gives meaning to the landscape to know whether a particular igneous rock formed when two continents collided about 425 Ma, or when quite different continents split apart at about 60 Ma. Igneous rocks are monuments to this tectonic narrative.

There are places on our planet where such rocks were created very recently indeed, and one only has to glance at them for their origins in the inner Earth to be obvious. Take a flight to Lanzarote and after half an hour in a car you can circumambulate a 300-year-old volcanic cone, then walk into its bowl-like caldera, surrounded by rocks that are visibly made of a solidified, viscous material so young it has yet to grow a mantle of soil. This near-desert is a kind of Eden, a glimpse of the birth of landscape itself.

Britain is not like this: our igneous rocks are old, and have been heavily eroded. Even on an igneous mountaintop they are products of a volcano's inner world: the plumbing of the Earth's crust, rendered visible only by the processes of erosion.

In general, igneous rocks make sparsely inhabited places. But granite has been an important building stone, and in places where it lies low it has been reasonably densely settled. And the dramatic landforms made by volcanic rocks have often made suitable locations for fortifications and other seats of political power: stone thrones. There is a contradiction between their stubborn fixity and the liquid viscosity of the material of which they are made; a contradiction that embodies the processes of making and remaking common to all stones.

These rocks are significant in another way, too. As products of the inner Earth, they are the source of many of the minerals that go to make up other rock-types. A lump of clay may be made of tiny particles of silica, magnesia and other minerals that first reached the surface as magma. This most malleable and useful of sedimentary rocks, mythologically the very stuff from which human life was made, can thus ultimately owe its origin to tiny grains of lifeless, hard magma.

Quartzites and limestones

The mighty *inselberg* of Canisp/*Canasp* rises a little east of Suilven. Its name may mean 'white mountain': a reference to the gleaming, crystalline sheen of its peak. This is made of a quartz-rich sandstone that has been metamorphosed, transforming it into quartzite.

This rock does not weather into soils, nor does it easily erode: it often forms mountaintops, a capping of bare, shattered stone beneath which hundreds of feet of softer rocks may shelter. Many of the mountains of Assynt are topped by it; the broken sandstone ramparts of Stac Pollaidh are the result of its removal by erosion, which exposed to weathering the Torridonian sandstone below.

Rocks like quartzite were of huge significance to prehistoric people. Around Ledbeg, 8 miles east of Stac Pollaidh, there are prehistoric cairns built from them, and apparently positioned to provide glimpses of the *inselbergs* of Cùl Mòr and Suilven.

With this rock we are moving into the Cambrian era, from 541 Ma. At this point, Rodinia had broken up, and the Lewisian and Torridonian rocks were located on the bed of an ocean called Iapetus. The sand that eventually became quartzite came from a nearby coast; later, layers of lime fell on top of it. Over time, this solidified into the other main kind of sedimentary rock: limestone.

This memorable material is a testament to a momentous change in the history of the Earth. An explosion of life took place during the Cambrian, distinguished by the appearance of body parts dependent for their hardness on calcium (bone is just one variant). The amount of calcium carbonate in the environment increased dramatically. Much limestone originated as the bones and shells of things that were once alive; it's almost as if this closeness to sentience has somehow passed into the rock itself, which forms consistently distinctive landscapes wherever it appears.

Limestone has been hugely useful to humanity; it dominates any list of the best stones for carving with; the lime it contains can also be used to make mortar. Lime makes an excellent fertiliser, its alkaline nature reducing the acidity of the infertile soils that dominate places like Assynt. For centuries it was the only effective disinfectant known; later it was used in many industrial processes. Burning to heats of around 900–1,100°C is the best way of extracting lime, and limestone landscapes can be dotted with former kiln sites. This is a rock that has generated its own building-type. The caves and hollows which form easily in limestone provided early shelter for humans, and bequeathed to us the evidence for their lives; the grasslands it supports have been a prime location for Britain's wool wealth. Without it, human lives without number would have been impossible, and many fine buildings would collapse.

The settlement of Durness, Sutherland, lies in the far north, where the north-west strip hits the coast. As one approaches it, the endless peat is suddenly replaced by bright green places that attract grazing, and even agriculture. Angular, sculpted-looking rock formations split the ground. The landscape has taken a near-Mediterranean turn. Its features are typical of the distinct geohistorical dialect spoken by all limestone places: 'limestonelish'.

Caves are one of the great attractions of this rock-type; and here is Smoo cave, an 37m mouth that gapes towards the sea. It was used both in the Mesolithic period and by Norse colonists. It is one of several such in the Durness limestone: *Uamh An Ard Achadh* ('High Pasture Cave') on Skye – where there are further rocks of the north-west strip – is one of the oldest habitation places in Scotland, including an Iron Age 'passage to the underworld', used for burials.

These caves are testament to another quality of the limestone. Unlike the other rocks we've explored, it is highly porous. It also dissolves easily;

though rainwater is usually only slightly acidic, it gradually eats limestone away, carving not only the strange rock-shapes around Durness, but also sink-holes and caves: rock formations for people to wonder at – and use. All the major caves of Britain are in limestone; Sue Clifford, author and environmental campaigner, has called it a giving, open rock, one that easily reveals its own interior.

In Assynt, most settlements which do not cling to the coast are on this limestone. Look for where it lies, and discover a long, narrow, discontinuous deposit that lines the eastern, inner edge of the country of Lewisian gneiss and Torridonian sandstone. Beyond, a more generic-looking Highland rises. Here we encounter my final extraordinary thing.

The Moine Thrust

Let's take a bird's-eye view of the entire northern Highlands. The country to the east of the Durness limestone is consistently and densely mountainous in a way that Assynt is not. It is dominated by a long, bashed-about ridge, cut through by ice-carved glens, yet still a major watershed. Rain hitting the west side runs west to the Atlantic; rain hitting the east side takes a longer route to the North Sea. The Scottish far north thus follows the Britain-wide rule that high ground tends to be towards the west and gentler slopes to the east. The rocks of this ridge, meanwhile, have an extraordinary origin.

By the Silurian period a great continental collision was under way. By this time the rocks were part of a continent known as Laurentia. Continents are made of terranes: primeval building-blocks of the Earth's skin, each with a discrete history; and as the mighty collision took place, one Laurentian terrane was thrust over another, bulldozing its way more than 45–60 miles west across what was probably more Lewisian/Torridonian country. In some places the rocks were turned upside down. If the eastern terrane hadn't stopped where it did, we would have no north-west strip.

This great shunt is known as the Moine Thrust. Its leading edge can in some places be touched: one such is a small escarpment, just 5 miles east of Stac Pollaidh, and easily missed in this country of rocks hardened under great trauma. This is Knockan Crag, and it played a central role in establishing that this event must have occurred, a discovery which opened up dramatic new possibilities for the kinds of processes the Earth might have been through. It has been turned into an impressive, all-weather centre for the interpretation of this landscape: a path lined with artwork leads to a rotunda containing both geological information and an impressive view. It is an open-air shrine to geology, a kind of scientific sacred landscape.

Geology and history

Knockan Crag is just off a section of the long road from Ullapool to the northern coast: the A835, A7 and A94. Like most roads, it makes its way along a path of least resistance that connects nodal points formed by settlements – and thus follows the low-lying, settlement-attracting outcrop of the Durness limestone, with the rocks of the Moine Thrust to one side and country of *cnoc*, *lochan* and *inselberg* to the other. History flows along such paths, in this case defined by the line where one primeval chunk of continent rode up over another, tying together settlements that might not exist were it not for rocks formed during the first flowering of complex life.

Inchnadamph, the centre of human authority in Assynt, is one such. This is a scattered place, set in a bowl of Durness limestone 9 miles north of Stac Pollaidh. Here is the tiny parish church for Assynt, burial place of the local lairds, the MacLeods of Assynt. Their seat, Ardvreck castle, rises from a promontory of the nearby loch, with the ruins of its urbane replacement, Calda House (1726) nearby. There is even a memorial to two geologists of the Moine Thrust, Ben Peach and John Horne. Explore further, and there are prehistoric burial sites and abandoned pre-modern townships.

Just as with geology, considerable gulfs of time can separate the monuments in such places. But what the visitor experiences is not an unconformity but a series of remnants of past eras, present all at once: a place with a capital 'P'.

The hard, exposed sandstone of Stac Pollaidh was marked by paths and cairns. Now we are on a gentle, low-slung limestone, and we are following a tarmac road through fragile but ancient centres of settlement and power. Such sites are the smaller siblings of every turnpike road and motorway, every cathedral city and conurbation to come. And Inchnadamph is, in a quiet, spread-out way, a 'dense place'; a place where the human reaction to the underlying geology in deep time is both visible and rich.

From the shape of the mountains to the location of its settlements, Assynt is defined by the rocks of which it is made.

Other Precambrians: toy wildernesses, sacred places

Here and in other ways, the north-west strip is geohistorically an extension of the 'slightly' younger Highland Scotland in which it sits. One might, though, consider it a kind of ultra-Highland: especially on the Western Isles.

This long archipelago is dominated by Torridonian-free expanses of Lewisian gneiss. Like a bulwark of hard stone, it protects the Scottish mainland from the Atlantic; and it is a cultural bulwark, too: Barra/ *Barraigh* and adjacent islands are home to some of the only communities in Britain to have remained Catholic continuously since the medieval period. On Lewis/*Leòdhas*, by contrast, the Presbyterianism is so fierce that some congregations refuse even to sing, instead chanting the Psalms in Gaelic. And the Isles are the main centre of Gaelic speaking in Britain.

Here on Lewis there is an outstanding monument to Neolithic responses to the rocks. Callanish/*Calanais* is a setting of standing stones in a cross in circle pattern, dominated by a central stone almost 3.5m high, 'curved like a skinny supermodel' (Mike Leeder and Joy Lawlor, authors of *Geobritannica*). The circle is approached by avenues – one of them 82m long – and shares the landscape with dozens of smaller such sites.

All seem to be arranged to work in concert with natural features: the view from the *Cnon an Tursa*, on the flank of which the main circle stands, emphasises such features as the rising and the setting of the moon over a range of hills 13 miles to the south.

All this is a jaw-dropping orchestration of human intervention, landform and the heavens; but it also a work of careful stone-selection. I know of nowhere better to study the aesthetic delights of gneiss: its mineraline bands like stretched treacle or snail-trails, the creation of forces of impossible power. Perhaps the beautiful Dounby maceheads, found on

Orkney, and made of gneiss rendered as smooth and shining as if it had been mechanically polished, were sourced from somewhere hereabouts.

This mighty ritual monument feels remote today, but its position overlooking the Atlantic is a reminder of the central role played by these western waterways historically. With that borne in mind, let's jump a full 137 miles south, to Iona, at the very tail of the north-west strip.

Iona

The 3.5-mile-long lump of gneiss known as Iona is one of Britain's most compelling sacred places, and a little universe unto itself. It's the kind of

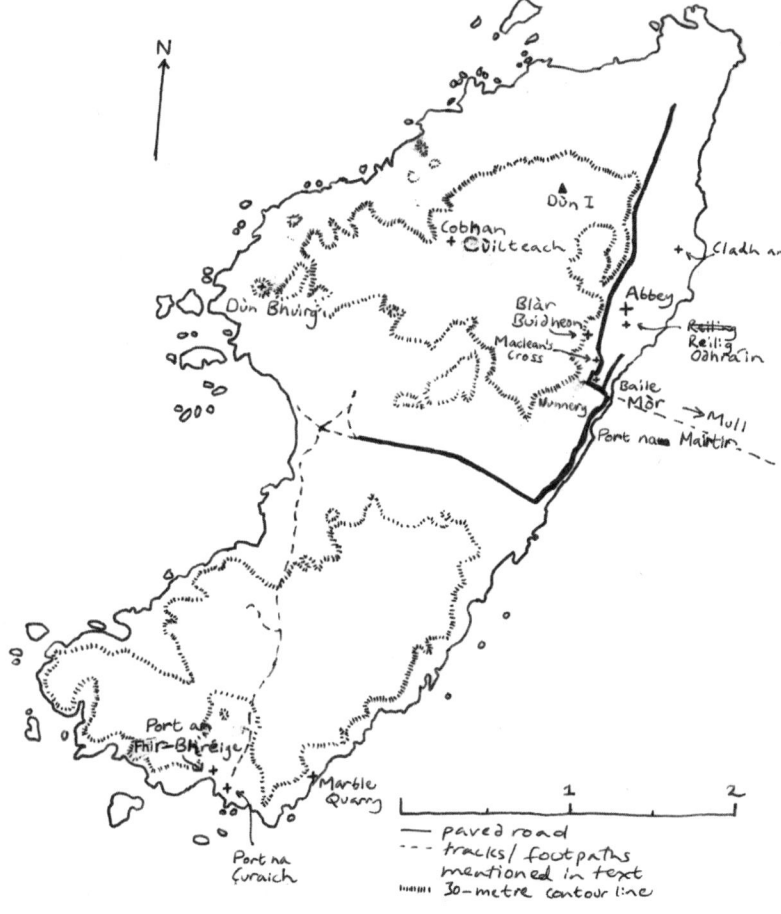

place that draws people; in the youth hostel I met a Californian lawyer who had brought his father's ashes, and a group of biologists from the tropical Chinese island of Hainan.

The medieval abbey here is one of the great historic buildings of Highland Scotland, the crosses around it some of Britain's greatest works of ancient sculpture. The hill of *Dùn Ì*, which rises behind them, is a satisfying scramble; the southern half of the island is empty. I thought I was alone on the beach of *Port a' Churaich* until I heard a voice shout 'Look!' and a pod of porpoises swam past.

But this beach was no wilderness. Cairns of sea-rounded pebbles littered it like devotional polyps, dominated by an enormous mound shaped like an upturned boat, collectively maintained by countless hands. I bent and picked up three pebbles of exceptional, translucent whiteness – 'St Columba's tears'; such rocks are known as fossilised grief.

In fact they were marble. This made them special in themselves. While various stones are marble-like, true marble, which is metamorphosed limestone (here, Precambrian limestone), is very rare in Britain. A clamber over nearby cliffs brought me to the rusting remains of an eighteenth-century marble quarry: its products went as far afield as Westminster Cathedral. The few other true marbles in Britain are also in the Scottish north-west, and also made of ancient limestones. But Iona marble has a mythical backstory.

Giants fill the British landscape; a dramatis personae of people, mythic and historical alike, imagined as colossal beings filled with the power to use mountains as footstools and scoop out unexpected valleys. They can inhabit eye-grabbing archaeological sites as often as they do unusual landforms. The Devil, closely followed by King Arthur, gets top billing in this remarkable gathering of 'stone heroes' – of whom St Columba of Iona is my favourite; his legends are more lithically responsive than most, responding particularly sensitively to the colour and texture of individual rock-types as well as the shapes of mountains.

Columba crossed from Ireland in 563, hoping to Christianise the Irish-descended Gaels of the kingdom of Dál Raita/Riada. The first known Christian mission to any part of Britain since the collapse of

Rome, the community he founded became Iona abbey – and his name fills the landscape of the island.

Tòrr an Aba, a tiny glacially scoured *cnoc*lette immediately west of the abbey, is where he is said to have had his writing cell; *Port a' Churaich* is where he landed (hence the boat-shaped cairn). The approach to his shrine at the church itself was a kind of lithic pilgrimage, paved with red granite from Mull, lined by great carved crosses and other stone monuments; and 'St Columba's tears' played a significant role in pilgrim devotions. People prayed as they rolled balls of it around the hollowed boulders known as *clachan bràth* ('prayer stones'): if the stone was worn through, it was believed, the world would end (an unfulfillable prophecy, given the hardness of the boulders relative to the marble). One of the altars in the abbey was a solid piece of this white rock: fragments of it were claimed to protect the bearer from misfortune. There is more of this to come.

Iona markets itself as an island off an island off an island: to get there from the mainland, one has to cross to Mull and then traverse 27 miles of slow roads to even get close; the rocks get older as one heads west, but only Iona is Precambrian: a geological place apart.

Approach from the seaward side, however and it is anything but isolated. Iona guards the very mouth of the Great Glen, the gateway to the interior of the Highlands. Like Callanish, it would have been a nodal point: at once possessed of an evocative liminality – and very much at the centre of things.

Perhaps sacrality is the ultimate compliment that human beings can give to landscape. Such places have been my lifelong obsession, especially when they include ambitious stone buildings. From a stone circle to a cathedral, in such places geology has been excavated and rearranged in an attempt to evoke the Divine. As we move south to England and Wales, there is more of this.

Precambrian England and Wales

There is a 135-mile gap between Iona and the next place British Precambrian comes seriously to the surface, on Anglesey/*Môn*. From here on, the rocks are much younger than those in Scotland. Most were formed around 560–580 Ma, a full 500 million years later than the Torridonian.

These English and Welsh Precambrian rocks are almost all the result of volcanic events which took place on the edge of a relatively small continent known as Avalonia. The chief exception is Shropshire's Long Mynd, a kind of Uluru/Ayers Rock of the Marches made of sedimentary rocks, their layers upended like hard grey splinters.

I love the way this place-name conflates the Welsh *mynydd* ('mountain') with the English associations of 'mind'. A kind of metamorphosed language, evocative of deep memory, of time out of mynd; a place with the mind of a mynydd. If there is one quality shared by all Precambrian rocks, it is that they have a long mind.

Like the mynd, almost all are isolated outcrops. Often they are cupped among protective sequences of Cambrian, Ordovician and Silurian material. And among them are a striking series of mini-Ionas: tightly circumscribed places of wild character, in which the sacred sits centre-stage.

There is Bardsey/*Ynys Enlli*, the island off the tip of north Wales's Lleyn peninsula, said to be the burial place of 20,000 saints: I came upon one of them once on an archaeological dig, shocked by the sudden intimacy as my trowel brushed against the calcium of a long-buried toe.

Or there is St David's, where Wales's greatest cathedral sits in a Precambrian valley, next to the little river Alun, once bridged by a slab of 'marble' called the *Llech Lafar* or 'talking stone'. It was said a corpse once broke into speech while being carried over it; the effort cracked the rock itself down the middle. Rocky Precambrian hills and tors rise from the plateau above, at once dramatic and small in scale; the cathedral tower rises among them from its valley-set site.

But let's head for Llanddwyn, on Anglesey. Soon after you cross the Menai Strait, pick up a low escarpment that runs west. In contrast to Snowdonia, the island is almost flat; but its tight, subtle rises hold clues to the presence here of no less than five separate terranes. Anglesey has the geological complexity of some entire continents.

Our ridge is made of a Precambrian metamorphic rock called blueschist (the colour comes from the mineral glaucophane). This formed in conditions of high pressure but relatively low temperature, deep below an area of subduction. A short detour from the scarp led me to Bryn Celli Ddu, a Neolithic burial mound which displays a series of glistening specimens of this veiny rock; its inner room is lit up by the sun on midsummer morning, linking the deep Earth with the heavens and the deep time of the Precambrian with the shallow one of an event which takes mere minutes to pass.

Pick up the scarp again, and find yourself heading straight for Newborough/*Niwbwrch*. Soon you have to walk, seeking, at the northern end of one of Britain's great beaches, a rocky, green, grey peninsula shaped like an arthritic finger. This is the two-thirds-of-a-mile-long tidal island of Ynys Llanddwyn.

Billowing rocks tie Llanddwyn to the shore: balloon-like formations known as pillow lavas. Ten minutes' walk later and one hits the sea at a cove where the rocks are a jewel-box of jammed-together textures and colours: red, green, white and pink. This is the Gwna Mélange, and it is as enigmatic as it is attractive: it may not even be Precambrian.

The landward end of this peninsula, the argument goes, was created as new crust welled up and spread; the *mélange* at the other end of the 'island' is the remnant of great submarine landslides, created as the crust descended again. This little place is a single sliver of continent, a tiny terrane-ette: a miniature embodiment of the engine of the skin of the entire planet.

And sitting on top of it all, among hillocks and clifflets which swing with low-slung drama from one side of the peninsula to another, there is a holy well to St Dwynwen, the fifth-century hermitess who is a kind of Welsh St Valentine; the battered remains of what was once an impressive pilgrimage church; a Celtic cross of 1903; and the remains of two successive lighthouses, one of which sits like a dramatic foil above the rocks.

In short, in this dense place, the layered detritus of human needs – salvation, protection, healing, love – are scattered across a finger of rock that embodies the fundamental forces of the Earth. And, like Iona, and Bardsey, and St David's, it is only superficially a wilderness. Nearby Newborough was a major centre of power, and these places have all been on major seaways, while for all their wildness they are too small to get

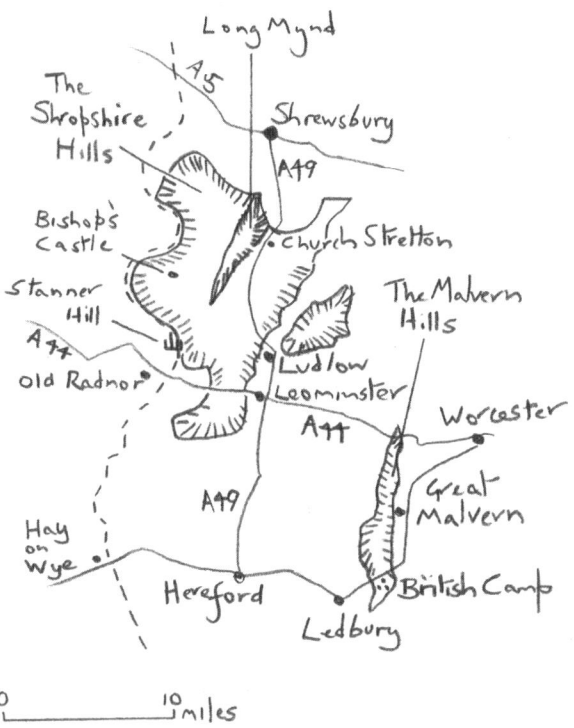

lost in. 'Deserts' perhaps, in the eyes of hermits, but also places safe enough to dream in.

In England's Malvern hills, this 'sacred baby wilderness' dimension becomes something rather urbane. For this is our first example of one of my favourite phenomena: the town or city that embodies its own geology.

The Malverns are a 7.5-mile-spine: an igneous row of mini-Alps, rising 'in pyrramiddy fashion' (Celia Fiennes, a traveller and writer, 1702) from fertile countryside, like a hard tongue slipped between the soft lips of their surroundings. If this is a glimpse of the basement forced to the surface – perhaps along another terrane boundary – it is the kind one gets in a horror film, just before the torch fails. Looking east from this ridge, gazing over the settled heartlands of southern England, there is said to be no higher point between here and the Urals.

Here, we find the Precambrian making borders. The line dividing Herefordshire from Worcestershire is made physical by the Earl's Ditch, an earthwork of Bronze Age origin that runs along the top of the ridge (an hour to the west, the border of England and Wales runs along the foot of Stanner Hill, which contains what are, at c.702 Ma, the oldest dated rocks south of Scotland).

Dreamers have long been drawn to the Malvern heights. William Langland, fourteenth-century author of *Piers Plowman*, lay by a spring beneath a 'broad bank' (the Iron Age hillfort known as British Camp?), where he had a vision of 'a smooth plain, thronged with all kinds of people . . . moving busily about their worldly affairs': the soft, young country that extends below.

St Werstand was an eleventh-century hermit. A refugee from Norse attacks, he founded one of two priories that grace these slopes. Both churches are built of younger rocks sourced either from the lower slopes or the plain below; but tour the buildings around them, and find that many are made of the diorite that makes up the Malverns themselves.

This dense, obdurately hard stone is the key to the history of the town of Great Malvern. Cooked up several miles below an active volcano, the Malverns are riven with fault-lines large and small. These have eroded into the notch-like passes used by those roads which cross the hills; and they provide a patch down which rainwater can percolate, and purify, and pick up minerals and finally burst out as 60–100 separate springs. They also explain the ability of these stones to be cleaved, once powered tools had been developed, into rough polygons, making structures such as St Ann's Well and Great Malvern station into dark symphonies of diorite.

Such buildings bear witness to the town's status as the centre of a kind of early modern healing cult. People flocked here to take the waters, and the priory became hemmed in with new buildings. The combination is a striking collision of the wild and the wealthy, the comfortable and the primitive: a toy wilderness.

It was against the backdrop of the Malverns that Edward Elgar wandered the local lanes, mentally composing his sweepingly Romantic musical visions of Englishness; that W. H. Auden taught; that local bands from the 'Dancing Did' to 'And Also the Trees' have coined a singularly place-inspired, rural twist on rock music. Surely the swooping darkness discernible in all these artists owes something to the shadow cast by this Precambrian upland. The Malverns are the geological Caliban of southern England, and in their way as dense with the geohistorical themes of the Precambrian as far-off Iona.

Building stones

Mostly, the rocks of the British Precambrian are too hard to have been actively favoured by architects. Only a few – on Tiree and Coll in the Hebrides, and a few places in Shropshire – have been more than roughly shaped. Elsewhere, though the red jaspers of Anglesey and the Lleyn have been used decoratively, builders had to make do with roughly fitted boulders, or import stone from elsewhere.

Their main strength lies in this very hardness. Igneous rocks, hard enough to cope with powered, wheeled traffic, are often quarried for roadstone. There are many small quarries in the Malverns, like bitemarks in the rising ground. But if the Malverns come as a shock when glimpsed from the orchardlands of Worcestershire, Charnwood is even more unexpected.

Here is a great island of moorland, rising in the heart of rural Leicestershire. It is a major centre for roadstone and aggregate. It may even be named for the useful hardness of its stones, if the 'charn' is related to the querns it once produced. In nearby Nuneaton, a tiny outcrop of Precambrian underlies, uniquely for rocks of the period, the kind of ordinary, suburban, built-up landscape most Britons inhabit – rocks used to floor Roman Watling Street.

Bardon Hill quarry in Charnwood itself is one of the five biggest quarries in the UK, supplying about a tenth of the aggregate in the country: nearby Ordovician Mountsorrel is even bigger. You probably drove over Precambrian fragments of Leicestershire moorland last time you hit your nearest motorway: shards of the most ancient parts of our island, serving to speed our way across it.

This quarry is also an unexpectedly moving dense place. Climb out of the suburbs of Coalville and at the top there is a tor, a communications mast and an Ordnance Survey triangulation point. Then, just yards from the trig point, someone has cut the rest of the hill away. Thanks to the activities of Aggregate Industries, the view is of a colossal hole in the East Midland landscape; a hole in which giant-tyred lorries crawl like distant silent toys.

Cast your eye down the sides of the hole, and get a glimpse below the lid of Place itself. The lower part of the quarry-sides is grey, and Precambrian; the upper edge of this is marked by a rising and falling line, easy to imagine as a cross-section through a series of steep granite wadis. Above this, everything is red: this is desert sand, which filled and smothered these rocky valleys 300 million years and five geological periods after the lower rocks were formed.

The hill you are standing on is merely the exposed peak of one of these buried Precambrian hills.

This is a place that tips you back in time, and like all such, even those that are the side-products of extractive industry, the experience is extraordinary: a series of lost landscapes, past places, vertiginous expanses of history: time contracted and jammed together into a kind of singularity; the undercarriage on which we live exposed – in this case, by delving human hands.

I have lingered on these comparatively small outcrops of English and Welsh Precambrian because they have a special power. The deep origins of the Britain in which most people live are muffled by millennia of softer, sedimentary rocks. The further south and east one goes, the truer this becomes. Precambrian moments thus come as a shocking revelation of what lies beneath: like a stone circle in a suburban estate, or a mosh-pit at a tea-dance. The rocks of the Malverns, St David's, Bardsey and Llanddwyn have a power disproportionate to their actual extent: a power we also encountered at Callanish and Iona, and in a sense the entire north-west strip, which is a kind of sacred place for the connoisseur of landscape. It is no wonder they have attracted mystics.

All these traces of the Precambrian are also accidental survivors of a pre-Britain, exposed only where tectonics and erosion have conspired to deliver them up to us. Yet these rocks have endured all that later geological history could throw at them. From Columba to Elgar, they have nourished the human soul. Perhaps the greatest unconformity of all is that in human terms, Precambrian is at once very hard, and very soft.

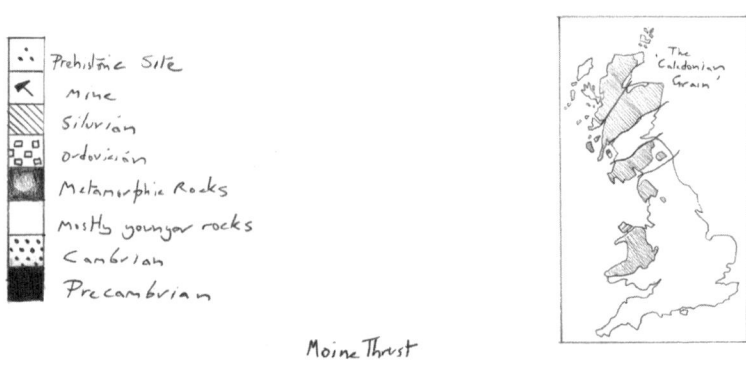

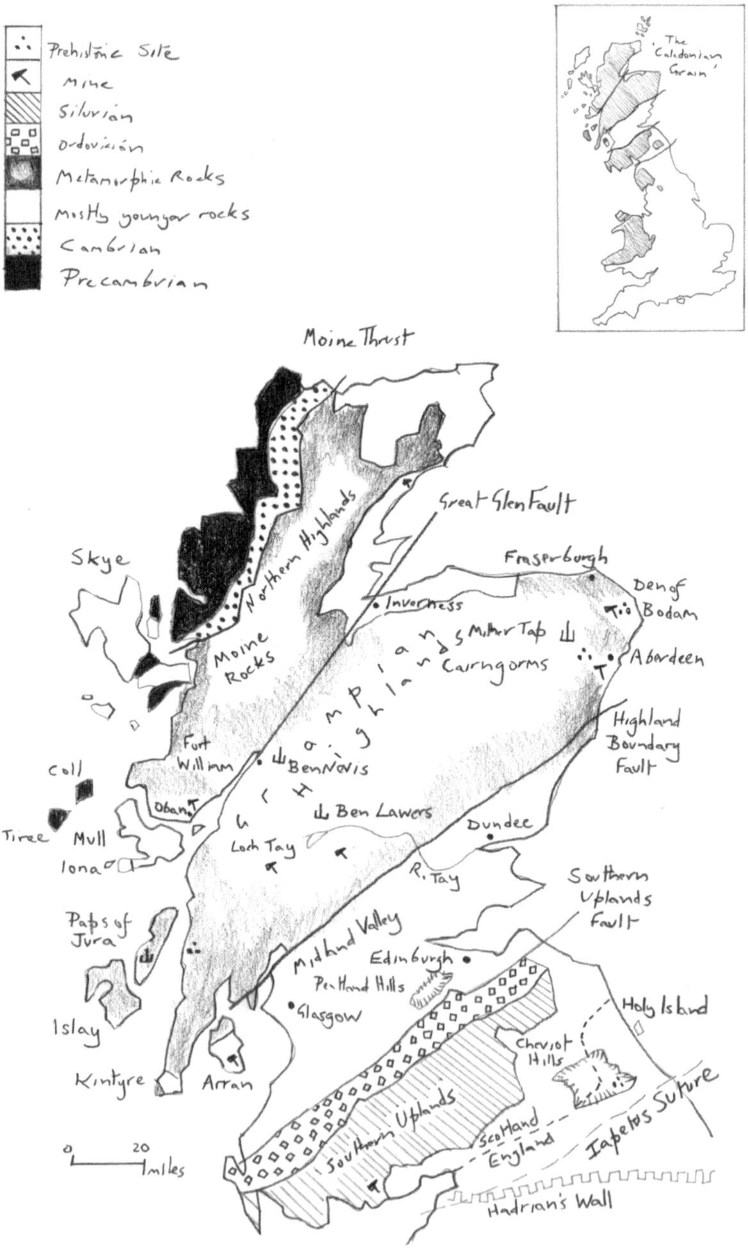

Legend (map key):

- Prehistoric Site
- Mine
- Silurian
- Ordovician
- Metamorphic Rocks
- Mostly younger rocks
- Cambrian
- Precambrian

'The Caledonian Grain'

Moine Thrust

Great Glen Fault

Skye

Northern Highlands

Fraserburgh

Den of Bodam

Inverness

Grampians

Mither Tap

Cairngorms

Aberdeen

Moine Rocks

Highland Boundary Fault

Coll

Fort William

Ben Nevis

Tiree

Oban

Mull

Ben Lawers

Iona

Loch Tay

Dundee

R. Tay

Southern Uplands Fault

Paps of Jura

Midland Valley

Edinburgh

Pentland Hills

Holy Island

Glasgow

Cheviot Hills

Islay

Scotland

England

Iapetus Suture

Kintyre

Arran

Southern Uplands

Hadrian's Wall

0   20 miles

Chapter 5

Cambrian, Ordovician and Silurian tortured rocks

541–419 million years ago

I first walked through the Llanberis pass as a twentysomething hitchhiker. I had been a little crestfallen to be dropped off at a spot that seemed to be halfway up Mount Snowdon. But as I followed the narrow, winding strip of tarmac down into a steep-sided valley, and shattered walls of stone towered ever-higher over me, I became possessed of a kind of exultancy.

The visual bombast of this place was overwhelming. As if the landscape had been formed not by the silent power of geology, but by some great operatic sequence of chorus and aria, or the eviscerating riff-and-solo of heavy metal. Yet the only actual sound was birdsong and the ever-present drip and tinkle of falling water. And even in the glorious state of mind this place inspired, I could understand why, not very long ago, most people simply thought of such country as a place of terror, to be avoided at all costs.

In 1775, Dr Johnson described the comparable landscape of the Scottish Highlands as 'matter incapable of form or usefulness, dismissed by nature from her care and disinherited of her favours'; fifty years earlier, Daniel Defoe found the English Lake District to be 'all barren and wild, of no use or advantage to man or beast', and possessed of 'a kind of unhospitable terror'. Such reactions were normal before the modern period.

As I descended the valley, things began to soften. Cottages and drystone-walled fields appeared; a pair of beguiling lakes filled the valley floor. Then, just as things seemed to be calming down, I came to a mountainside that seemed to have been slit by some cosmic razor.

Precipitous descents and pinnacles came in giant steps, each floored by great arenas of mounded detritus. Mighty embankments of the same stuff made routes between them. From these shards of discarded rocks to the steepest of cliffs, everything seemed possessed of an inherent sheerness, steep and smooth, a shade of grey suffused with a subtle, oily purple.

This was the 550m-high 'working face' of the Dinorwic slate quarry: a place with a sublime magnificence every bit the equal of nearby Snowdon – but entirely artificial. Dinorwic is the product of a colossal human hunger for the rock of which this part of Snowdonia is made: slate.

Slate is a metamorphic rock, one that preserves some of the traces of its sedimentary origin. It starts life as mud or clay: soft stuff, made of countless tiny particles. But these muds have ended up about 6 miles underground, where temperatures of 250–300°C have put them under the kind of pressure that only colliding continents can exert. Eventually, their constituent grains are forced to lie flat. The resulting rock is dense, brittle, impervious, and can be easily split along the angle formed by these flattened particles; an angle which sits at right angles to the direction from which the pressure came: its 'cleavage plane'.

Slate is thus imbued with a kind of distended tension, as if tectonic forces are waiting within it to be released. It splits thinly, yet remains strong. It shrugs off any rain that falls on it, and is light, and thus relatively cheap to transport. All this makes it the ideal roofing material. The thinner the slate (and Snowdonian slate can be split to just 4mm), the lighter the roof, and the less substantial the walls beneath; building becomes quicker and cheaper. It is no surprise to discover that the industrial era was the heyday of Snowdonian slate – with powered transport enabling widespread distribution from its mountainous home, terrace after terrace of new housing across Britain came to be roofed with it.

But slate is a rock-type as much as a roofing stone: it may be used on floors, or even, in some areas, make entire buildings of large, crisp blocks. Yet every time a slater splits a piece, this rock falls apart along a line of weakness generated by ancient tectonic pressures. Millions of homes across the country are thus dependent on the flattened embodiment of ancient tectonic events; in this case, the 'Caledonian' events that led to the assembly of Britain.

Caledonian drama

This is a story that birthed landscapes and resources that have resonated through human history. A story in which all but one of the structural building blocks that make up Britain came together. A dramatic story that starts in the late Precambrian, has the 120 million years of the Cambrian (541–485 Ma), Ordovician (485–444 Ma) and Silurian (444–419 Ma) at its heart, and ends early in the Devonian. From the dawn of life to an era when fish swam in the oceans. And, perhaps because Scotland itself is their most vivid embodiment, 'Caledonian' is the collective term for these events.

Rocks made in the Caledonian era cover a third of Britain, extending over 400 miles north to south: from the north coast of Scotland to Pembrokeshire/*Sir Benfo* in Wales. They include the Lakes as well as the Grampians, the Cambrian mountains/*Elenydd* as well as Snowdonia/*yr Eyri*. The three highest patches of land on the island – Ben Nevis (1,345m), Scafell Pike (978m) and Snowdon/*Yr Wyddfa* (1,085m)– are made of rocks created at this time; as were the majority of our roofing slates, and most of the granites that line our harbours and pavements: our oldest nationally significant building stones. There are stray outcrops in southern England, too, especially in Leicestershire and the Marches, where England's rare Precambrian rocks are often nested in slightly larger outcrops of this date.

This is a story of the collision of two continents. One, Laurentia, contained all the rocks of the Scottish north-west strip, as well as others that would come to make up much of Scotland. The other, Avalonia, contained all the rocks of Precambrian England and Wales.

Laurentia and Avalonia were separated by the ocean of Iapetus, which by the late Ordovician was 1,200 miles wide. But now it began to close. The northern continent of Laurentia headed south-east; the southern one of Avalonia north-west. The layers of seabed sediment between them were squashed and concertinaed, and often, metamorphically transformed.

Everywhere, huge mountain ranges went up as the crust buckled: Himalayan in scale, they are collectively known as the Caledonides. Basins formed, too: some were corrugations of the pressurised crust, others the result of the crust stretching out as the mountain-building phase came to an end. Magma welled up from deep underground, erupting as massive volcanoes and lava flows, or slow-cooling below the surface into masses of granite. Terranes which had once lain far apart were pressed together, creating massive fault-lines, zip-lines in the Earth's crust: the Moine Thrust is one of these; the Great Glen, further south in the Highlands, another.

The most fundamental of these boundaries is also the most deeply hidden: it is called the Iapetus suture. It marks the point of final conjoining, which took place in the late Silurian (about 430–420 Ma), about 30° south of the equator: roughly the latitude of South Africa, or parts of Australia (the longitude of such events is often unclear). This was more a gentle docking than a great tectonic trauma, and continental movement continued thereafter. Yet as a result, the rocks of Scotland/Laurentia were joined to those of England and Wales/Avalonia. They have not been sundered since.

These events, then, could be dramatic: but they could also be slow and unremarkable. Millions of years could separate episodes of eruption or phases of mountain-building. But once the final docking had occurred, the Iapetus Ocean was gone forever and a large new continent was born: Laurussia.

Our Precambrian north-west strip is a fragment of Laurentia, almost expunged when another terrane of the same continent was forced over it; the Precambrian rocks of England and Wales mostly originated an ocean away, as Avalonia moved north. Both now became part of a single entity.

The events that drew them together were marked by a single angle of approach, a kind of cleavage-plane for an entire nation, which runs at roughly 140–150°, from north-west to south east, and marks the landscape to this day.

I call this the 'Caledonian Grain'. It means the Great Glen, the Iapetus Suture and (to a lesser extent, thanks to a last-minute nudge from a continent known as Baltica) the Moine Thrust run roughly parallel to each other. The long, droopy nose of the Kintyre peninsula follows the Caledonian Grain, as, 200 miles to the south, does the finger-like Lleyn/ Llŷn peninsula. The coastlines of North Wales and north Pembrokeshire run at about the same angle. There are many more examples, for this grain sets the underlying rhythm of the British landscape. It is Britain's bassline.

Britain's bassline

The fault-lines which create such grains are fissures in the skin of the Earth, created under tectonic pressures. They direct the form of mountain ranges, the locations of valleys, the courses of rivers, and the paths of human history. These are everywhere, and vary hugely in depth and extent; they run especially deep where terranes join.

Each such fault is a kind of scar-line, a line of weakness. It can be reactivated by later phases of tectonic change. And erosion will seek out and eat at it whenever it can. Faults of extraordinary antiquity can thus guide the formation of landforms, which is a relatively recent story. Such faults are at once clues to the underlying structure of the land, testaments to the great tectonic narrative that underscores all geology, and shaping features of the landscape itself.

These faults thus form an underlying pattern to the island as a whole. The grain they form, just like a cleavage plane, generally runs at right angles to the direction from which tectonic pressure came. But, like the grain in a piece of wood, it can be varied in detail and flowing in form. And the Caledonian Grain is the most profound of them. It is increasingly visible the further north and west one goes; to the south and east it is buried under younger rocks.

There are three further grains to come – 'Variscan', 'Atlantic', 'Alpine' – and each is also a result of a major phase of tectonic change. (Many others have come and gone, of interest to geologists but no longer having an obvious and visible impact in the landscape.) Their overlying sub-rhythms syncopate with this primal one in a great tectonic counterpoint. Between them they give the island its 'rhythm section': a kind of heartbeat of Place, which underlies its human history. And they help guide the setting of the younger, softer rocks that sit on top of them, and which play the melody lines in the music of the landscape.

But without this first Caledonian Grain, Britain itself would fall apart. Unlike almost any other phase of our story, its major faults are also terrane boundaries. And the cleavage plane along which each piece of Snowdonian slate has been cut is its local expression, even if mighty structures such as the Moine Thrust and the Great Glen are its most visible results. The whole island resounds to its deep tectonic dub.

Geohistories of the grain

On the ferry from Mull to Oban, I looked down the very throat of the Caledonian Grain. The Firth of Lorn made a great mouth-like gulch, down which mighty valley-side succeeded mighty valley-side into infinity, with no sign of twist or turn as the firth became the Great Glen. This deep valley then runs straight as a Caledonian die for 55 miles, from one side of Scotland to the other; dividing the Highlands into northern and southern halves. The glen itself is about 2,130ft deep, its base filled by a sequence of nine lochs; but the faultline it follows cuts fully 25 miles into the Earth's crust. It is perhaps the most blisteringly obvious geological feature in Britain.

Here, two Laurentian terranes met as Iapetus closed; a scar-line so profound it has remained seismically active. Indeed the rocks on each side of it have shunted hundreds of miles in relation to each other over the millions of years since they were created.

It is no surprise, looking at this landform, to find it is the great natural routeway of the far north, a natural Panama Canal of Highland history. It connects the eastern Highlands with the western ones, and the Irish with the North Sea: history runs backwards and forwards along it like a shuttle. Roman soldiers may have passed along it, before abandoning their attempt to subdue the northernmost parts of Britain. Early bases for Christian missions to the far north – Iona and Portmahomack, both founded by St Columba – sit at either end of it.

In the early modern era a series of fortifications known as 'the chain' bound this Caledonian scar with military power, from Fort William in the south-west to Fort George in the north-east. Fort George was built by General Wade after the defeat of the Jacobites at Culloden in 1745; the glen-following A82 and B862 were among the 250 miles of Highland roads he laid out. These roads helped enable the wholesale dismantling of Highland culture from the 1740s. In 1803, in an attempt to stimulate the economy of a fast-depopulating area, the Caledonian canal was built to link the string of lochs that floor the glen. Today, Oban in the west and Inverness in the east are key elements in the human infrastructure of Highland Scotland.

The glen is not unique: the Menai Strait is a kind of miniature version of it, carved into a grain-following fault that runs between terranes whose distinct earlier histories help explain the contrast between flattish Anglesey/Môn and mountainous Snowdonia. Bangor and Caernarvon are its Oban and Inverness: each have been both gateways and focuses for power. Bangor was an ancient religious centre and cathedral city, and Caernarfon was Edward I's planted capital of a recently conquered Gwynedd, and site of the earlier Roman fort *Segontium*.

In England, an even smaller, inland Great Glen runs though Church Stretton in Shropshire, separating the Long Mynd from Caer Caradoc: it forms a strategic route through the Marches, plugged midway by the castle at Church Stretton itself, just as Urquhart sits partway down the Great Glen. Today the Church Stretton valley is followed by the A49 and the railway line to Shrewsbury; it marks one of the few points in England where the possible joining points of terranes are visible on the surface. Yet it is through such faults that both the Malverns and Charnwood forest poke their rocky heads: they are effectively the highest peaks of a deeply concealed Caledonides.

Such faults can generate boundaries as well as routes. To the south of the Highlands, a terrane slipped downwards between two faults. Younger sedimentary rocks later gathered on it. Thus was formed the Scottish Midland valley, often called the Central Belt, which is that nation's main centre of population and economic activity.

Bounding the Midland Valley to the north, the Highland Boundary Fault brings Highland Scotland to an end with a juddering halt. It marks the most fundamental division in Scottish history: that between the clan-dominated Gaelic-speaking society of the Highlands and the more urbanised, feudal, Scots-speaking one of the Lowlands.

Bounding it to the south, a great bulwark of hills follows the Southern Uplands Fault. Here the Southern Uplands themselves begin, and with them, the distinctive culture of the Borders. All this follows the Caledonian Grain, as do some of the Caledonian-era volcanic hills which rise within the Midland Valley, such as the Ochils, Sidlaws and Pentlands.

The Iapetus Suture is further south, beyond the Southern Uplands. Less blisteringly obvious than Scotland's other terrane boundaries, it runs from deep below the Solway Firth to a point a little south of Holy Island – but it is geohistorically even more significant. It was only in the tenth/eleventh centuries that the kingdoms of Scotland and England emerged, and came to share a border; by 1237 that border ran from the Solway Firth to the Tweed, more or less as it does today: very nearly the path taken by the suture line. This has remained the most significant national division in the British body politic. And it was preceded by a comparable line, once equally significant: the northern limit of the Roman empire.

It is easy to get a little Scotland the Brave about the coincidence between this island's most significant political divide and its most ancient and fundamental structural feature. But the suture makes an unwieldy political metaphor, for it is both the embodiment of a deep and primordial separation and testimony to an also-ancient unity. And these features – the Great Glen; the Highland Boundary and Southern Uplands faults; the Iapetus Suture line and the England/Scotland border – all run at the same angle. It is as if Scotland's history ran from north-east to south-west: a nation on the grain.

Lost Himalayas

The Grampians are Scotland's mightiest mountain range. Here, expanses of rock stretch infinitely upwards; in rain, cataracts are draped like string across precipitous mountainsides; such waterways shine should sunlight hit them. Tiny valleys and corries, little landscape-ettes, can be glimpsed high up among the giant shoulders of stone. Such country can receive over 3m of rain a year: the kind of treatment that would wash away the softer lithologies of southern England; yet the waterfalls cut the narrowest of grooves in these resilient, ancient rocks. Unless you are somewhere unusual (the peat-filled basin of Rannoch, for example), you will rarely apprehend the shape of a mountain from a distance. That is, unless you climb one; then, the intervening glens can seem to disappear, and you find mountain after mountain sitting at about 730–915m. 'The horizon's gates unlock and lock / and the valleys open out / Like a volume's turning leaves' (Edwin Muir, lightly edited).

Most of the rocks of which the Scottish Highlands originated are Precambrian sediments, laid down on two separate terranes in ancient Laurentia, then pushed together as Iapetus closed. The Great Glen is their dividing line: the rocks to its north are known as Moinian; those to the south, Dalradian. Thanks to 'orogeny', the faintly erotic geological term for mountain-building, these sediments ended up 15–20 miles below the ground, where they were twisted into unlikely positions and bodily transformed as terranes conjoined, birthing the Caledonide mountains high above. Whole thicknesses of rock could be bent over, like a carpet-ruck many miles long. Today these mountains form the most extensive tract of metamorphic rocks in Britain, and its largest area of mountain.

There are igneous rocks, too; many of the very highest points, Ben Nevis included, are the deep innards of volcanoes whose calderas lay several miles above. The Cairngorms, Britain's highest plateau, are the exposed top of a great mass of magma, which, during the late Silurian and early Devonian, welled upwards from far below before slow-cooling perhaps 3 miles underground into an enormous granite mass known as a batholith.

Batholiths are often products of tectonic change; even when not exposed on the surface they can buoy up the rocks above them. Largely buried batholiths help explain both the great height of the central Lakes and that of the northern Pennines.

The high central Lakes and the Snowdonian mountains, Britain's other major mountainscapes, are also dominated by Caledonian-era tortured sediment and igneous rocks, though here the events took place on the southern side of Iapetus. Britain's highest country thus originates as the deep undercarriage of former Everests, Nanga Parbats and Krakatoas; as if the landscape was turned inside out.

But there is another category of highland made by the rocks of this period: massively bare, high hills such as the Southern Uplands, the northern Lakes, and the Cambrian Mountains. At best these make big, beefy arrays of smooth-sided heights; at worst, they can be formlessly bleak.

This hill country is made of sedimentary rocks that have been bulldozed and upended, but not comprehensively transformed; the remnants of the closing Iapetian seafloor, its Scottish and English sides once hundreds of miles apart and now forced into proximity. Stand on Skiddaw in the Lakes, gaze 30 miles north to the Southern Uplands, and you are gazing across two sides of a lost ocean.

Then there is a unique category of landscape I call 'highland lowlands', in which any of these rock-types can occur, but on low ground which may be relatively densely settled, and which thus shares some of the geohistorical character of lowlands elsewhere in Britain. This is a rare combination of rugged landform and dense history, and a distinctive group of geohistorical themes cluster round it: subsets of the wider themes suggested by the Caledonian-era rocks, in which mountains play a central role.

Mountains and man

All the major uplands have things in common. Human activity has avoided the tops (though one might come across an abandoned *shieling*, in Wales a *hafod*, a stone bothy once used as summer accommodation when grazing animals). Valleys, by contrast, become the very veins of history. Where glens, *cwms* and dales connect relatively straightforwardly to nearby lowlands or major waterways that story can be rich indeed.

The Highland stretch of the Tay, Scotland's longest river, is followed for some distance by the railway and the A9, another route carved by General Wade and today the transport lifeline of the far north; it then bends east, carving one of the few east-west ways through the central Highlands. This has been a veritable motorway of human culture. Around Loch Tay the slopes of the 1,204m Ben Lawers are made of schists –

metamorphosed muddy, shaley rocks – which have weathered into calcareous, farmable soils, and there are signs of human activity from the Mesolithic onwards.

In the eighteenth century, there were 120 settlements around this loch. They would have been dominated by a distinctive Highland building type, still sometimes seen in the Hebrides, if now downgraded to outhouses: the 'blackhouse'. Oblong, thatched, with 3m-thick walls, its corners rounded to avoid having to shape the intractable local boulders of which it is built. There are two rooms: one for cattle, the other for people. Traditionally, Scottish houses were white with 'harling', a slurry of lime, water and pebbles that sealed them from the elements; the term 'blackhouse' may have arisen as these structures ceased to be the main dwelling and became neglected.

Today there are barely half a dozen settlements around Loch Tay. This is a story that repeats itself across the Highlands: we've already touched on the missing townships and farms of Assynt. It is the result of the Clearances, in which large numbers of people were displaced, often forcibly, so the land could be used for grazing and hunting. Radical depopulation resulted, but the change went deeper than that.

With the planting of new towns, the promotion of crofting as the main form of rural settlement, and the placing of many settlements on unproductive coastal land, the modern Highland landscape was born, even as an older, much more populated landscape vanished. The Highlands today are thus just as much a reflection of industrial-era history as are metropolitan Glasgow or Liverpool; founded on human trauma, as are the genteel slaving-funded terraces of Bristol.

This story – thrilling landscapes, settlement focused on valleys, and a human history as complex and challenging as can be found anywhere – recurs in many places. Its architectural traces can be distinctive, too. In the high Lakes, drystone walls climb impossibly up hillsides – heroic works of the Enclosure era. When in the 1810s–30s, Wordsworth wrote that the local farm buildings had 'risen, by an instinct of their own out of the native rock', they were in fact relatively new.

Such houses make another distinctive vernacular. The large, whitewashed, residential 'fire house' is surrounded by smaller barns and byres. It has an enormous, curved-cornered chimney breast built of mortared stone. The low-pitched roofs are covered with local slates, the uneven surfaces of which are loved by mosses and lichens, making each a variegated ecosystem. Most of the stones used in these buildings are rescued from local river beds, making their walls a symphony of local geologies.

Stone heroes

High in the mountains, where physical monuments are few, the stone heroes can be the most palpable sign of a human presence. They fill the mythosphere, evoked whenever we say the name of hilltops such as Cadair Idris: the seat of the giant called Idris. We have already met Columba, presiding hero of Precambrian Iona.

Many of these figures are anonymous. The three conical Paps of Jura are perhaps the most striking of a disconcerting crowd of hills named for disembodied breasts. Others, like Idris, or Jock O'Bennachie, inhabitant of Aberdeenshire's Mither Tap, are specific to a given place.

All the above figures inhabit the Cambrian, Ordovician and Silurian rocks. Of the forty or so natural place names I have found (in English alone) named for Arthur and the Devil, a dozen lie on these geologies: the next most popular – with five each – are on the Carboniferous and the Cretaceous, both of which also make distinctive hills and one-off landscape features. Add in Gaelic and Welsh, let alone linked figures such as the 'barrow' or *wyddfa*, for which Snowdon is named in Welsh (built over a giant slaughtered by Arthur), and this mountainous country truly is their homeland.

Mountain place names can also vividly describe their form: Scafell is probably Old Norse for 'the fell with the bald summit'. Those, such as Pumlumon ('five peaks'), or Moel Goch ('barren red hill') that are Welsh/ Brythonic in origin use a language that has been spoken continuously in one place for longer than any other British place-name-making tongue. As natural features tend to acquire their names early, those of Welsh mountains may be very old indeed.

These languages have had a remarkable afterlife in the geological sciences: the names for the Cambrian, Ordovician and Silurian periods come from the Latinised form of *Cymry* ('Welsh') and two major early Welsh tribal groupings, the Ordovices and the Silures, while the Dalradian rock-system is named for the Scottish early medieval kingdom of *Dál Riata*. As a result of the work of nineteenth-century scientists, words with their roots in Iron Age and early medieval Britain are used by geologists across the world.

Romantic rocks

It was perhaps the Romantics who first claimed that people other than hermits, monks and madmen might benefit from the elemental awe inspired by such places. Here, no part of Britain was more influential than Lakeland: a highland whose restricted extent and rich resources have made it the most geohistorically dense mountainous district in Britain.

William Wordsworth explored the high interior as a youth, and in adulthood set up home at Grasmere, just into the Lakes' high igneous central zone. While it was his poetry that made this landscape famous, it was his best-selling *Complete Guide to the Lakes* which provided access to it.

By the 1880s, in a marker of the extent to which the landscape was being tamed, the climbing of rocks, long done only out of necessity, was becoming a sport. Wastwater was an early centre. Fast forward to 1923 and the Fell and Rock Climbing Club purchased 3,000 acres of high Lakeland, and gave it to the National Trust as a war memorial. A commemorative service is still sung on top of Great Gable there every year on Remembrance Sunday.

It is in stories like this that we see, alongside the taming of the mountains by leisure and sport, something rather interesting: a kind of sacralisation. Today, tourism dominates the economy of many of these areas – if by that one counts everything from the shooting industry on the great estates, to the coach parties and gift shops of Aviemore and Ambleside, to the lonely rapture of the determined Munro-bagger. Yet running through this story, and echoed far back in time, is a sense that the seeking out of the old, hard, high places is also a spiritual pursuit.

The stone heroes, with their supernatural size and power, might be one symptom of this. Another is the way prehistoric monuments often seem positioned in relation to significant eminences: the Simonside hills, which ring the Cheviots – those heights that balloon near the Scots border, remnants of a mighty late Caledonian/early Devonian volcano – are thick with cup-and-ring marks and other prehistoric monuments, as if honouring the dark granitic dome in the middle. Mountains are sacred in many cultures – China and India have whole networks of them – but eminences with an explicit sacred tradition are rare in Britain. Yet it is possible they were once much more common.

For the modern take on this, head to Snowdon. The eroded remnant of one side of a volcanic caldera, this 1,085m mass is not for the faint-hearted; yet its peak is host to a shifting population of serious hikers and day-trippers who have nipped up on the railway. Explore further, and find makeshift shrines among the discarded coffee cups on the summit cairn, temporary memorials to those who loved this unusually accessible mountaintop. Somewhere in our souls, the mountains remain holy.

Dividing places and geological bulwarks

Caledonian-era rocks have also formed impervious geohistorical dividing lines in the landscape, definers of difference. They are, for example, heartlands of Celtic language and culture. Welsh first-language areas cleave strongly to such rocks in central Wales and Gwynedd; in Scotland, the Highlands were long Gaelic-speaking. Today that language is at its strongest in the Precambrian Western Isles and (geologically much younger) Northern Skye; but perhaps its survival is partly a result of the great expanses of Moinian and Dalradian mountain that separate this region from English and Scots centres south of the Highland Boundary Fault.

Here, the 'squashed oceans' of the Southern Uplands and Cambrian mountains play a particularly intriguing role. These are mountains to get lost in, hills that rear up like dour, featureless shadows. In the Southern Uplands, burns dissect impenetrable, ice-steepened slopes. Waters run dark, fast and hard. Little drystone shielings sit in the corners of many fields. The very rock names are of a type that suggests whaleback, rain-sodden uplands: shale, grit, mudstone, greywacke. Flatten out these great sheaves of upended sediment, and this stretch of mountain 45 miles from north to south becomes a portion of sea floor at least 930 miles wide.

The uplands are home to the distinctive regional identity of the Borders, celebrated by Sir Walter Scott, and long marked administratively by the English and Scottish Marches (not to be confused with the Welsh Marches); and legally by Border or March law. The territory is studded with defensive buildings, including architectures unique to it: defended houses known as 'pele towers'; grander fortified homes known as 'bastles'. For 300 years, from the fourteenth to the seventeenth century, a gangster *reiver* ('raider') culture prevailed across the region, and into the northern Pennines.

Isolated farms and prehistoric barrows, alongside the occasional ruined *hafod* mark the high, bare hills of the Cambrian mountains. Here Owain Glyndŵr established himself as a force to be reckoned with, defeating Henry IV on the slopes of their highest point, Pumlumon Fawr (752m), 'the top boggy and the view over a dreary and almost uninhabited country' (Thomas Pennant, a naturalist and traveller, 1778). This very historical stone hero is locally associated with a pair of quartz stones, and the cliff said to be marked by the hoofprints of his horse.

With their high rainfall and impervious rocks, these mountains are also host to important water reservoirs, supplying South Wales and the English Midlands; Liverpool's 1965 creation of a reservoir at Llyn Celyn, further north in the foothills of Snowdonia, caused the abandonment of one of the last all-Welsh speaking communities and was a trigger for the revival of Welsh nationalism. Years of resentment followed; Liverpool issued a formal apology for the event in 2005.

England has long been the largest and wealthiest territory on this island; in holding their own against it, it is striking that both Scotland and Wales have certain geographical qualities in common.

In the early medieval period, British or Gaelic kingdoms dominated much of the country from Wales through the Lakes to Scotland, giving the Caledonian-era rocks considerable cultural continuity. As English hegemony expanded this began to change, but the hard-to-conquer mountains have played a protective role, helping these cultures survive. The Southern Uplands in particular are a palpable geological border defence, protecting the Scottish Midland Valley from incursions from the south.

Routes through such territory are strategically significant: many battles have been fought along the Roman path of the A1 to Berwick, or the A68/Roman Dere Street through Lauderdale.

But Welsh and Scottish power also depended on the possession of significant fertile lowlands, for example in the Midland Valley and Glamorgan, where large settlements could be established and wealth generated. Perhaps the possession of both is the geohistorical key to the survival of these nations. The kingdom of Gwynedd was long the most powerful in Wales, and the seat of Llywelyn ap Gruffudd in his fight against Edward I of England. Snowdonia is its eyrie (the Welsh, *yr Eyri*, means precisely that), its significance marked by the way Edward I's castles at Conwy, Caernarfon and Harlech ring this highest ground, where 'nature created, in our rocks and mountains, fortifications . . . quite impregnable' (Pennant).

But Gwynedd also contained significant lowland, and the heartland of 'upper Gwynedd' (*Gwynedd uwch Conwy*) covered both Snowdonia and the highland lowland of Anglesey and the Lleyn. Relatively fertile and densely settled, these areas long played a role alongside the mountains in preserving the territory's power; Anglesey, after all, was the site of the British 'last stand' against the Romans. Perhaps there is something symbiotic in this relationship of highland and lowland. Perhaps a small nation on the defensive needs both. And in Scotland and Wales, the lowland is often on these ancient rocks.

'Highland lowlands'

Argyll

The bewitching landscape of western/central Argyll came as a revelation to me. Like many southerners, I think of mountains when I think of the Scottish Highlands. But here, little reaches higher than 300m. Sequences of long peninsulas and low valleys stretch out along the Caledonian Grain; the sea's wet shivery fingers follow it deep inland.

Here I walked in some of the best-preserved remains of the primeval Atlantic rainforest – Scotland in its brief breathing space between the departure of the ice and the arrival of the humans – and found myself in places of ancient growth, low landform and ever-present water: the peace was almost electric.

These parts of Argyll have much in common with other areas of highland lowland. While not mountainous, the old, hard rocks create areas of moor, forest and rocky outcrops: country that, while it contains far more farmed land than true upland, is rarely bucolic or easy. The sheltered, complex coastline helps make this a key centre of power: from these sheltered lochs, a boat could work its way across the islands and coasts of western Scotland, or over to Ireland: the Mull of Kintyre is nearer to Belfast than it is to Glasgow.

Argyll was the base of the powerful Campbell clan, Dukes of Argyll, as well as of the Lords of the Isles; the offshore island of Islay was their main seat. As well as having excellent access to the seaways of the west, it is bestowed with fertility thanks to its ancient limestones, rare glimpses of unmetamorphosed Dalradian rock. Other nodal points of power included Sween castle on the mainland, and the cathedral on Lismore, another limestone-rich Hebridean island.

Schists dominate the Argyllshire landscape, rocks softer, more erodible, generating soils more farmable than the Moinian and Dalradian mainstream. The Argyll Group of Dalradian rocks, of which most are apart, stretches to the east coast and also contains most of Highland Scotland's metals, minerals and building stones.

There are stretches of igneous rock, too: such as the Tayvallich volcanics which lie at the gateway to Kintyre. These were born late in the Precambrian, as lava spread onto the floor of an Iapetus Ocean that was still in its opening phase. Their low, parallel, grain-following hills and glens reflect the different erosion rates of fast-cooled basalts and slow-cooled granites; and of the hard quartzites and soft sediments which settled between lava pulses. It is the remnants of the latter that help bring fertility to these valleys. They tell a story which could sit equally happily in the last chapter, but which is included here because they submit so utterly to the grain, and played such a key role in the emergence of Scotland.

Here, as the mouth of a glen opens towards the wetlands of the Moine Mhòr, lies Kilmartin: one of the richest Neolithic/early Bronze Age landscapes in Britain. Great mounds of river boulders make the chambered burial cairns on the valley floor; massive rocks make such stone settings as Nether Largie; there are stone surfaces carved with spectacular arrays of cup-and-ring marks, and a henge – rare for Highland Scotland.

Kilmartin is special, but highland lowland is often rich in prehistoric monuments. There may be several reasons for this: the land attracted settlement, being more fertile and forgiving than nearby upland made of the same rocks. The rocks themselves included innumerable slabs and boulders, freed or loosened from their parent rock by (often ice-age) erosion and thus not needing quarrying. Later areas of settlement are relatively few, and dominated by pasture, so ancient remains have survived where architecture and the plough have destroyed them elsewhere.

Here in Kilmartin, the past swung into significance again in the early medieval period. Just to the south, in the middle of the wetland, a hill of Tayvallich volcanics rises like a Precambrian omphalos. This is Dunnadd, the former seat of the *Scotti*: Gaels from Ireland, whose kingdom, Dál Raita, was centered on Argyll and played a key role in the formation of Scotland. A heartbreakingly eloquent bit of geo-culture lies at its rounded, rocky peak: the single footprint (said to be size 8), hollowed into the rock, which played an important role in king-making ceremonies.

People in many cultures have fixed the footprints of the great and powerful in stone: from those of the Prophet Mohammed at the Dome of the Rock in Jerusalem, to the ubiquitous footprints of Buddha found in the East. In Britain, Scotland is the epicentre of the phenomenon: at least a dozen are known, including footprints of St Columba on Arran and the Mull of Kintyre; the idea probably comes from Ireland. They give a touching intimacy to the human associations of the rocks, while also embodying the colossal power with which stone heroes are endowed.

North-east Scotland

North-east Scotland is another emblematic stretch of highland lowland. The high Cairngorms come down in a series of steps, the glens turn to straths, and we enter a great hip of land, a plateau interspersed with rocky hills that rarely rise much above 200m.

This is a region apart. Fraserburgh is the only place on our island where the local dialect (Doric) was so strong I struggled to understand what was being said to me. Parts are very fertile – there are vast, young, unhedged fields of grain in Buchan. There is a bigness to the roll of this lowland, a sense that it could yield up hills of real drama with a shrug if it wanted to.

Here, more than a dozen patches of Caledonian-forged granite are set among complex expanses of Dalradian metamorphic rocks; one colossal quartzite structure is roughly followed by the historic county of Banffshire. The granites and quartzites tend to make patches of moor-like hill country, but otherwise the lie of the land says little about what is going on beneath the surface: until one reaches the coast, where the spectacular 'yawns' or rock arches and headlands revel in such names as Arnot Boo and Blowup Nose.

Elsewhere, the geology can be followed by looking at the changing texture of gateposts and garden walls, a game you can play in many parts of Britain. Even if changes in the rocks are not reflected in the landforms or the buildings, they can line the edges of people's gardens like a map.

This built landscape embodies the contradictions inherent in the term 'highland lowland'. On the one hand, this is low country only in the Scottish sense: rocky hills are frequent, and one can rarely forget how close are the massifs which become the Cairngorms. On the other, much of this country looks like that which dominates Scotland's true lowlands, which are mostly on younger (Devonian and Carboniferous) rocks.

In lowland Scotland, smaller settlements are often scattered *kirktouns* and *fermtouns/clachans*, a school or place of worship (or, once, a mill or a smithy) the main marker of their centre. Often even these have been replaced by large farms. Towns are common ('burghs'), but usually younger than those in England: in north-east Scotland a great wave were founded c.1720 to c.1850, during the Clearances. One exception is north-east Scotland's major city: Aberdeen. Of twelfth-century origin, this is the largest settlement in Britain to stand on rocks older than the Carboniferous (Dundee, sited mostly on Devonian rocks and with 40,000 fewer inhabitants, is the only competitor).

Scottish historic towns, partly because they are relatively young, and partly because Scotland's *feu* system encouraged landlords to standardise their buildings, have a certain architectural sameness in comparison to their English equivalents. Their centres are also dominated more by major public monuments, and less by ancient churches, than in the southern country. Stylistically, there is a lot of Neoclassical and Scots Baronial, with its stepped gables and pointy turrets. Monuments and memorials make dramatic vertical foils to nearby uplands; I call this the 'Scot's flourish', and it can be seen everywhere from Edinburgh to Glenfinnan. In spite of this, the scatter of castles, ruined abbeys, old parish churches and prehistoric sites reminds us that we are in a long-settled land.

In north-east Scotland, however the 'farmed' look of landscape is a relatively recent creation. This was 'once a most barren spot, but by the industry of the inhabitants brought to its present state' (Pennant). This transformation, in the era of enclosure and improvement, left 'Consumption dykes' in its wake: thick, wall-like mounds of cleared stones several hundreds of yard long, embodying the transformation of rocky moor to well-farmed land. The Royal Forest of Stocket, west of Aberdeen, was a game-filled moor until it was given to the city by Robert the Bruce as a reward for its loyalty; these 'Freedom lands' were enclosed in a 26-mile sequence of sixty-seven boundary markers known as March Stones. Fifteen of these remain, eighteenth-century in date. But much older stone settings add a remarkable dimension to this landscape.

Recumbent stone circles

The sun was sinking as I approached the stone circle at East Aquhorthies, 16 miles east of Aberdeen. The country became vivid in the dying light: to the west the country around Inverurie was a great verdant bowl; to the east, the dark peak of Mither Tap O'Bennachie (the 'mother top of the Bheinn na Ciche', or more simply 'the hill of the breast') was a presence at once beckoning and intimidating. And ahead of me lay a 'wondirful gret croune of stanes' (Bishop John Leslie, 1578).

This stone circle was unlike any I'd seen before. A single great rock interrupted its circuit: it lay flat on the ground like some prostrate giant, sentinel stones standing to either side like watchful guards.

Neither feature is seen in other parts of Britain; yet there over seventy such 'recumbent stone circles' in north-eastern Scotland – and all but a handful sit on the region's Dalradian/Caledonian highland lowland.

A central burial cairn made many of these monuments a fusion of stone circle and barrow. Traces of cremation pyres suggest rites in which heat and dynamism stood in contrast to the cold permanency of the rocks. Architecture like this makes transitory rituals permanent, turns loss into stone.

The recumbent stone circles are as unique as the Caledonian-era lowland that is their home. But they also have much in common with monuments of the era elsewhere. They are intensely responsive to the surrounding landscape: East Aquhorthies is part of a great cluster that gathers around the meeting of the rivers Don and Euie at Inverurie, where a henge once stood. Twenty or so of these also keep the Mither Tap in their sights, while somehow avoiding making direct gestures towards that ominous peak.

Great care must have been taken as the builders selected these stones from among the many glacier-dropped boulders in the area. Quartzite is a repeated theme: the mighty recumbent at East Aquhorthies, red granite covered by a quartzite skin, was an oddly reptilian presence in the falling light. At Auchmaliddie the flankers are made of this bright, hard rock, and quartzite pebbles were scattered around Tomnaverie. It seems likely this rock-type had specific meanings, perhaps to do with the way it seems to capture light.

Caledonian-era quartzite also forms holy mountains and stone thrones. On Jura, the triple glistening peaks known as the 'paps' are hard mammary eyecatchers, visible from many parts of Scotland's west coast. The name of one, Beinn Shiantaidh, means 'holy mountain'. Far away to the south, on Anglesey/*Môn*, the bare white calvaria known as Holyhead Mountain/*Mynydd Twr* is surrounded by prehistoric sites. The medieval St Gwenfaen might cure the sick if two pebbles of the white rock were thrown into her nearby spring. As her name means 'white stone', or 'saint of the holy stones', she herself seems as much lithic as human.

Back on Anglesey, I was entering a Welsh highland lowland that continued south along the coast all the way to Pembrokeshire, 100 miles to the south. There, the Caledonian rocks come to an end – and we encounter two of Britain's most remarkable geohistorical stories.

Bluestones and Landsker lines

Like the Mither Tap, the Preseli/*Preselau* hills of Pembrokeshire, south-west Wales are a strong yet shadowy presence: almost intuitively a source of power.

The hills climax in a long, north-facing Caledonian Grain-following escarpment about 400m high, lined with barrow-like tors of shattered Ordovician rocks: they line the ridge and scatter the slopes below as if they have slipped down it. The whole area drips with prehistoric monuments.

I climbed one of these tors, Carn Goedog. Up close it almost seemed to separate into columnar slabs, each a piece of igneous stone known as spotted dolerite or bluestone. Such easily extracted rocks were generally a useful source of building materials for the religious architects of

Neolithic and Bronze Age Britain; but here we are in the presence of something special.

This outcrop is one potential quarry-site for the most famous man-made erratics in Britain: up to forty-four rocks, most of them of this 462-million-year-old material and each about 1.5m–2m high, which today stand in a circle 135 miles away, on the 80–90-million-year-old Cretaceous rocks of Wiltshire.

At some time before 2900 BC, these rocks were used to build the first stone circle at Stonehenge. The question of how and why this happened – in effect, whether the stones arrived in Wiltshire by human or natural agency, and thus whether the cause is historical or geological – is one of the most significant conundrums in the story of humanity's relationship to the rocks. But there they are, a low ring of ancient upright stones, standing within the ring of much larger, younger and more locally caught sarsen stones that dominates the monument, and marked out by a gentle blueness when wet.

Of the two cases, the geological one is weakest. Transportation by ice is the only natural process that could have brought the bluestones here: but the ice never reached beyond the Severn, nor are there ice-transported bluestone erratics in the areas that it did reach.

Substantial progress has lately been made on the 'history' side of the argument. It has even been claimed that the bluestones have previously formed a stone circle on Preseli itself. And the potential quarry-sites of most have been narrowed down to a handful of tors.

After leaving Carn Goedog, I visited another of these: Craig Rhos-y-felin, a rounded thing sitting next to a stream. Here, lying on the grass next to the tor is what has been claimed to be an abandoned monolith, prised free of its parent rock and left behind (it may have cracked), waiting for some Neolithic Obelix to carry it away.

The bluestones must have mattered to the builders of Stonehenge: just one sign that for these people, stones were embodiments of places and their identities. The Devonian rocks of the ring of Brodgar on Orkney come from at least seven sources across the archipelago's mainland, as if each was an emblematic segment of separate district.

Pembrokeshire is also home to a remarkable geohistorical story rooted in medieval politics. In the middle of the county a great change takes place. The southern limit of the Caledonian is marked by a spirited little series of volcanic outcrops – and then the plateau evens out, as the Carboniferous rocks begin. This 100-million-year gap marks a major geohistorical boundary.

At first the change is not very visible. But the grain is changing, too: the lie of the land starts behaving as if tectonic pressure is coming from slightly west of due south, rather than south-east: this is the Carboniferous-era Variscan grain. Soon moorland falls away, and deep, ria-like estuaries appear, many of them making good harbours. Villages and market towns replace scattered farmsteads; medieval churches replace Nonconformist chapels. We are in a country that as early as the seventeenth century was being called a 'little England beyond Wales'.

I had a lot of fun here, snaking my way along any lane that came close to the Ordovician/Carboniferous boundary, and seeing how the place-names differ either side of it: English to the south (Roblston, Camrose); Welsh to the north (Coed y Bach, Gignog). On the north side of the line I counted a dozen obviously English names among twenty Welsh ones; and in the same area to the south, a single Welsh name among forty that were English. Welsh is spoken in north Pembrokeshire, and English in the south; people speak of the 'Welshry' and the 'Englishry' (or just, 'down below').

There are thus two Pembrokeshires: a northern one, Ordovician and older, moving to a subtle version of the Caledonian Grain – the southernmost outpost of patterns that apply all the way to Cape Wrath; and a southern one, made of much younger rocks, and moving to a new beat – and the division is as much cultural as geological.

This geohistorical division has been called the Landsker line, from a Norse word for a natural boundary. It is the divide between older rocks and younger ones, infertile and fertile, inaccessible and accessible, highland lowland and more typical lowland; and between British and Anglo-Saxon, landscapes filled with prehistoric and early medieval monuments, and landscapes more visibly medieval and later. The line, which runs roughly west to east from the coast at Newgale to near

Laugharne, Carmarthenshire (and then continues across the Gower peninsula), has shifted over the centuries, but remains remarkably intact. Its existence is ultimately thanks to the Normans, who moved Flemings and English into the area, pushing the locals into the less forgiving country. It is a vivid illustration of how the rocks of the Caledonian era have underlain the making and unmaking of nations.

There is a further dimension to the early history of the highland lowlands: many were important sources of prehistoric hand-axes. In north-east Scotland, the Den of Boddam was the only Neolithic flint mine in northern Britain. Other tools came from Graig Lwyd, above Penmaenmawr at the foot of Snowdonia; the Preselis; and in England, the Charnwood/Nuneaton area. And in the highest part of Ordovician Lakeland sits one of the oldest and most dramatic industrial sites in Britain.

The first industrial landscapes

I have twice tried to climb to Pike O'Stickle ('pointed summit on a steep mountain'), a large, tor-like knub of rock that peers vertiginously over Great Langdale in the very highest part of the Lakes.

The first time, I tried to go up the scree slope that runs down from it. The day was peerlessly hot and, pinned to the steep, endlessly loosening surface, I was fried alive. My mobile phone vanished, perhaps claimed by spirits who understandably objected to me trampling on one of what may look like the countless natural screes that line the sides of Lakeland valleys – but is in fact one of the most remarkable archaeological sites in the land.

The second time I approached it was in the depths of winter, and this time I climbed Langdale up a well-worn footpath. When I finally topped the plateau, I found myself bounding like a spaceman over deep fields of snow. Buoyed by the confidence that goes with achievement, I decided to take a shortcut back, only to get lost: snow had covered the burns by which I'd oriented myself, and distorted the shape of the surrounding hills. I ended up twisting my ankle while jumping a hidden, snow-covered waterway, and later finding myself on a narrow, icy ledge that I'd thought was going to be the path down. This is the kind of country that can kill people.

I had, however, stood next to the knuckle-like Pike itself, and gazed down the apparently vertical scree slope that had defeated me before. Just a short distance from its top a dark, artificial-looking cave opened like a boil in its side.

This shallow cave is carved into rocks known as epidotised tuffs, or 'hornstone': solidified volcanic ash which once rained heavily into a closing Iapetus. This hard, greenish, attractive rock forms a 'dark, intermittent procession of outcrops' (Nicholas Crane) at about 1,650–2,900ft, running for about 11 miles along Langdale, Scafell and Glaramara: some of the most challenging country south of the Grampians. Yet no less than 21–30 per cent of the provenanced Neolithic stone tools in Britain are made of them.

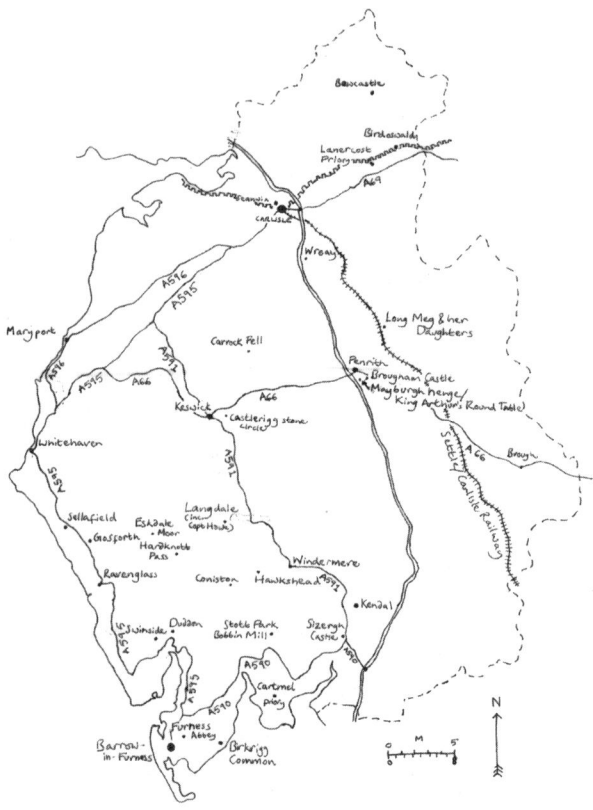

The Pike is the most visible of the rock's quarry-sites: the little cave is probably a shelter; the scree slope a colossal mass of discarded stone. The experimental archaeologist James Dilley tells me that the tuff is easier to knap, quicker to polish and less brittle than the ubiquitous flint; and its smooth, greenish surface may have evoked the much-prized jadeite axes of the Alps. Nevertheless, a massif that contains one of the highest points in Britain seems a remarkable place to site a quarry. Clearly, these people loved this rock.

Trade in these rocks may even be the key to the location of the area's Neolithic monuments: one can imagine a gateway at the Edenside henges of Mayburgh and King Arthur's table, foreshadowing Penrith and the M6 as strategic points in the soft, younger country to the east; a nodal point at the beginning of higher, older country at Castlerigg stone circle, near Keswick (where each rock seems chosen to echo the outline of a nearby hill), and an endpoint in Great Langdale, perhaps marked by great boulders at Copt Howe, one of which is covered in Neolithic rock art. Perhaps this was a sacralised, as well as an industrialised landscape, its very inaccessibility a factor in the pull of the rocks.

This site, at its most active from about 3800–3500 BC, marks several 'firsts'. Never before had such a specific stone-type generated such an intense feeding frenzy among human beings, resulting in the removal of a large amount of stone from a specific location and its spreading throughout the island. And – with the flint mines of Cretaceous south-east Britain – this is the first landscape to be visibly and permanently transformed by industry. A direct line of evolution leads from here to Dinorwic, and indeed to every mine or quarry in the land. And it is just one of the resources generated by Caledonian-era events.

Metallic riches

We think of the Lake District as a place of great natural beauty, but it was long full of industry. You can easily stumble on the small 'delves' or quarries, ruined buildings and grown-over slagheaps that are the remnants of metal extraction. Grander examples include the dark ruins of Bonsor mine, a memorable feature of the climb up the Old Man of Coniston, from here were wrested 35,000 tons of copper in 1856 alone. The ruins of the Greenside lead mine near Ullswater, once one of the most important in Britain, are comparably forbidding. The transport of lead ore is a likely reason for the Roman road over Hardknott pass, which follows a route so steep that it can intimidate in spite of its modern covering of asphalt.

Lead, after all, was essential for everything from pipes to bullets. No wonder Elizabeth I, determined to maximise native resources if the Spanish threat was to be faced off, imported German and Dutch miners to the area; they built some of the first wooden rail-guided wagon-ways to help transport loads of ore. Defoe's sense that this is a useless landscape; Wordsworth's praise for its untarnished wilderness – both suggest a certain wilful blindness.

A unique industry fed on the graphite found near Seathwaite in Borrowdale, among the largest and most historically important such deposits in the world. This soft, distinctive 'metallic earth or hard glittering stone', as William Camden, historian and topographer, called it in 1607, was already being mined from 'wad holes' in the sixteenth century. Graphite is inert and heat-resistant, and generated a host of uses as the industrial revolution got under way; not least as moulds for cannonballs. But its oldest and most prescient use is probably a result of the simple discovery that it left a grey and reasonably permanent mark when rubbed on a sheep. Eventually, methods were developed of encasing this soft marker in wood so as to stiffen it: the 'lead' pencil was born. For a long time the chief source of graphite for pencils globally was Borrowdale; and the best ones came from the factories in Keswick.

Tectonic change and metal and mineral deposits often go together. When magma rises, it may bring with it a hot, rich stew of materials which can then be chemically altered by the changing environments they encounter en route. The resulting materials might then be deposited in the fault-lines which provide routes through such rocks, forming lodes, veins and seams for human beings to follow.

For the earliest signs of such metal-hunting, go to Wales. Copper, the earliest metal to be discovered, was being extracted in about 2500–1600 BC from Copa hill in Cwmystwyth, a dark, smashed-up Silurian valley in the Cambrian mountains, 'narrowly with rocky mountains enclosed'

(John Leland, poet and antiquary, c.1535–43). The alteration by smelting of the geochemistry of the peat here is Britain's first known evidence for atmospheric pollution; the valley was also mined for lead, both by the Romans, and by the Cistercian monks of Strata Florida abbey: a charter of 1184 mentions 'possessions under the land'. In the industrial era it was a source of silver and zinc, too; the site today is littered with remains going back to the very discovery of metal itself.

It's possible, though the evidence is less clear-cut, that copper was extracted even earlier than this at Parys Mountain, Anglesey. Today, this Silurian hilltop is more a post-industrial wasteland than a geological formation – but that is an industrial-era story, for from the 1780s, under 'copper king' Thomas Williams, Parys – for a few intense decades – eclipsed even Cornwall, becoming the single greatest source of the metal in the world. Parys Mountain copper played a major role in the copper-bottoming of the boats of the Royal Navy, and later of everything from tea clippers to slaving ships; the process made ship maintenance easier, and improved speed and manoeuvrability – one senior official claimed it doubled naval power. These ores thus helped secure British economic prowess.

Once, hunger for its copper gave the hill 'a most savage appearance. Suffocating fumes of the burning heaps of copper arise in all parts and extend their baneful influence for miles around' (Pennant). Today the impression of artificiality is increased by the remains of an engine house and a windmill (both to pump water from the mine); and the striking shades of scarlet, green and yellow that fill the ponds formed by the ever-present rain. The hotter shades are from oxidization of the iron used to process the ores; the green, today rare, is the copper itself.

Other metals and minerals found in the rocks of this period include silver, often present in the lead ore known as galena; and lead, copper and zinc, also often found together. But there are many others, including cobalt, arsenic, nickel, manganese, and such lesser-known materials as barytes (of fundamental importance to the oil industry for its use in drilling) and antimony. Sir Isaac Newton long hoped this metallic material was the alchemical Philosopher's Stone, capable of creating the most precious 'stone' of all: gold.

This rare, beautiful, untarnishable metal has mattered to people both culturally, as a marker of beauty and power, and for its inherent value. Without a gold crown, a king is not a king; while entire economies have depended on gold-based cash.

One of the only sources of gold in Britain lies in the Argyll-group Highland rocks around Tyndrum and Aberfeldy, an important area for metals and minerals generally. Further north, the (failed) Helmsdale/Kildonan gold rush of 1869 led to the creation of a short-lived clapboard town, Baile an Òr, in Sutherland. But another metal-rich area was the main historic source of gold in Scotland – it is centered around Wanlockhead and Leadhills in the Southern Uplands. These industrial settlements are said to be the highest villages in Scotland; Leadhills is little more than a long line of white cottages at the head of an industry-raked valley, yet it was the site of one of the first public libraries in Britain in 1741.

The only modern sources of gold south of here are in Wales. The little-visited upland of the Rhinogs is also Britain's most extensive Cambrian landscape, separated by grain-following estuaries from Snowdonia to the north and Cadair Idris and the Cambrian mountains to the south, and rich in minerals and metals. The nineteenth-century goldrush here stimulated the virtual rebuilding of the characterful little town of Dolgellau; the gold for royal wedding rings is still sourced in the area.

But the oldest goldmine in Britain is at Dolaucothi, near Pumsaint in Carmathenshire: the southern edge of Silurian country. Already known in the Iron Age, the gold here might explain the determination with which the Romans fought to defeat the Silures and Ordovices. The highly organised operation established from AD 70/80 included a Roman fort (possibly *Luentinum*, from 'washing', after the use of water to sluice the gold from the ground and then sort it) and ambitious leats totalling 7 miles in length.

A wonderful medieval geo-legend is based in this landscape, featuring five saints on a pilgrimage to St David's, who are attacked by an evil magician who lives in the mines. He conjures up a storm in an effort to put them off; all but one are saved by sheltering under a rock which to this day has the marks of their heads and shoulders impressed on it. The fifth was taken into the mines, where he lies asleep.

The *Carreg Pumsaint*, the 'stone of the five saints', which inspired this tale does indeed have an odd shape, but the hollows on it were created by the workers in the Roman gold-mines, who used it to crush rocks in search of the precious ore. While the stories of stone heroes often interpret unusual landforms, or obviously ancient sites such as barrows, it is rare for these geological fables to seek to explain an early site of industry.

Rare limestones

Not all the rocks of these periods have been as tortured, twisted and bulldozed as these. In Shropshire and the Black Country, a Silurian limestone crops out. It makes our second limestone landscape, and in it we can discover more aspects of 'limestonelish'.

On the road from Much Wenlock to Craven Arms in Shropshire, I was in a landscape with the same crisp, green, calcium-rich character I had seen at Durness. I was following Wenlock Edge, one of a pair of ridges of unnerving straightness, like the crests of waves breaking along the Caledonian Grain. Where frost and ice had broken the rock from its cloth of soil, small, bright crags of white limestone split the surface: 'wen' is from *gwyn*, the Welsh for white. But to glimpse the innards of this stone, it's better to head 30 miles east, to a group of hills which break from the suburban housing of the Black Country: one provides a stone throne for Dudley castle; another is the Wren's Nest.

To climb this hill is to discover gorges and cliffs as spectacular as any of the caves around Durness. But these are not natural: for the Nest has been gouged and tunnelled within an inch of its life, in a great feeding frenzy that sought lime for use as flux to help purify iron ore in the smelting industries that flourished on Carboniferous rocks that surround the hill. The process revealed to the world the inner structure of the hill: the ripple-marks left by great storms on the Iapetus sea floor; herds of trilobites bustling in the Iapetan shallows, now fixed in rock.

It is human industry that has made this lost world visible, and its nineteenth-century discovery stimulated major advances in the incipient science of geology. So it is fitting that a fossil trilobite, the 'Dudley locust', is the emblem of the local town.

Wenlock limestone also makes a decent building stone. Indeed its gentle greenish shade defines Much Wenlock: another settlement that, like Great Malvern, is visibly built from the bones of the Earth beneath it. We return to where we began, with building materials.

Building stones

Keills chapel sits at the merging point of water, land and vapour. Hard by its Argyllshire lochside, it is a simple structure built – like almost every building in Dalradian and Moinian Scotland, it sometimes seems – of the slabby, hard-to-shape rocks around it. But outside it stands a lavishly carved eighth-century cross almost 2m high, and within, dozens more carved stones line the walls.

These medieval grave-markers practically squirm with shallow, smooth carvings: knights clad in what are probably thick rolls of linen rather than chain mail; the boats and swords that were the keys to power and wealth in the region; crosses of knotty foliage; beasts that seem to have crawled out of illuminated manuscripts.

All this is carved into slabs of the 'green beds', greenish-blue epidorite schists of the Argyll Group; this site, towards the end of a long peninsula, may even have been a centre for their distribution. For though they are most common in mid-Argyll, such carvings can be found in many locations among the highlands and islands of Scotland's far west. Many were quarried on the shores of lochs Sween and Fyne. They are among the only carvable rocks in the western Highlands.

These early medieval crosses and later tomb-markers have two things in common: sophistication of design, and flat, smooth, graphic carved surfaces. Perhaps this is rooted in the limitations of these layered but fissile rocks, which are easily quarried in great flat slabs, and relatively soft on exposure to the air – but apt to collapse if carving goes too deep.

Such rocks sit towards the upper end of a hierarchy of stones used for building and carving. Most stone – like that of Keills chapel – is only suitable to be piled up as rubble, or perhaps to be given a single flat side. Such rocks can be found in many parts of Britain: in Caledonian-era Shropshire there seems to be a new variety every few miles.

Better still is 'dimension stone', rock that is cuttable into rectilinear pieces or ashlar, as with the Wenlock limestone: often, as here, some beds are more carvable still, and could even qualify as freestones.

These are rocks that can be cut in any direction, making them suitable for deep, fine carving. Ideally, a freestone can also take significant compressive weight, making it suitable for structural as well as sculptural use. Stones with these qualities sit at the top of the hierarchy of building stone. The grains of which they are made are typically relatively small, uniform in size, and cemented together strongly. They are thus always of sedimentary origin (even marble, one of the most carvable of stones, is ultimately derived from a sedimentary rock).

The very best freestones are often limestones, the calcium in which glues particles together particularly well. But excellent sandstones are not unusual, and include the two oldest freestones in Britain: Egryn, from the foot of the Rhinogs, often seen in old buildings within striking distance of this coast; and Caerbwdy, quarried at a Pembrokeshire cove, where I feasted on fish and chips and stared at lumps of the pink/purple rock used in St David's Cathedral. Neither of these is of first-rate quality: it is their Cambrian age – they are 526–499 million years old – that makes them special.

In truth, however, most stones of the Cambrian, Ordovician and Silurian succession can barely be shaped at all. James Loch, one of the nineteenth-century Commissioners of the Sutherland Estates, described the local rocks as 'almost unfit for building', because of 'the labour of procuring them, and the expense [sic] of forming them into shape'. Buildings of stone in Caledonian upland areas can be dour, unless money has been spent on imported materials, or better rocks happen to lie nearby: in the Southern Uplands, red and tan Devonian, Carboniferous and Permian sandstones are not far away, and give many buildings an appealing combination of slabby walls and colourful, finer-grained 'dressings', as more finely wrought areas such as window-surrounds and cornerstones are called.

The massive rocks that are the Caledonian norm have a power of their own. In Wales, Dolgellau is defined by the greenish tones of the local variant; not far away, Harlech castle is almost a geological presence in itself, sitting on the fault-bounded cliff from which it was built.

There are also a few rocks that have attractive colouring and can be polished and used ornamentally. These are often called 'marble', though they are geologically not marble at all. The Cambrian Mona marble of Anglesey is a green, white-veined igneous serpentine, used in Grecian-style furniture by its great promoter, George Bullock. Bullock supplied furniture to Longwood house, Napoleon's place of exile on St Helena, so the emperor may have contemplated his uncertain future at a table in the South Atlantic topped with a little piece of Anglesey. There are comparable materials in parts of the Highlands, north-east Scotland (Portsoy marble was used at Versailles) and Herefordshire.

Of these rocks, only Portsoy is relatively well known. But Caledonian-era geologies also produced the two geologically oldest superstar building stones in Britain.

Slate building stones

As you explore quarries such as Dinorwic, buildings of slate begin to separate themselves from this mangled world. There is the enormous mill complex near Llanberis itself, now the National Slate Museum. High on the shoulders of the mountain above, are the scattered houses of the squatter settlements built by quarry workers and their families. There are also dormitories for workers; dressing halls for shaping slates; *Gwaliau*, smaller processing shelters; and *caban*, spaces where workers could rest. Perhaps the men who sat in them discussed the £100,000 a year made by local quarry owner Lord Penrhyn, when their own average earnings were about £52. The radical ideas spread by such men spearheaded the industrial-era resurgence of Welsh culture.

But the architecture of slate is everywhere in this region. In the 1830s, as the industry hollowed out the Ordovician slates on the southern side of Snowdonia (which were mined rather than quarried) Blaenau Ffestiniog transformed itself from a scattering of farms to the second largest settlement in North Wales; a miniature city, creeping like a grey slatey spider over its hilly valley, its foci around the marketplace and the sites of chapels.

Places like Dinorwic and Blaenau possess a great, shattered harmony between the landscape and its extraction; between where people lived, where they worked, and what the mountains look like. This is as powerful a feedback loop between humanity and geology as any in Britain.

Then there are the ports – Port Penryhn, Port Dinorwic, and others – and the mighty houses of the quarry owners – the English Pennants and Assheton-Smiths, the Welsh Oakeleys. None is more vainglorious than Penryhn Castle (completed 1837), a work of Romanesque hauteur outside Bangor. It is a testament to the wealth of the Pennants, who under Richard, first Baron Penryhn, invested slaving money in developing their eponymous quarry. Here, in a valley adjacent to Dinorwic, the biggest slate quarry in the world developed, in the mid-1850s; when Dinorwic produced 90,000 tons of slate, Penryhn produced 120,000.

Snowdonian slate was known as early as the Roman period. By the fifteenth century it was being exported as far away as Ireland and south-east England. But its heyday was the industrial-era explosion of British cities, when the quarries of Snowdonia employed some 8,000, and the rock roofed much of the country, and as far afield as America and Australia. The rebuilding of Hamburg after a fire of 1842 consumed vast quantities of it, ironically later destroyed by British bombing.

But slate has had many applications. Penryhn castle boasts a four-poster bed made of it. In local farmhouses and cottages it generated a delightful vernacular art form, in which elaborate patterns were engraved on prominent slate lintels. Then there is the 'wedding stone' or 'rock cannon', a stretch of slate bored with holes. Filled with gunpowder, these become giant reusable geological firecrackers, used to mark social events and celebrations. In the younger slates of Cornwall, they are called 'merriment holes', which sounds vaguely obscene.

The marking of slate with chalk was for centuries the most ubiquitous of all educational technologies: it combined thin slices of Caledonian Wales with sticks of Cretaceous south-east England. Slate has been used for flagstones and gravestones, billiard tables and electrical switchboards.

Almost all the other true slates in Britain are also the result of Caledonian events. In Scotland, a strip of rocks of the Argyll Group was aggressively quarried at the 'slate islands' of Easdale, Seil, Luing and Belnahua in the Firth of Lorn, and at Ballachulish on Loch Leven. These slates can have a silvery sheen, and many are naturally studded with little square jewels of yellow pyrite (Fool's Gold); while pretty, they make the material more likely to fail. Nevertheless, they were exported to the industrial centres of the Midland Valley, and across the world. The aristocratic Bredalbane family, the local landowners, also owned Nova Scotia, and there is much of this slate in eastern Canada.

Easdale island has been a source of roofing material since at least the twelfth century, and the hunger for slate came close to entirely removing it. Its single large hill is now a spine of rock eaten into on both sides by great mouthfuls of quarry which open to the sea in great flooded pools; the low, white workers' cottages, meanwhile, largely sit on made ground. The big sheltered pools and piles of flat discarded stones here today attract both wild swimmers and the world stone-skimming championships.

The impact on the adjacent islet of Ellenabeich was even more dramatic. Quarrying removed its middle, leaving only a low circle of rock between it and the waters of the firth. After this was breached in a great storm of 1881, all that remained was a kind of slatey reef. Waste material from the quarry, meanwhile, had been deposited between Ellenabeich and the much larger island of Seil: and it is on that entirely artificial ground that the settlement of Ellenabeich sits today.

Easdale produced more slates than anywhere in Scotland until upstaged by Ballachulish in the 1860s. The latter quarries, opened in 1693, came to be the source of 15 million slates a year. There were also major slate quarries in north-east Scotland, and along the edge of the Highland Boundary Fault.

English slates are rare, though those of Lakeland are for many the finest in Britain. It is said they will last twice as long on a roof as those from Wales. Like the hand-axes of Langdale, they originated as Ordovician volcanic ash, compacted on the Iapetus seafloor. Then there are the slates from Swithland, on the edge of Charnwood Forest:

their legacy is a series of huge, water-filled quarry-pits, one of them 55m deep. The industry died with the takeover of Welsh slate.

Indeed Snowdonian, and to a lesser extent Easdale/Ballachulish, slates caused the extinction of a huge variety of stone roofing materials. These included rocks that are not geologically slate, but which can be split unusually thinly while remaining reasonably strong. These are 'stone-slates', also used for flooring flags and gravestones, and sourced in rocks of many geological periods. They are particularly attractive for their rough, rocky texture, and the extent to which they harmonise with the landscape from which they come. Some – as around Findlater and Toumintoul in north-east Scotland, or Harnage in Shropshire – are of Caledonian-era origin. The disappearance of such materials under the onslaught led by places like Dinorwic became, as Richard Fortey puts it, a 'national conspiracy against regional character': a lithic monoculture.

Granite building stones

Slate was not the only superstar building material to have been created in the great, subterranean Caledonian mill. And here, instead of a shattered mountain, we are returning to north-east Scotland, and the great city of Aberdeen.

The hard silver heart of this city is revealed in its massive buildings, their crisp, erosion-resistant details 'at once ancient and freshly minted' (Ted Nield, author of *Underlands*). The place has a metallic glint, which can shine menacingly after rain, or become bewitching in moonlight – and it comes from the large minerals they contain. For this is an entire city defined by the local rock.

A taste for carving this obdurate material started early, for the region is the homeland of the enigmatic Neolithic carved stone balls, many made of granite and each only a few inches across. Until the nineteenth-century invention of powered tools, only the local Picts and the sixteenth-century Cornish came close to matching such finesse in shaping this stone. Local granite boulders were used for buildings from the medieval period, but quarrying is not recorded until 1603.

Granite's heyday began with demand for it in London, 400 miles/650km to the south. Precocious in development and without good building stone of its own, the metropolis has sucked in man-made erratics like a sponge. Its streets torn up by carts and hooves, in 1766 it was calculated that the use of Scottish granite setts could save the lives of up to 3,000 horses and reduce maintenance costs by up to £12,000 a year.

With good granites close to the coast, the quarrying and sett-making industry of north-east Scotland began to boom. Soon granite was being used in other situations in which compressive strength and imperviousness were required, such as harbourfronts. But its potential was more than just practical; as Dr Johnson commented, granite was 'beautiful' as well as 'hardy'.

In the 1830s, the Aberdonian mason Alexander MacDonald invented a steam-powered granite polisher. The result was the first widespread use of shaped and polished granite since the days of ancient Egypt. Just as with pharaonic carvings, the resulting objects have a certain resplendent sobriety, their sheer, massive lines projecting power and authority. Carved granite has always had the macho air of a triumph of will over matter.

Mighty plinths of polished granite supported monuments to Sir Walter Scott, the Duke of Wellington, Prince Albert and others; by the 1890s they could be seen as far afield as Wellington, New Zealand (Queen Victoria), Pretoria, South Africa (Paul Kruger) and Louisville, Kentucky (Scots-born senator James Guthrie). A fashionable granite headstone could 'transmit the Inscription Engraven on it to distant Ages', as Macdonald put it. In 1893, 89,341 such were exported to the USA; In 1900, the delivery of a granite copy of an ancient temple to Egypt, for use in a memorial to prime minister Khedive Nubar Pasha, set the seal on Britain's usurpation of an ancient granitic/imperial/commemorative nexus. Though Scandinavian and American sources were by then eclipsing it, and the nation's roads had long been covered with asphalt, the nationwide construction of war memorials after 1918 gave the material another lease of life.

In the meantime, granite architecture had become fashionable. Here again, London took an early lead; in the early nineteenth century it was used in the British Museum and for the fountains in Trafalgar Square (added partly to constrain political protests). Soon, polished granite frontages were projecting self-assurance and affluence in many places. In 1894, £13,000-worth of the rock was extracted, and more than half was exported as far afield as China. Emigrant Scottish granite workers were helping develop granite industries in America, Russia and elsewhere.

By this time, the granite industry had reshaped Aberdeen itself. A city which had supported just eight master masons in 1784 was home to sixty or seventy in 1850; they employed 1,400 people. And the city itself had been transformed.

In 1741, a city ordinance declared that buildings should be of stone to guard against fire. With an example already set by Robert Gordon's Hospital (1723), granite structures proliferated. A series of granite bridges allowed the settlement to spread beyond limits long defined by the Dee, the Denburn and the Don. Bannerman's bridge (from 1766) was one of the first-ever flyovers; Union bridge (1805) had one of the largest single-span arches in the world. Union Street became, as the poet Alistair Mackie put it, a 'mile-lang monument to the grey skinkle [lustre] and mica een o the quarry hole', which 'bleezed greet in the wink o its million een'. By the end of the 1840s Aberdeen was simply known as 'the granite city'; the use of any other material drew complaints.

I made a special detour here to see Marischal college, said to be (with the Escorial palace, Spain), the largest granite building in the world. Completed in 1906, the architect, A. Marshall Mackenzie, used the medieval Perpendicular gothic style, but this is no pastiche. Granite favours smooth lines and simplified forms, and Marischal would be almost modern in its abstraction were it not for the sheer vertical ribbing of its detailing and the icy flair of the stone of which it is made. As an architecture shaped by the unique qualities of the rock from which it is built, it is without parallel.

Meanwhile, the area around Aberdeen was becoming the capital of British quarrying. 'Half o' Aiberdeen has come oot o' that hole', it was said of the quarry at Rubislaw, today a great absent monster surrounded by loose fencing in a western suburb of the city.

This is the sunken inland ocean from which a total of 6 million tons of stone was ripped, and I had to see it for myself. Leaving a youth hostel apparently filled with migrants and oil workers rather than hikers, I peered into a void 148m deep, its base 49m below sea level. Sunlight cannot touch the great pool that fills it. Though it began as a small hillock, today you could put Castle Rock in Edinburgh into Rubislaw and still have space for more. In a marker of Aberdeen's continued dependence on geological resources, the discovery of North Sea oil was announced on the same day in April 1970 that Rubislaw was closed.

The high quality of the white-grey stone produced at Kemnay quarry 15 miles away made it larger still. Indeed by 1900, quarries ringed the city, and there were more around Peterhead, and other places where granite lay within reach of the coast, or to which railway lines could be laid.

There are other useful granites of the Caledonian era, especially in the Highlands: Glensanda quarry, the largest in Europe, is a source of hardcore and roadstone. Attractively coloured granites include those from the Ross of Mull, cut within sight of Iona and used on London's Holborn Viaduct. The quarries at Criffel in Galloway were so good for quays and bridges that they were purchased by the Liverpool Dock Trustees; the nearby town of Dalbeattie became a mini-Aberdeen. A small outcrop of the Lakeland granite batholith near Shap has yielded one of Britain's finest granites, its pink crystals making it ripe for decorative use. And there are further important granites in south-west England, though these are geologically much younger.

Aberdonian granite and Snowdonian slate share a common origin in the processes that created the structure of the island itself. Every granite plinth to a Victorian hero is carved from a lump of frozen magma that welled up below the lost Caledonides. Every slate roof is made of rocks compressed as continents conjoined. Our homes are roofed with lithic embodiments of the events that united Britain.

The clay of life

Most Caledonian-era building materials are hard: they have had to be to survive so long. But there are a few clays. Like all such materials, they have been used to make bricks – and much more besides.

Clay is a soft, poorly consolidated sedimentary rock, made of particles which ultimately derived from igneous, silica-rich sources. Its qualities vary subtly from one deposit to another – making one clay more plastic and another more able to withstand heat, or giving them a variety of tonal qualities.

Hold clay, and you can shape it into almost any form. Impervious, bowls or cups of it can hold liquids. Fire it to more than 900°C and it becomes hard, long lasting (unless dropped on the floor). Many of the resulting objects are also beautiful, a transfer of geology to aesthetics through the moulding power of the human hand.

Clay in its unfired form can be used for buildings: the ancient clays of Wales, known as *clom* or *mwd*, contributed to the near-lost British tradition of earthen architecture. And the material's imperviousness has given it a vital role in industrial- and modern-era works such as embankments and dams: 3 million cubic metres of the stuff can be consumed when building 9 miles of dual carriageway.

But it is fired clay, in the form of bricks and tiles, that lies at the heart of clay's significance for architecture – those in Radnorshire and Montgomeryshire are Silurian. Though the iron they contain usually turns brick red while they are being fired, they vary depending on the presence (or addition) of materials such as sand, ash and limestone/chalk. Like all clay objects, they are at once geological and artificial; something very hard, made from stuff that is very soft.

They also have an unexpected intimacy about them. Bricks, like cups, like bowls, are designed to fit the human hand: the dip or 'frog' in them, marked with the name of the company that made them, makes them easier to carry. Things of humble beauty, still in everyday use.

From birth to revolution, change can be sudden. Perhaps the tectonic events that gave us volcanoes and earthquakes are the geological equivalents. But change can also be slow, gradual, undramatic: the daily churn of politics, the growth of a child – and in geology, processes of erosion.

As we come to the end of the epoch-making geohistory of the Cambrian, Ordovician and Silurian rocks, we move from the former to the latter. Something softer, more giving, comes in the wake of the assembly of Britain: our first typically lowland landscapes are the result. It is a story with an intimate geological and historical relationship to the highland-forming rocks we have just explored.

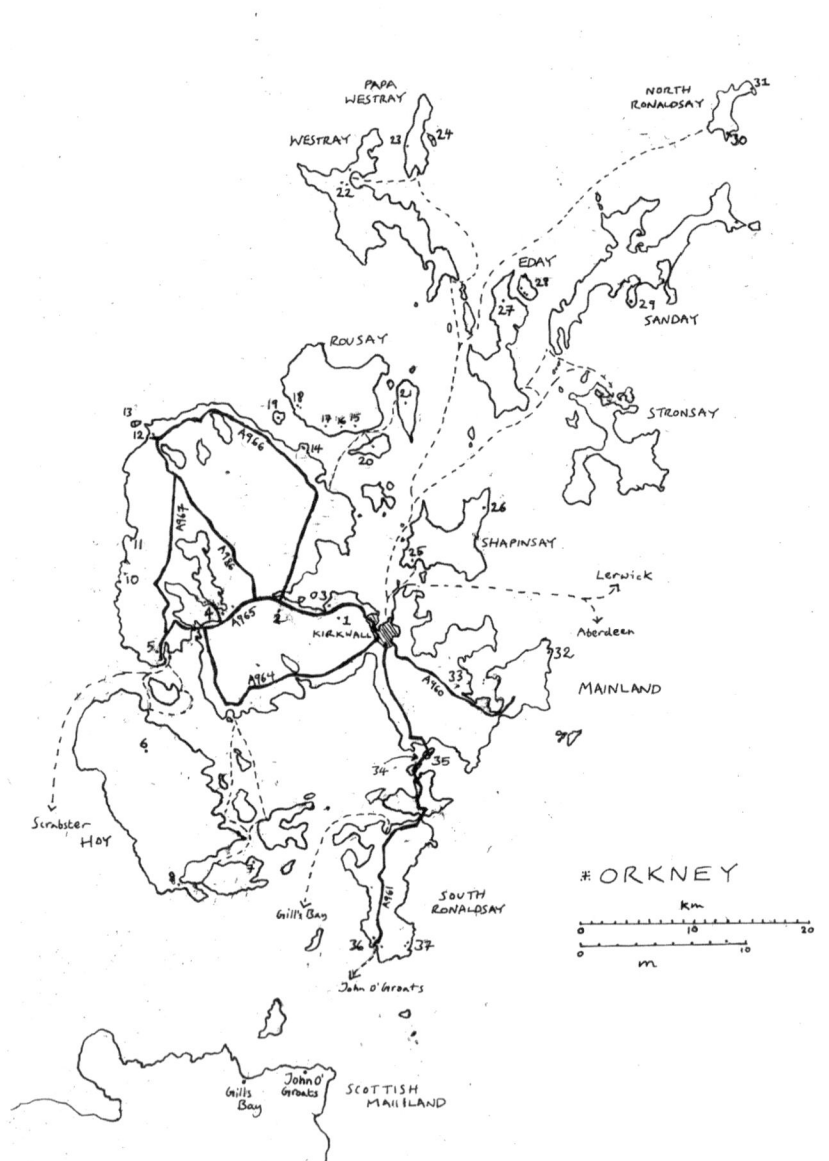

PAPA
WESTRAY

NORTH
RONALDSAY   31

WESTRAY   23   24   30

22

EDAY
28

27   29
SANDAY

ROUSAY

18   STRONSAY
13   19
12   17 16 15
A766   14
20

26

SHAPINSAY

25   Lerwick

A147   0 3
4   A765   2   1
5   KIRKWALL   Aberdeen

A964   33   32

A960   MAINLAND

7

34   35

6

8

Scrabster   HOY

Gill's Bay
SOUTH
RONALDSAY

ORKNEY

km
0   10   20

0   10
m

36   37

John o'Groats

John o'
Gills   Groats   SCOTTISH
Bay   MAINLAND

Chapter 6

Devonian Old Red deserts
419–358 million years ago

I visited Orkney shortly after the death of my mother. I decided to take my time in this place, and salve my wounds with solitary exploration. As I moved around in what – it quickly became clear – was the defining place of the Old Red Sandstone, the rock itself seemed imbued with a quiet kind of grieving: for the 'Old Red' is the detritus of the death of mountains.

Even as the Caledonide mountains went up, they started to erode. They did so very fast. The mountains were young, high, exposed, and unprotected by soils and plants, few of which yet existed. From the late Silurian, through the Devonian and into the Carboniferous, massive amounts of mountain-dust – sand – were washed from them.

Much of this fell into the basins which were also the creation of Caledonian-era pressures. By the end of the Devonian the mountains were little higher than they are now, while at their feet lay an emerging new rock, in deposits that in Orkney alone might have been 1–2 miles deep. Invisible to those who inhabit them, many sedimentary rocks lie remarkably deep, and normally what remains is a fraction of what there once was. For all their beauty, these landscapes are also testaments to removal and to loss – as, in a sense was my experience of Orkney itself.

Geohistorically, the Old Red Sandstone – which I'll simply call the Old Red from now on – has a profound binary relationship with the mountainous uplands we have explored so far. Not only is it mostly made of fragments of them, but it forms a history-rich littoral to these older rocks, a kind of geohistorical margin. Everywhere, the Devonian is close to upland, but fertile and easy to settle, generally making low-lying landscapes and weathering into well-drained soils (in the north often complemented by a layer of much younger earths generated in the wake of the ice ages). There are grainfields in Caithness, and orchards in Herefordshire. Both sit in the shadow of Caledonian-era upland.

These are gentle landscapes, but ones that are edged with highland hardness: well-settled country which also lies close to challenging and empty environments. While being our first true lowland landscape, the human history of the Devonian rocks is partly defined by its role as a route past, or anchor for power in the region of, nearby highland country.

Devonian rocks are found in three areas: but the first, in Devon, are – ironically, given the name of the period – rather different to the rest. These south-western rocks are seawater deposits, and they formed several hundred miles south-east of 'Britain'. Their story is embedded in that of the Variscan events of the Carboniferous and early Permian periods – we'll come back to it.

This leaves the classic areas of Old Red: rocks originating in freshwater rivers and lakes, rocks which formed at the foot of Caledonide uplands.

One large patch lies adjacent to the Cambrian mountains, and has Herefordshire as its heartland. Here we are in the border zone between England and Wales known as the Marches; narrower arms of the rock reach deep into Wales.

The other major area is in Scotland, where scattered 'islets' of Old Red are found in valleys around the Southern Uplands, and line the foot of the Highland Boundary Fault. They then increase in size and historical significance as they head north along the eastern side of the Highlands – until one reaches an actual archipelago: Orkney.

Orkney and the Old Red

Orkney is a place suffused with the qualities of its rocks. Scattered islets with flat-topped profiles lie like slabs in the water, as if they had been planed off. Equally slab-like rocks edge their shorelines: red monoliths struggling to break free of imprisoning cliffs, or lying scattered on the coast, like the remains of some tragic accident. The layered flatness of hills and rocks alike gives the whole archipelago a certain subaqueous quality. The light makes a soft dance between low, flat-topped hills and the vapours of the waters and of the skies.

From long barrows to whaling towns, the islands are filled with monuments of many eras. It can seem as if the velocity of time itself is increasing here, closer than anywhere in this book to the axis around which the Earth spins. I stood on the northernmost point of the island of Papa Westray and knew there was no landfall between me and Arctic ice. Sky and sea can seem to come as close as *ultima* is to *Thule*; the wind is constant (I was told, only half-jokingly, that if it stops, people fall over).

The archipelago is culturally and historically almost as much a part of Scandinavia as of Britain. The tourist will find no clans or tartans. There are crofts, but they are relatively large and productive, filling the landscape with stone-built farms; more like an intensified version of Old Red Herefordshire than anything else in Scotland's Highland zone. It is all a bit of a surprise, coming from the south through seemingly endless expanses of mountain and peat, to find the far north-east so relatively bucolic; yet were it not for those mountains, this sandstone would not exist.

While its identity is a proud variant of 'Scottish', there is a sense in which Orkney is just Orkney; or perhaps that it is a rather special variant on what it is to be 'British'. Fitting, then, that the Old Red is our first truly British rock. Now that the main constituent parts of our island have been assembled, everything will be potentially visible in any part of Britain, forming a series of layers lying on top of the old, hard 'basement' of Silurian-and-older rocks.

The sense that this is a world apart is everywhere. The largest of Orkney's seventy or so islands is called 'Mainland', as if the 700-mile-long land mass to the south were an incidental extra. There is a 'mountain range', in the shape of Ward Hill (481m) and adjacent uplands on the island of Hoy. They are made of solid Old Red, but a plinth of volcanic rock helps give them their height. There is also a 'sea': Scapa Flow, a great sheltered anchorage, its bounds fixed by faults which either follow the Caledonian Grain or run at right angles to it. Old Red often responds to this grain, gathering as it does in basins shaped by Caledonian-era pressures; and the Old Red of the far north is particularly prone to clean, right-angled fractures.

This is a place defined as much by the water as by the land; the 'ebbes and streames of contrair routing tyds' described by the sixteenth-century Scots poet William Fowler. Its rocks formed on the floor of the 19,000-square-mile 'Lake Orcadie'.

The Old Red rocks laid down on the bed of this mighty expanse of water are also those that have the greatest geohistorical intensity. They extend from Shetland to south of Elgin on the Moray coast: a full 200 miles north to south. On the Scottish mainland they dominate Caithness, and then become a great 'L' shaped fringe to the Highlands, running south down the east coast and then east along the Moray Firth. Their lacustrine origin is made explicit by frequent seams of fossilised fish, 'Caithness fish beds' with bony, coal-like spines, which can look as if some enormous fish grill had been left in the sun for a few hundred million years. Such life was teeming in the waters of the Earth.

The sands of the disintegrating Caledonide mountains, often themselves flattish grains of clay or mica, fell slowly through still waters, settling on the lake floor. The layers of 'bedding' that result are a characteristic of sedimentary rocks; the angle at which they sit known as a 'bedding plane'. Unless later tectonic developments distort them, these planes are horizontal: they enable nature (in the form of frost or water), or people (using levers and tools) to potentially split and release the rock in horizontal chunks.

These horizontal planes are particularly emphatic on Orkney, where later events – the removal of overlying layers, the rising of the crust – caused them to develop the right-angled faults which explain both the flattish profile of the islands, and the slab-like rocks that can so easily be turned into standing stones and drystone buildings.

One can get a vivid glimpse inside these rocks on the ferry from Stromness, Orkney, to Scrabster on the Scottish mainland. As you pass Hoy, the cliffs fall a sheer 346m: these are the highest sea-cliffs in this book (the highest cliffs in the UK, at 426m, are on St Kilda), and a cross-section through the Ward Hill massif. The Old Man, a single pillar of rock a few yards wide and 137m high, makes a dramatic vertical foil; 15 million people watched its televised ascent in 1967. Many have climbed it since.

These rocks come on like a ruddy stone sunset veined by dark horizontal clouds. These lines mark periods when the environment of the lake-floor changed for a while, altering the character of the rock. They render the bedding planes more visible.

No matter how consistent and strong a sedimentary formation is, at some point such a line will interrupt it; and often these are lines of weakness. The distance between them often determines the ultimate size of blocks of stone that can be removed from the rock. And such stones are strongest when laid so that their bedding planes remain horizontal. The blocks in an ashlar wall thus directly reflect the changing conditions on the bed of a sea, lake or river millions of years ago.

The redness of these cliffs is also an expression of the Devonian environment. Laurussia was moving across the kind of latitudes occupied by the Kalahari today: a desert zone then as now. Heat, combined with exposure to water and oxygen, turned the outside of many grains of sand reddish: usually, in the case of the Old Red, a rusty kind of purple.

But this rock can also be yellow or tan in colour; it can even be apple-green where there was less oxygen, or grey where the water was deep and the sun far away. In Devon there are limestones; at the foot of the Highland Boundary Fault, 'conglomerates', made of lumps of Caledonian rock washed in great fans from the heights, and cemented together like some lithic fruit cake. But red sandstone is the period's normative rock: Laurussia is sometimes called 'the Old Red Sandstone continent'.

Maybe it was some kind of elision of my emotions and the rocks themselves, but death and its commemoration became for me a defining geohistorical theme of the Orkney landscape. It's not only that the rocks are the colour of blood, and visibly cemeteries of sea-creatures and mountains alike. It is also that the islands are littered with monumental burial structures from the distant past: Neolithic burial mounds; medieval churches honouring the martyr-saint Magnus; harbours and coasts that are a great graveyard of naval history. Most of the 835 people lost in the 1939 sinking of HMS *Royal Oak* still lie at the bottom of Scapa Flow; they are by no means alone.

In places the landscape itself seems poised on the edge of destruction, or at least catastrophic change. On the coast of Papa Westray the door of a 5,000-year-old home looks over a stretch of sea that was not there when it was built; nearby, the stones of a ruined broch perch atop a prehistoric midden, from which they clatter back into the basin from which they were born.

Prehistoric Orkney

The clouds were low when I visited Hoy. On the steep side of Ward Hill I lingered at the very point where cloud shut down any sense of the wider landscape, and my senses closed in. Perhaps the peak should remain hidden, for this is another of our lost 'holy mountains': a place which the surrounding ancient monuments seem again and again to be trying to talk about. In recorded history a few fragile myths were associated with the hill – it was a refuge of the goblin-like fairies known as 'trows', for example – but there is nothing to prove it was once a spiritual centre for the entire archipelago. Yet as I explored, that often seemed to be the case.

Hoy does not only include Orkney's highest points and most dramatic cliffs; it also has deposits of hematite, used by early people to polish leather and make fire; and later, to make iron. Red ochre derived from it is the likely source of the pigment used to colour the interiors of Orkney's Neolithic stone buildings. The other minerals of Orkney are found not far away on Mainland, on small rocky Precambrian rises above Stromness. And both these sites overlook the part of Mainland which, in terms of human culture, makes Orkney globally significant.

Here a great broad bowl of Old Red land is filled with water, separated into two lochs by an isthmus today so narrow there is barely room to walk a few people abreast: Stenness on one side; the Ness of Brodgar on the other. In around 3000 BC this arresting landscape was one of the cultural epicentres of the British isles: the site of a great ritual complex in which upended Old Rocks were arrayed in the Old Red landform.

The standing stones on Stenness are sheer Old Red slabs, their clean, right-angled forms up to 4.5–5m high, yet only 250mm thick. They form a frame through which the midwinter sun rises over Ward Hill; even their silhouette seems to echo the form of this distant upland. Cross to the Ness of Brodgar and encounter a 104m-diameter stone circle, one of the largest in Britain.

There is something abstract, sentinel, impossible, about these monuments, backed by the low animal presence of hills and water. The rectilinear form of the rocks makes you almost expect Stanley Kubrick to appear and engineer a battle of poorly dressed-up apes.

Athwart a low hill, the great burial mound of Maes Howe overlooks everything with an air of patrician authority. Externally this is a mighty domical barrow, 26m wide and 7m high; but within, there is a long drystone corridor which opens into a single room over 4.5m high. Enormous angular slabs of Old Red stand at each corner of this artificial cave; Old Red flagstones are used to make a relic-chamber-like opening in each wall; more, carefully dressed with simple tools, corbel out overhead, a great Neolithic dome. Once again, the hills of Hoy play a crucial role: for at the midwinter solstice the rays of the sun rise above them, cross the 3.2m Barnhouse standing stone (also on Stenness), and flow directly down the passage into this inner chamber.

To walk between these sites, as the waters and horizons shift and the smooth, steep mountaintops of Hoy come and go on the horizon, their relationship to the standing stones locking and unlocking, is to be in what is arguably the greatest calibration of landform, geology and ancient man-made structure in Britain: a great open-air sacred landscape. It is even possible that this architecture of standing stones and stone circles was invented here, before spreading south.

There may be many reasons for this astonishing precocity. It is possible that Orkney had few trees as early as c.3500 BC, encouraging people to use stone. But it surely did no harm that large pieces of rock were effectively lying, around pre-quarried by natural processes such as frost, and that they were naturally strong, slim and flat. One quarry-site for the Brodgar ring has been found, a low rough outcrop on a hill called Vestrafiold in the north-west part of Mainland. Simple tools, wooden wedges and a little bed of clay to slip the rock onto were enough to remove them.

The people of Neolithic Orkney knew how to select the best-quality stone, and decorate it with incised patterns. They also understood that it should be laid along its bedding plane. Their stone tools included man-made erratics from as far afield as Arran and Langdale. Such objects were later the subject of a whole body of folklore – prehistoric stone arrow-heads, for example, were 'elf-shot' that could make cattle ill. People passed newborn babies through the prominent hole that is a feature of one of the Stenness stones, or shook hands to promise weddings and seal contracts.

But on Orkney, the Neolithic pressure rarely lets up. The island of Rousay, dominated by a single mountainous hill, seems to have been a veritable land of the dead, its coast lined with enormous drystone mounds, palaces for the ancestors whose interiors are divided into separate stone stalls in which bodies were placed. Most today are capped with twentieth-century concrete vaults. I cycled between them, fighting my way into the sodden teeth of the most ferocious rainstorm, and discovered what good places they were in which to shelter; at once as bleak as a multi-storey car park and as spooky as a pyramid. 'We all go under the hill', as the Orkney poet George Mackay Brown put it.

Orkney is also the only place in the British Neolithic where stone architecture is not just the province of ritual and of the dead. Skara Brae on Mainland is a stone-built Neolithic village, its thirteen drystone houses include slab-sided sideboards and shelves. The stone-edged hearths and lintels often seem to have a solstitial orientation.

On the Ness of Brodgar a palatial complex is currently being revealed in which perhaps thirty roofed buildings sat within a magnificent enclosure with walls 5–6m thick. The grandest structure, 19–25m across, contains a 'dresser' of alternating red and yellow stones. When it was ritually closed in about 2450 BC, piles of rounded pebbles were used to convert the complex into a kind of cairn. In such places there is an astonishing intimacy with the daily lives of long-vanished people; an intimacy which only makes their utter absence more palpable.

One of Orkney's most memorable Neolithic monuments sits in a peaty valley right next to Ward Hill. The Dwarfie Stane is a block of Old Red 8m long and 2m high, presumably dropped by a melting glacier. In one of the most laborious acts of stone working of the British Neolithic, it has been hollowed out to make a short, low passage, with a space either side the size and shape of a small bed. Both the internal arrangement and the way the space is made – carved rather than built – are unique in Britain.

I crawled in, lay down, and the dead crowded in around me: the tomb's unknown intended occupants; my mother, who I had so recently held as she faded in a Truro hospital bed, and who had had a memorable holiday on Orkney. The layered presence of generations of visitors, their names etched into the rock; including one 'H. Miller'. Suddenly I was lying next to a remarkable Victorian.

Hugh Miller was a native of Cromarty on the Black Isle, that Old Red peninsula near Inverness. This self-taught geologist, writer and campaigner had a passion for the Old Red Sandstone: he even wrote a book of that name. He was originally a stonemason: his Old Red gravestones in the kirkyard at Cromarty can be identified by their edging of wave-like scalloped mouldings. Mermaids plagued his nightmares: perhaps they slithered out of a Devonian lake.

Outside the tomb I came across an even more unexpected graffito: lines of Persian, left there by Major William Mounsey, who used them to tell us about the two nights he spent here and thus 'learnt patience', having been plagued by midges. Remarkably, the Dwarfie Stane itself seems a creation of such connections, for its closest comparators lie in the eastern Mediterranean.

Stone graffiti is especially common on carvable rocks such as the Old Red. From scratched dates and initials on the walls of country houses, to the medieval devotional glyphs etched by local peasants into church arcades, to the cup-and-ring marks of the Neolithic, they render permanent the presence of forgotten crowds of ordinary people.

In Neolithic Orkney, the Old Red is about more than mourning and monumentality. It embodies memories, and human lives; it makes homes as well as tombs. It can be carved, shaped, arranged. And it seems possessed of a kind of cosmopolitanism, at once an edgeland and a heartland. The dying mountains, it seems, have birthed much life.

After the Neolithic

These great hymns to Neolithic lithophilia impressed those who came later. Some 1,500 Bronze Age round barrows cluster around them; and the brochs and round houses of the Iron Age often reuse or are sited near them, too. Places like the Broch of Gurness, overlooking the sound between Mainland and Rousay, built a few centuries BC and surrounded by a proto-village of pure drystone.

While brochs can be found from the Southern Uplands to Shetland, the Old Red is the homeland of this monumentally oppressive building-type, with the overwhelming majority clustered in Orkney and Caithness. Here these great tubular towers must once have virtually lined the coast, squatting smoking ogres on the Old Red clifftops. Some remained in use well into the early medieval era. Once again, the coincidence of fertile soils and geologically prepared flag-like stones had triggered ambitious drystone architecture.

The Old Red can also be lavishly sculpted: a story that starts on a high, with the sixth/seventh-century-AD Pictish symbol stones. My jaw fell open when I stood in front of the Rosemarkie stone at the Groam House museum on the Black Isle; it did so again in front of the Dupplin cross, which dominates the little church at Dunning, not far from Perth. Surely, I thought, the contained and complex graphic power of such carvings made them the greatest of Britain's early medieval standing stones and crosses.

They are certainly the greatest artistic legacy of the Picts, the polity which, with the Gaels of Argyll, contributed most fundamentally to the formation of the Scottish nation. And if their distribution is anything to go by, the Old Red was a major cultural focus of these people; roughly two-thirds of the 250 or so known lie on the Old Red Moray coast, Strathmore, and northern Fife.

Not all are Old Red. The 3m-high Maiden Stone is an astonishing-for-its-era work of granite carving standing at the foot of the Caledonian-era Mither Tap, which the Picts turned into a mighty stronghold: a whole series may have ringed this fastness. Comparable stones encircled the

Pictish strongholds on the New Red Sandstone at Burghead on the Moray coast; and the Old Red at Dunning.

The earliest phase of this art-form speaks a consistent, enigmatic, almost grammatical language based around a vocabulary of about forty-five abstract symbols and spirited stylised animals. Later it becomes explicitly Christian, the carvings impressive not only for their size, but also for sucking in sources from as far afield as Rome and Byzantium. Once again, the Old Red rocks seem associated with a precocious cosmopolitanism.

The unique culture of the Picts spread as far as Orkney and Shetland, where it was eclipsed by Scandinavian invasions – the development which makes the next vivid layer in the Orkney landscape.

Viking Orkney

From the point of view of the north Atlantic, Orkney is a nodal point, a key stepping-stone for anyone who might want to move between Ireland and Scandinavia, or connect Denmark to the Isle of Man (let alone Iceland, Greenland, or North America). One wonders whether the Vikings could have held their empire together at all without the existence of this substantial, highly defensible tract of fertile sandstone country, located between their scattered possessions.

Probably first arriving in the eighth century, the Norsemen reshaped this landscape to such an extent that almost all Orkney's place-names are Scandinavian. Ward Hill (from the Old Norse *varðil:* 'beacon, watch tower') is one of many so-named eminences in Viking Scotland, each a lookout station for approaching enemies.

In the twelfth century, the Norse clothed the islands with grand Romanesque churches. The shattered remnant of one at Orphir, Mainland, is a northern outpost of a contemporary fad, also seen in England and Scandinavia, for churches whose circular form evoked that of the Church of the Holy Sepulchre and the Dome of the Rock in far-off Jerusalem: cosmopolitanism once again.

I'm not the first to use Neolithic burial mounds for shelter. One day in 1153 a group of Vikings escaped a ferocious snowstorm by hiding in Maes Howe. Though two were said to have gone insane, they spent at least some of their time scratching testaments to their fleeting visit into the rocks.

These marks have much in common with later graffiti: boasting about your tag ('These runes were carved by the man most skilled in runes in the western ocean') or indulging in a bit of laddish obscenity ('Thorni fucked. Helgi carved' – you can almost hear the leering sniggers). There are records of the 'treasure' found within, and exquisite interlaced beasts, as fine as anything one might see in an illuminated manuscript. Runes carved by Viking visitors turn up in remarkable places: there are even some in Hagia Sophia, Istanbul.

Even today the charged verticality of runic script draws the eye; it seems designed for incision on stone. It is a reminder how crucial mark-making on stone and clay is to the history of writing: many scripts, from Mesopotamian cuneiforms to Roman capitals, are designed for it, in contrast to the cursive world of ink marks on soft surfaces.

But the defining presence in Viking Orkney is its saint, Magnus, the Earl of Orkney, executed on the little island of Egilsay by a rival claimant to the earldom. The death took place between 1115 and 1118 on a bare, rocky hilltop that, it was said, immediately became green and fertile. A fine church was built nearby, and remains an impressive geometrical presence in this peaceful place. And about twenty years later, a mighty cathedral was built as a shrine church for him at Kirkwall, Orkney's capital. This building might, for centuries, have been the most impressive work of architecture north of the Great Glen.

Although its architecture is British – with specific inspiration from Durham – Kirkwall cathedral is best understood as the greatest expression of this self-confident outpost of Scandinavia. It is a geologically and architecturally stratigraphic building, its 'Old Red' Romanesque phase visibly separate from the yellow-white stone used to complete it in the thirteenth-century Gothic style. This yellow-white 'Old Red' stone from Eday is Orkney's native freestone: just one of many good building stones supplied by the rock, from the Black Isle (where there were once more than thirty-six stone quarries) to Banffshire, from Jedburgh to Herefordshire.

Devonian building stones

Few of these stones were popular far from their place of origin. Instead they create settlements visibly in harmony with the geology on which they sit. The warm glow of such Borders towns as Melrose, Dryburgh and Jedburgh owes much to them, as do the bricks made from Devonian mudstones and clays in Dundee and Herefordshire. There is even a polishable sandstone at Llangain, Carmarthenshire. The ensuing periods, running right through to the Cretaceous, are to produce almost all the great building stones of Britain.

The most significant Old Red building stone is a reflection of the qualities that made the material so popular in Neolithic Orkney. Splitting easily into flat slabs while remaining strong, the Old Red produced some of the most durable flagstones in Britain, used for flooring and stone-slating alike. Orkney produced them, as did Arbroath on the Strathmore coast; but it is on Caithness that they became a major industry. The county sheriff, James Traill, opened a quarry and developed a port; the village of Castletown became a quarry workers' town. Over 35,000 tons were exported in 1901/2. Caithness flags, each a younger, more shaped cousin of the standing stones of Orkney, are said to have floored the Strand in London, and a meat-processing factory in Argentina.

They also mark the local landscape, for the fields of Caithness are separated by serried ranks of smooth Old Red, like teeth, or gravestones, or a closely spaced stone row. Many houses have flagstone shelves and cupboards, updates of those at Skara Brae. Castlehill harbour remains an evocative, flag defined place, from its carefully laid quay to the serried ranks of abandoned stone-for-export lined up alongside it.

The Old-Redness of Romanesque Kirkwall cathedral lingers long in the memory. Magnus' bones were rediscovered in 1919, walled up in one of the circular columns of this dark church; it is an enjoyable architectural aside that, though Durham made them famous, its elephant-leg columns with round capitals were first used in Britain in another Old Red cathedral, or next to it: the chapel of the eleventh-century bishop's palace in Hereford. The idea had come from the continent, another sign of Old Red's voracious geographical appetite.

Atlantic Orkney

Stromness is Orkney's most remarkable town. This stone-built place is more like a lithified version of the transitory settlements in *Moby-*

Dick than an outpost of urban Britain. The streets are paved in great flat slabs of Old Red from Orphir. The back garden of every shore-side house becomes a slipway, a kind of grown-up version of the Norse-origin *nausts*, boat shelters and slipways sometimes found carved in the Orkney cliffs. Developing as a port from the sixteenth/seventeenth century, its very existence is a testament to Orkney's third period of international significance after the Neolithic and the Viking age.

From this period the islands became a key staging-point for transatlantic whaling and imperial expansion. Eliza Fraser of Stromness was shipwrecked in Australia, and claimed to have been captured by Aboriginal Australians; Dr John Rae, another local, learned his survival skills from the Cree and explored much of northern Canada on foot and dug-out canoe, finding the North-West Passage. By the end of the eighteenth century, three-quarters of the Hudson's Bay Company workforce in north America were men from Orkney; many of their descendants still live in Canada; many married local Inuit. More cosmopolitanism.

Whether as souvenirs or ballast, large numbers of stone tools made by indigenous peoples were transported to Orkney as a result of such contacts: a remarkable series of man-made erratics. North American arrowheads turn up often in the earth around Stromness. Captain Henry Linklater decorated his garden with shining dark lumps of Canadian Labradorite.

Linklater's grave lies in a modern cemetery on a shelf of Old Red just outside Stromness. The heights of Hoy stand on the horizon. The Labradorite pebbles that cover it have travelled 2,000 miles; gazing on their ebony rainbow glimmer, one understands why indigenous peoples were claimed to believe it contained imprisoned stars or Northern Lights, though the tradition may be a fabrication.

George Mackay Brown, the poet who 'transforms everything by passing it through the eye of the needle of Orkney' (Seamus Heaney), is buried in the same cemetery, a reminder of the richness of the Orkney mythosphere. Many, from the sculptor Dame Barbara Hepworth to the composer Peter Maxwell Davies, have been inspired by the place: Davies lived at Rackwick, a small village squeezed between the glowering Hoy uplands and the stroppy Atlantic. Old Red poetry, Old Red music, Old Red connections.

Orkney's strategic significance continued into the twentieth century. Thanks to the need to defend the North Atlantic and the North Sea, Scapa Flow was the site of the scuttling of the German naval fleet in 1919, and the base for the Home Fleet during the Second World War. Its low shoreline is in places dominated by twentieth-century military detritus, buildings with a kind of hasty concrete brutalism that depended on the scooping of millions of pebbles from the nearby shore; 580,000 tons went to building the Churchill Barriers, which guard the harbour and form roadways between Mainland and the southern islands.

Next to one of these is the Italian Chapel, an exquisite work of Italian Trecento Gothic that started life as a pair of Nissen huts on a prisoner-of-war camp. The inmates, led by Domenico Chiocchetti, turned this corrugated iron building into a beautiful place of Catholic worship. It remains a major attraction, even though the camp around it has gone.

Like the remnants of Neolithic and Viking Orkney, this sacred structure overlooks water, and is connected to far-off places. Like them too, it stands in glorious isolation, having outlived the more temporary structures that once surrounded it. It is a further memorial to Orkney's unexpected cosmopolitanism, and to Orkney's dense, brittle stratigraphy; its association with intensely lived lives and deaths. A place at once at the centre of things and far from them.

Corridors of power

This role as a transmitter of power and ideas is perhaps the Old Red's dominant geohistorical theme, visible everywhere it appears.

In Scotland's Highland zone, it is often the very humus in which the institutions of the state have grown. Head south from Caithness on the A9 or the railway, and see how these two arterial routes of the Northern Highlands follow the narrow strip of Old Red that runs down to Inverness.

This city, the capital of Highland Scotland, sits in the very elbow of Highland Old Red, where it turns east along the Moray coast. Until the seventeenth century it, and the royal and baronial burghs of Wick, Nairn, Dingwall, Tain, Forres and Elgin, were a sequence of settlements for which there were no other comparators in the far north. All are on this outcrop of the Old Red, as were the medieval centres of episcopal power at Dornoch, Fortrose and Elgin.

Jump south 60 miles and another stretch of Old Red runs along the foot of the Highland Boundary Fault. Here, the Old Red underlies Strathmore, that great natural corridor connecting the Midland Valley to north-east Scotland. This is fertile, expansive country; like a big, broad, loud version of the English Marches.

For many, Dr Johnson included, the route along Strathmore into north-east Scotland was the safest way of approaching the Highlands. In *Macbeth,* when Birnam Wood made its way to Dunsinane, it was across this Old Red valley that it marched. Cawdor, too, is on rocks of this period, here near the Moray Firth not far from Culloden, the Devonian setting for the breaking of the power of Highland culture in 1746.

With power, wealth and politics alike flowing along Strathmore, it is no surprise to find here the only major city to stand on Devonian rocks: Dundee. Many buildings here use Old Red building stones; and the Victoria and Albert Museum (2018) is one the most striking geologically inspired works of recent architecture. Its design visibly evokes the layered Old Red cliffs of Caithness, far to the north. Here the cliffs at Duncansby Head are extraordinary ribbed assemblies of pyramidal forms, visibly piled-up layers of trapped sands: 'natural masonry', as Thomas Pennant put it in 1769.

From Strathmore, the Devonian rocks stretch along the foot of the Highland Boundary fault, just about reaching the west coast. Rivers pour out of great gaps in the escarpment, following Old Red-era erosion-paths out of the Highlands. We will see more major river-mouths – from the Moray Firth to the Tay, the Severn to the Exe – opened by water in soft red sandstones Old and New.

In AD 78–84 the Roman emperor Agricola tried to capture the Midland Valley. The chain of 'Glenblocker forts' he created predates the Antonine and Hadrian's walls further south, and each plugs one of these valley-mouths. The area has been militarily contested for centuries since; I have counted at least ten major battles fought in the vicinity of Perth, the historic city which guards the route of the Tay out of the Highlands and onto the Old Red on which it sits.

The corridors of power continue as we move on to the Borders. The Roman-origin Dere Street was historically the most important route between Scotland and England: the valley it follows through the Southern Uplands, Lauderdale, is carved in a line of Devonian conglomerates.

We can now do a 250-mile jump to another borderland, the English Marches, where again the Old Red is a transition zone between high and low, and a route between regions. The Herefordshire Old Red almost seems to push westwards both the English/Welsh border, and Offa's dyke, that boundary between Anglo-Saxon Mercia and the British territory beyond. The great Marcher lordships who held the area in the medieval period had centres of power in Old Red Hereford, Raglan and Monmouth. Such castles were at the cutting edge of medieval defensive architecture: more cosmopolitanism.

From this central zone, peninsular jaws of Old Red, here slipping darkly back into the Silurian, make further passages through high country: one reaches towards Cardiff, and thus ties the lowlands of the Marches to those of south Wales; the other provides access west to Pembrokeshire. They helped make Caerleon/*Isca* on the Old Red the key bridgehead for Roman power in southern Wales, and guide the A40 up a deep and narrowing Old Red valley, following an ancient fault-line past historic centres of power at Abergavenny and Brecon. The 2m Altar Stone at Stonehenge appears to be Devonian, and from somewhere in this region, as if picked up *en route* by people moving from Preseli to Wiltshire.

The sheer ice-carved brows of a great ridge gaze over the A40. Nearly twice as high as the hills of Hoy, they form the only true Old Red mountains. Pen y Fan (886m) is the highest peak in southern Britain; part of a series of massifs of 'horrid rocks and precipices' which 'even darkened the air with their height' (Defoe). These heights, which have the Brecon Beacons at their heart, stand on a high platform of Carboniferous rocks, protected by a hard Devonian capping.

Follow the corridor through these uplands and into Carmarthenshire and Pembrokeshire, and find more strips of Old Red. Here the rock does much to create the relative gentleness of the country south of the Landsker line. These southernmost Old Red rocks finally peter out in Somerset; like so much in this part of Britain, they are now running with the Variscan Grain, the next great wave of tectonic change.

For more Old Red cosmopolitanism, visit the exquisitely carved purple-grey church at Kilpeck, Herefordshire. This perfectly proportioned twelfth-century building today sits in rural isolation, but once a castle and a settlement stood either side of it. The extraordinarily crisp carvings that enrich it meld Celtic, Norse and Anglo-Saxon influences, just as the local place-names are linguistic mongrels of Old English and Welsh (Kilpeck itself; Leintwardine, Garway).

Some of the images on this church were fresh from the pilgrim route to Santiago in northern Spain; Richard Fortey, palaeontologist and natural historian, says their curling, stylised foliage tendrils are very like the incipient plant-life of the Devonian itself. There is more of this 'Herefordshire school' carving at Hereford cathedral, a church which nevertheless can feel parochial compared to its mighty peers elsewhere in England – until one reaches the north transept, which is an achingly metropolitan structure built by a Savoyard courtier of Henry III.

The cathedral holds the famous *Mappa Mundi*, a medieval map of the world that is like a kind of great diagrammatic Wikipedia, condensing knowledge of the planet into a single image. We are a long way geographically and historically from the Dwarfie Stane, yet spiritually and geohistorically there is much common ground.

The themes of this chapter are often more visible in Scotland, and at Scone near Perth they congeal into a single rock. This is arguably the most politically contested man-made erratic in Britain.

The Stone of Destiny

The royal seat at Scone came to prominence in the tenth century, when the Gaels of Argyll forged a proto-Scottish nation: Alba. Moot (or Boot) Hill here is said to be the site on which Scots kings were inaugurated; the greatest of many such *tom a' mhòid* ('Court Hillocks') in the country. The roughly rectilinear 152kg stone sat atop this mound, a literal stone throne, used in crowning ceremonies.

The stone is a dense place in and of itself. According to legend it was carried to Egypt by Jacob's sons, and thence to Spain and Ireland: there it was used for coronation ceremonies on the Hill of Tara, where it could be relied on to groan loudly if anyone attempted to crown a pretender.

It is in fact a lump of very local Old Red, possibly first squared off in the Roman era. It bears the traces of no less than eight further layers of human intervention, of which among the more *recent* are the holes made to insert rings in it to help transport it to Westminster in 1296 (the last Scottish king to be crowned on it was John Balliol in 1292). The contemporary Coronation Chair was created by Edward I specifically to house it: directly below the seat on which every English, and latterly British, monarch since has been crowned there is a Stone of Destiny-shaped gap.

The Coronation Chair is still in use, but the cubby-hole below its seat is empty. The stone was stolen by Scottish Nationalists on Christmas day 1950, recovered a year later, and finally returned to the Scottish nation by Prime Minister John Major in 1996. This man-made erratic is now held in a kind of heritage tat-cum-national shrine in Edinburgh Castle; a kind of geological trace-element of Scottish nationalism.

This lump of rock is also a kind of omphalos for the historical themes of the Old Red: made of the grains of ground-down highlands that fell to form lowlands; its place of origin a centre of human power that guarded routes between the two. A rock with an ancient history, deeply implicated in the emergence of political and religious power, and suffused with a precocious cosmopolitanism. A rock blood-red with politics – and, perhaps, a kind of grief.

I have in my hand a letter my mother posted from Stromness in July 1972. Writing home from a holiday with her best friend, she described 'a grey straggly street, paved all over', and an archipelago of 'wide rolling turf hills, huge skies, and water everywhere because of islands, inlets, and numerous inland lochs'. She had tried to get to Hoy, but the ferryman had complained that he had to bring everyone back: 'it would be better if people went and stayed forever'. We all go under the hill, indeed.

Human beings, like islands, are each a world apart. Ultimately, only physical objects will outlast us. Of all materials, stone has the greatest ability to resist this erosive power; even today, after 5,000 years, the stone-setters of Maes Howe and Skara Brae, Stenness and Brodgar are able to tell us something of their lives, beliefs and ideas.

Each rock-type is also a universe unto itself. The Old Red has formed the very arteries along which history flows, a quiet fullness on the fringes of the great mountains. It is now to be covered by further layers of sediment. Each will have its own personality; and with the next, our geohistorical themes will switch from the prehistoric-to-medieval periods to more recent centuries. Because, more than any other geological period, the rocks of the Carboniferous shaped the world we now inhabit.

Legend:

- Carboniferous
- Igneous
- Mountain
- Prehistoric Site
- Historic site
- Quarry / Mine
- Battle field

Glasgow

Edinburgh

The Cheviots

Newcastle

Pennines

Carlisle

York

Forest of Rowland

Leeds

Liverpool

Peak

Chester

District

Nottingham

Telford

Birmingham

The Valleys

Forest of Dean

Swansea

Cardiff

Bristol

The Mendips

0   50 miles

Chapter 7

Carboniferous industry
358–299 million years ago

I

Geological energy

In the summer of 2022, in the final throes of drafting this book, I travelled north to do some final site visits. But all was not well on the journey there. First, the railway tracks began to melt; then the overhead wires caught fire. Our metal box full of people sat stationary for several hours. It wasn't long after that that they closed the line altogether, as heat of unprecedented intensity swept the country.

The next day the UK recorded its highest-ever temperatures. By then – significantly later than planned – I was in a hired van, and busily burning my way through a tank full of diesel. By the time I reached the Borders, the heat was pouring down like something solid; movement and thought alike had become clogged and slow. I had intended to climb the Eildon Hills, but now their steep, exposed slopes seemed quite beyond me. My body was reaching its limits – as was the infrastructure of the nation.

For many, that day – the nineteenth of July – was the moment the climate emergency arrived in Britain. Yet global heating is only the most recent of the consequences of our discovery of the energy latent in geology. This story begins in Britain, with the birth of industry;

it is dominated by the rocks of a single period: the appropriately named Carboniferous.

The British Carboniferous is a period of huge geological variety. It gave us coal, and much else, too. The era's varied rocks created a great mixed landscape, seeded with resources whose historical significance coalesced at the time of the industrial revolution. The period can seem like a timebomb, its potential locked up for 300 million years, until its eighteenth-century detonation. The fall-out from its explosion changed the world, and its consequences are as urgent now as they have ever been.

Ironbridge

A couple of years before that day in 2022, I went to Shropshire to witness that moment of detonation. Here, just south of Telford, the River Severn eats a gorge into a plateau of Carboniferous rocks. The steep valley-sides are lined with distinctive houses of smudgy brown-red brick and the detritus of industry, all visually tied together by a beautiful metal bridge. In the eighteenth century this was known as Coalbrookdale – the valley with the small, fast rivers, where there is a lot of coal. It has come to also be known as Ironbridge.

Before this place had a bridge, or buildings, or a name, it was a landform. The gorge was carved out by a River Severn driven onto a new path by ice-age glaciers. This natural act of excavation created a landscape pregnant with possibility, both because of the river itself – and because of the rocks it exposed on the valley-sides.

The Severn was a veritable motorway of water, bringing within reach large parts of the English Midlands, and extending to Bristol, a staging-point to almost anywhere west: Ireland and the Mediterranean; Africa and America. The brooks which ran into it at Coalbrookdale carved brief, steep valleys down which water flowed fast: it could be harnessed to generate power. Timber was plentiful. But neither transport nor energy would have been needed were it not for the rocks that lined the valley-sides like a layer-cake.

These rocks form a litany which is to be repeated in many Carboniferous places: limestones (here Silurian Wenlock limestone), sandstones, mudstones and clays, all Carboniferous – and threading their way through these rocks, nodules and seams of iron, and layers of coal.

By the seventeenth century this small coalfield was the second most important in England. But coal was a relatively unpopular fuel at that time. It was iron that was the dale's main export.

All this began to change when a young Quaker ironmaster, Abraham Darby, established an ironworks in one of the dale's side-valleys. Here, in 1709, he discovered a way of producing iron by fuelling his blast-furnace with coke. This is coal that has already been half-cooked in charcoal, making it burn faster and harder. The innovation transformed the efficiency with which the cast iron could be produced. His son, Abraham Darby II, turned the foundry into England's most important. Such expansion creates a spiralling demand for the products of the Earth: more iron ore, more coal.

These were not the only useful things present in the valley-sides of Coalbrookdale. The limestone could be used to remove the sulphur generated by the process. The sandstones resisted heat well, and were used for hearths, casings and moulds. The clays could be fired to make tobacco pipes, brick, tile and porcelain. Some were heat-resistant 'fireclays', useful for lining furnaces and kilns. Limestone and sandstone alike included decent building stones.

Soon the ironworks was producing everything from cooking pots to cannons to steam-powered engines: indeed they were a centre for technical innovation, and played a major role in producing the pumping engines which, by removing water, enabled mines to go deeper than they ever had before – further increasing the accessibility of coal. By the end of the century five ironworks and three porcelain factories filled a landscape which was becoming famous.

Seekers of intense Romantic experience came to Coalbrookdale to witness the 'altogether horribly sublime […] mills and all their vast machinery' (Arthur Young, agriculturist). This was a place as awesome in its energy and its power to surprise as any mountain cataract. A town was developing, housing what Young called the 'scummies and dregges of many countries', attracted by the employment on offer. Houses climbed the valley-sides, their chimney pots made of local iron. Such features look unusual even today, and must have seemed almost shockingly innovative at the time.

This was a new kind of place. It was centred not on a river crossing, a castle or a church, but on the resources of the earth, and their extraction, processing and transportation: quarries, kilns, furnaces, factories, slipways, wharves. And in 1779–80, Abraham Darby III (grandson of the first Abraham) built here the world's first major bridge made entirely of metal: the 100ft 6in/30.6m-span Iron Bridge.

It rises from footings of local sandstone, its metal joints derived from carpentry, its ogee curves and skeletal braces suffused with Gothic elegance. From this experiment in an architecture of metal, every iron-framed mill or Victorian train shed spins out; as well as such marvels as the Crystal Palace, and ultimately (though the structural properties of steel are rather different) the skyscraper. Yet metal-framed buildings are as dependent on geology as those made of stone: it is merely that the products of the rocks have been more greatly transformed. A metamorphic architecture.

Darby's pride in his local place rings out from the bridge, in the giant metal words 'this bridge was cast at Coalbrook-dale'. Today you can gaze on it from the town's many cafés, and then explore the many museums, the recreation of industrial-era Britain at Blists Hill, and the shrine to the birth of industry erected around the remains of the oldest surviving Darby furnace. They are monuments to the moment the modern world began – and the symbiotic potential of the stratigraphically arranged pile of Carboniferous rocks on the wooded valley-side, as exposed by the erosive power of a late ice-age River Severn.

Ironbridge offered its residents industry and innovation, misery and enlightenment, poverty and riches. Yet ultimately, it was a place where geology was king; along with its sibling, landform. Industry came to Coalbrookdale as a result of the almost uncanny roll-call of potentialities offered by the rocks, aided by the waters that drained them; homes and culture followed.

A comparable story was to play out across Britain. By the nineteenth century, combined with Britain's maritime prowess and the wealth generated on the back of the slave trade, the geohistorical potential of places like Coalbrookdale had made this island the most powerful place on earth, transforming its landscape in the process. Darby's process had helped create the industrial revolution; our present climate crisis is just one of its long-term consequences. And it was all dependent on the Carboniferous rocks of Britain.

Even before their geology was understood, the potential of these rocks was being remarked on. 'Nature has placed the beds of iron and the beds of coal alongside of each other, and art has taught man to make one to operate upon the other', wrote Cobbett in the 1830s of the Pennines, Britain's largest Carboniferous region. 'The water and the coal seem to be engaged in a struggle for getting foremost in point of utility to man.' The reason for this lies in the shifting nature of the Carboniferous environment.

Carboniferous geologies

Determined to scout out the view from the top, I returned to the Eildons a few days after my abandoned visit. The weather had cooled, and this time I did go up. But just as I reached the saddle that separates Eildon Hill North from Eildon Mid Hill, a great wall of airborne moisture descended: fast, solid-looking, intimidating.

I had hoped to look over a Border landscape: the Southern Uplands; the Cheviots; the Tweed, flowing towards the North Sea through the flatlands known as the Merse. In fact I stood by an increasingly damp cairn, surrounded by claustrophobic grey.

It seemed extraordinary that conditions could change so rapidly. But perhaps the hills and the clouds were not so different from each other. The slow progress of the continental plates and the rapid shifting of the air are both driven by energy in convection. The stasis of the rocks and the dynamism of the atmosphere are illusory: both are in a state of constant, interdependent flow and change. Bring continents together and volcanoes are a result; move moist, warm air over the sea and a haar rolls in. Release carbon from the Earth and the climate heats; melt the ice caps and the sea-level rises. The universe is really just ever-changing chains of energy.

We too are embodied, dynamic energy-systems, more substantial than clouds, less so than stone. Indeed, respiring within our hard skeletons, we have something of the nature of both. Our remains could become components of future rocks; perhaps, one day, fossil fuels.

Such movements of energy are everywhere in geology. The Eildon hills are igneous: hot magma, pushed energetically into the crust and losing its power as it cools into cold, hard rock. The surrounding sedimentary rocks owe much of their character to the movement of water, and the way it transports and drops sediment. The North Sea has not always lain to their east; the Merse was once a marsh. Perhaps one day it will flood. Crust, climate and oceans are in constant flux; a universal truth – but one perhaps particularly evident on islands and near coasts.

As the Devonian came to a close, our Britain-to-be was gradually submerging. It eventually became a series of islands of largely Caledonian-era rocks on the edge of the continent of Laurussia. In such places, what was ocean might later be land washed by rivers, estuaries and deltas; what was dry land become marsh or swamp. The litany of rocks we saw at Ironbridge was a typical result: at the beginning of the period, limestones formed in deep water; in the middle of the era, sandstones dominated, deposited in fresh water; and later on, softer sandstones and clays took over. This sequence works, as a generalisation, for all our Carboniferous landscapes; and in all, the late Carboniferous rocks include a material that is new to us: coal.

Coal

There is magic in the geology of coal. Plants eat light. They use its energy to breathe in carbon, complex molecules of which they then combine with nutrients to construct the fibrous, woody material which gives them their strength. When they die and start to rot, the carbon goes back into the atmosphere. But if the rotting is arrested or slowed, the carbon remains stored, where eventually it may be covered by sediment, and compressed and heated until it becomes coal. The process is particularly prevalent in the Carboniferous, when forests (often inhabited by early land-based reptiles) were one of the planet's dominant life-forms, and bacteria capable of digesting them had yet to evolve. Oil is formed in a comparable way, but with plankton rather than plants forming its source material. Indeed it is a general truth that the presence of plant-derived carbon in rocks transforms their usefulness.

Swamps and wetlands are ideal places for this to occur. Here water gathers and becomes stagnant, often because the rock or clay beneath is impervious and the landform flat. As nearby plants die, their remnants are washed into this oxygen-free setting: decay slows, and the swamp becomes clogged with plant matter: peat. Add 10,000 years of heat and compression and 10m/30ft of this dark, matted, rooty, damp material become a metre/3ft of black, dense, dry coal. Its quality varies hugely: lignite is less than 35 per cent carbon and perceptibly wood-like; anthracite is over 90 per cent carbon, dense, pure, and almost smoke-free.

Swamps are particularly ephemeral entities. Over the millions of years of the late Carboniferous, an area of freshwater swamp might be replaced by a shallow sea, depositing sand on top of the peaty morass; then dryish land might draw nearer, mud replace sand, and plants begin to put down roots – before the swamp returns. The sequence can repeat itself many times over. And though coal might only comprise 4 per cent of all this, other useful materials might also develop in the surrounding rocks.

The sands-and-roots stage – effectively fossilised soil – might become fireclay; less plant-material-rich phases, clay. While iron is ubiquitous – much of the planet is made of it – the ore can become usefully concentrated in rocks; here a combination of erosional processes and chemical reactions with decaying plant material assisted the process. While this iron is not especially pure, the fact that a mine sunk in search of coal would often find it made the whole business more economically worthwhile. Collieries, foundries and brickworks often stood together.

So each coal seam is a compressed swamp, and a battery of stored energy from a distant past. Formed about 300 Ma, its useful deposits may be gone within the next 300 years. From Abraham Darby onwards, exploitation of this cheap, relatively transportable rock became one of the engines of the industrial revolution.

The Variscan Grain

In the Carboniferous, tectonic processes once again become an important part of our story. Laurussia continued its stately progress north, crossing the Equator at this time; it also conjoined with other continental masses, leading to the formation, around the beginning of the succeeding Permian period, of the supercontinent of Pangea. Like Iapetus before it, an ocean – the Rheic ocean – disappeared. These events are second only to the Caledonian ones in their implications for the British landscape; complex in detail, we can give them the blanket name 'Variscan'.

This time, the epicentre of events is slightly off-screen. The Variscan equivalent to the Caledonides snaked its way from Germany to Spain. The rocks in the nearest part of Britain, the far-south west, were effectively created as a side-effect. Igneous events are very visible here, and also in northern Britain. And everywhere, sediments that had been laid down in horizontal layers were flexed and bent as new suites of faults developed and old ones were reactivated.

The Variscan events created a grain that runs very roughly at 170°, from just south of south-east to just north of north-west. Britain's south-west peninsula points along this variant of the Variscan Grain as emphatically as the Lleyn or Kintyre do the Caledonian one. Indeed the south-west is such a Variscan land apart that we'll explore it separately: but the grain, as ever varying in its specifics from place to place, has left its mark on all the landscapes of the period.

Carboniferous landscapes

I burnt a lot of carbon in the course of writing this book. The 1,400 miles I covered that hot week in July were part of over 64,000 miles of exploration, all of it dependent on fossil fuels and forged metal. The speed conferred by this familiar but shameful mode of transport does have one advantage: it enables one to appraise the big picture of the lie of the land. With a bit of preparation, and a willingness to park up and disappear on foot (or, on occasion, folding bicycle) to look more deeply or reach less accessible landscapes, the front seat of a car/window seat of a train is a great place to build up a picture of the overall shape of what's around you. So let me rush you through a road tour of Carboniferous Britain.

The Scottish Midland Valley

Let's start in the north, where the Carboniferous defines one of Scotland's most important regions: the Midland Valley, or Central Belt. The expansive rural aspect of this densely populated country is everywhere punctuated by sudden hulking uplands. The low ground is underlain by a range of Carboniferous limestones, sandstones and mudstones, the surface distinction between them (and indeed with the Devonian country that takes up the northern third of the valley) muffled by a deep blanket of glacial-era earths. All this owes its existence to the Caledonian events, in which an ancient terrane sank downwards between the bounding Highland Boundary and Southern Uplands Faults, and was subsequently buried under these younger sediments.

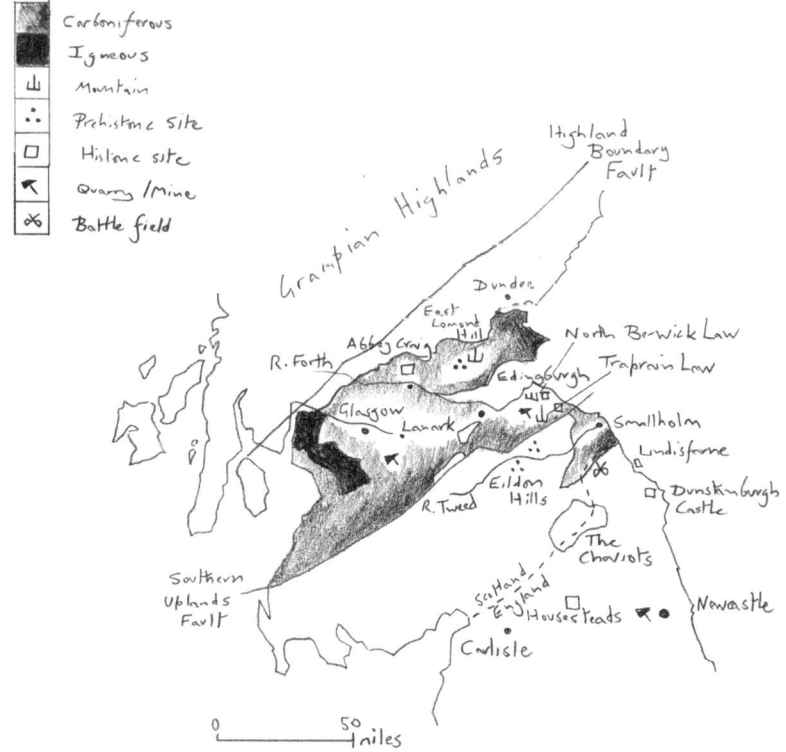

Even before the industrial era this was a territory full of 'busy scenes of commerce and rural economy' (Pennant). Today, settlement is most dense where the Carboniferous coal was found. Here – in a great patch that stretches from Glasgow two-thirds of the way to Edinburgh, north towards Stirling and south to Lanark; and which has significant separate outcrops in Ayrshire and East Lothian – I crawled through post-industrial towns such as Bathgate and Livingston. The high streets were decaying; former colliery, foundry and factory sites were marked by leisure attractions, out-of-town shopping centres and business parks: the Botox of post-industrial Britain.

Such patterns apply everywhere in Carboniferous Britain. But here these places were cheek-by-jowl with some of some of Scotland's most significant historic sites: the royal burgh of Stirling was only 10 miles from Falkirk, once home to Europe's greatest iron foundry; Dunfermline was both the burial place of medieval kings and a major industrial centre. The Clyde and the Forth were separated by a littoral just 30 miles wide, briefly the northern border for the Roman empire, leading to construction of the Antonine Wall in AD 142–165, and later, an early southern boundary of Scotland itself; the Highlands were long believed to start at Stirling, and even considered an island. The country's most important canal, built from 1790, linked the two rivers.

It was as if London, Canterbury and York and Manchester, Birmingham and Newcastle, were all in the same tightly bounded area, an area also including the Severn and the Thames, and all of it largely on rocks of a single period.

This, in other words, is the heartland of the Scottish nation. Of the twenty most populous settlements in the country, only Inverness and Aberdeen lie outside the Midland Valley; and within it, only Dundee and Perth are on Devonian rocks rather than the Carboniferous ones. These include Edinburgh, the nation's capital, and Glasgow, its largest city. Indeed, the majority of the nation's population live here, their sense of being in a valley rather than the 'central belt' obscured by the sudden uplands: Pentlands, Ochils, Campsie Fells. These are made of igneous rocks, some created in the Caledonian events, others the Variscan ones (Variscan igneous rocks can cross into the Permian in date, but are part of a single tectonic narrative).

The Pennines

In England's far north, I crawled in low gear up the 893m Cross Fell. This vast escarpment, the highest point in the Pennines, breaks like a great wave over the younger rocks of the Vale of Eden; I was a tiny bodyboarder, climbing the wall of some gargantuan geological breaker, its top sprinkled white with snow. Beyond stretched out the oceanic expanses of the high Pennines.

Here was a landscape of bleak and formless grandeur, dominated by big, smooth-sided hills and peat: 'the most desolate, wild and abandoned country in all England' (Defoe). Walk into these hills, and any given top seems endlessly out of reach, the way forward riven by small peat-gorges known as 'hags'.

This is a sandstone landscape, its most emblematic rock the hard, impervious 'Millstone Grit', dominated by big, hard grains of silica laid down on the floor of an enormous estuary. Further south, this rock often forms clifflets ('edges') and tors: the outcrop known as the Roaches, in Staffordshire, hulks up like broken teeth, gleaming darkly even as it tears your trousers.

These places can seem barren, but they long formed important sheepwalks; their rocks have been used in industry and architecture; and because they shrug off water, they have been prodigious sources of power for settlements in the lowlands and valleys, or 'dales', below.

There are dales in many parts of northern Britain. But a suite of them in Yorkshire is known specifically as the Dales, and it was as I explored them that I encountered the first of the three great limestone landscapes of the Pennines, cut by east-running rivers that ate through the gritty sandstone and revealed the softer rock beneath.

Crisp limestone edges lined the fringes of Wensleydale; open sandstone moor lurked above. As I descended, the road following a central river, I found myself in grazing country, punctuated by market towns and filled with a dense drystone architecture of field-walls and two-storeyed barns known as 'laithes': hay above, stock below. Side valleys were 'hopes', deep gorges, 'denes' or 'gills', narrow clefts and channels, 'cleughs'. It was a delectable landscape, repeated in a stepladder of such valleys.

Further south, I entered Britain's only true limestone mountainscape. Hills such as Ingleborough cragged upwards like great karstic shards, their peaks protected from erosion by sandstone caps. Dramatic arenas such as Gordale Scar turned out to be cave-systems that had collapsed. There were haunting limestone tablelands, scored by water into dense grids of tiny, ankle-busting gorgelets known as 'grykes', separated by short stretches of broken, flat-topped rock known as 'clints'. Sudden voids might be anything from a few feet to several yards across: each of these 'swallet/swallow', 'shake' or 'sink' holes was a tiny placelet, deliciously festooned with calcareous plant-life, and potentially concealing extraordinary subterranean grandeur.

At Gaping Gill the Fell Beck descends a full 110m into a hole so large it could contain York Minster – only to re-emerge from a cave just under 1.5 miles later. Remarkable landforms stimulated remarkable names: Quaking Pot, White Scars, Black Shiver Ridge. Drystone walls marched imperious over the slopes, defining territories and limits for grazing: each was a little gallery of abstract limestone forms, often framed by sandstone gateposts. This was a landscape made spectacular by its own solubility; a sculpted, hollowed-out country, at once hard as nails and caught in a state of disintegration. A metaphor for geology itself.

Such Pennine places were different from the Scottish Midland Valley. The distinction between bare, dark sandstone country and the bright, skeletal limestone one was everything here: there, it had barely registered. Here, igneous rocks were rare; there, they were common. The Scottish Carboniferous made lowland country, settled deep in time: these uplands were only of marginal significance before the eighteenth century.

These generalisations are largely true of the rest of the English and Welsh Carboniferous outside Scotland, but the Pennines are their mightiest expression. They are a great spine, running 150 miles north–south down northern England. The massif disburses centres of power and identity to the lowlands either side, creating distinctions that apply deep in time: Roman and medieval Chester/*Deva* and York/*Eboracum*; the white rose of Lancashire and the red one of Yorkshire; industrial-era Manchester and Leeds; modern Scousers and Geordies, north-westerners and north-easterners; the M1/east coast main line and the M6/west coast main line.

Variscan valleys

As I crossed and recrossed it, this backbone of the North divided itself into vertebrae. Each was separated by a particularly significant gap, each following a significant Variscan fault, each taken by a major road. The northernmost was drained by the South Tyne, and followed by the A69 Newcastle–Carlisle; the A66 took the next to the south over the Stainmore Pass; and in the next, the A59 and A65 were the major ways through an area of complex faults and broken-up uplands – Forest of Bowland, Pendle Hill, Ilkley Moor – drained by the Ribble and the Aire.

These passes have been vital conduits of history. Many had been taken by Roman roads; no less an east–west structure than Hadrian's Wall ran along the edge of the northernmost. Further south, the Leeds and Liverpool Canal (from 1770) was the first attempt at a trans-Pennine waterway. They also helped make sense of the landscape; Cross Fell was in the first vertebra, the limestone of the Dales and the mountainous limestoneland north of Skipton in the second. And the third and southernmost vertebra, much changed.

The Peak District

The high northern Pennines are buoyed up on hidden batholiths of Variscan granite. The southernmost vertebra is lower; it is also both the largest and the most geohistorically dense.

This country began as a low, wasp-waisted sandstone upland which was a major conduit in itself. Here, Mesolithic people followed migrating herds across the Standedge Pass; there are more Roman roads and, as Leeds and Manchester burgeoned to either side, some of the most heroic works of the industrial era forged their way across this peaty gap: the Rochdale and Huddersfield Narrow canals (1804 and 1794–1811), and the Leeds–Manchester railway line (completed 1841). They have in turn been upstaged by the M62, conduit for millions of journeys across the English north.

Then the wasp-waist broadened out, and I was in the Peak District; said to sit within an hour of a third of England's population, this area became, in 1951, the first of Britain's National Parks.

Perhaps its popularity explains the fact that here, uniquely, the contrasting sandstone and limestone Pennines have a name: Dark Peak

and White Peak. And both these territories have a certain intensity of character. The sandstone country of the Dark Peak is dramatised by broken gritstone outcrops; it surrounds the limestone of the far south like a dark oyster around a white pearl.

The White Peak forms a plateau, interrupted by occasional tors of limestone hardened by magnesium ('dolomitic limestone'). The surface is scored by an almost exhausting network of drystone walls, their silver-grey geometry bringing out the restless subtleties of the land surface. Valleys are sudden, cliff-lined gorges, as at Dovedale. Older villages – Youlgreave, Winster, Parwich – hide in their bases; before the industrial era there were few other settlements, and this was open country – albeit scarred by the traces of metal extraction. Many valleys were dry; springs might be marked by the ancient tradition of well-dressing, in which spring-heads are redecorated annually. At Matlock on the western side, the Derwent cut an impressive gorge.

Such watery features are characteristic of this soluble rock. It is thanks to the Carboniferous Limestone that the Pennines host a disproportionate number of mineral waters and spas: Ashbourne, Buxton, Harrogate. And elsewhere water cuts the same limestone into further sheer-sided gorges: the

Wye at Tintern, the Avon at Clifton, Bristol. Like the Derwent, these rivers were historically prodigious sources of both power and transportation.

Other historical themes were also true of limestone in general. The calcium bones of the earth were rarely far below the surface, making for rich pasturelands. The many cracks, voids, faults and fissures in this rock made it a seed-bed for metal ores: the resulting industries remain a visible element on the White Peak landscape, and were once significant in the Dales, too. Further north, Weardale, a narrow limestone valley in the sandstone northern Pennines, had been supplied with heat and mineral-rich fluids by the buried granite below. Lead, iron, silver, zinc, barytes, witherite, fluorspar, and even gold developed here, with Alston, Britain's highest town, its atmospheric capital. In 1768, the valley hosted 119 mines.

Such resources impressed early commentators. 'The surface of the earth looks barren', Celia Fiennes noted of the Pennines, 'yet those hills are impregnated with rich Marbles Stones Metals Iron and Copper and Coale mines in their bowels'; it was 'an immense subterranean treasure, never to be exhausted', added Defoe. Both were surely thinking of a broader region than that most of us think of as the Pennines today.

The Pennine Fringe

Further Carboniferous rocks lie either side of the main massif. Their historical significance is hard to overstate. Here the landscape is lower, settlement denser, and moorland has become less common. The gritstone disappears: sandstones and mudstones make tightly rolling, steep-sided hills. It is here that coal and iron are found. In the far north, a long western extension almost rings the Lakes, giving birth to the industrial towns of Barrow-in-Furness, Whitehaven, Workington and Maryport.

I call this entire Carboniferous Pennine-edge the 'Pennine Fringe'. Here, in places such as Lancashire, Northumberland/County Durham and Yorkshire, were England's main coalfields, the largest of which ran a full 60 miles north–south down the eastern side of the main massif.

As well as iron and coal, such country held fireclay and building stone here; and it was into this landscape that the sandstone heights poured their burden of water, providing power for early mills.

Such mills were the most visible sign of industry; they often followed rivers into the main massif, dragging with them strings of settlements. On the western, Lancashire side, Colne, Nelson, Burnley, Accrington, Blackburn; on the eastern, Yorkshire side, Hebden Bridge, Halifax, Dewsbury, Wakefield.

With industry on the valley-bottoms, settlement was often pushed uphill: the skyline bristled with terraced houses, Nonconformist chapels and other structures. 'Mill and work at bottom, chapel and Heaven at top, and the wild moors surrounding all,' as the author Glyn Hughes puts it. All the greatest industrial-era settlements of the English Midlands and North were on or near this Pennine Fringe; they marked out the Carboniferous like a U-shaped join-the-dots. To the west: Preston, Bolton, Manchester and Stoke, and to the east, Newcastle-upon-Tyne, Bradford, Leeds, Sheffield and Derby; at the bottom: Birmingham and Coventry.

Here, the main massif has come to an end, and Birmingham/the Black Country and Coventry grew up in association with two largish, tear-shaped Carboniferous outcrops. Smaller ones extended east into Leicestershire (the village of Coleorton there is appropriately named), and also west and north through Shropshire to the North Wales coast. Coalbrookdale is on one of these; the industrial town of Wrexham another.

All in all, the Pennines and their fringe were a single Carboniferous phenomenon, their rocks presenting water power, metal ores, coal and other advantages to a waiting human world: the Coalbrookdale story writ large.

Of anticlines and synclines

The arrangement of rocks in the Pennines is partly a result of the Variscan events. As well as generating the east–west faults which separate its vertebrae, they bowed flat layers of Carboniferous sediment upwards by up to 1–2 miles, like a great half-tube. Over time, erosion sliced off the top of this: as a result, the youngest layers lay exposed on either side, and the older ones towards the middle.

As these older rocks also happened to be the hardest, the middle was more resistant to erosion. It became the high ground of the classic

Pennines, with its mid-Carboniferous sandstone dominant, and older, early Carboniferous limestones peeking through where this had been eroded away. The youngest rocks, which were also the coal-bearing ones, lay to either side: the Pennine Fringe. Though today they are lower-lying than the rest, these rocks once arced over all the others. This makes the Pennines an example of a ubiquitous geological phenomenon known as an anticline.

Because of this, the coal slopes downwards to either side of the main massif. The high-quality Barnsley, or Top Hard, seam is at the surface near Sheffield; but head east to Barnsley and it has slipped 300–400m underground. It is twice as deep again, with much younger rocks now on the surface, by the time we get to the very un-Carboniferous city of Lincoln. It is only latterly that mining at such depths became feasible, for example in the flat, young country near Thorne in the Humber estuary.

A syncline is the opposite of this. Here the rocks have been bowed downwards into a basin, and then eroded. The pattern is reversed: the oldest rocks are on the edges and the youngest in the middle. The industrial centres of Scotland sit in a series of such basins; in each, old Carboniferous Limestone dominates the outside, then there is a ring of mid-Carboniferous rocks, and the young, coal-bearing rocks are in the middle. The resulting landform, however is uniform – but in Wales, it is not.

The Welsh Valleys and the south-west

Here I drove down a series of steep-sided valleys: Ebbw, Rhondda, Rhymney and more. Each was a river-carved gash in an open moor, and each was lined with vertiginous ladders of terraced housing, punctuated by Nonconformist chapels. In effect, a series of miniature linear conurbations had strung themselves out along the slit-like landforms, creating a landscape so unique it has given its name to an entire region: just as the Dales are a subset of all dales, so the Valleys are a very specific series of valleys.

The Valleys score their way north–south down a bean-shaped Carbon-iferous upland, its longer side stretched east–west with the Variscan Grain. Still the place where almost one third of the Welsh population live, they were the industrial centre of Wales, just as the Pennines with their fringe were for England and the Midland Valley was for Scotland.

As all this was a syncline, the oldest rocks were on the outside. To the north, a capping of hard Devonian rocks made the Brecon Beacons. Early Carboniferous limestones ringed the rest of the outer edge, their metal ores most dominant in the north-east. In the middle lay the mid- and late-Carboniferous suites of sandstones, shales and mudstones, with their usual complement of useful features, including – exposed on valley-sides cut by the rivers that flowed off the high ground to the north – coal.

Further south and further west from here, the Variscan grip on the landscape strengthened, placing the rocks in complex arrays. In south-west Wales, softer Devonian and harder Carboniferous rocks alternated, the contrast between the two creating the memorable coastline of the Gower peninsula: the famously beautiful Rhossili bay is a soft Devonian gulf fringed by harder Carboniferous ridges.

In Gloucestershire, the Forest of Dean was a tiny repetition of the Valleys: an upland with the older, metal-rich limestone on the edge and a younger, softer, darker coal-bearing heart. The coalfields around Bristol lay cupped in narrow uplands of Carboniferous limestone, of which the high Variscan ridge of the Mendips, rich in lead and silver, is the best-known. Here, the 'deep, frightfull chasm' (Daniel Defoe, novelist) of Cheddar gorge was a spectacular, dry version of those of the Derwent, Wye and Avon. South and west from here began the profoundly Variscan territory of the far south-west: a country we will be coming back to.

II
Carboniferous geohistories

Before the age of industry

Medieval and prehistoric 'limestonelish'

A few years ago, a friend led me into the Earth. We crept into a Mendip swallet hole, and headed down tube-like subterranean tunnels. Sudden mouth-like gulfs opened out; tiny dark throats ran off them. It was like being swallowed by a beast of mysterious complexity. My safety helmet bashed the wet noses of stalactites, their tips watery solutions of the limestone itself, lengthening imperceptibly as they dried: rocks forming before my eyes. In this hidden, tight, occasionally spectacular world, one could almost feel the water dissolve the landscape's interior, transforming into stone as it went.

Here was the glamorous shine water gives to rock; the coloured blush of mineral ores, and the fretting and ribbing of part-digested surfaces: an urgent proto-architecture in which early people could discover the power of stone spaces. And everywhere, the disorientation of darkness and constriction, the drama of opening out and revelation.

Limestone is the great cave-forming lithology, and Carboniferous Limestone caves have protected a disproportionate number of prehistoric remains. The 'Red Lady' of Paviland, Europe's oldest ritualised burial, was laid to rest in the Carboniferous Limestone of Gower, with other important early sites in the Peak and at Cefn, near St Asaph in North Wales. Carboniferous Limestone is also associated with a tool-making stone, the flint-like chert.

And here in the Mendips, in a cave in Burrington Combe known as Aveline's Hole, is the site of Britain's oldest known cemetery: twenty-one or more bodies, placed there 10,200–10,400 years ago, decorated with red ochre and buried with a collection of Jurassic-era fossil ammonites. The Rev. Augustus Toplady wrote the hymn 'Rock of Ages' while sheltering beneath a rock just yards from Aveline's Hole. He might have agreed with these local ancestors that some force of supernatural power must explain this place of crag and hollow mountain.

Later on, the limestone continued to inspire. The White Peak, with its relatively low elevations and large quantities of shattered stone, is host to such compelling Neolithic monuments as the henge at Arbor Low. And in Pembrokeshire, I stumbled on a spectacular medieval stone hero, in the shape of St Govan.

His home lies at the head of an inlet in a coast dominated by Carboniferous Limestone cliffs. This little chapel of St Govan seems to grow like a squat stalagmite from the cliff itself; and an opening behind its altar led me to a large, ribcage-like array of grooves and ridges: the kind of thing limestone erosion often causes. These, it was said, were the imprints made by this Irish monk's chest as he hid from pirates. Govan stayed on, and the site became a hermitage. The grooves were enormous: he must have been both giant and gymnast.

A less exalted series of stone heroes inhabit Hope Dale in the Peak. Here the limestone Peak Cavern is popularly called the Devil's or Peak's Arse: the sudden malodorous wind it is said to eject does not seem to have put off the lead miners who built a small village in its mouth.

But here we are in Hope Dale: the point where Dark and White Peak meet. Nearby Mam Tor is a towering sandstone hill whose name means 'mother tor'. The soft shales on its lower reaches are causing a kind of structural collapse in the hill itself, meaning this unstable mum is casually demolishing herself. Tarmac smithereens of the A625 lie scattered on her sides.

Hope Dale, like many mixed landscapes, was a great centre of power: Mam Tor is topped by a late Bronze Age hillfort; nearby Peveril castle was the medieval royal stronghold for the Peak. The *Pecsaete* would have known it: an early medieval tribal group named for the landscape – a rare distinction, but one shared by the *Wreocensaete* in the Precambrian Wrekin, and the *Cilternsaete* in the Cretaceous Chilterns.

Of polities and power

The medieval world is particularly vivid on the Carboniferous lowlands of the Scottish Midland Valley and the low-lying Pennine Fringe of north-east England. Unusually for the Carboniferous, these areas were major centres long before the age of industry. The varied Brythonic, Anglian, Norse and Gaelic place-names of the Scottish Midland Valley reflect the ever-changing spheres of influence here, and perhaps echo the way the landscape itself is divided up by igneous hills. The Anglo-Saxon kingdom of Northumbria once stretched from the Forth to the Tees. Newcastle-upon-Tyne, with its Neoclassical terraces of tan sandstone, could easily be a Scottish city. But the signature geohistorical story of these areas relates to their igneous rocks.

Igneous thrones

There was a reason for wanting to climb the 422m Eildons: they are one of the most striking geohistorical entities in this book. They can seem to hold the reins of the landscape, making sense of the mixed country that extends around them. All hills should look like this: multi-peaked, pyramidal, spare: the term 'commanding presence' might have been invented for them.

This is an extraordinarily strategic location. The England/Scotland border is not far away; the Tweed leads to the east coast at Berwick; Lauderdale, that crucial route between Scotland and England, heads north from here through the Southern Uplands. The whole area is dotted with centres of conflict and power. More battles than anywhere else in Britain have been fought in the region around Berwick-upon-Tweed. Scottish abandonment of a lava ridge 12 miles away was the cause of their defeat at Flodden field in 1513.

The Eildons themselves have attracted human reaction in near-continuous layers since prehistoric times. A massive and very early Iron Age fort encloses Eildon Hill North; it was later replaced by a Roman signalling tower. *Trimontium*, 'place of the three peaks', lies at the foot of the hills: it was the centre of imperial authority north of Hadrian's Wall. By the medieval period the focus had slipped a mile north to Melrose, with its magnificent Cistercian abbey; and a wonderful series of geo-legends had accreted itself to Eildon.

King Arthur is said to sleep beneath these hills. This is not the only story in which hills are associated with sleeping heroes: remember Silurian Pumsaint? One suspects caves and barrows, prehistoric burials and fossils are cross-fertilising in the mythic imagination. One Gaelic term for a rounded hill, *sithean*, is derived from the belief that fairies inhabited such landforms.

But Eildon's interior has hosted another more intriguing figure: Thomas the Rhymer, a local laird who met the queen of the fairies somewhere in its bowels and returned gifted with powers of prophecy. Perhaps he predicted a hilltop burning in unprecedented heat, and a writer lost in a fog. Perhaps all these sleeping heroes will one day be uncovered by the waking hand of erosion, ready to deliver us from our geology-derived crises.

Plugs and sills

After I finally left Eildon, I drove to Smailholm. Here, a 'shattered tower' rises dramatically from a ridge of 'naked cliffs rudely piled', according to Sir Walter Scott, who grew up just below it. A textbook example of the defensive architecture of the Borders, the 'naked cliffs rudely piled' on which it stands are a ridge of Variscan basalt: as at Eildon itself, igneous rocks have here been used as a platform for defence, for buildings that make power visible.

They are not alone. In fact I sometimes wonder whether the Variscan-era igneous rocks of the Midland Valley and northern England are not, per square inch, host to more stone thrones than any other rock-group in Britain. Repeatedly making sudden, steep-sided hills, cliffs and ridges, this is geology that encourages humanity to flex the muscles of power.

Many such hills are the rigid remnants of a volcano's inner plumbing. The volcanic plug at Dumbarton, downriver from Glasgow, leers over the Clyde from its bleak post-industrial setting. Fortified in the Iron Age, it became *Alt Chluaidh*, the rock of the Clyde, the power-focus of the British kingdom of Strathclyde, and later a royal castle. It may be the oldest attested continuous site of human habitation in Scotland.

Yet Dumbarton was just one of over 1,000 small volcanoes known to have existed in the Midland Valley, many of which left such features behind. There are fourteen volcanic vents in East Lothian alone: here, the Bass rock is an island shaped like an upturned bowl, its grey flanks dominated by a ruined castle; the nearby orange-red Tantallon Castle sits on another former vent; Dunbar Castle on yet one more.

One starts to wonder if the 'Scot's flourish' starts with the building of defensive structures on isolated igneous knolls. Lothian's igneous North Berwick Law and Traprain Law are both topped by Iron Age hillforts.

Features known as 'sills' play an especially vivid role in this story. These are great sheets of magma that forced themselves through existing rocks like vast, buried, tongues, often running along bedding planes.

They cooled rapidly, often into dolerite; where erosion has exposed them, they become sudden cliffs up to 15–30m high, dramatically interrupting the flow of any landscape in which they sits: geological bulwarks.

Two are particularly significant: the Midland Valley Sill in Scotland, and, in northern England, the Whin Sill. Really a whole suite of intrusions, the former extends for about 620 square miles below the ground, and its exposed edges crop up in a great U-shaped series of sudden steep clifflets in the centre and east of the Valley. East Lomond hill in Fife carries a major Iron Age hillfort; Abbey Craig, Stirling an early medieval one. This is the location from which William Wallace is said to have prepared to battle Edward I; it is topped by the Wallace Monument, an 1860s Scots flourish and a prelude to Castle Rock, less than 3 miles away.

This is the site of Stirling castle, one of the most important royal strong-holds in the nation, sheer on three sides but on the other approached up a relatively gentle ridge along which stretches the twelfth-century burgh, where the Holy Rude parish church is as magnificently named (for English speakers at least) as it is designed. An exactly comparable arrangement applies at another igneous crag of the era, Castle Rock in Edinburgh.

For all its geohistorical significance, the Midland Valley Sill sits in a landscape in which rocky outcrops and sudden hills are not unusual. The opposite is true of the Northumberland coast. This is a place so spacious one's eyes can feel pinned open; except where the Whin Sill throws sudden linear shivers across the land, itch-like ridges of a buried world.

'Whin' is a term for a dark, hard rock; it may also imply a place where gorse grows. There is said to be 1,700 square miles of it below the ground; exposures occur from Cross Fell to Lindisfarne. One such must have seemed to Roman surveyors to be almost geologically designed to repel and impress anyone approaching from the north, for it is followed by fully 15 miles of Hadrian's Wall, clinging photogenically to the sill's lip near Housesteads/*Vercovicium*.

But that is not its only outburst of defensiveness. A sudden cliff-edged plateau of the sill provides the setting for fourteenth-century Dunstanburgh castle. Nearby, another sharp-sided nub of it is the platform for Bamburgh, a great royal stronghold that was preceded by the hillfort known as *Dun Duarioi*. Ridges of the sill form the natural groyne which helps keep the sands of Holy Island/Lindisfarne in place; these in turn caused the mummification of the region's greatest saint, Cuthbert. His first church may just have perched on a whin ridge that runs above the twelfth-century abbey ruins. Tudor Lindisfarne castle sits atop another such rise.

A common ancient root, *berg*, gives us words for 'hill', as in iceberg; burial mound, as in 'barrow'; and urban settlement/seat of power, as in 'borough'. Landform, history and power are verbally intertwined.

Cuthbert has given his name to some little stone crinoids or sea lilies, Carboniferous fossils which could be threaded to make rosaries. But he has a Variscan igneous territory of his own on the slab-like outcrops of the Sill known as the Farne islands. Here he spent several years in contemplation; and here, too he enacted several bird-related miracles, presumably inspired by the archipelago's colony of terns, whose nesting sites cover the columnar rocks.

The igneous thrones of the north, then, have been attracting human attention since prehistoric times. But it is of course industry, and the potential of a sequence of sedimentary rocks, that is the major geohistorical theme of the period.

Industry and after

It is hard now to imagine what the most intense industrial-era landscapes were like. In the Black Country, James Naysmyth reported in 1830, 'The earth seems to have been turned inside out. Its entrails are strewn about: . . . covered with cinder-heaps and mounds.' There were pits and furnaces everywhere; people had 'fierce white eyes' and were covered in smut. Even the plants were dead, or grey.

Here lay the thickest coal seam in Britain (5.5–7.5m of what are in fact twelve to fourteen close-packed seams); almost at the surface, the coal was apt to set fire to itself, leaving acres of hot earth smouldering. There were 540 pits in 1865; 26,620 people worked in them; work as dirty and difficult as can be imagined.

The area's very name is a translation of industry into toponym. It is said to originate from the blackness of soil, coal and daytimes alike: the night was simply red. This winning and burning of black rocks and brown ores gave rise to a throat-curdling mass of chimneys. As well as Carboniferous coal and iron, there was the much-quarried and tunnelled Silurian-era Wenlock limestone of the Wren's Nest: in terms of its scale, the combination of the three proved even more potent than at Ironbridge.

Abraham Darby was born below this hill, and earlier experiments with using coal to make iron took place there. Darby's life jumps from one Carboniferous location to another: Dudley, the edges of Bristol, Coalbrookdale. His very geohistory was Carboniferous. The same could be said of Richard Arkwright, and many other early industrialists – and indeed millions since.

The Black Country eventually engulfed a whole series of once-separate towns and villages, all on the Carboniferous: Dudley, Walsall, Wolverhampton. Birmingham, a few miles to the east, was a separate centre of manufacturing and marketing centered on Triassic rocks. The two settlements eventually became a single Birmingham and Black Country, or West Midlands, conurbation. Matthew Boulton and James Watt's Soho Manufactory (1766) and Foundry (1795) were positioned between the two, the foundry a mile nearer the Carboniferous rocks, the factory nearer Birmingham. Here were pioneered steam-powered machinery, mass-production manufacturing, and the use of coal gas to make lighting. Thanks to the latter, in many mid-nineteenth-century towns and cities, the very night had been conquered in a way unprecedented in human history.

All this is without the textile industry which, around Glasgow and in West Yorkshire and Lancashire, added mills to the dense landscape of coal pits, iron foundries and heavy manufacturing.

Even this had a geohistorical dimension. Wool was a major feature of the economy in any area with good pasture. But through much of the Pennines there were also consistent, powerful sources of water power, and it is on the Pennine Fringe that the textile industry took off at scale. Cotton eventually replaced wool on the western side of the Pennines, and around Glasgow and Paisley: the damper Atlantic climate and west-facing ports that caused this change are both expressions of landform, and ultimately the result of geological developments.

Iron, lead, steel

Long before the age of industry, metal mattered. Indeed the Bronze Age mines of the Great Orme in North Wales are among the most memorable mining sites in Britain.

This eye-catching promontory pokes out from the dark Caledonian-era rocks of the coast, much like the serpent's snout after which it is named. Made of Carboniferous limestone, it is possessed of a kind of treeless brightness. Any passing human would be curious about such a place; and such an explorer might also have been surprised to find smears of green, soft rock running along cracks in the grey-white stone. This is malachite, the raw material needed to make copper; smelt it with about 10 per cent tin, and you have bronze.

The ore is softer than the surrounding rock. It is the product of fluids that leached their way up from the hotter regions below, following fault-lines which occasionally billow out into caverns; such lines can be thick enough for someone very adroit, perhaps a child, to follow, using bones and rocks from the nearby beaches as tools. On occasion, terrifyingly, miners lit fires below ground to soften up the deposits.

By about 2000 BC, a major industry was developing here. Perhaps 871–1,741 tons of metal were eventually produced: enough to make millions of objects. Opencast at first, the entire hillside became a nest of holes and passages, as if hollowed out by wriggling human worms: you can follow some of the 5 miles of man-made caves said to run below the headland, descending 70m into the rock. No one would go deeper here until the nineteenth century, when mechanical pumps doubled the mine's depth.

To make the bronze, tin had to be brought, probably from Cornwall; timber for smelting, from the wooded ground that is now Llandudno and the Conwy valley. Objects forged from the resulting metal have been found as far away as Holland and France. The holes and fires that peppered the peninsula must have made it look even more dragon-like in the Bronze Age than it did to the Norsemen who named it. It is one of a trio of well-attested prehistoric metal ore mines in Britain: there is Silurian Copa Hill, in the Cambrian mountains – and another on the Carboniferous limestone, at Ecton Hill in the White Peak, where around 2000–1700 BC mining led 20–30m underground, removing up to 500kg of ore.

As we enter recorded history, we find more centres of industry on the Carboniferous: Peak and Mendip silver and lead and Forest of Dean iron are particularly prominent. Silver and lead, both of which can be found in the ore known as 'galena', were being quarried in the Mendips by AD 49, just seven years after the Roman invasion. The Roman Fosse Way seems partly laid out to enable access to them. Roman 'pigs' or ingots of this have been found as far away as Normandy.

Medieval aristocrats and churchmen profited from such resources: the bishop of Bath & Wells and the prior of Witham controlled much Mendip mining. The miners of the Forest of Dean were looked to by Edward I for their skills as sappers. The significance of the White Peak as a source of lead is emphasised by a potentially Anglo-Saxon carving of a miner in the church at Wirksworth, that town described by George Eliot as 'grim, stony, and unsheltered'. It was the capital of the mining area known as the 'wapentake'.

Here, Charles I was told in a petition, 'many thousand people are dailie imployed in the lead mynes, to the greatt proffitt of your Majestie'. Many local fields remain marked by the detritus of extraction: quarries, lines of spoil-hcaps, small ruined buildings. Little sheer-sided gorges or trenches known as 'rakes' are the work of humans, following and removing lines of ore across the landscape. Comparable marks are known as 'scowles' in the Forest of Dean, and made the Mendip landscape 'gruffy' with disturbed earth. Discarded stone was re-sorted in search of more ore, work often done by women. Spoil-heaps are thus one of the few physical signs of women's extensive role in mining and quarrying.

Exploitation of the metal resources of the White Peak was ultimately in the gift of the Crown and its local aristocratic representatives. An elaborate administrative system developed, focused on the Barmote court, which still meets in Wirksworth's Moot Hall. The system allowed ordinary people to prospect and stake claim to seams; these people were known as 'Peakrills', the small operations they ran were 'meers'. Often, individual miners would club together and become shareholders in a new mine: a pattern that held true nationally, and led to the growth of many of the distinctive 'squatter' settlements in mining and quarrying country. Further examples on Carboniferous rocks line the sides of Weardale, and cluster in pockets of the Forest of Dean.

Eventually, larger companies gobbled up the smaller ones. These could be vast: Mill Close Mine at Darley Bridge in the White Peak was the biggest lead mine in the country in 1901. They made their overlords very wealthy. The Dukes of Devonshire owned mines throughout the Peak, the northern Pennines and the Lakes. Their mine at Deep Ecton, one of the deepest in Britain, was said to have produced 10 per cent of the world's copper (as well as lead) before being upstaged by Silurian Parys Mountain on Anglesey. Their mineral wealth helped fund their gracious Carboniferous sandstone palace at Chatsworth (1687) and the dark, Peak-version-of-Bath spa at Buxton (1779). The White Peak came to be a source of other useful things, too: the lime in the limestone, in demand for fertilisers and in the chemical industry; fluorspar, important to the metal industry, in medicine, and for enamelling.

A comparable institution to the Barmote court survives in the mining district of the Forest of Dean. Anyone born in St Briavel's hundred who has worked in a mine for a year and a day has the right to dig for the area's products: coal, iron, stone – and ochre.

This 'brush ore' was very pure, pasty, iron-rich and red. It was sometimes found in thick deposits known as 'churns'. At Clearwell Caves, six separate iron mines worked 20 miles of spectacular natural caverns – caves still used for 'colour mining', producing natural red, yellow, purple and brown pigments. These are the likely source of the 'Terra Rossa d'Inghilterra' used by Michelangelo and other Italian Renaissance artists.

The thought that Italy's greatest painter might have placed smears of the Forest of Dean on the walls of the Sistine Chapel is a remarkable one, but also a reminder of how fundamentally human the very act of colouring something is; and how important such rocks are to its story. The Carboniferous Limestone is in many places a source of pigments, especially black and red, including the ochres for which the 'Red Lady' of Paviland is named. Such sudden bursts of soft red and purple in the rocks must have looked like the very blood of the earth.

Industrial synergies

Lead is linked to silver, iron to ochre: as the industrial era dawns, such relationships between resources become increasingly significant, and generate remarkable geohistorical patterns. There is a direct connection between the White Peak lead mines and the decision by Richard Arkwright to locate a water-powered cotton mill next to the Derwent at Cromford, a site which sits alongside Coalbrookdale as a birthplace of the industrial revolution.

This was a 24-hour-a-day factory housed in a seven-storey building, and Arkwright's decision to locate it here was surely influenced by the presence of Cromford sough, which had been dug to drain the mines there by Sir Cornelius Vermuyden and brought a reliable and powerful supply of water down from the White Peak plateau. Arkwright built a townlet for his workers, and a castle-like residence nearby, making the place at once both feudal and capitalist, aping the past and the radically new.

In other places, industries grew at a midpoint between sources of raw materials. With coal in the Valleys but copper and tin ore in Cornwall, and the former easier to transport than the latter, copper-smelting and tin-plating were concentrated around Swansea: between the two, but nearer to the coal. Merthyr Tydfil grew where the local deposits of iron ore and coal came close together: 6,000 people once worked in the Dowlais ironworks there.

Such economies of scale stimulated the remaking of natural patterns. In Staffordshire, Josiah Wedgwood needed to get flint from the chalklands of the south-east, China clay from Cornwall and gypsum from Derbyshire to make the porcelain-like products of his factory on the Etruria marl, a Carboniferous clay. Perhaps it is not surprising that he was a key mover in the creation of the game-changing Trent and Mersey Canal, in 1766 cutting the first sod on a project that was to forge a link between those two vital rivers.

Pots and knives

Bottle-shaped kilns of dark brick can still be glimpsed beneath the run-down high streets and regeneration projects of the 'six towns' known collectively as the Potteries, of which Stoke is the most important. The industry developed where a Pennine Fringe ridge of coal-bearing rocks runs north–south, parallel to a valley of Etruria marl: this geological colocation created a conurbation whose very identity is derived from its geological resources.

Likewise, there is a spot where the Millstone Grit of the Dark Peak throws the eager power of the Pennine rain into five rivers, all of which tumble and fall into a single bowl of Pennine Fringe land. The power of these waters is complemented by the usefulness of gritstone for grinding and sharpening. Coal and iron ore deposits surround the bowl on three sides; there is lead immediately south and west. Perhaps no surprise, then, that the town of Sheffield, which sat in this cauldron of potential, was already known for making sharp-bladed metal tools in the medieval period. In the nineteenth century it became the most important steel manufactory in the world.

The frequent colocation of iron and coal was perhaps the most important synergy of all. As a result of Darby's discoveries, the entire iron industry recentred itself on the Carboniferous, abandoning older centres such as the Weald. Such synergistic shifts of focus are vividly seen in the Scottish Midland Valley.

Scottish synergies

Scottish coal was originally sourced around the Firth of Forth, where in the medieval period it was being used in salterns and exported to London; an export trade that was for a long time second only to that of the English north-east. Here, 'seacoal', gathered as black rocks left by the receding tide, was a major source; yet as early as 1618, one colliery already stretched a mile under the sea.

As mining technology improved, transport links got better and iron and manufacturing became more important, the industry spread to more deeply buried seams inland. Here coal, iron, and the trading city of Glasgow, with its access to the Atlantic and its burgeoning textile industry, lay close together. Scottish coal lay in complex, fault-riven layers, many with memorable names: Earl David's Parrot, Coxtools, Humph, Creepie, Kiltongue. Meanwhile, the ironworks established at Carron just outside Falkirk in 1760 became one of the largest in the world, consuming as much coal as the entire city of Edinburgh.

The development in the 1850s and 60s of the Bessemer and Seimens steel-making techniques required higher-grade ores than could be found in most Carboniferous locations, and iron extraction moved again, on to younger rocks where the ore was also more deeply buried. In 1860, 63 per cent of British iron was sourced from Carboniferous rocks; by 1937, this had shrunk to 1 per cent. But the ores of Scotland (and also of the Cumbrian coast) were exceptions, and by 1885 the nation was producing 20 per cent of British steel, much of it destined for the shipyards on the Clyde, which built more metal-hulled boats than the rest of the world combined.

Scotland had textile mills, too, thanks to its many fast-running waters. Near Lanark, the river Clyde cuts cliffs as the harder Carboniferous rock becomes softer Silurian/Devonian; the resulting waterfalls give it great power. In 1786, at the foot of these waterfalls, Richard Arkwright and David Dale founded what they hoped would become a 'Manchester of Scotland'. The result, New Lanark, became the nation's largest cotton mill, and the site of the 'primitive Socialist' experiments of the succeeding millowner, Robert Owen. The Falls of Lanark also drove what is claimed to be Britain's first large-scale hydroelectric power station (1927).

An even more significant Scottish innovation gave rise to a unique monument-type. Drive south-west from Livingston, West Lothian, and enter a landscape of housing estates, deep green pastures, and sudden industrial and commercial areas on the sites of former mines.

Here, near West Calder, an almost shockingly geometrical group of five conical eminences rears on to the horizon; even now, tinged green with plant growth, they stand out all the more for being a marked shade of orange. Seen from above, each has a tail, emanating from a single point, like a clutch of rodents tied together. Attempt to climb these man-made 73m 'mountains' and find rock fragments shifting under your feet like a Highland scree-slope, and clinking drily like dry wood. Each is an exhausted fragment of a sedimentary rock suffused with potential fossil fuel: oil shale.

This is the Five Sisters Bing (a *bingr* is a 'heap' in Norse; *beann* Gaelic for 'mountaintop', *ben* the Scots for 'hill'). It, and the nineteen others that survive, owe its existence ultimately to the Scottish inventor and philanthropist James 'Paraffin' Young, who discovered that oil could be made from these rocks: the heat the process involved turned them from dark grey to orange. At the Five Sisters, the point where the rats' tails join was the site of the Westwood Oil Works, one of the youngest of these operations.

The refining business founded by Young in the coal-mining area around Bathgate was the first commercial oil refinery in the world. The profits were enormous, and by 1870, ninety-seven competing works had been set up, producing in the late nineteenth century 25 million gallons/114 million litres of crude oil for a worldwide market. The vast refinery at Grangemouth owes its origin to this industry; today it is dependent on tankers bringing supplies from overseas. Carboniferous shales remain the main focus of attention for potential UK fracking; and Carboniferous coal-bearing rocks are an important source of the gas we extract from the southern North Sea. We are back with fossil fuels.

North-eastern prowess

In the north-east, the oldest use of the 'black stuff' in Britain has been identified in Iron Age smelting sites. A healthy export business is already attested in the Middle Ages, and by the eighteenth century up to 83 per cent of local coal was being shipped out of this area. Much of it went to London, which had exhausted other sources of fuel, but it also went to other east-coast locations, and even to Europe. The area was not overtaken in productiveness until south Wales reached peak production, in the early twentieth century.

The seams of the north-east were often accessed from the sides of river valleys; though County Durham was the biggest producer, the Tyne helped make Newcastle the centre of the trade (the expression 'Coals to

Newcastle' is first recorded in 1538). The steep sides of the river valleys meant coal was loaded from enormous timber piers known as staithes, the vivid setting for the ending of the 1971 film *Get Carter*; the 'Wigan pier', a jokey name popularised in music halls and made famous by George Orwell, was a Lancashire equivalent.

Politics and power

As early as 1666 the coal producers of the north-east had successfully held Parliament to ransom by suspending mining in protest against imminent price regulation; the political significance of the coalfields was only to increase. Twice in the twentieth century, striking miners' unions induced a state close to civil war. The strength of these workers is embodied in their union offices: in South Yorkshire, those of Barnsley (1874) are a proud Gothic fantasy in Carboniferous stone, known as 'King Arthur's castle' after the miners' leader Arthur Scargill. In Rotherham, not far away, there is a monument to the other extreme of the Carboniferous experience: Wentworth Woodhouse (from c.1724), the largest family home in England. The Wentworths were an aristocratic mine-owning dynasty, and their house sits right on top of the Barnsley seam; after nationalisation a spoil-heap from opencast mining overlooked the earl's bedroom window.

In general, working conditions for miners were appalling, especially before the reforms of the 1840s. In Scotland, from 1606 until 1799, any 'vagabond' or 'sturdie beggar' could be forced into the pits and salterns of the Firth of Forth, and be unable to leave employment without permission.

The ending of such practices in the course of the nineteenth century was a major achievement, one in which the workers themselves played an active role; it ushered in the century-long period in which working-class life was transformed from a world of random exploitation to one of regular hours, ever-improving access to education and healthcare, and relative economic stability: a world that is beginning to feel like a historical 'blip'.

Of course, this was no utopia: coal burnt on an industrial scale became heavy smog, which cloaked much of Carboniferous Britain and the areas around it. Underground, methane often accompanied coal deposits; if just 5–15 per cent of it was present it could explode on exposure to air, causing underground conflagrations in an atmosphere already full of coal dust.

In the worst colliery disaster of all, 439 men died in an underground gas explosion at the Universal Colliery, Senghenydd in the Aber valley in 1913. South Wales was also the site of the 1966 tragedy at Aberfan in the Taff valley, where the spoil-heaps of the Merthyr Vale colliery had unwisely been positioned where permeable shales met impermeable Pennant sandstones, and natural springs burst out. Their very roots were unstable, and on 21 October up to 140,000 cubic yards/107,000 cubic metres of waste collapsed down the hill in a great slurry, killing 116 children and twenty-eight adults in the valley below.

Welsh culture

These Valleys had only truly opened up from around 1830, when canals, railways lines and docks connected them to the Glamorgan coast; yet in 1913, 20 per cent of the 3 million tons of coal extracted in Britain was dug by the area's almost-quarter-of-a-million miners. The coal here improves in quality as one heads west, where Variscan pressures helped create rich, if heavily faulted, deposits of anthracite. During the First World War, 90 per cent of the coal that powered the navy came from one place: the Rhondda valley. British military power depended on industrial prowess, and in turn on its geology; 'every knuckle of soft ore / A bullet in a soldier's ear', as the poet Norman Nicolson put it.

Such areas developed strong communities, with proud and unique cultures. The Valleys were at once profoundly Welsh and inherently industrial; Socialist and Nonconformist (there are said to have been 151 chapels in the vale of Rhondda in 1905). If it were not for them, Welsh-language culture would have remained restricted to the highland fringes: even today their western zone is the largest Welsh-speaking area outside Silurian-and-older Wales.

III
The Carboniferous mythosphere

Where would we be without electronically amplified, recorded or created music, without photography or film, without the energy that powers the internet, or the settings for much of the literature of the last 200 years – not to mention the machines and transport networks that printed and distributed it? There is a sense in which our cultural universe is both powered and defined by the historical impact of fossil-derived energy.

Many aspects of this culture have specific roots in the British Carboniferous. Science burgeoned: William Smith's discovery of stratigraphy, fundamental to geology, was the result of his professional need to predict where coal might lie. Even before that many of the great discoveries of the era depended on a kind of proto-geology, in which people were testing and investigating the properties of earth materials: Darby and coke is just one example. Political movements are a feature of the age, and Communism was founded on Friedrich Engel's study of conditions in industrial-era Manchester and Salford, where his father owned a mill.

But the cultural implications are everywhere. In the art of Joseph Wright of Derby and the literature of D. H. Lawrence, inspired by Carboniferous mills, forges and coalfields. In the music of Heavy Metal, born in the Black Country. Tim Burton set his film of *Charlie and the Chocolate Factory* (2005) in a vividly evoked fantasy industrial-era city; Hayao Miyazaki of Japan's Studio Ghibli transmuted the landscape of the Valleys into the fantasy world of his animated film *Castle in the Sky* (1986).

In sport, we have Rugby league, overwhelmingly concentrated in Carboniferous and Carboniferous-dependent industrial towns. In architecture, whole new building types. From Yorkshire parkin to Staffordshire oatcakes, Cornish pasties to fish and chips, new foods supplied fast energy to those working long hours in mines and factories, foundries and mills. It is ironic that this food is itself Carb-heavy.

It becomes increasingly possible to use 'Carboniferous' as an adjective for a great wave of cultural change which is still breaking over us. One could say that everything from Paddington Station to Brexit,

Led Zeppelin to the Labour Party, are geohistorically 'carboniferous'. Those Welsh choirs are carboniferous. And there is an aspect of the Carboniferous landscape that injected a very non-urban aspect into the mythospherical souls of those who live on these rocks.

Carboniferous wilderness

The people of Carboniferous Britain live with an ever-present wilderness in their backyard. The Scottish Midland Valley is scattered with bare volcanic hills and hemmed in by major uplands (the edge of Glasgow is less than 15 miles from the Highland Boundary Fault); the fells of the English Pennines whisper an ever-present threat of freedom over the constricted terraces and abandoned mills of the Pennine Fringe. Run out of the backstreets of the Valleys and you are on open ground, if today heavily planted with forestry. Drama and emptiness are around every corner. As Elizabeth Gaskell put it in 1857, the 'wild bleak moors' of the Dark Peak can either be 'grand from the ideas of solitude and loneliness which they suggest, or oppressive from the feeling which they give of being pent up by some monotonous and illimitable barrier'.

Whichever is the case, this is a geology which places an intense emptiness alongside an intense built-ness, making for a mythosphere rich in possibilities. In Scotland, no Lowlander can be unaware of the Highlands. Further south it is the gritty mid-Carboniferous sandstones – otherwise the *least* useful in the litany of Carboniferous rocks – that articulate it most powerfully. Perhaps such places as the Dark Peak and the Trossachs are the spiritual and cultural safety valves of the industrial revolution. One can hear the longing for release to the Highlands in the music of Glasgow's Blue Nile; the stubborn, shattered grandeur of the gritstone in the music of Joy Division (half of whom came from Macclesfield, from the edges of which one can be among rocky gullies in minutes). Not for nothing do stereotypes of the northern English often include the word 'gritty'.

Perhaps the first stirrings of this come in that great fourteenth-century poem, *Sir Gawain and the Green Knight*, whose geography seems to evoke specific details of gritstone Staffordshire. The poem is written in a Middle English from this part of the world. The green knight's castle of Hautdesert lies in a slightly tamed landscape adjacent to wilderness, an embodiment of the Pennine Fringe. His own combination of greenness and a sharp-axed threat almost embodies such landscapes. The adventure moves to a Dark Peak world of 'rogh knokled knarres with knorned stones', in which the green chapel is 'a crevisse of an olde cragge': a geography that fits the area between the Roaches and Lud's Church, an extraordinary sandstone cleft where logic suggests no valley should be (the landslip that caused it may be connected to the instability of hard gritstone sitting on top of softer sandstones). Lollards are said to have preached in this narrow chasm, lighting the touch paper on a historical chain that would lead first to Protestantism and ultimately to Nonconformism – whose chapels, ironically, were to become signature buildings of Carboniferous Britain. Indeed, Nonconformism is arguably a kind of carboniferous spirituality.

Four centuries later, it is hard to think of a personal name more evocative of the Dark Peak than Heathcliff, or a more isolated gritstone farmstead than Wuthering Heights, said to be based on Top Withens, the ruins of which occupy the side of a dark scarp a little over 3 miles from Haworth. 'My love of Heathcliff remembers the eternal rocks beneath – a source of little visible delight, but necessary,' as Cathy puts it.

For me, the sense of a social order going through an advanced trauma seems to pervade this book. The Brontës moved into Haworth parsonage in 1820, and *Wuthering Heights* was published in 1847; exactly the period when Haworth changed from a Pennine village to a swollen, town-like mill settlement, filled with newcomers. Heathcliff himself is an outsider. Even today, prettified within an inch of having any character at all, Haworth makes a good stand-in for hundreds of small settlements on the tipping point between Pennine Fringe and Dark Peak. The signs in Japanese that lead from the edge of the village to Top Withens are a remarkable demonstration of the power of this gritstone tale. Indeed 'gritstone carboniferous' could almost be a term for a whole aesthetic: a kind of bleak romanticism fuelled in equal measure by mills and moors.

The Dark Peak likewise looms over the writing of such place-inspired creative talents as Ted Hughes (Calderdale); Henry Moore (Wharfedale); J. B. Priestley (Bradford); Simon Armitage (Huddersfield); Tony Harrison and Alan Bennett (Leeds); and Barbara Hepworth

(Wakefield). Glyn Hughes, a native of Cheshire, wrote an entire volume entitled *Millstone Grit* (1975). The urge to freedom that these fells seem to inspire in the surrounding urban communities lies behind various mass trespasses, such as that on Kinder Scout in 1932, which sought free access to the Peak's high places, and led to the creation of the Peak District National Park.

The Dark Peak's mythosphere takes a grim turn in places such as Saddleworth moor, and its associations with the Moors Murderers: the very embodiment of The Smiths' 'Manchester, so much to answer for'. Yet the darkness is not always macabre. These are places of emptiness and freedom, and it sometimes seems the Pennine spirit affects even the light: a photographer friend swears by its qualities, as cloud systems break up and re-form with endless drama over England's exposed spine.

Industry and light alike inspired the painter Joseph Wright of Derby: works such as *Landscape with a Rainbow*, 1794, and *Arkwright's Cotton Mills by Night*, c.1782–1783, capture a Derbyshire – rural on the one hand, industrial on the other – at the very moment of its carboniferous transformation. His *An Experiment on a Bird in the Air Pump* (1768) is particularly extraordinary. The scientist at the centre of the painting is removing the air from a glass vessel, making a bird within it struggle for life. He may look as if he is still part natural philosopher or mage, but what he holds is the power that comes with experimental enquiry.

Around him, an audience gathers, their faces thrown into sharp relief by a hidden candle. They show fascination, grief, wonder – and a brooding contemplation of the implications of this new approach to the natural world, as if aware that it will bring in its wake everything from electricity to the atomic bomb, from the smog to the melting railway lines.

Wright knew something extraordinary was happening, and perhaps uniquely captured it in paint: but of course it is L. S. Lowry who depicted its day-to-day implications. His rural landscapes (for example *A Landmark*, 1936) are overlooked evocations of the Pennine upland that surrounded his home city. But he is most famous for depicting the city itself; and though the flatness and mud of his Salford scenes bespeak their setting on the adjacent Triassic New Red Sandstone, their bleakness could just as easily be that of places like contemporary Newcastle, Sheffield or Glasgow, places that inspired literature from Elizabeth Gaskell (Manchester) through Arnold Bennett (the Potteries) to D. H. Lawrence (the Nottinghamshire coalfields): the urban landscapes of the Carboniferous.

Cities

Seen from space, Britain's major cities mark out the Carboniferous: in England, the great series of settlements that run in a 'U' around the Pennine Fringe; Glasgow and Edinburgh in Scotland; in Wales, Cardiff and Swansea, the ports that enabled the export of the coal and iron of the Valleys.

Indeed, Carboniferous is the geology on which most of us live: at a rough estimate, 30–35 million of Britain's 67 million inhabitants. With very few exceptions – perhaps the most significant are London and Portsmouth/Southampton – our major settlements either developed directly on these rocks or were economically dependent on their products and set on adjacent ones, chiefly Permian/Triassic.

These settlements are testament to the extraordinary population movements that went with the great carboniferous moment. Glasgow had 10,000 inhabitants in 1600, 77,000 in 1801; it then doubled in twenty years, and by 1901 had reached 761,000. In such places the new ways of living nascent at Coalbrookdale, Cromford and their ilk were writ large, as entire populations adapted to lives as timetabled as factories. In such cities, especially early on, 'misery walks abroad in skin, bone and nakedness' (Defoe).

It is also true that those settlements that have weathered the post-industrial storm least well are literally mono-lithic, in that they often lie far from other rocks. Even before the economic death-knell of the Covid-19 pandemic I found parts of some of these former towns of mills and mining frightening in a way that was at once palpable and hard to define. Bradford is one of my favourite places in England; it has a thriving cultural life, and its swaggering mills, mosques and hills give it a special carboniferous drama. But when I visited post-pandemic I found many suburban high streets, while never exactly prosperous, effectively shuttered up; what had seemed 'deprived' now simply looked abandoned.

While the causes are complex, the geographical facts are simple: place an early twenty-first-century map of deprivation, or Brexit-majority voting, or the 'Red Wall' of the 2019 election, or Covid-19 mortality, over a geological map and these Carboniferous-dependent industrial settlements loom large. Such communities have been radically shaken by the geohistorical decline of our 'late carboniferous' world; many are equally tired of being stereotyped by such developments.

The centres of the major cities, meanwhile, are generally thriving, multi-ethnic places, filled with fine buildings of many traditions and eras. Let's visit two of them.

Glasgow and Edinburgh

We're in Scotland. Glasgow, looking west down the Clyde, can stand in for the 'typical' industrial-era urban behemoth; and Edinburgh, facing east down the Forth, is one of the great geohistorical urban entities to be found anywhere.

Almost a third of Scotland's population live in the region of the former city, which is also among the half-dozen most populous urban areas in the United Kingdom. Like Leeds, the rocks that it sits on may be Carboniferous, but they are merely adjacent to those which are rich in coal and metal ores: this is a location to which they could be brought, and processed, and the resulting products traded onwards, here down the Clyde and out to sea.

The story starts long before the age of industry, and with a sudden Variscan hill. This 59m outcrop of an igneous sill had a green hollow (*glas cau*) next to it through which the Molendinar burn flowed to the Clyde. As early as the sixth century a cathedral had been founded in this dip. This is the 'Townhead'; the hill itself has become the famous Necropolis, Victorian burial place of 50,000 people.

But another small settlement developed further down the burn and nearer to the Clyde. Here we are on the humped hills of glacial earth, with Carboniferous rocks beneath them, that are typical of the Midland

Valley. It was from two centres, then, that first informally, and then in great planned leaps from the late eighteenth century, a stretched grid of streets was laid out parallel to the river.

The town already sat among Scotland's wealthiest dozen burghs in the sixteenth century. By 1700 it was second only to Edinburgh. Atlantic trade boomed after the Act of Union in 1706 improved access to English colonies. Subtly but importantly quicker to reach from the American east coast than Liverpool or Bristol, the city became a nodal point for tobacco, sugar and cotton, most of it dependent on slave labour. The dredging and widening of the shallow Clyde enabled larger boats to come to harbour; the construction of the Forth and Clyde and Monkland canals (the former completed in 1791) brought coal and iron ore into the city centre. Cotton manufacturing in the area boomed; later, heavy engineering too.

It is possible that the shallowness of the Clyde encouraged the city's dependence on local building stones, which do much to give Glasgow its distinctive character. Certainly, as the city grew it mined the pale Carboniferous sandstones beneath its own feet. This is a stone-built city to a greater extent than its English peers, with their many brick buildings; its housing was also noteworthy for being marked by tenement blocks rather than terraces.

As early quarries were worked out or built over, new ones further out were established; the pits left behind became the sites of Buchanan Street and Queen Street stations. New stone-sources appeared; especially after the coming of the railways in the 1840s, which first brought in Midland Valley sandstones from further afield, and later Scottish slates, Aberdeenshire granite, New Red Sandstone from the Borders and English Carboniferous sandstones. New textures, darker browns and bright reds were added to the city's pale-to-brown palette.

In the course of all this development several new parks were created. A former whinstone quarry was cut through in the course of the 1887 creation of Victoria Park, revealing the fossilised stumps of eleven extinct *Lepidodendron* trees. These are remnants of a Carboniferous forest estimated to have had 4,500 trees per square kilometre, many of them up to 30m high. The whole world-changing, coal-making cycle starts with such plants: the literal roots of the industrial era.

Edinburgh remains more palpably an old, and very dense, place. It, too sits in a rolling country of Carboniferous sandstones and glacial earths, broken by remnants of Caledonian and Variscan volcanoes. Here these make mini-mountains, giving the raw landscape a sculptural quality even before people set to work turning one of these ridge backs that heave to the sky (to paraphrase Scott) into a stronghold.

Arthur's Seat (251m) is the largest presence; the mountainous innards of a volcano, within walking distance of a major city centre. No fewer than four Iron Age fortifications grace its peaks. Volcanic vents are marked by formations such as the Lion's Head; the Midland Valley Sill cuts right through it, forming Salisbury Crags. And nearby is Castle Rock, a plug from the throat of another part of this Variscan volcano.

Here a mile-long sandstone ridge climbs to an igneous peak, coming to a juddering halt at the snout of a 122m-high cliff. Between the rock and the mountains, there is the less dramatic igneous platform known as Calton Hill. And the landform offers up one further flourish, in the shape of the Nor' Loch, a steep, moat-like valley, gouged along the northern side of Castle Rock by an ice-age glacier.

This is a kind of Scotland-in-miniature: mountain, loch, and lowland layered with glacial earths; and everything running more or less with the Caledonian Grain.

It was David I who laid out a burgh on Castle Rock, in the process wiping away evidence for occupation which may go back to *Din Eidyn*, 'the fort on the hillslope', and earlier. The long sandstone slope became a high street, with Holyrood Abbey, later Palace, at one end and the castle on its igneous peak; in the 200 years before 1700 it became the most prosperous settlement in Scotland and the principal stronghold of Scottish kingship. Constrained by the rock itself, aristocrats and merchants built a sequence of high, stone-built, tenement-like houses along the line of the Mile, giving the centre a tight, staccato rhythm unlike any other settlement. The Nor' Loch valley was flooded as a defensive measure.

Then, in the eighteenth century, in a great triumph of human effort over geology, the Nor' Loch was drained, and a bridge (the North Bridge, finished 1772) thrown across it, allowing Edinburgh to expand onto the more accommodating sedimentary-Carboniferous-and-till landscape beyond.

Edinburgh New Town was a planned eighteenth-century settlement of vaunting elegance and rational poise; a civilised sedimentary counterfoil to the igneous drama on the crag: yet as its axis runs parallel to Castle Rock, it still cleaves to the local grain.

It was just one expression of a city that had developed a brilliant intellectual culture, significant not least for its geological discoveries. It was on Salisbury crags that James Hutton argued that some rocks had cooled from lava; on Blackford Hill, that the nineteenth-century Swiss scientist Louis Agassiz argued that glaciers had played a fundamental role in shaping the land.

But even enlightened Edinburgh could not resist the lure of the 'Scots flourish'. On Calton Hill from the early nineteenth century there grew a series of recreations of ancient Greece that were at once both a national acropolis, and a viewing point for the architectural and geological glories of the city; a Parnassus of the north. Meanwhile the great gap of the Nor' Loch, and the steep gorge-like valleys followed by the pends and wynds on Castle Rock itself, were bridged in a sequence of spectacular interventions – the South Bridge, George IV Bridge, Waverley Bridge. The views these create across, down and up the gulfs and crags and buildings of Edinburgh are among its greatest visual thrills.

From the mid-nineteenth century the drained loch became the path of the railway line: to arrive at Waverley is still to feel as if you are climbing out of a canyon. A series of grand gothic crags were added to the urban ensemble: the Tollbooth church (1839); the Scott Memorial (1840); St Mary's Episcopal cathedral (from 1874). Their blackened sandstone spikes, each a 'Scots flourish' of the first order, are as darkly emblematic of Scottish urbanism as the Torridonian pinnacles of Stac Pollaidh and Suilven are of the Highlands. And all this time, local landlords were laying out impressive suburbs.

As a result, the city is surrounded by at least sixty-seven quarries, of which perhaps the most important were at Craigleith. Once 110m deep, and now the site of a Sainsbury's – I filled up on diesel there several times while writing this book – their stone was used for the statue of Nelson on his famous London column and exported as far afield as America. The fossil tree now outside the Natural History Museum in London was found there.

As the city spread, it sucked in stone from further afield: Caithness and Arbroath flags; Aberdeen and Peterhead granites; Easdale and Ballachulish slates; Carboniferous sandstones from Northumberland and Kincardineshire. There are hot-looking Permian/Triassic sandstones from Dumfriesshire; and even a couple of buildings of Portland stone from Dorset. A pair of entrance piers of 1886, now on Melville Drive, were designed to show off the qualities of such incoming stones, with a different material on each of their eighteen courses, each inscribed with the name of its parent quarry.

But it is the Carboniferous sandstones that tie the city together visually, making the whole place, from its landform to its buildings, a hymn to local rocks igneous and sedimentary alike. By 1900, even allowing for the pollution coming in from Leith and the coalfields, Geology and History could be forgiven for giving each other high-fives: one of the great urban spectacles on the planet, tied together by its richly textured, tan-coloured, Carboniferous building stones and dramatic natural features.

Edinburgh arguably outdoes even granite and Aberdeen and limestone Bath as a great hymn to the power that landform, geology, history and architecture can have when they act in concert; and its building stones are the glue between the rocks and the human achievements.

Carboniferous building stones

It is not only Glasgow and Edinburgh that are defined by Carboniferous sandstone. No other material comes closer to knitting together the built fabric of Britain. Its crisp, often pollution-darkened shades of beige, tan and off-yellow can be seen in Manchester and Paisley, Leeds and Newcastle, Bolton and Bathgate alike. Decent building stones can be found within reach of most major settlements, and there are good freestones, too. From the eighteenth century onwards, the demand for such rocks was voracious. In the mid-1840s there were 238 stone quarries in Yorkshire alone. Their grains are often cemented hard with silica, causing significant health problems for quarry-workers (many Edinburgh quarry workers were dead by 35).

Some of the Carboniferous sandstones are so fine-grained you can barely see the individual pieces of sand; others are visibly filled with swirls of rusty iron-red. Shades of grey can appear, derived from the carbon in Carboniferous plantlife. Those that are very hard, such as the gritstones, are good for dams, bridges and the like.

In older homes, one often sees rough local stone used for walls, and better material from a more distant source reserved for window-frames or corners. White Peak settlements such as Youlgreave and Tideswell use local grey-white limestone for walling and the tan sandstones of the Dark Peak for corners and window-frames – a colour-chart of the Peak itself. In general, a square stone window-surround in one stone, set in a rubbly wall in quite another, is something of a visual signature of the architecture of northern Britain.

Some of the oldest quarries in Britain seek these sandstones. There are Roman quarries around Hadrian's Wall, with original graffiti and inscriptions. There is a Roman tomb in Bordeaux carved from English Millstone Grit.

Pennine sandstones have other unique qualities. The name 'Millstone Grit' comes from that rock's special usefulness as a natural abrasive. The most important sources were the Dark Peak edges above Sheffield, a source of querns as early as the Iron Age. These later became so important a supplier of millstones that, as early as the thirteenth century, they were often simply called 'Peak stones'. Millstone Edge is a memorable monument to the industry, for at its base there are piles of abandoned millstones: slumped, regular circular forms that stand in contrast to the sharp-edged cliffs from which they were won.

The Carboniferous sandstones also included many sources of flagstones and stone-slates, leaving settlements in the Pennines and the Scottish Midland Valley rich in stone-flagged roofs. The most important of these, 'Yorkshire stone', dominates the pavements of London and other cities.

This strong, impervious sandstone can split along its many clayey bedding planes into slabs as thin as 2–3cm in depth, while withstanding the pounding of a thousand busy feet. It comes in subtle khaki variations, and wears into raised lines that curl across the surface like the coast of some forgotten continent. Quarried in many areas around Bradford and Leeds, the epicentre of the industry was around Elland, near Halifax. Locally called 'thackstones', these rocks could be ordered in standard sizes with delightful names: 'Jenny why gettest thou', 'Rogue why winkest thou', 'Short haghattee'.

In the south-west, Pennant is a late Carboniferous coal-bearing rock. Its name comes from the Welsh for the head of a valley or a stream, and it is often found on the springlines that separate permeable shales from impermeable sandstones. An almost duck-egg blue variety can be seen on the pavements of Bristol. But this stone is also the most famous Carboniferous building stone of Wales, seen in such defining structures as Caerphilly castle.

The Carboniferous limestone, hard and brittle, is less popular as a building stone. Hopton Wood, extracted near Wirksworth, is a major exception. This is a superstar stone, beloved by sculptors such as Jacob Epstein, Eric Gill, Barbara Hepworth and Henry Moore, and distributed across the world by the Commonwealth War Graves Commission, who often use it in their cemeteries.

Carboniferous Limestone is important in Wales, perhaps because it lies adjacent to the Cambrian/Ordovician/Silurian mountains, whose native stones are poor. Edward I's Gwynedd castles are perhaps the greatest Carboniferous Limestone buildings in Britain. Although they stand on ancient, hard rocks, most are located next to waterways down which stone could be imported, often from the eastern peninsula of Penmon on Anglesey.

Several Carboniferous limestones can be polished to look like marble, but the most well known is from Frosterley, Weardale – it comes up a glossy black, rammed with enormous white crustacea. The shafts that run up the walls in the Chapel of Nine Altars at Durham cathedral virtually boil with this black-and-white seafood orgy. 'Derbyshire Fossil', much of it again from near Wirksworth, is thick with plant-like crinoids and other fossils, and has been used for internal cladding and paving. Its patterns bloom like little fractal flowers, making a shiny stone garden of the walls of the Royal Festival Hall in London (1951). But Derybshire marbles can come in pyrotechnic arrays of colour, lavishly displayed in local country houses such as Chatsworth and Old Bolsover Castle.

Some of these White Peak rocks really look like precious stones. The most unique is Blue John, sourced only around Castleton, a delicate fluorite mineral that crystallised from saline fluids deep in the Earth. Translucent, veined and a deep purple-blue, it has been used since the eighteenth century to decorate the walls of country houses, and to make jewellery and other ornamental items.

'Bristol diamonds' were quartz nodules found around Clifton Gorge, and their name came to be applied to other stones that look precious, but aren't. Cannel coal from Lancashire, an oil shale that burnt like the candle for which it is named, was polished and formed into boxes and other objects, for it 'looked like black marble' (Celia Fiennes). Even softer, and much more widely exploited, were the many Carboniferous clays.

Brick and clay

About a third of all clay extracted in Britain is Carboniferous, and about 30 per cent of modern bricks (and all clay drainage pipes, a technology crucial to the improved sanitation of the nineteenth century) are made from this material. Most of it came from the clays and shales (and a silica-rich stone known as ganister) that separated seams of coal; those made from fireclay and crushed ganister could resist the heat of a furnace, and were also popular for sanitary ware: sinks and toilet bowls.

Brick, meanwhile, was a fundamental enabler of the era's growth: the fast food of mass construction, making everything from Victorian terraced houses (22,000 bricks each, or 61sqm of clay per street), to canal bridges and railway tunnels (14 million bricks per mile). Its source-clays were often dug from the very mines whose coal was used to fire them, and whose workers were driving the demand for new housing in the first place. Many bricks were made by women: one nineteenth-century observer noted that three-quarters of Black Country brickworkers were female.

Accrington 'bloods' are among the most famous Carboniferous-sourced bricks (and tiles): very strong, and deep red from the iron in the local fireclay: they were used in the Empire State Building. Staffordshire Blues, from the Potteries, are particularly fire-resistant, being made from shales and mudstones also rich in iron; they have an expensive-looking deep blue sheen.

By the late nineteenth century Ruabon ('Terracottapolis') near Wrexham was the biggest terracotta-making centre in the world, its industry based on Etruria marl-type clays, a prime tile-making material. Wrexham produced Victorian terracotta in nightmarish variety, seen for example in such scarlet Gothic fantasies as the Victoria Law Courts, Birmingham (1887–91) and the Prudential Assurance building, Holborn, London (from 1876).

In Scotland the ability to make bricks from the detritus of the oil-shale and coal-mining industries helped shift the brickmaking industry's focus from glacial earths of geologically recent origin to Carboniferous mining areas. Such clays had a special reputation for heat-resistant bricks and terracottas; the works at Armadale were among the biggest in Britain.

Here, 'Blaes' or 'composition' bricks, were simply made of crushed and compressed quarry waste. Coal ash and clay were sometimes combined and used in the same way in England; outside Bristol, bricks made from the slag of a brass foundry were used to build the black, castellated eighteenth-century gate to Arno's Court; Horace Walpole called it 'the Devil's cathedral'.

Exotica

The insatiable appetite for stone of the big industrial cities, and the advent of steam-powered transport, led to a vast increase in imported stone, making such settlements perhaps the greatest gatherings of man-made erratics in Britain. Snowdonian slate, Aberdonian granite and Yorkshire paving slabs became superstar stones as a result. Cardiff colliers brought European granites, schists and gneisses (often from Britanny or Scandinavia) in as ballast, turning the walls that line the city's backstreets into an extraordinary display of rocks. Today there are granites from Argentina rather than Aberdeen and gneisses from Brazil rather than Assynt in the architecture of Glasgow. Our great carboniferous cities can be as geologically polyglot, built of immigrant stones, as are their populations. Perhaps this shifting of stones, initially around the island and then the planet, is a carboniferous phenomenon in itself.

Conclusion

From its seedbed on this offshore, edge-Atlantic island, the energy embodied in the British Carboniferous transformed the face of planet Earth. The resulting ways of living have become 'normal' when they are entirely artificial; or, perhaps, derived from the discovery of a potential locked up in a specific sequence of rocks in a specific place – and thus very natural.

There were, of course, thousands of years when humans lived on these rocks without inventing the factory or the powered machine. But a remarkable set of historical circumstances found itself with a happenstance colocation of geological potentialities, and the result was a world-changing chemical reaction, between the Carbon-based life form known as the human being and the Carboniferous resources beneath its feet.

It can come to seem, as this story unfolds, as if the evolution of the landscape had, in a single geological period, seeded it with humanity's greatest geo-opportunity – one which is also rapidly turning into our greatest geohistorical challenge. As if these rock formations were lying in wait, like an apple on a forbidden tree, for their potential to be consumed.

As a result, from caves to coal to building stone, the rocks of the era are more visible, more extracted than those of any other geological period: as if history had turned geology inside out.

This is true of settlement patterns, too: most Carboniferous landscapes were marginal before the industrial revolution – and some still are. These are places in which upland forms a constant shadow; places that became troubled communities as the mills and the mines and the foundries closed down.

But perhaps the most remarkable thing, taking a long view of the Carboniferous, is the intensity of the events that played out on them. The level of exploitation – of rocks, of people, of much of the entire planet –

in the eighteenth and nineteenth centuries gives this great lithophiliac historical era a nasty edge: one-sided, even abusive.

For 2–300 years, humanity crawled, flocked, gathered in great clumps alongside, over and under these rocks like excited insects. The Pennines in particular are like a great central nervous system, their sandstone and limestone vertebrae by turn barren and bone-like; their edges spreading energetic messages in liquid, carbon and metal to a hinterland in which human activity burgeoned like bacteria either side of the spine of some great and nourishing corpse.

It's an animal thing to find resources and exploit them. But many of the most useful bits of the carcass have been eaten away, and we are only at the beginning of the kind of crisis that results from taking the carbon out of the Carboniferous.

If it were not the fact that we are sentient, and thus experience suffering, our fate would be no sadder than that of a coral reef locked up in a limestone crag: a figment of the cycles of heat and cold, deposition and destruction, in which all things are caught up. Or perhaps the stones are grieving, too.

History is mostly sedimentary; the past layering itself gradually into human culture. But occasionally it erupts with igneous, tectonic fury; and when that happens, it cools equally rapidly as the geohistorical energy depletes. This is not so much death as transformation: for as we know, all energy has to go somewhere.

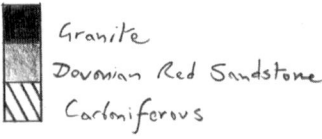

Granite

Devonian Red Sandstone

Carboniferous

Lynmouth

Exmoor

Bridgewat.

Netherstorey

Taunton

Umberleigh

Rough Tor

Tintagel

The Beacon

Jamaica Inn

Bodmin

Dartmoor

Exeter

Exmouth

Kents Cavern

Torquay

Chysauster

Carn Brae

St Ives

Castle an Dinas

St Just

Truro

St Auskl

Colehele Manor

Tavistock

Plymouth

King Tor

Grimspound

Crockern Tor

Lands End

Falmouth

Godolphin

St Michael's Mount

Poltesco

Penzance

0   10   20
                 miles

Chapter 8

The Variscan twist

There is a cove in Cornwall that I probably know better than any place on Earth. Its rocks can go from a pitted black to the deepest sunset orange in just a few feet. Its cliffs are shot through with great buckling, twisting patterns. I have lost precious toys in its soft, pale sand; found its bright rocky particles perfect for building castles and dams.

I once tried to put into writing every memory I have of this place. As I wrote, I was amazed how the brain opened up routes to levels of detail I didn't even know were there. The colour of the drawers in my grandmother's kitchen, just a mile or so down the road. The slip of the rock as one's foot made an unreliable landing. The smell of a block of vanilla ice cream, held like a brick between two wafers.

I also noticed how these memories echoed history itself; there was a long prehistory, in which the memories, lacking chronological structure, had no stratigraphy: a kind of geological basement of the mind. An adolescence as foreign as it was defining, as if undergoing some metamorphic transformation, a teenage orogeny. An adult life in which decades of visits – with friends, and then my own family – seemed to flash by, their sedimentary layers compressed by the pressures of time.

Today one of my favourite things is to float beyond the breakers and feel the ocean lift and dip with infinite power, gazing on the cliff as it rises and falls. The unrelenting waves work on every fault, fissure and shift in the rock, making the coast into a mightily sculpted series of headlands and sea-caves. Amid this grand procession of natural forms, a ruined engine house is a geometrical presence; a mineral lode visibly cuts through the cliffs below, hollowed out by centuries, perhaps millennia, of human activity.

Bolster the giant knew this place, too. This enormous creature could reach the rocky hilltop of Carn Brea, 6 miles away, in a single step. His home was the Beacon, an isolated hill atop which, as a child, I played at leaning into the sou-westerly gales to see if they would hold my weight.

Bolster was in love with a local girl, St Agnes; but Agnes wasn't interested. In a small valley that hangs above my cove, she cut him a deal. If he could prove his love by filling a small hole in the ground with his blood, she would consent to his advances. Bolster lay on the heathery grass, punctured his body, and bled.

What he didn't know is that the hole drained into a sea-cave, and anything that ran through it would merely make its way across the beach and into the Atlantic. Eventually Bolster faded into death, even as his blood congealed into a red blush still visible if you walk into the cave from the beach.

I once recounted this story to the curator at the church of Sant' Agnese fuori le mura in Rome. I even saw the catacomb below it where the body of the real Agnes had been laid in the soft volcanic rock. She was amazed to hear that her local virgin martyr somehow had an alter ego on a far-off Atlantic coast. But then, given its relatively small extent, the far south-west is a part of Britain that punches well above its geohistorical weight.

The rocks of my little cove were born on the Devonian floor of the Rheic ocean (or a related sea), perhaps 250 miles south-east of what is now Britain. But in the course of the Carboniferous they were shifted, compressed and buckled as continents closed in on each other, the ocean shrank, and the Variscan mountains went up.

By about 305 Ma, early in the Permian, Laurussia was no more and the supercontinent of Pangea had been born. But about 20–30 million years later, as the crust settled back post-impact, magma from below pressed up deep under the young mountains. As it cooled into granite superheated, mineral-rich subterranean fluids made their way into the many faults and fissures in the surrounding sedimentary rocks; chemical stews in which metals and minerals bloomed.

The Beacon is underlain by some of this granite; Carn Brea is another outcrop of it. As for the cove, though the rocks in it are classified as sedimentary and Devonian, what strikes one visually is not the environment in which they were created, but the Variscan trauma they have been put through.

The red on the side of the sea-cave is not the scabby detritus of a lovelorn giant, but metal ore. The engine house not far away is the most eye-grabbing of the mining remains that dot the area. Parts of the clifftop have become a desert. Though for me this place is a kind of Eden, it was once for some a hell on earth.

That story is in microcosm that of the entire far south-west. A typical Cornish cliff will be a slaty mass of compressed rock, weathered to forbidding slaty browns and blacks: in places, once-horizontal bedding planes will be contorted into Variscan knots, accompanied by sudden mineral splashes of colour.

Such sedimentary rocks dominate the western part of the south-west peninsula. They lie around and on top of a great granite batholith, the emergence of which had a dramatic impact on them. Today the region is at once both a favourite holiday destination and a place troubled by post-industrial decline.

The result is a country with three geohistorical landscapes: the more-or-less distorted sedimentary norm, Devonian and Carboniferous in origin, which forms lowland, the differences between its constituent rock-groups having only a subtle effect on the lie of the land; the granite, which forms higher stretches of peaty moor; and the areas around the granite, where the sedimentary rocks have been most deeply affected by the granite's birth. Geologists talk of a 'metamorphic aureole'; I like to think of a related geohistorical idea, the 'Variscan Fringe'. This Cornish twist on the Pennine Fringe was the heartland of industry. My little cove is a Variscan Fringe landscape. The granites of the Beacon cooked its multicoloured rocks and helped create their ore deposits.

Much here is a testament to the area's uniqueness. The engine house is a building type unique to Cornwall. It is an expression of an industrial story that created no cities, lacks coal, and was significant long before the age of industry. Of a geology that put in place the final piece in the structural story of Britain. And the dominant reason for the region's quiet otherness is that here we are closer than anywhere in Britain to the Variscan continental collision.

The Variscan difference

A major fault-line lies deeply buried below the Bristol Channel: the south Wales coast roughly follows it. It probably marks the leading edge of the Variscan continental collision. Another such line, which bends south as it heads west, is followed by the south coast of Cornwall and west Devon – and it may mark the very suture-line along which continents conjoined. The south-west peninsula sits between the two, its landscape as defined by the Variscan story as parts of Scotland and Wales were by the Caledonian ones. The results in both are comparable: landscapes distorted by mountain-building; igneous events; rocks formed from squashed ocean floors; granites and slates; metamorphic rocks (though sedimentary rocks that have been heavily distorted are here far more common than true metamorphics) and metal deposits, here on a grand scale.

The Variscan story becomes increasingly visible as one heads down the peninsula. Somerset, Dorset and east Devon are mostly composed of rocks younger than the Variscan era. Here, erosion has often been guided by Variscan faults, leaving the rocks arranged in complex and beguiling combinations which often respond to the grain. This part of the south-west is one of Britain's richest and most extensive mixed landscapes.

By the time we reach Exmoor, the rocks themselves are being visibly distorted. Further west on Dartmoor, the rocks are a creation of these events, and the Variscan story dominates everything west from there.

Western Devon and Cornwall is the territory we will concentrate on for now, with occasional dips back into north Devon. A long finger of cooked and contorted sedimentary rocks, sitting astride a granite mass, and all there because of a continental impact coming broadly from the south-south-east. It can begin to look as if this country simply sits on the northern edge of a major crustal join, like a spadeful of rocky earth chucked onto the lip of a trench, and held in place by a granitic glue.

This is a territory that goes its own way, heading off into the Atlantic on the Variscan Grain. A region at once Celtic and English; at once less part of the Anglo-Saxon world than any other part of England, yet not as separate as Scotland and Wales. Even the prevailing winds blow with the geological grain, coming as they do from the south-west, running up the peninsula as if the climate itself followed the fault-lines of the planet. This is a place of subtle differences, an entire region dancing the Variscan twist.

The sedimentary norm

Much of the far west is far enough from the granite to lack major ore deposits, and thus be relatively untouched by industry. It is deep pastoral country, made of variously shunted Devonian and Carboniferous rocks. Valleys are deep and curvaceous; in spite of its gentle, hilly complexity, almost all rises stop at about the same elevation, and there are few natural landmarks.

This land is full of subtle Variscan exceptions-to-rules. The Devonian system globally is named after the county of Devon, where it first began to be fully understood: yet the Devonian rocks of that county stand apart from the Old Red Sandstone norm. The further one heads into the narrowing west, the more the landscape combines the market towns and villages common in the rest of England with the scattered, centreless country of hamlets, farmsteads and isolated churches more typical of Wales.

Throughout, the highest ground is to the north, meaning that the longest rivers flow south, the Tamar, which marks the border between

Devon and Cornwall, being a particularly emphatic example. The high north coast faces the Atlantic; its cliffs are high and rugged, and there are many small coves or 'porths' – mine is one of them – and few good harbours. The southern coast slopes into the more sheltered waters of the English Channel: a gentle place of deep valleys and wide river mouths that creep and slink deep inland.

Coasts are always significant places, but rarely are they a more defining geohistorical entity than in this finger of land, reaching out towards Ireland, and Brittany, and the open Atlantic. Head due west from Land's End and your next landfall is in Newfoundland.

Coastal places

Though it was once place of noise, steam and hardship, today my little cove has nothing in it but a café, a National Trust car park and a beach bright with the mica washed from nearby rocks. Other nearby beaches are not so lucky: bungalows and eating places squeeze their way down to Trevaunance, where various attempts to build a harbour were scotched by the ferocity of the waves, leaving battered mounds of squared-up granite in the cove. The little porths of the north coast presented a challenge to a mining industry dependent for energy on coal shipped from south Wales.

Such coasts brought to the peninsula many of the saints whose names drape the Cornish landscape with memories of forgotten holy men, as often Welsh, Irish, or Breton in origin as Cornish: Tudy, Mabyn, Ivo. St Piran, the tinner's patron and the county's patron saint, floated here from Ireland on a millstone (its petrology is not recorded). His flag, a white cross on a black background, is inspired by the story that Piran once watched tin melt out of a hearth of blackened rock, then set into a white cross: a geological banner.

On the south coast everything changes. Cliffs are rarely high. The Lizard juts south, made of particularly complex, hard and ancient rocks which turn much of the peninsula into a low moorland.

These rocks record the very beginning of the Variscan events, and include a deep red or green material that has a glossy, lizard-skin texture: serpentine. This a rare fragment of the deepest crust, created about 5 miles below the ocean floor. From 1866 a factory in Poltesco was making polished souvenirs and architectural items from it, and craftsmen still work it today.

Further along the coast, gentle valleys of water reach deep into the interior, creating decent harbours: Falmouth, Fowey, Plymouth. The latter city, today a major navy base, was England's first slave-trading port and the final departure point of the Pilgrim Fathers. Throughout, there are significant early modern chains of defence: no wonder, as Fowey was burned by the French in 1457, and Penzance by the Spanish in 1595. The peninsula's finger-like landform may have connected it to the Atlantic coasts of Europe; but it has also been a vulnerability.

The coast took on a new significance as railways and later the car brought mass leisure to the Cornish beaches: the Great Western Railway reached St Ives in 1877. As a result there are those – and I am one of them – who have returned to the same place several times a year for their entire lives. This is a very peculiar kind of status, neither tourist nor resident, neither 'grockle' nor 'emmet'. It means my little Eden has grown with me. Only a few places in Britain have a comparable significance for so many people: the south coast of Fife and the north Norfolk coast, on Carboniferous and Tertiary rocks respectively, are among them.

Other sedimentary landscapes

Moving inland, Exmoor is an east-west Variscan blob, its sediments squeezed upwards between faults and capped by gritty Devonian 'Hangman Grits'. Deep, wooded combes lead to England's highest cliffs. With its impervious capping, shaley interior, and steep slopes, this is a landscape with a propensity to flooding: most disastrously at Lynmouth in 1952, when thirty-four people died.

In north-west Devon there are the Carboniferous rocks known as the Culm, the hills of which run emphatically with the Variscan Grain. In South Devon the rocks of the Rheic ocean floor are less disturbed than elsewhere: the South Hams are deeply folded places, profoundly rich and green; and there is a large area of (rather impure) limestones, which yielded good building stones and contains cave-systems, such as Kent's Cavern, a Neanderthal habitation site.

There are also, from place to place, outbursts of rock from Variscan volcanic events: Launceston and Exeter castles sits on igneous stone thrones. Tintagel castle, a major centre of power in medieval Cornwall, sits on a podium of lava and slate, its 'high terrible crag environed with the sea' (Leland). And between Dartmoor and Bodmin Moor rises my personal omphalos, Brentor: remnant of a Carboniferous undersea volcano, and one of the only features in the entire region that is neither granite moorland nor sedimentary plateau.

Even without the tiny twelfth-century church that sits at its 334m peak, this would be an eye-catching landmark. As a parish church the building is almost inexplicable, the least convenient location in the area – and it generated a winning geo-mythological legend.

It seems the devil moved the building site from the base of the tor to the peak of it every night, until an impatient St Michael appeared, showered Satan with rocks from the tor, and sent him packing. As the builders decided to leave the church of St Michael where the devil had put it, it is not clear who won this particular struggle. In any case St Michael, the intermediary between Heaven and Earth in medieval religion, is consistently associated with high places, especially sudden, conical interruptions such as Brentor and St Michael's Mount. He thus joins our litany of Stone Heroes.

We are now in West Devon, and from here on into Cornwall the rocks become sequences of slaty, compressed Devonian rocks, collectively known as 'killas'. They can seem dour – until one gazes at length at a Cornish cliff, or at the subtle varieties of fawns, greys and browns in manor houses such as Cotehele, 'secret, intimate, lovable', and 'built out of Cornwall' (Alec Clifton-Taylor, architectural historian).

Mythospheres of the far west

Such qualities bleed into the literature of the region. Exmoor has generated not only Lorna Doone, but also Coleridge, who explored the moor from his base at Nether Stowey, and wrote *Kubla Khan* while dosed up on laudanum in a farmhouse on its northern edge.

Here the flanks of the moor begin a steep and forested tumble into the Bristol Channel: a landscape whose dark, north-facing cliffs make for a 'sunless sea', approached along 'forests ancient as the hills / Enfolding sunny spots of greenery': a line which almost embodies north Devon. Coleridge had with him a travel yarn known as *Purchas his Pilgrimage*; perhaps this extraordinary work, for all its exotic references, is secretly Exmoor translated through an opiate haze.

But in general, perhaps it is the variety of moods supplied by its landscapes that has done most to inspire literature in the far west. From Du Maurier to *Poldark*, we find both wild north and soft south; granite moor and busy industry; elemental coast and pastoral countryside. Each plays their part, helping make this relatively small part of Britain mythospherically so very full.

Perhaps 'variscan' works as an adjective for all this, much as carboniferous makes a good adjective for the Great Industrial Moment; and of course the two are closely related, for the Variscan events are the underlying tectonic narrative of the Carboniferous, even if its endgame extends into the Permian. And it is the metal and mineral deposits that resulted that are the area's most signal contribution to British history.

Tin, copper and more

The engine house near my cove is one of Britain's most evocative ruins. Perched on the cliff-edge, it has featured on everything from pasty wrappers to postage stamps; and its architecture is instantly recognisable. This is a tall, thin structure with a tall chimney on one corner, and a large opening in the wall furthest from it. It and others like it have become a visual code for 'Cornwall'.

Few building-types of any kind, let alone industrial ones, are so closely associated with a specific region. It is an irony that they were designed to assist the removal of the innards of the land of which they have become an emblem.

When in action, these buildings were anything but romantic ruins. Each is an exoskeleton, as the archaeologist Adam Sharpe puts it, for an enormous steam engine, and the great arm-shaped iron beam it powered. The beam pivoted on a large opening in one 'bob' wall, half in and half out of the building itself. Typically, it reached over an adjacent mine-shaft, from which it pumped excess water. Often built of rough stone from the mine itself, with brick on the upper chimney and granite strengthening, the work these engines did allowed miners to pursue tin and copper ore, often descending by ladder, up to 3,000ft under the ground and below the sea, in appalling conditions. As many as 2–3,000 are known to have existed; by the 1860s, when the architectural form had crystallised, they would have contained engines of the type invented in Cornwall by Richard Trevithick.

A Cornish building-type, housing Cornish technology, all to facilitate the removal of Cornish ore. Is there something in the geology of this small county that made it a particular centre for innovation? Certainly the region's wet climate and steeply faulted rocks made flooding a major issue, and its dependence on imported coal made fuel efficiency especially important. The industrial-era discovery of copper below the tin encouraged deeper mining; mines went deeper still when the tin was found again. All this must have encouraged innovation, in particular the search for effective pumps.

But the significance of Cornish ores long predates the Trevithick engine or the engine-house. In prehistory its metal ores may have made the area one of the most important places in Europe. Cornish gold has been found in one remarkable Bronze Age object from central Germany, the Nebra Sky Disk; as tin is both rare and essential for making bronze, there is every possibility that Cornish tin had just as wide a distribution, that ore from this island was one of the keys to the Bronze Age.

Tin may be the reason for some of the first written mentions of Britain. It, or Spain, is the likely location of the 'tin islands' (Cassiterides). In the first century BC, Diodorus of Sicily wrote of a promontory at the far corner of Britain where there are 'earthy seams' from which tin was quarried, smelted and purified.

The mineral lode that runs down the cliffs near my cove might just be the result of early mining. It is very conspicuous, and you only have to scramble down to it to see it has long been hollowed and followed without mechanical assistance. It also has an intriguing name: Towanroath vugga: 'the witch or giant's hole'. In such old workings later miners might particularly fear the power of the 'knockers', or spirits with whom they shared the mines.

Tin remained important in the medieval period. Extraction was done by forcing water through tin-rich deposits, separating heavier stones from lighter ones: 'hushing' when water is sent at speed through loose material, often by damming and then releasing it; 'streaming' when done alongside a natural waterway, the water of which may be redirected. The demand was huge, as many household implements were made of pewter, an alloy in which tin is the largest element. West country tin was traded as far afield as France, Italy and the Baltic. I have seen estimates of as many as 5,000 tinners working in Cornwall by 1400. 'Stannary' law was a legal system of its own, with tin taxed in nodal towns such as Liskeard and Bodmin, parliaments such as that held at Crockern Tor on Dartmoor, and courts and prisons, such as Lydford castle, Devon.

With the industrial era, the focus moved to copper, for which Cornwall came to meet two-thirds of global demand. Mines became architectural complexes – whim houses, stamps, buddles, blowing-houses and smelters, all for processing ore, all arguably more visible today than their equivalents in other areas where metal ore was mined. Deep mining was focused on the Variscan Fringe, with the metamorphic rocks around Camborne the first and major centre; but by 1850 mining areas extended in patches from Penwith to west Devon. By then, 12,000 tons of copper were being produced each year – and as late as 1900, by which time the copper market had collapsed, 10,000 tons of tin.

These metals had multiple uses: tin for cans, tin foil, and solder; copper for the bearings essential to smooth-running machines, brass-making and on the hulls of ships. This metal was to become vital to a society increasingly dependent on the wires that carry electricity. The copper-smelting and brass industries of Swansea, Birmingham and Bristol, and the tin-plating works of Wales and Liverpool were dependent on Cornish ores.

A successful mine or 'wheal' could be astonishingly profitable; two weeks of working for copper at Wheal Virgin, Gwennap, in 1757 cost £100 – and made a return of £5,700. Men such as Joseph Austen, AKA Treffry, the 'King of Mid-Cornwall', became fabulously wealthy; country houses such as Godolphin were built by mineral lords. The Duchy of Cornwall benefited hugely, too. Lesser 'adventurers', miners clubbing together to fund a new wheal, and below-ground 'tutworkers' and 'tributers', all of them effectively freelancers working for their portion of profit, might have more unpredictable careers.

The industry's decline began early, as sources elsewhere in the world developed. In the second half of the nineteenth century roughly 300,000 Cornishmen are estimated to have migrated. They took with them an unmatched expertise in deep mining; it was said, 'look in a hole anywhere and you will find a Cornishman looking for metal'.

The Cornish engine house went with them, so the building-type most associated with the county can also be seen in Mexico and Michigan. In South Australia, the copper mining villages of Burra (Redruth, Lostwithiel, Copperhouse) became an antipodean Cornwall. A variscan architecture gone global.

This diaspora also exported other aspects of Cornish culture: a powerful Methodist tradition (there are 600 surviving chapels in the county); distinctive foods, such as the pasty. This is effectively a meal enclosed in pastry that is crimped so dirty hands can hold it below the ground. And although the collapse of Cornish mining spread Cornish culture worldwide, it left in its wake what was arguably the world's first post-industrial landscape, with all the demographic issues that entails.

Lead, silver and zinc, often formed later than the Variscan events, were also sourced in the far west, along with an astonishing litany of other materials, including antimony, arsenic, bismuth, cobalt, fluorspar, gold, manganese, mica, nickel, tungsten and uranium. Iron and other metals were mined on Exmoor. Cornish iron is exceptionally pure, and the oldest dated source of the metal in Britain (eighth century BC) is Cornish. Marie Curie isolated radium from pitchblende sourced at Wheal Trenwith near St Ives. 'Culm' means 'coal', and north Devon is host to a thin Variscan line of clayey anthracite: the appropriately named village of Umberleigh was a source of the resulting pigment, 'Bideford black'.

It is with these prodigious supplies of useful Earth-materials borne in mind that we can explore the landscapes most marked by Cornish industry; landscapes rich in many other ways, too.

The Variscan Fringe

The Variscan Fringe is not as clearly defined as its Carboniferous sibling. It emerges out of the sedimentary norm as one draws closer to granite, and metal and mineral deposits increase; often the rocks themselves cross the barrier from highly distorted sedimentary rocks to true metamorphic ones. While ore was sourced both on it and in the granite itself, the Fringe is where the richest deposits exist, and mining was concentrated. As a result, a landscape otherwise comparable to the rest of the non-granite far west acquired a strong industrial overlay.

This is where engine houses and the like are clustered. There are also many swollen villages, their terraces of granite and killas rubble. And there are the stannary towns, settlements shaped by the economies of metal extraction deep in time, combining the scale of a market town with something of the character of an industrial one. Tavistock in West Devon, where I spent my teenage years and encountered Brentor, is a good example.

'Tavi' is set in a pastoral country of the deepest, wettest green. Dartmoor is a constant grey presence. The abbey here grew rich on mineral wealth, which passed to the Dukes of Bedford after the Dissolution. In the nineteenth century they built attractive estates of industrial-era workers' cottages and re-engineered the town centre, cleverly incorporating surviving abbey buildings. If my cove of twisted rocks is an Eden, buildings of green, Hurdwick lava stone with granite dressings – magma that spilled onto the surface and magma that welled up beneath it, side by side – sit alongside those of London and Wiltshire, the other two places I have lived, as the lithology that feels most palpably like 'home'.

These are fine towns, but the far west has no major industrial-era cities. Though it once contained two of the most important steam engine foundries in the world, the port of Hayle is no Liverpool; Portreath, no Cardiff. Redruth/Camborne is the nearest thing to an industrial conurbation, yet the two combined are no larger than a mid-ranking northern town such as Macclesfield. The capital of Cornwall's most important mining area, this place embodies the idea of a Variscan Fringe: it stands on metamorphic rock, and its boundary almost clings to the exposed edge of the granite.

In this area lay some of the most fabled names in Cornish mining. Dolcoath, long the most important of all; South Crofty, the last to close. Some places still look as if a Total War between humanity and geology had only just finished, leaving behind a landscape of stone redoubts, bottomless pits and mounded desert wastes.

Throughout all such towns one sees many examples of the far west's distinctive vernacular: buildings of, or dressed in, granite; walls hung with slate to protect them from the rain. As rocks whose very existence depends on tectonic pressure, these are the Variscan Fringe's chief contributions to building stone.

Slate and building stones

West country slate was a major industry, especially before the industrial-era takeover of Caledonian slate. Devon slate was used in Roman *Isca/* Exeter; 800,000 slates from the county were sent to Winchester in 1187. The quarry at Delabole (Cornish for 'the pit of flakey/leafy stone'), just north of Bodmin Moor, has been active for over 600 years. Its exceptionally good slates come from a hole now 430ft deep and 1.2 miles in circumference; they have roofed the Victoria and Albert Museum in London.

A few quirky far-western building stones stand out from the killas norm, and all are products of the Variscan Fringe. 'Shilf' was made from mixed slate waste and mud or straw; 'scoria' from mining slag. 'Rollies' were cobbles from beaches. Polyphant, porphyry and catacleuse, the latter hard, green and spangled, were used decoratively: all are igneous results of Variscan pressures. Ashburton marble is south Devon limestone half-metamorphosed by Variscan heat. Not quite a true marble, it has a sumptuous, almost brash, coloured veining, beloved of Victorians for church fittings, and in 1861 used by George Gilbert Scott in London's Foreign Office.

All these rocks reflect Variscan pressures in different ways. But visually the granite, slate and killas are the overwhelming architectural signature of the far west. A typical Cornish church is a building of hard ascetic granite, or, failing that, killas with granite dressings; it stands in a churchyard full of smoothly incised slate headstones: a memorial aureole gathered around a sacral igneous mass. The architectural embodiment of the county itself, and one in which the products of its great granite batholith play a defining role.

Granite landscapes

The Cheesewring on Bodmin Moor looks as if CGI rather than geology had conjured it from the Earth. This roughly 10m-high tor is made of huge lumps of granite shaped by ice-age erosion into big, flat pillows: from a distance they look as though they might slowly melt back to magmatic life. Those at the base are smaller than those above, making the whole thing appear as if it is about to keel over. The overall effect is at once artificial, abstract and oddly organic. It is the most bewilderingly vertiginous of all tors.

A stone-stacking contest between the giants Uther and Tue hovers in its mythosphere; and prehistoric people built in association with it a colossal circular enclosure of smaller rocks, known as Stowe's Pound.

Approaching from the south-east, the effect is even more dramatic: for the whole thing teeters on the edge of a large industrial-era quarry, stone from which is said to have been used at Tower Bridge, London.

This is a landscape of magma, ice, dynamite and the ancestors; a granitic place in which the prehistoric and industrial eras are loud but rough-edged geohistorical voices that butt up hard against one another. This juxtaposition of raw geology with two contrastingly lithophiliac periods of human history is a powerful one – and it is emblematic of the landscapes of the far west's granitic spine.

This is, with the Cairngorms, Britain's main granite landscape. Not truly mountainous yet too infertile to sustain heavy settlement, the granite is a distinctive kind of 'highland lowland'. In a sense it is also the key to the entire story of the far west. It was a centre for ore extraction in itself; the ore deposits of the Variscan Fringe would not exist without it. The rocks of the entire peninsula cluster around it as if hardened and protected by its presence, 'formed by Nature to resist the otherwise irresistible power of the ocean' (Defoe). Yet it is really a colossal, buried lump of rock.

This batholith is enormous. First detectable just east of Dartmoor, it runs west for at least 140 miles, like a twisted, south-west-pointing finger. Joints and knuckles of rock rise as much as 3,000ft above the main mass; though they formed at least 2 miles below the surface, today they poke their heads up above the softer rocks of the sedimentary plateau; impermeable, each makes moorland, or former moorland. If some stone-hero-sized Barbara Hepworth had been commissioned to produce a sculpture entitled 'granite batholith on a Variscan Grain', a shape like this is what she might have produced.

Like a skimmed rock, the granitic moors hop from east to west, getting gradually smaller and lower as they go: Dartmoor (highest point 621m); Bodmin Moor; West Penwith, the site of Land's End; and the Scilly islands, rarely over 40m high, a flooded moorland whose tors and ridges almost seem to be sinking into the sea. There were once other, smaller moors: the two most important were Hensbarrow, north of St Austell; and Carnmenellis, south of Camborne/Redruth. They have largely been transformed by industry.

These granites are hard, brittle, grey, massive, rough, and rammed with slugs and smudges of mica, quartz and feldspar, silver-white and black flecks of which dominate its surface (one Bodmin Moor variety was called 'Pepper and Salt'). Sometimes there are shades of soft pink. A grid of narrow fault-lines known as joints traverse these rocks; they developed as the magma cooled.

Between their birth and the onslaught of the ice age in comparatively recent times, erosion removed the colossal amounts of the sedimentary rock that covered them, lowering the land-surface until the granite peeked out above the ground. The ice, when it came, did not cover this country, but subjected it to violent pulses of freeze and thaw. Already weakened by great climatic swings, exposed granites were rotted and disintegrated; nubs of rock were left on hilltops and crests, their right-angled joints splitting them into sections. The Cheesewring is a dramatic example. The architectonic, unearthly presence of such tors is such a signature aspect of the west-country landscape that the very word 'tor' – a high structure, mound or rocky heap ('tower' is related) – originates here.

We are thus glimpsing these rocks as if in mid-disintegration. Indeed they are surrounded by eroded material, spreads of rotting tor that are especially geohistorically significant. Their most obvious form is clitter: boulders of varying size, so densely skirting some tors that the sure-footed can jump from rock to rock on these 'clitter fields' without getting their feet wet in the peaty earth. Pre-quarried by erosion, such rocks might have been designed to be exploited by prehistoric and medieval monument-makers.

Prehistoric landscapes

Stowe's Pound is not unique. In the late Neolithic, the moors were enriched with monuments that respond to and enrich the natural landscape in remarkable ways. There is a kind of lithophilic genius to such sites, and Roughtor on Bodmin Moor may be their highpoint.

From many angles, Roughtor looks like a mountain, crested by shattered tors (Roughtor itself, Little Rough Tor, Showery Tor). Brown Willy next door is the actual highest point on the moor. It is easy to imagine such places as the abode of powerful ancestral forces, scattered with the tor-architecture of giants.

Even the more normative structures in the area relate to these two hills: early long cairns, which maintain a respectful distance from them; later stone circles, which use them to indicate solstitial rising and setting points of the sun. No fewer than six of these focus on Brown Willy, the summit of which is capped by a large Bronze Age cairn. It has recently become popular to build sub-Andy Goldsworthy piles of balanced stones on this tor; a home-made landscape art that has become so popular it threatens the archaeology.

But it is the cairns that are most remarkable. They are made of great mounds of clitter, often shaped like, enclosing, or even hiding, natural granite tors, as if trying to match or enhance the achievements of the geology: 'enculturating' the natural landscape', as the archaeologist Christopher Tilley puts it. Fragments of quartz and coloured clays have been found deliberately spread around them. 400 such cairns are known on Bodmin Moor alone.

Each of the tors on Roughtor has one. Showery Tor is a natural 5m stack circled by an artificial wall-like ring of mounded rock fragments, originally perhaps two-thirds the height of the tor itself. If these are stone thrones, the intention is not defensive: this is at once a religious architecture and a powerful kind of art. The sense that it was Roughtor as a whole that mattered is confirmed by the presence of the Bank Cairn, a great snaking mound about 400m/1,300ft long, built entirely of mounded clitter, approaching it from the direction of the moor-edge; it is possibly a processional way.

Also unique, and even more ancient, are the tor enclosures, a kind of variscan take on the causewayed enclosure. There is one on Roughtor – and another on Carn Brea, which sits on the edge of Carnmenellis, and also boasts an Iron Age hillfort, a medieval castle-ette, and an enormous granite cross, memorial to local mineral lord Francis Basset; all set in a post-industrial landscape that comes on like some arsenic-poisoned ancient city.

Stone rows in the region seem to be particularly ambitious; that on Stall Moor, Dartmoor, is 2 miles long. More fragile rows of cleared rocks and slight earthworks are traces of a dense and highly planned grid of fields known as reaves, laid out across the landscape in the Bronze Age and originally extending far beyond the moorland areas where it is now visible. Later, in the Iron Age, at places such as Grimspound on Dartmoor and Chysauster on West Penwith, you can explore well-preserved drystone granite villages and almost feel as if you are walking with our ancestors. Clearly, granite has shaped the man-made monuments of the entire region.

Moorstone and building stone

The clitter fields of the moors continued to fuel impressive architecture in later centuries. Available lying around in usable pieces, strong and aesthetically appealing, and situated in a region that was poorly endowed with other good building stones, 'moorstone' became a major medieval and early modern building material, 'white, with certain glimmering sparkles', and 'found upon moores and wast grounds, which serves them instead of free-stone' (Childrey, antiquarian and academic, 1661).

With settlements on the granite, such as St Just in Penwith, Cornwall can seem built entirely of this material, the human and natural landscape

(Left) Stone-stacking is a centuries-old practice stretching back to prehistoric times.

Right) A granite boulder, identified by its rough texture nd speckled appearance. Granite originated as magma that ooled slowly deep underground.

(Above) A close-up shot of a drystone wall.

(Left) A weathered stone archway. It is erosion, in concert with the qualities of the rocks themselves, that orchestrates the lie of the land.

(*Above*) This wall in Shropshire indicates evidence of stone carving, a craft that dates back to the Neolithic period.

(*Below*) A Precambrian stone slate found in Anglesey.

(*Above left*) Sandstone is one of two main types of sedimentary rock. Sedimentary rocks are like metamorphic rocks in that the material from which they were made was originally something else. Through them we get a glimpse of a distant past.

(*Above right*) A New Red Sandstone wall.

(*Below left*) The stunning New Red Sandstone found in Dawlish.

(*Below right*) Jurassic limestone, as seen in Ham Hill, Somerset.

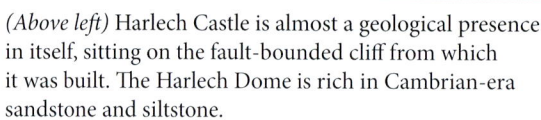

(*Above left*) Harlech Castle is almost a geological presence in itself, sitting on the fault-bounded cliff from which it was built. The Harlech Dome is rich in Cambrian-era sandstone and siltstone.

(*Above right*) New Red Sandstone found in Liverpool.

(*Below*) A field wall close to Siccar Point, with stones of red sandstone and greywacke from nearby.

(Below left) A granite boulder covered in lichen on the Isle of Arran.

(Below right) Anglesey's Precambrian rocks are almost all the result of volcanic events which took place on the edge of a relatively small continent known as Avalonia.

(*Above right*) Dunadd Kilmartin Glen, a medieval site of the crowning of Scottish kings. Their footprint can be seen in the rock itself.

(*Below right*) A close-up of the footprint.

(*Above right & below left*) Devonian granite found respectively in St Cleer and St Neot, Cornwall.

(*Above left*) Red sandstone buildings are often found in nineteenth-century architecture based in Edinburgh, Dumfries and Glasgow.

(*Below left*) Freestones are rocks that can be cut in any direction, making them suitable for deep, fine carving. The grains of which they are made are typically relatively small, uniform in size, and cemented together strongly. They are thus always of sedimentary origin.

(*Below right*) In Holderness, East Yorkshire, field boundaries, walls, and sometimes entire buildings are made of these shining rounded rocks of many colours, textures and origins, from fragments of the Whin Sill to chunks of Scandinavia.

sitting in intense grey harmony. Drystone walls of moorstone mark out enclosed land; around Princetown on Dartmoor, convicts were forced to work it into properly squared blocks.

But granite architecture can be found throughout Cornwall and west Devon, perhaps especially in the Variscan Fringe, where there is more settlement than on the granite, and the moorstone is close at hand. Churches and manor houses alike are formed of great shaped pieces of the rock, a muscular architectural vernacular, with an abstract simplicity of form and a fetish for monolithic columns, like standing stones shaped and brought inside.

A real pride in this material is detectable. Launceston is some distance from the granite, and surely had access to good freestones via the Tamar; yet at St Mary Magdalene church (1511) there is a bull-headed determination to use this most intractable of building stones to cover the exterior walls entirely with carved decoration.

As techniques were developed for splitting the rock using iron wedges, and transport links improved, so granite quarrying flourished, until it was second only to that of Scotland. There are impressive industrial-era quarries at places like the Cheesewring, or on Dartmoor, King Tor and Merrivale; they often burrow into hillsides in search of unweathered rock.

Much of the outside of Truro cathedral – a Gothic Anglican riposte to the strength of Methodism in Cornwall – is granite from Mabe and St Stephen. London Bridge uses Dartmoor granite. The Duke of Wellington's sarcophagus in St Paul's Cathedral is of Luxulyanite, a black variant of granite on Bodmin Moor, where there were thirty-nine quarries and the granites were much prized for their polishable fineness of grain.

Even finer-grained is the distinctive rock known as White Elvan, made of thin dykes (Elvan means 'dyke') that squirted their way into the granite after it formed. It could be finely carved, a quality rare in Cornish rocks; remnants of quarries make distinctive little gorges following the dykes, for example, around Pentewan, south of St Austell. It is seen in Cornish country houses such as Elizabethan Trerice, or Georgian Antony.

The rotting of the tors did not stop with clitter. Smaller fragments of granite were washed into valleys, where they became part of a gravel known as growan. Any tin ores that had been present in the granite were transported into it, too: common, easy to find and extract, the growan was an early focus for the tin industry.

Tin

On Bodmin Moor and Dartmoor, moorland streams are often lined by substantial, natural-looking banks. Dig beneath their thin peaty skin and find they are made of sorted growan. These are the remains of early tin streaming, upstaged when industrial-era mining took off in the Variscan Fringe. But one unique industrial-era landscape of extraction developed on the granite itself, eventually covering two-thirds of Hensbarrow, the granite country north of St Austell.

China clay

As a child, the 'St Austell lumps' were always a source of amazement to me; a man-made orogeny of white pyramidal mountains, dominating one side of the road as one crawled along the A30. Artificial Alps, they reflect the presence of some of the world's largest deposits of one very specific and unusual form of rotted granite: China clay.

Though most have since been levelled to make ziggurat-like, flat-topped hills streaked with green, these 'sky tips' can still impress. Explore more deeply, and discover lagoons set in deep excavations, turquoise in the sun and tan under cloud; and white quarry pits up to 80m deep. This is an industrial landscape whose colours can have an almost Mediterranean intensity, and it is still active. The Eden Project is situated in one former such site. Yet without the drinking of tea, this industry-that-replaced-a-moor would not be there at all.

The China clay was formed long after the Variscan events, when the feldspar in some granites was transformed by hot, salty water; to use it, the other constituents of the rock, mica and quartz, have to be filtered out. The quartz 'stent' waste was piled into the lumps; the mica was placed in artificial lagoons and lakes to avoid polluting groundwater. The St Austell lumps landscape is the result of waste disposal on a grand scale.

In the seventeenth-century, Europe fell in love with two Chinese practices: the drinking of tea, and the elegant, strong, brittle, almost translucent white cups, saucers and teapots that went with it. No one

THE VARISCAN TWIST 203

in the West could work out how this ceramic – porcelain – was made. Some, Josiah Wedgwood among them, used materials such as bone, mica and ball clay to produce rough equivalents; attractive enough, but not the real thing.

European demand for porcelain was thus a bonanza for the Chinese, who as early as the Ming dynasty (1368–1644) were producing objects to suit Western tastes, complete with Christian religious scenes and heraldry: the fine art equivalent of chicken chow mein.

In the early eighteenth century, working from descriptions of porcelain-making written by a China-based Jesuit, a kind of experimental proto-geology got under way, melting Chinese objects to work out their constituent parts, and searching the landscape for equivalents.

The main material being hunted for was a fine-grained white clay, sourced in China at Gaoling ('high ridge') in Jiangxi province: kaolin, or China clay. A related harder rock known as *bái dūn zi* ('white block from the earth'), which became known as pudense, or China stone, was also sought.

The first European source found was in Germany, where true porcelain was first made in 1706. In 1745 another source was discovered being used by First Nation Americans, and imported to England by a Plymouth-based chemist, William Cookworthy. Cookworthy then found local sources on the granite moors, especially the growan of Hensbarrow, where the China clay made white deposits in moorland valleys, and an equivalent to the harder China stone made low hills. After years of experiment with how to mix, form and fire these materials, he patented his porcelain recipe in 1768.

In 1775, Josiah Wedgwood and others broke the monopoly and began leasing quarries. The resulting trade between Cornwall and the Potteries aided the development of ports around St Austell – Par is one – and, at the other end of the journey, the building of the Trent and Mersey Canal. Attempts to manufacture porcelain in Cornwall itself were frustrated by the cost of importing coal to fire the kilns. Eventually, 75 per cent of the world supply was shipped from the county.

Other uses of China clay proliferated. The depression created by the Napoleonic wars led to its widespread use to adulterate flour. The material has been used in textile-making, in sanitaryware and tiles; inert in its reaction to other chemicals, it has various industrial and medicinal applications. From 1946, 40,000 'Cornish Unit' prefabs were made from China clay waste; many houses of the material still stand. White paper was almost one-third the material for many years, and remains the major reason for its extraction.

By 1914, 159 quarries were in operation. Devon and Cornwall remain one of the biggest producers of the material globally – 1.5 million tons in 2014, out of an estimated 163 million tons since production began – though the industry is under strong pressure from overseas. This geology may yet acquire a new importance, as it is also a source of lithium, crucial for the manufacture of the batteries that could help us reduce our dependence on fossil fuels.

Granite outliers

In some places the batholith only briefly breaks the surface of the surrounding rocks. The Beacon, where the granite itself is barely visible, is one example – but St Michael's Mount is the most remarkable. This spectacular tidal island lies in a natural harbour at the very gateway to West Penwith. It was an early focus for trade in tin (and, before that, Cornish polished stone hand-axes, which were distributed throughout much of southern Britain). With its priory-capped tor-covered eminence, and submerged remains of prehistoric forest, the site remains a compelling, dense location, ostensibly dropped into place by yet another angry giant, Cormoran. It may have been the *Ictis* described by Diodorus of Sicily, from which locals made civilised by their cosmopolitan contacts sold to traders from as far afield as the Rhone and Marseille.

Other mini-moors – such as Kit Hill near Callington, with its folly; Castle-an-Dinas near Roche, with its hillfort – make obvious stone thrones. Then there is Roche Rock; one of the weirdest rock formations in Britain, erupting from a peri-urban setting of playing fields and abandoned China clay edgelands. It is topped with the remains of a fifteenth-century hermitage 'wrought . . . with great labour, out of the obdurate rock' (cartographer John Norden, 1584).

A granite mythosphere

The soul of John Tregeagle, a seventeenth-century magistrate and lawyer notorious for his dishonesty, as legend tells it, sought refuge here. But soon his spirit was banished to a beach near Padstow, where it had to plait ropes from the local sand. Originally, it is said, the harsh local representative of a past lord, this stone hero jumps from one Cornish natural phenomenon to another. As we have seen, the region's other stone heroes are often associated with the granite.

Such stories are just an indicator of the power of these moors. Daphne du Maurier mythologised Bodmin Moor's Jamaica Inn; many artists, such as Peter Lanyon, have been inspired by West Penwith.

One can see why when sitting on Carn Gulva, a tor on the northern crest of this western peninsula of the western peninsula that is Cornwall. Here one can look down at the grey sea crashing on the cliffs a mile away, and see glowing darkly between moor and coast a thin strip of dense green farmland, and the engine house of Carn Gulver mine.

The intense and haunting beauty of this combination of ocean, cliff, farm, mine and moor is obvious; less so is the fact that the great granite lumps which bound the fields were placed there in the Bronze Age, and are still functioning field boundaries today.

This is one of the most quietly magical landscapes in Britain. The Penwith sequence – well settled southern plateau, brief but intense northern moor, ancient-cum-industrial coastal strip – can feel as if all the themes of the British landscape are coalescing on the run-in to Land's End, a motherlode of essence-of-place. Here, at Britain's furthest corner, the Variscan twist blooms into an exquisite dance.

As we leave the far south-west, we also leave behind Britain's true uplands. Such landscapes have in general become less high as we have moved south, while also, whether in Precambrian Pembrokeshire or early Permian Dartmoor, Penwith or the White Peak, becoming ever richer in visible traces of human history. We will not see another hill that is much over 450m.

We are also leaving a series of narratives that underly the geohistory of much of western Britain. These have been places in which Celtic cultures play a central role, and the visible Roman impact is relatively slight; where the seaways enable one to hop along peninsulas and islands from Orkney to Finisterre and from Land's End to Dingle Bay. Instead, new themes will come centre-stage.

The rocks we have looked at so far fall into two categories. First, the old, hard, igneous and metamorphic rocks of the 'basement'; although they underlie the entire island, these only dominate in the landscapes of the north and west. Second, and lying on top of them, the Devonian and Carboniferous rocks academic Arlëne Hunter calls the 'older cover'; mostly sedimentary, but with narratives also caught up in tectonic events. In the course of this journey we have moved through two great phases of continental collision, during which the constituent underlying parts of our island have been assembled.

Though there are further waves of tectonic change to come, almost everything we will now explore is sedimentary, and sits in relatively simple layers on top of these rocks: the 'younger cover'. This is the upper layer of the skin of an island which, as archaeologist Jacquetta Hawkes put it, is basically an ancient skeleton with a flesh-like sedimentary covering. The younger cover dominates the south-eastern and most populous third of the island: an area whose landscapes we have hardly addressed.

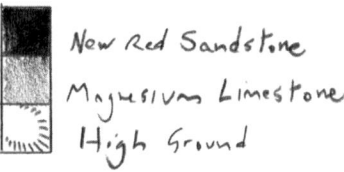

New Red Sandstone
Magnesium Limestone
High Ground

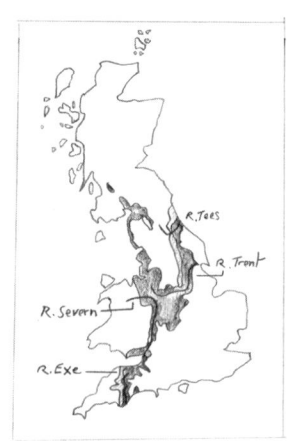

R. Tees
R. Trent
R. Severn
R. Exe

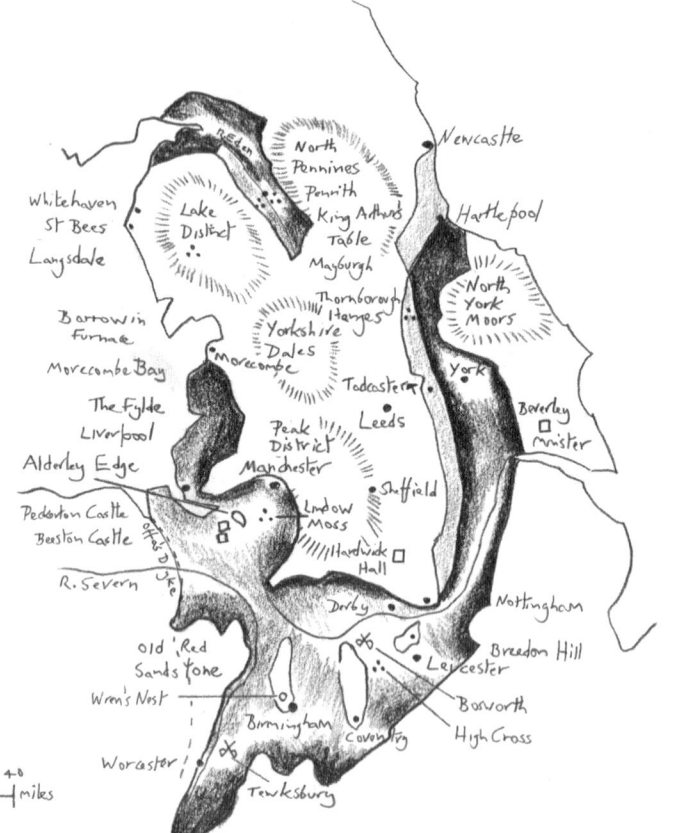

R. Eden
Newcastle
North Pennines
Penrith
Whitehaven
St Bees
Hartlepool
King Arthur's Table
Lake District
Langsdale
Mayburgh
North York Moors
Thornborough Henges
Barrow in Furness
Yorkshire Dales
Morecombe
Morecombe Bay
York
The Fylde
Liverpool
Tadcaster
Beverley Minster
Leeds
Peak District
Alderley Edge
Manchester
Sheffield
Pederton Castle
Beeston Castle
Lindow Moss
R. Severn
Hardwick Hall
Derby
Nottingham
Old Red Sandstone
Breedon Hill
Wren's Nest
Leicester
Bosworth
High Cross
Birmingham
Coventry
Worcester
Tewksbury

0   20   40
|____|____|__ miles

Chapter 9

Permian and Triassic New Red deserts
299–201 million years ago

It's easy to get bogged down in the Midlands countryside. Fields are a green so deep it is almost sopping. Hedges are as thick as a greenwood in summer and as dark as peat in winter. Villages seem made entirely of either black-stained timbers or rotting red stone. The ground's impervious surface is thick with streams and waterways. Winding lanes are half-flooded; everything feels old and dark, crumbling back into clay or grainy, cavity-filled sandstone. The rocks are known as 'mudstones' and 'marls', which just about sums it up.

There are sandstones, too. They make, low, heathy bluffs, where suddenly everything is dry. An edge of wildness blows through their stands of birch, oak and beech; the woodland seems to fling us back to the greenwood.

This sandstone Midlands can have a certain quiet hardness about it. The low ridges are as often the sites of towns as they are of woods: Warwick, Nottingham, Bridgnorth. As you move around you note a curious balance between industry and rurality, as if much of this country is not quite fully either.

Deep countryside here often becomes suburbia almost before you notice it. Suburbs in turn are punctuated by anonymous edgelands, their dank fields separating modern housing and industrial estates. I went to Tutbury,

Staffordshire, a beautiful market town – with a large Nestlé factory nearby. The nearby National Forest is an attempt to transform former industrial wasteland into a wooded, leisure-oriented landscape. A little further east, the spreading country around the Trent would be a deep England in itself – were it not punctuated by enormous cooling towers, cathedrals of electricity. In many places, enclosure has left the ridge-and-furrow of medieval strip fields rippling across many modern ones, a reminder that the industrial era created traumas rural as well as urban.

The Midlands, in truth, is one of England's unsung landscapes, a region many pass through on their way somewhere else. But the area has real geohistorical depth; and many of the themes that apply throughout the succession of Permian and Triassic rocks seem to coalesce here, as if in some great geohistorical basin.

In general the rocks of these periods are intensely responsive to human input; polite, where the rocks we have explored until now have been bolshy, supple where they have been hard. Though they are remarkable for their consistency of character, there are subtle shifts of voice from one area to another. The subtly variegated dialects that result are murmurs in comparison to the bombast of the Ordovician or the Moine Thrust, but once heard they become rich in their own right. I fell gradually in love with them.

If there are contrasts here – between urban and rural, mobile and fixed – then perhaps they are rooted in the greatest contradiction of all. That these well-settled places have their geological origin in the driest and least hospitable environment imaginable: one of the greatest deserts this planet has ever known. A geological alchemy has turned a dry, lifeless expanse into a damp, muddy, fructile landscape, and made sand dunes into heathy ridges. But we know what happens when we mix water and sand: mud.

Desert detritus

Glance sideways as you pull through the 2-mile long, 80ft-deep cutting that leads to Liverpool Lime St Station, and you might glimpse the cross-section of a sand dune. A surface textured with tiny sand-grains, each rounded by desert winds. Sweeping lines cut across it, each a former dune-top. You can almost feel your eyes sting in the hot, dusty air.

The New Red Sandstones are basically varieties of fossilised desert. Looking at them one can distinguish fast rivers suddenly rushing into rocky wadis, from lakes that evaporated rapidly beneath a hot sun; dunes built by the wind, from inundations by shallow, briny seas.

In origin, the 'New Red' – here used as a catch-all for a long and related sequence of Permian and Triassic rocks – is comparable to its Old Red predecessor: continents have collided, young mountains have eroded rapidly into equally young basins; the iron in their sandy deposits has reddened in the hot air of a desert. Just as the Old Red was made out of the Caledonian mountains, so the New Red is mainly the detritus of the Variscan ones; as the Old Red formed in a desert zone south of the equator, so the New Red formed in a comparable location north of it, approaching the latitude of the Sahara as the Triassic comes to an end. Sun-blasted sands, eroded from Variscan heights.

This is a period given to grand geological gestures: Pangea reached almost from one pole to the other, witnessed extraordinary extremes of climate which eroded rocks rapidly, and was host to enormous deserts. The resulting sediments pass seamlessly through the 252 Ma Permian/ Triassic boundary; British geologists often simply talk of 'Permo-Triassic' rocks.

For life on Earth, however, the transition was anything but smooth. The end of the Permian marks one of the greatest extinction events in history: 92 per cent of all marine species and 75 per cent of those that lived on land disappeared. Climate change was a key cause, and another such event marks the Triassic/Jurassic divide. The triumph of the reptiles was one result.

Sandstones and clays

Throughout, the two rock-types of the Midlands – the sandstones and the mudstones/clays – dominate. The sandstones form the ridge through which the Liverpool railway line is cut, and which does much to create that city's memorable setting. They also, on occasion, produce some fine building stones.

These rocks can be an almost painfully danger-signalling, fresh-blood shade of scarlet. Most are the remains of river beds and the like rather than sand dunes. Perhaps the most widespread formation is the Triassic Sherwood Sandstone, which dominates the Midlands.

These rocks have spawned bright red buildings and related place names from Redcliffe to Redditch. But they can also be dark brown, desert-yellow and rose-pink. Sometimes they are studded with water-rounded pebbles, dark jewels in scarlet settings: each is a river-eroded fragment of a lost Variscan (or even Caledonian) height, looking as fresh as if it had just been dropped by a child in a sandpit. Where there are large numbers of these – the so-called 'Pebble Beds', moisture slips into the earth, making it relatively poor agriculturally. Here stand some of the New Red's larger areas of woodland and heath: Cannock Chase, Sherwood Forest.

At other periods, the clays dominate. The most widespread are Mercia mudstones. Impermeable rocks like these formed as great a challenge to the railway-builders of Liverpool as the sandstones, trapping the developing city behind meres – boggy freshwater lakes – and peat bogs known as 'mosses', 'black and dirty . . . frightful to think of . . . will bear neither horse or man' (Defoe; though in this area the mosses are caused more by deep glacial earths than the mudstones themselves).

These 'rocks' are often generically called marls: the thick, sticky sense associated with the word is appropriate. They were laid down in shallow, briny lagoons and stretches of sea. The country they make can seem superficially dull; low-lying, but without even the distinction of true flatness – until you let them seep into your soul.

Among their legacies is the New Red's main economic resource: salt. Briny pools in the Pangean desert evaporated fast, leaving large amounts of this mineral behind. Liverpool was once so dependent on the export of salt from Cheshire that most people simply knew it as 'Liverpool salt'.

Though the sandstones and mudstones dominate, other formations bookend the story. At the start of the Permian, there are breccias – like conglomerates, but comprised of larger pieces: stony lumps, flushed from fresh Variscan heights. At the end of the Triassic, sea replaces desert, and limestone replaces sandstone; these are the Liassic rocks, which continue well into the Jurassic. The most important variant, however, comes in the late Permian, when there is a sudden ingress of the sea; a rock known as the Magnesian Limestone is the result.

There is a sense that with the New Red we are coming to the end of something. This is the last of our desert-origin, red sandstones. Like its predecessors – Torridonian, Old Red – it is the result of an episode of tectonic mountain-building. But it is also part of something new. We are leaving a world that, for much of our story, has been almost unfathomably unrecognisable; in its place, something dimly familiar, rich with plants and large land-animals, is gradually replacing it. The world of the younger cover.

The younger cover

The New Red Sandstones of Dumfries and those of Exeter (and Liverpool, and the Midlands); the honey-yellow Jurassic limestones of Lincolnshire and those of Somerset; the white chalk of Yorkshire and that of Dorset: a traveller blindfolded and taken to each pair of locations would have trouble telling them apart.

These are the defining rocks of the younger cover, a 234-million-year sequence of relatively simple geologies, layered from older to younger and exposed in strips that run roughly parallel across south-eastern Britain. Just under 15 per cent of England and Wales is covered by Permo-Triassic rocks, 18 per cent is Jurassic and 20 per cent, Cretaceous.

Younger cover rocks formed slowly, as tiny particles settled on top of one another and were compressed; they erode away evenly. The resulting landscapes are relatively low-lying: the New Reds rarely climb above 230m. And they often form long, continuous ridges or 'escarpments', especially in the Jurassic and Cretaceous, where they become such a defining feature we talk of the 'scarplands'.

Concentrated in the south-east of Britain, these are our first mainly English rocks; however their small-but-significant outposts in the far north and west suggest there was once much more of them. Those in the Highlands form bright green smudges of sea-edge fertility and human activity; one reaches the tiny coastal settlement of Applecross across the sulking emptiness of the Torridonian uplands, and finds there a patch of Triassic and Liassic rocks, the scene of human activity from the Mesolithic onwards, and the seat from which the seventh-century St Máel Ruba evangalised much of the ancient north-west strip.

In spite of their large outcrop, these are layers of rock in retreat; often, their scarps mark the 'leading edge' of what remains. They can leave outposts behind, sudden islands of younger rocks in a landscape of older ones; or erosion can make holes through which harder, old rocks poke. Rub away the Permian and Triassic, and the Carboniferous lies beneath: rub away the Jurassic, and you find Triassic.

The Carboniferous (and Silurian) Black Country sits in a sea of New Red, the Wren's Nest and associated hills rising from the Midland plain. Breedon Hill, Leicestershire, is another Carboniferous stone throne – a sudden, electrifying hill that has been half removed by industrial-era quarrying (much of it for a hardcore specifically suited for speedway circuits), yet still manages to support both a hillfort and a memorably large and ancient church.

These are in general fertile rocks, yielding both pastureland and arable country. As Leland wrote of one such landscape, the younger cover is often a beneficent sequence of 'meatly woody and enclosed ground . . . and plain champaigne, fruitful of corn and grass'. Champaign or 'champion' country, with its large arable fields and few woods, is often suggestive of rural bounty.

These will be territories over which history moves with relative ease, and leaves thickly layered traces. Where there are relative uplands, they can be rich in ancient remains; in lower country, especially on the clays, younger historical layers – Anglo-Saxon, medieval, industrial – are more visible.

These rocks are also strategically significant. Almost every major migration from Europe to the British island has hit them first, and settled them most thickly. And they emphasise our geological connectedness to the rest of the continent. The English New Red is also the *Buntsandstein* of northern Germany; the Channel Tunnel reconnects the chalklands of Kent with those of northern France.

Finally, they have a way of storing up important resources. The sequences of sandstones and clays of the New Red lie at the beginning of a long alternation of impermeable soft rocks and permeable harder ones. Such sequences make natural reservoirs, the permeable storing material like a sponge, the impermeable sealing it in. Though they contain comparatively little in the way of metals and minerals, they host the most considerable series of aquifers in Britain, helping sustain dense populations.

They are also a source of gas and oil. These are derived from the remains of algae, plankton, bacteria and plant material, buried rapidly and subjected to temperatures of 100–150°C 2–3 miles below the ground. They can be born in one source rock but migrate to another, where they are then kept in place if there is a capping of impervious rocks. The rocks of the younger cover play an important role in these processes, without which there would be no native source of natural gas, no North Sea oil, no fracking. The economy and politics of Britain since the late twentieth century would have been very different.

These stores of energy have partly survived because they have not been disturbed by major tectonic events. But the crust never sleeps: the rise and fall of basins continues, creating places for fresh sediment to gather, and germinating structures which will come, much later, to be filled by seas that are still with us.

The rocks of the younger cover underlie the historic heartlands of wealth and history in England. They are less significant in Scotland and Wales. And the New Reds are a fitting introduction to them. After the macho histrionics we have explored so far – all that grinding, melting, hardness and mountain-building – they can come as a relief. These are particularly quiet, giving lithologies, surrendering themselves into valleys and fertile country; allowing themselves to be hollowed and carved, and become the sites of great cities – rocks which often form soft landscapes, and sustain rich histories.

New Red landscapes

From their Midland heartland, the Permo-Triassic rocks fan out in three directions. The result is a 'Y'-shaped territory, its two arms running either side of the Pennines; its tail reaching down towards the south-west. They thus fill basins next to the Carboniferous heights as if they were clogged gutters of their detritus. From Morecambe in Lancashire, or Hartlepool in Tyne & Wear, you could walk to Birmingham without leaving them, before continuing on almost as far as Gloucester.

And this is not the end of the New Reds: with a few hops of up to 25 miles, you could extend the left-hand arm of the 'Y' north, to parts of Cumbria and southern Scotland; or follow its tail south and west through Somerset and South Wales to the south coast of Devon. With its long arms and easy country, and in spite of the historic reputation of its roads ('those terrible clays' – Defoe), the New Red's very distribution invites movement.

Throughout, certain themes recur. These are often places of rich pasture and fertility: the steep green hills of south Devon can seem to ooze fat, lactose and thick, floury scones. Hundreds of miles to the north it is a shock, in the world of peat and ancient gneiss that is the Isle of Lewis, to find tall trees around Lews Castle; but this little corner of sheltered fertility is a tiny toehold of New Red. It is no coincidence that Stornoway, the chief settlement of the Western Isles, is here. We saw something similar at Applecross.

Elsewhere the contrasts are more subtle: especially where the New Red butts up against the Old Red, as between Burghead and Lossiemouth on the Moray coast – the site of a major Pictish fort – or in the borderland that is the English/Welsh Marches.

There is a brightness and clarity to the New Red northern Marches of Shropshire and Cheshire that only becomes clear as you pass from them onto the darker, Old Red southern ones of Herefordshire and Gloucestershire. Offa's Dyke and the England/Wales border follow the edge of the New Red with faithful clarity in the northern half; but then lose that precision in the muddied, complex world of the Old Red southern one.

Scotland and north-west England

The discontinuous patches in the left-hand branch of the 'Y' become quite large in Scotland and England's far north-west. In the Borders around Dumfries, a group of fertile, often fault-lined basins of Permian New Red separate the Southern Uplands from Galloway. Each makes green, rich, grazing country; like a fragment of Worcestershire dropped among the greywackes; their line is followed by the M6/M74 and the west coast main line.

The Solway Firth opens its soft mouth into these rocks, which mark the England/Scotland border even as they help smother the deeply buried Iapetus Suture. This is our first major New Red river-mouth, but by no means the last: from the Severn and the Trent to the Exe and the Tees, many important waterways and broad estuaries have made their way along this basin-filling, easily eroded rock.

Like the Old Red, the New makes waterways, and also corridors and passages. And like the Old Red we might expect to see political, economic and cultural power reaching its fingers along such routes.

This is very evident in Cumbria, where the New Reds have a great trumpet-shaped footprint, about 40 miles wide along the Solway coast, and narrowing south-east for 55 miles to the southern end of the Vale of Eden.

Carlisle here was a north-western outpost of English (and before it, Roman) power; its castle and cathedral testaments to the curious, eroded-yet-powerful qualities of New Red buildings. In Penrith, Celia Fiennes found the stones 'look'd so red that at my entrance into the town [I] thought its buildings were all of brick'.

Here, the Vale of Eden is a great tongue of New Red towns and green pasturelands, dominated to one side by the great, sheer Carboniferous wave of Cross Fell. The river Eden cuts a red-lined gash through the valley, digging gorges into the rock and deep glacial earths. It is not the only sudden, tight, fault-lined New Red valley: the Vale of Clwyd in north Wales is another (Ruthin there means 'red fort').

There is one more patch before we join the New Red's main, continuous outcrop. On the Cumbrian coast, a patch runs from Barrow-in-Furness almost to Whitehaven, interrupting the Carboniferous rocks that ring the Lakes. At Barrow the great hulks of the submarine sheds are almost a geological presence in themselves, and a reminder that this was a New Red ship-building and iron-founding town, fed by the Carboniferous iron ores of Furness: an embodiment of a New Red/Carboniferous relationship that is a major aspect of the rock's geohistory.

Then, in Lancashire, the continuous outcrop starts. The distinction between land and sea blurs in this clay country: the 'wet Sahara' of Morecambe bay; the former wetlands of the Fylde.

Cheshire and the Midlands

As we approach the Midlands, we hit the New Red Cheshire Basin. The historic city of Chester here is one of the great New Red settlements, half-timbered, its crumbling cathedral and city walls almost scarlet. This was for centuries one of the major seats of trade and power in north-west England.

Cheshire and its environs are places of pools, little stands of trees, green fields, and sudden broad, earthen gorges set in a gradual, wave-like rise and fall of glacial earth: 'flat, rich but unpleasant' (Pennant). It is home to the salt deposits that have been the chief New Red resources, and of the mires and mosses. Now mostly drained, these were once collectively the third-largest area of peat bog in the country, and the scene of mysterious Iron Age or early Roman human sacrifices – Lindow Moss has yielded the individual black-humouredly known as 'Pete Marsh'. Peat is visibly a once-countryside in a way that coal is not (one can see the fibres of ancient plants in it) and these bodies are much the same, corpses as fixed in mid-decay as a peaty tree root.

Sherwood Sandstone scarps ring the Cheshire plain. The 227m Mid-Cheshire Ridge is topped by six hillforts, medieval Beeston castle, and nineteenth-century Peckforton castle, said to be England's youngest fortified home. Alderley Edge is draped in geohistories so thick you can almost touch them. Smooth, yellow-red tables of bare stone are exposed around its highest areas; from Stormy Point, one can see the lights of Macclesfield and Manchester. Armada warning beacons were lit here atop a Bronze Age round barrow.

To the south, Carboniferous-and-older hills draw close together, and the Grand Trunk and Shropshire Union canals, the railway from London Euston, and the M6 all squeeze through the narrow, ice-age carved New Red corridor known as the Cheshire Gap. We enter the rock's Midlands core.

This is a territory that stretches perhaps 40–50 miles east to west and 65–80 miles north to south, from Stafford to Leicester, and Derby to Worcester. The mosses and meres are absent here; and gypsum replaces salt as the main resource. We have been here already, and we will back, for in the story of the New Red, this country is hard to avoid.

Heading north-east

For now, let's head north up the eastern arm of the 'Y'. The Magnesian Limestone lines its western edge; the A1 and M1 follow the deposit as surely as the M6 did on the other side. Nottingham is a major medieval and industrial-era settlement on a Sherwood Sandstone ridge; York, comfy and at ease in its eponymous Vale, dominates one of the most fertile, historically rich districts in Britain.

The city was the capital of Roman *Britannia Inferior*, the central settlement of the Viking Danelaw, and later the effective capital of northern England. The medieval Merchant Adventurers' Hall is one testament to the wealth generated by those who sponsored Carboniferous/ Pennine lead mining from here, before Leeds eclipsed the city as surely as Liverpool and Manchester replaced Chester.

This branch of the New Red finally runs into the sea on the low-lying coast south of Hartlepool. Here, the mouth of the Tees is the New Red's north-eastern last gasp. Here I walked among peri-industrial dunes, the lights of industry winking on the reclaimed land nearby.

South-west England and south Wales

Moving south and west from the Midlands, we pick the trail up again. This is the long tail of the 'Y', and we're following the Severn, and with it, the M5. As we go, New Red often shades into Lias and back to New Red again. The rocks continue uninterrupted below the nearby Severn: much of south Glamorgan is New Red and Lias, too.

Lowland South Wales can be compared to the Scottish Midland Valley in its significance for Welsh history. It is the site of the Principality's three largest settlements, as well as an extensive stretch of fertile country – surely key factors in the survival of Welsh nationhood. Yet with its easy connections east into England, it is a more porous, open landform than its Scots equivalent; perhaps it is no coincidence that Scotland has retained the greater independence.

Back in England, the New Red is increasingly becoming a broken-up phenomenon, flowing among complex Variscan synclines and anticlines: the mixed landscapes typical of the eastern half of the south-west. It makes it way around the Carboniferous Mendips, merges into the Lias as we cross the Somerset Levels, then runs on to Devon.

This country is the New Red's last great hurrah. The Crediton Trough, a long, thin spear-shaped extension of the New Red followed by the A377 and A3072, reaches deep into Variscan/Carboniferous country. Crediton lies at its gateway; until 1050 it was the seat of a bishopric, which was then relocated to Exeter, the historic city at the head of the Exe estuary.

On its ridge of New Red rocks and Variscan lavas, Exeter effectively occupies the boundary of the eastern/mixed landscape and western/Variscan south west. Of Roman origin, it was long the chief settlement of Devon and Cornwall; people based here might once have needed to communicate in Anglo-Norman, old English, Latin and Cornish alike. Apart from the Jurassic/Cretaceous medieval cathedral – its stone sourced from no fewer than twenty separate quarries – the older buildings here are a New Red the colour of wine, sometimes complemented by harsh, veined lumps of the local basalts. The New Red rocks finally leave our story, which has its northernmost expression in the Western Isles 545 miles to the north, on the English Channel, just south of Torquay.

Here we are approaching Britain's most extensive stretch of New Red cliffs (though the highest are at St Bees on the Cumbria coast): 20 miles of them, from Sidmouth to Torquay. These are memorably followed by the Great Western Railway: one of the most spectacular and frequently disrupted train rides in Britain.

Look to the landward side, and see a depthless succession of cemented Permian sands, burnt to a high-resolution scarlet and crossed by seams of dark pebbles that mark the paths of lost Pangean rivers. Above the cliffs, the deep green of the clifftop visibly crumbles away. Ahead, the train pulls through sequences of short tunnels, cutting with ease through cliffs, stacks and promontories of this pliable rock. On the seaward side, the breakers of the English Channel eat away at it further, and sandstone reduces back to sand.

Only once in all this time does the rock-type change fundamentally. At various points, shallow seas ingressed into parts of the Pangean desert. When these evaporated, they became more saltbowl than sea, and, at their peak, for about 20 million years in the late Permian, they left behind a layer of limestone which is today an easily overlooked feature of the British landscape. Before we draw out the geohistories of the New Red, this rock deserves a separate treatment.

The Magnesian Limestone

Hardwick Hall (1590–7) is an unmissable sight from the M1, a massive dark mass atop a long escarpment. Look harder as one sweeps north, and one might notice drystone walls and barns in the fields around the motorway; perhaps, even, a distinctive roll to the land. Easily missed, this is neither the rounded Carboniferous country to the west nor the flattish New Red one to the east.

Such is the slender landscape identity of the Magnesian Limestone: the only major Permian or Triassic sedimentary formation not to be placcable under the broad heading 'New Red'. Most of its outcrop is very narrow, east to west; it runs roughly parallel to the eastern side of the Pennines, often forming a west-facing escarpment. If you noticed it at all, you might simply think you were on some last gasp of the Pennine Fringe.

In fact this formation is quite a phenomenon; though rarely making ground that is more than 180m high, or half a dozen miles wide, it runs – sometimes a true ridge, sometimes indistinguishable among other hills – a full 130–140 miles north to south. In other words it is a thin, narrow north–south line – except in the far north, where in County Durham it widens to make a true limestone landscape.

Like the Cambrian, Silurian and Carboniferous limestones we have already explored, these rocks are typically a pale, dense warm tan or a hard grey-white. They were born in a shallow tropical sea, and many are dolomitic. With their dry valleys, sink-holes, gorges and caves, much about the resulting landscape is normal-for-limestone. Yet their geohistorical themes also look forward: for this country prefigures the scarplands of the Jurassic and Cretaceous.

Castles, hill-forts and towns cling to the Magnesian Limestone ridge. Its dry, elevated, linear landforms make natural routes; and it contains liberal quantities of excellent freestone. For all these reasons, the Magnesian is, in spite of its limited extent, a geohistorically significant formation.

In its wide north-eastern outcrop the scarp, its base followed for a period by the A688, looks west into the coal country of County Durham. The Magnesian Limestone (like much of the New Red), sits directly on top of the coal-bearing Carboniferous: once mines could go deep enough to cut through it – starting at Wearmouth here in the 1820s, but later also in north Yorkshire and in Nottinghamshire – parts of Permo-Triassic country of all kinds became extensions of the Pennine Fringe.

The limestone climbs rapidly to a waterless peri-urban plateau with drystone walls and quarries among the farms and ridge-and-furrow. It was quarried here for its special suitability for post-Bessemer steel making. It hits the North Sea in a glacial earth-covered riot of layered cliffs, caves and stacks cut by deep denes. Sunderland is a major industrial-era city sited on these rocks, sucking in the Jurassic iron ores of the North York Moors and nearby sources of Carboniferous coal. The town walls and parish church of Hartlepool are built of this rock; the glass industries around Sunderland consumed its lime, along with sand and coal. Local beaches still throw up delightful pieces of Anthropocene 'geology' – sea-smoothed 'pebbles' made of translucent coloured glass, which at Seaham are used to make a range of attractive objects. Lord Byron, who married Lady Anne Milbanke at Seaham Hall, complained about this 'dreary coast'; his ancestral home, Newstead abbey in Nottinghamshire, is a characteristically crisp work of Magnesian Limestone, 121 miles to the south, almost at the southernmost extreme of the formation.

Heading south, the formation narrows, but its ridge is lined by a series of historically important places, often located where rivers break through after running off the Pennines: Ripon, Knaresborough, Pontefract on the ridge's west-looking scarp; Doncaster, Worksop, Mansfield on New Reds at the east-looking foot of its dipslope. Around Ripon and Darlington the limestone includes gypsum, a soft material that caused the sinkholes said to have inspired Alice's fall down a sudden deep shaft into Wonderland. Alice's adventures in the Permian; perhaps the Jabberwocky is an early giant lizard, appropriate to the era that saw the first large reptiles. The same material underlies the mighty Neolithic henge complex at Thornborough, which was whitened using it.

Around Creswell, Derbyshire, there are a series of waterless, cave-lined gorges typical of limestone. Creswell Crags is the most famous, and justly so, for the prehistoric inhabitants here are behind the oldest art in Britain: Palaeolithic engravings of animals and geometrical forms, some of them arranged to exploit fractures and gaps on the rock-surface for artistic effect.

Magnesian building stones

The Magnesian Limestone comes to a final halt just a few miles north of Nottingham. But by then it has passed some of the finest freestones in Britain, quarried in several places, especially around Tadcaster in Yorkshire, and Mansfield in Nottinghamshire. These are our first serious limestone freestones; they won't be the last.

The chief buildings of the city of York are hard, silver-grey presences among the half-timbered streets; the mighty, cold Minster, gently yellow in sunshine, but cloud-grey when damp. They are basically well-ordered piles of limestone from Tadcaster, transported here across the New Red Vale. Much of this material was first quarried by the Romans – so important was the site for its lime that the probable Latin name for Tadcaster was *Calcaria* – only to be recycled into later buildings. Like some ancient sediment, each block may have been cut, transported, made and remade several times over. And York is not alone: a host of finely detailed, grey-white architectural wonders standing on younger, softer rocks, from Beverley Minster to Wressle Castle, are made of Magnesian Limestone; the Bishop Dike near Selby might even have been cut to transport it.

Further south, White and Red Mansfield, the former more pale grey and the latter orangey tan in shade, are the most important building stones. It is the high proportion of quartz they contain that makes them so durable; it gives them a gleaming sparkle in the right light. The White variety is magnificently displayed in Southwell Minster, as well as the railway viaduct at Mansfield itself; the Red one was preferred for decorative elements. It is used on the Shire Hall, Nottingham, and at St Pancras Station, London.

This London connection is not new. With access to rivers leading to the east coast, Magnesian Limestone was used in the medieval period at the Tower of London and Westminster Hall: a crisp, pale presence that presages the later London mania for Jurassic Limestone from the Isle of Portland.

But Magnesian Limestone has problems when exposed to pollution. The sulphur dioxide in coal smoke becomes sulphuric acid when combined with oxygen and water: acid rain, which eats below the surface of the rock, turning it to spongy dust behind its fissile skin. At the same time its surface turns a drab dark grey-black, with odd white patches, like a diseased lung. This is a general problem with limestones – acid solutions dissolve calcite – and millions of pounds have been spent on conserving Magnesian Limestone York Minster and the Palace of Westminster, where the rebuilding of 1839–52 was controversial for its stone-choice from the start.

Magnesian Limestone is a material that looks both forward and backwards. It shares its inscrutable texture and silver-grey colour with older limestones, bringing such qualities into the heart of our historic towns; yet its accessibility, usefulness, and receptiveness to the slicing of the chisel look forward, to Limestone's last great hurrah: the Jurassic limestones of south-eastern Britain.

There is another quality that this rock shares with the rest of the younger cover: it has often guided the paths of roads. Here, the north–south strike of the Magnesian Limestone has made it a particularly convenient 'hard shoulder' above the New Red clay, taken advantage of by chunks of the Roman-origin A1 and A10 as well as the modern M1; embodiments of the way in which history speeds through Permo-Triassic landscapes.

And where these roads are not on the limestone, they often use ridges of Sherwood Sandstone. It is to this New Red mainstream that we can now return.

Digging deeper

Wanting to bore deeper into the New Red's Midland heartland, I took myself to Repton, Derbyshire. The village sits on a ridge of Sherwood sandstone, surrounded by mudstones, over which slides the river Trent.

This mighty river outdoes even the Severn as the great waterway of the New Red, rising on Carboniferous rocks near the Potteries, but then tracking low-slung Permo-Triassic rocks diligently in a great 'U' around the Pennines.

For centuries the Trent marked where 'north' became 'south' in England, generating such administrative roles as 'Keeper of the King's Forests north of the Trent'. In other words this New Red area sits at England's heart. There are various ways of deciding where the geographical centre of the country is: but the traditional answer was High Cross in New Red Leicestershire, and all the other candidates are also on these rocks. Such mythospherical embodiments of the nation as Robin Hood and William Shakespeare came from New Red Nottinghamshire and Warwickshire respectively. We are in a literal middle England.

As if to prove that, here half-timbered cottages, a medieval church and a public school all nestle next to one former course of the shifting Trent, at once secure in its quiet rural prosperity; and historically well connected, thanks to the defining presence of the river.

But things were not so easy here in 873, when the Great Heathen Army of the Vikings marched into what was then an important royal centre in the Anglo-Saxon kingdom of Mercia. They dug a circuit of defensive earthworks between the already-ancient Anglo-Saxon church and the river, and overwintered within them. Fully 264 of the Norsemen died here, and were buried beneath a mound. Little is visible today other than the remains of a medieval priory, which in turn has become the school, and the Anglo-Saxon church, a remnant of the ancient kingdom of Mercia.

Mercia is one of the presiding entities of the New Red. Its large, central footprint was dominated by these rocks; and for a period it was arguably the most powerful entity in Britain. King Offa had treated Charlemagne himself as a peer; briefly made New Red Lichfield the seat of an archbishopric, rivalling Canterbury and York; and minted coins that, with their imitations of Kufic script, evoked the young, energetic empires of Islam. The kingdom could easily have gone on to swallow up other entities and become the centre of a unified England, were it not for the Vikings. They quickly came to the eastern part of the territory; major clusters of Norse-origin place names there are one legacy. A shrunken Mercian state held on in the west.

This east–west division of England's New Red central lowlands is an ancient one. Before the Romans, the *Corieltauvi* dominated the eastern Midlands and the *Cornovii* the west. In medieval England the Midlands had two mighty dioceses: New Red Coventry & Lichfield in the west, with their rouge-red and thickly magnificent churches; Lincoln in the east, its cathedral in crisp, bright limestone. Today, the East and West Midlands are separate English regions. The difference between the two is as palpable and yet hard to pin down as an incoming change in the weather. On the western side the New Reds butt up against Old Red and yet more ancient rocks, Rome's influence fades and Wales begins, rain-supplying oceans of history all around; to the east, the New Reds shade into further rocks of the younger cover, the land stretches east towards Europe, and incoming cultures roll easily across the inviting land.

The sense that you are working your way deep into England's early medieval origins here is to an extent true of much of the younger cover. The whole territory has palpably been redefined as each wave of history rewires the patterns left by previous ones; historical versions of the waves of sedimentation, deposit and removal that its rocks embody. Yet I always feel particularly close to the Anglo-Saxon dimension of this in the rural West Midlands: where Mercian is what it speaks. Lichfield and Tamworth, longer-lasting seats of Mercian power than Repton, are both here.

In places like these one can feel knotted in the undergrowth of an English history that ripples backwards and forwards in time: a sense richly evoked in Geoffrey Hill's *Mercian Hymns*, a passage from which forms the epigraph to this book. As I explore, I seem to be worming 'heavenward for ages amid barbaric ivy, scrollwork of fern' (*Mercian Hymns*, V).

The wildwood is never far away here. In Nottinghamshire, fabled Sherwood sits atop a low sandstone shelf. In Worcestershire, Shakespeare's Arden stood east of Stratford on the New Red clay. Needwood began not far west of Repton: a now-absent forest translated into human form annually when the priapic Horn Dance makes its way around the fields and houses of Abbots Bromley. Men dressed in faux medieval costume hold aloft the brightly painted skulls of eleventh-century reindeer, their antlers prancing like branches of thick oak. The hedgerows sprout trees, as if the fields had just been cleared. The 'tons' and 'leah/leys' – Rep*ton* and Abbots Brom*ley* – often indicate clearings made in woodland.

Royal forests on New Red rocks once stretched continuously from near Bristol to the edge of the Peak; then continued up its right-hand arm from the Humber to the North York Moors. Many were on the clays. The term 'Forest' relates more to an institution than a landscape type; an area of land, wooded or not, in which the Crown controls resources, especially game. These were politically and economically important places, at once carefully managed and mythospherically full of associations with the wild.

Back in Repton, and it is time to enter the oldest standing structure in this landscape: the church. Above ground this is a much-patched building of the thirteenth to fifteenth centuries, its grey-red sandstones blackened and patched. But the chancel long predates the Conquest, and narrow staircases descend into the floor, as if burrowing into the sandstone itself.

You are entering a crypt that has been here since the eighth century. It was here when the Vikings came, and incorporated the church into their defences. It is itself an artefact of layers. A Mercian king Wiglaf was buried here, as was his son, Wystan, murdered by a rival in 849 and subsequently acclaimed a saint. There have been many alterations since: and at some point the Anglo-Saxons transformed it into a kind of saint's shrine. Coiled columns rise from an uneven floor; some of the oldest vaults in Britain rise low above our heads. The whole place is an artificial New Red cave, filled with dank and early power.

Spread a map out on the crypt floor, and start to see something fallopian in the New Red outcrop, its great Midland gathering the nation's very womb. If Britain is a body-shaped island, its Caledonian and Variscan limbs stretching west, its Jurassic-and-younger rump facing east, then its navel is here in the Midlands. One might expect things historical to germinate in such a place, but the search for a single point of origin slides across the landscape. Early medieval Lichfield, or Tamworth? Eighteenth-century Birmingham, or even, on the Carboniferous, Ironbridge and Cromford? Perhaps there is no one answer, for this territory is at once deeply rooted and highly mobile. But one possibility is this little space in Repton, where one can almost feel the pulse of the New Red's beating heart, here below the ground, at England's expansive New Red crossroads.

Movement

The Trent shifts past Repton. The A38, a major road of Roman origin, follows it. Everywhere, these rocks form routes and ways through the wider landform, forging dense and easy networks between the many settlements. In this they have much in common with the Old Red, but where that rock formed slim arteries through forbidding country, the New Red lets history flow along broader, less constrained corridors. Take the two together and it can seem as if human movement has left a great red trail across Britain.

We've watched the major routes of modern England – M1, M6, M5 – follow the arms of the New Red 'Y'. In the Midlands, motorways conjoin in a concrete nest in the form of Birmingham's Spaghetti Junction: a modern embodiment of the region's historic role. Pre-motorway trunk routes – A1, A38, A34 – likewise followed the New Red's arms, and are often of Roman origin. Watling Street/the A5 is one of several important Roman roads that cross New Red country – it does so for fully 90 miles.

The New Red rivers host some of the most historically important harbours in the land: Bristol and Liverpool, Chester and Cardiff; even little Stranraer is sited on a Permian strip separating Galloway from the Rhinns. A remarkable number of England's earliest surviving stone bridges are on New Red sites, such as at twelfth- and thirteenth-century

Exeter, Tewkesbury, Bristol and Nottingham; at Kirkby Lonsdale in Cumbria and Stoneleigh in Warwickshire; and Swarkestone, just a few miles from Repton – crossing points of the Exe, Severn, Bristol Avon and Trent respectively.

The New Red's open landform also makes it a place in which conflict acquires a peculiar geographical dynamism. According to the military historian and geologist Trevor J. Halsall, the number of battles fought on New Red (and late Carboniferous) rocks is quite disproportionate to their extent. New Red Dumfries was plundered or occupied by the English half a dozen times between the fourteenth and sixteenth centuries; the Scottish army had a comparable impact on New Red Carlisle. Eleventh-century Normans and thirteenth-century Plantagenets alike used New Red Chester as their logistical base for assaults on North Wales. In the Midlands, key battles in both the Wars of the Roses and the Civil War – Shrewsbury, Tewkesbury, Bosworth, Towton, Worcester – reflect the shifting of the balance of power across the broad New Red; places where armies could cross the New Red's broad, slow waterways, such as Newark-on-Trent, had special significance. After the battle of Worcester, Charles II hid in an oak tree, a woody New Red hiding place that spawned a thousand Royal Oak pubs.

New Red Nottinghamshire was a frontline fracture in the English body politic during both the Wars of the Roses and the Civil War, and a left-wing friend used to call it 'the class traitor county', for its role in the miners' strikes of the twentieth century. Centres of political power shift in status in these landscapes: ancient centres of power such as Lichfield, Tamworth and Warwick – or, indeed, Repton – were left aside as Coventry and Birmingham came to dominate.

To see just how deep in time such tendencies can run, I went to a spot just outside Penrith, Cumbria. Here is a bottleneck of density: the M6, the west coast main line, medieval Brougham Castle and the Neolithic henges of Mayburgh and King Arthur's Round Table almost crash into each other as they cluster around the river Eden. The castle was a vital defensive location for the barons of the English north; it may lie on top of a Roman fort. Mayburgh is a Neolithic monument on a massive scale, its banks 4–7m high. It was made by mounding some 5 million rounded cobbles from the river bed into a mighty arena. All this sits where routes conjoin – not only north and south, but also east and west.

If these monuments were a nodal point for the trade in the Ordovician hand-axes of Langdale, it would presage the New Red's most striking geohistorical role, as the trading centre and distribution point for the resources of the older, harder rocks around it. This can be said in a general way of many New Red market towns – Penrith itself, Dumfries, Taunton; it also means that for tourists, the New Red is how most people approach highland country, from the Malverns, to Dartmoor, to the Lakes.

This synergistic relationship of upland and lowland rocks is likely to be replicated in many places, given that sedimentary lowlands often develop in the basins that go with mountain-building; but in Britain it is dominated by the relationship of New Red with Carboniferous. It is a synergetic relationship between the potentialities of two groups of rocks that has enormous geohistorical significance.

Synergy

The New Red/Carboniferous synergy is one of the most remarkable relationships in our story, made all the more fitting because the Variscan events tie together the stories of both. Largely made of tiny fragments of Carboniferous uplands, the New Red is the hard made soft, the sword made ploughshare. And if the Carboniferous gave birth to industry, the New Red is its geohistorical midwife.

Everywhere other than Scotland, the New Red makes lowlands next to Carboniferous uplands; landform that encouraged movement, trade, manufacturing and the growth of large settlements. It was on these that the products of the Carboniferous were brought to market and processed at scale. The rock's easily manipulated earths and soft rocks, navigable rivers and many urban centres came into their own. Geology and landform played into the hands of developing industry.

Though intimately tied to the Carboniferous, the historic core of a remarkable number of great industrial-era settlements – from Liverpool and Birmingham to Cardiff and Manchester – is on the New Red. Many were already significant market towns, and thus centres of finance, manufacture, distribution and marketing in their region; now they were catapulted to global significance: the first modern cities.

One starts to wonder what the historical consequences would have been if the New Red had not bordered directly on its resource-rich predecessor, and had not been so easy to move across, its surface so amenable to the gouging and digging that went with canal, railway and road-building. Surely the epochal economic 'lift-off' of the eighteenth and nineteenth centuries would have been harder to achieve – perhaps would not have happened at all – if the Carboniferous resources had lain isolated in a mountain fastness.

Umbilical canals and railways

The canals play a particularly illustrative role in this story for their special dependence on the lie of the land. A canal needs to draw its water from an existing waterway, and like a river it needs to flow downhill; to control the flow, the descent has to be gradual. They are thus happiest on relatively level ground.

The early canals in particular do their best to connect to, or render navigable, existing, natural waterways; and they spend as much time as possible avoiding the need to build embankments, cuttings or tunnels. They like valleys, soft rocks and relatively gentle terrain: the qualities of the New Red. Its supplies of clay, loam and sand were also helpful, for preventing leakage (though the New Red's marshy areas and hard-to-embank marly soils were disadvantages). The overriding function of the canals, however, was the transportation of bulk materials, especially coal, specifically mentioned in ninety of the 165 canal acts passed in 1758–1801: and this meant access to the Carboniferous uplands.

So the Bridgewater Canal (1761), the first true industrial-era artificial waterway, was built to transport the Duke of Bridgewater's coal from its mine in the Carboniferous rocks at Worsley to New Red Manchester. But the Bridgewater Canal built on a series of earlier achievements, and each is also mostly on the New Red, with the Carboniferous an ever-motivating presence: the Sankey Brook Navigation (begun 1755), transported Carboniferous coals and ores, and New Red salt, to New Red Liverpool. Before this, in Ireland, the Newry canal (1742) ran from

Carboniferous Tyrone to New Red Newry; back in Britain, and the ambitious cut dug by Exeter traders in the 1560s to bypass the Countess of Devon's weirs on the Exe also went across New Red rocks.

As we move into the later eighteenth-century heyday of the canals, the New Reds also dominate (the exceptions are mostly on the softer, younger rocks of the Fens and eastern England). The most far-reaching achievements connected key New Red rivers: by 1777 the 93-mile Grand Trunk Canal, the longest yet built, connected the New Red Mersey to the Humber via the New Red Trent; the New Red Severn and the Thames had joined the network by 1790. All this centred around the Midlands, which were to become an industrial-era Spaghetti Junction of artificial waterways.

By this time we are entering a 'heroic' age, in which landscape impediments become a challenge to overcome rather than avoid, and we see deeper incursions into the hillier country and harder rocks of the Carboniferous (and the Jurassic as well), along with mighty works of earthmoving.

At a very rough estimate, perhaps about 900 miles of English canals eventually ran over Permo-Triassic rocks, as opposed to 600 miles on Carboniferous ones. (And a little over 720 miles on rocks that are younger still, usually around London and the south-east; and just 90 miles on older lithologies, mostly Devonian). Transport of Carboniferous coal to New Red settlements is a dominant theme throughout. The canals are the artificial, riverine expressions of the Carboniferous/New Red synergy.

One could tell a similar story with regard to the railways, especially in the early years when climbing gradients was a major issue. The most significant of various pre-steam timber overland railways was built in 1603–4 to facilitate the movement of Carboniferous coals from Strelley, near Nottingham, to New Red Wollaton, en route to the Trent. The world's first steam-powered railway, from Stockton-on-Tees to Darlington (1825), transported the Carboniferous coals of the latter to the riverine New Red distribution point of the former. The first true passenger railway (1830) ran from New Red Liverpool to New Red Manchester. As the network expanded, entire towns developed as servicing and manufacturing centres, and they too had to be on low, flat country. Swindon New Town may be on Jurassic clays and Crewe on Triassic ones, but the root cause is the same.

In summary, the Carboniferous is the origin of resources, but it is the New Red that shifts and communicates them. The geo-logic of the industrial revolution is a combination of fast-running Carboniferous water, coal deposits and metal ores – and, in England and Wales at least, the ease of transport offered by the adjacent Permo-Triassic rocks. And geologically all these rocks, Carboniferous, Permian and Triassic alike, are knitted together in an underlying tectonic story: the formation of Pangea.

Such synergies relate to geological resources, too. Coalville, Leicestershire, is a town that would not exist were it not for the mining of Carboniferous coal from beneath a Permo-Triassic cover. The power stations and cooling towers of the New Red Trent valley were built to distribute electricity made using Carboniferous coals; the pylons that march from them, motorways of energy. Even some of the metal and mineral deposits in the Carboniferous rocks are the result of fluids, often briny, percolating down from the evaporating heat of the New Red desert. And as the country shifted from a rural nation to one dominated by industrial-era cities, countless millions must have followed New Red routes to get to their new homes on the New Red rocks.

As these cities developed, miners from Cornwall ended up in Teesside; Welsh railway workers occupied an entire quarter of Swindon; and key identities, such as the Manchester and Liverpool Irish, were born. All this presaged the multiculturalism that is such a glorious aspect of our major cities today. If Britain is polyglot in stones and people, it is in the industrial-era cities that this is most visible, and it is to these unprecedented settlements that the canals and railways ran.

Cities

Every major industrial-era settlement that is not on Carboniferous rocks is on adjacent Permo-Triassic ones; the chief exception, as ever, is London, and its related coastal conurbations. Perhaps about 9 million people live in cities the historic core of which is Permo-Triassic. We've swept the nation in pursuit of New Red landscapes: let's do so again, jumping from city to city to explore the character of a series of urban expressions of the Carboniferous/New Red synergy.

It is worth remembering just how dramatic the industrial-era transformation of such places was. Manchester had 22,000 residents in 1773, 75,000 in 1801, and 300,000 fifty years later; Birmingham went from 5,732 inhabitants in 1650 to 35,000 in 1760; by 1811 this had almost doubled. We've seen how Liverpool, the port that grew from a minor town to one of the apexes of the slave trade, is approached by rail along drained mosses and sandstone cuttings – it forms an ideal gateway to the story.

Liverpool

The city's New Red site is clasped between Carboniferous coals, which start just a few miles to the north, and the Triassic salts of Cheshire; these spawned chemical industries which were drawn to its vicinity.

The spacious grandeur of Liverpool city centre is defined by two New Red landforms; a broad, shallow valley has been carved into the soft rocks by ice and filled by the Mersey; a gentle rise behind it. The former became a major Atlantic port with a broad, grand harbourfront; the latter is the ridge of Sherwood Sandstone through which the railway carves itself.

The city's architectural statements sit on these two sites: grand commercial structures down on the Harbourside (Liver Building, 1908); on the ridge, the spiky grandeur of the two cathedrals. This hill supplied much of the city's building stone until well into the eighteenth century, but development beyond it was constrained until turnpike roads, early canal projects, river improvements and railways spanned what lay beyond: 'the bog where human foot could not reach', as Alexander Somerville put it in 1847.

St James's cemetery, right next to the Anglican cathedral, is one of my favourite New Red places: a layered sacred landscape for the industrial era. It was born as a quarry: the stone used for the Old Dock of 1715, the world's first commercial enclosed wet dock, came from here; as did that for many of the city's most significant early buildings.

Its stone exhausted, the site was redeveloped from 1827 into a park-like cemetery, its quarry-faces lined with cave-like mausoleums. There is a Greek-style Oratory chapel, as if this was some mercantile/industrial Delphi; the artificial entrance canyon next to it is visibly layered with the wind-blown sands of a barren equatorial desert.

And from the very lip of the cemetery rises the mountainous Anglican bulk of Sir Giles Gilbert Scott's cathedral, begun in 1904 and built of 30,500 cubic yards/23,300 cubic metres of New Red, much of it from Woolton, to the south-east.

It's all a fitting setting for the tomb of William Huskisson MP, the first human to be killed in a railway accident: a newfangled, Carboniferously powered machine, hurtling with industrious power across the recently conquered marshes and mosses, bringing death in its wake even as it linked the young cities that burgeoned on the Lancashire plain.

Manchester

Moving inland, we come to the first true industrial city, its New Red site tucked into an elbow of the Carboniferous Pennines. Carboniferous coal-bearing rocks begin within a mile of the centre, and enclose it on three sides; the Pennines beyond are an intense upland shadow, from which the power of the Carboniferous virtually falls into the city's New Red bowl.

The easily excavated sandstone-and-glacial-earth of the city centre has been cut through and bridged by a crumbling web of natural waterways, canals and railway lines, stage-sets for the mighty Victorian buildings which breed behind, above and between. The buildings, especially from the late nineteenth century onwards, became exceptionally tall as land-values soared; they include palatial warehouses, tokens of Manchester's centrality as a place of distribution as well as of manufacturing.

Manchester hosts some surprisingly dense places; at Castlefields, near the junction of the rivers Irwell and Medlock, a reconstruction of the gate of the AD 79 Roman town sits hard by the starting points of both the first passenger railway line and the first industrial-era canal.

The oldest part of the present city lies a little north of here, where a quay on the Irwell is overlooked by a low sandstone cliff. Here stands the cathedral, originally a grand fifteenth-century collegiate church, and testament to the fact that this was already one of the most important settlements in the region, its economy rooted in the wool of the Pennine sheep-pastures.

It is events from the seventeenth century onwards that truly put Manchester on the map. Cotton mills proliferated. An enormous shanty town of hastily built slums, canals, mills and factories rolled across the flat New Red countryside, its character still evoked by place names such as Moss Side.

During the nineteenth century, a wave of civic pride, embodied by the city status attained in 1853, washed over Manchester. The city rebuilt itself, improving housing and creating proud – in some cases visionary – civic cathedrals to health, culture, governance, education and industry. Soon it was effectively the second capital of England. The can-do attitude of the era is exemplified by the Ship Canal (1894), an excavation on the scale of a major river, cutting through the New Red expanses until it bypasses Liverpool; it turned land-locked Manchester into Britain's third most important port.

Architecturally, the city's oldest buildings use Sherwood Sandstones, many sourced in Castlefields; but even then, Carboniferous Binney Sandstone from Collyhurst, 1 mile away, makes an appearance. Later the city is dominated by the Carboniferous sandstones: the Town Hall (1868–77) is built from them. But like all industrial-era cities, Manchester sucks in stones from across Britain and the world. There is Portland from Dorset on the Central Library, recent buildings include such exotica as gneisses and granites from Kanakapura, India, and the Black Hills of Dakota, USA.

Today this is all as burgeoning as any city in Britain; yet shattered, overgrown corners still sit cheek-by-jowl with new, computer-designed towers, 'turrets of Victorian wealth' (Mark E. Smith), palace-warehouses and canal-canyons; a city that has been continuously eroding and regenerating since 1800 or so, a nexus of Triassic and Carboniferous geohistorical sediment.

Birmingham

Now we reach the cardiac core of the New Red Midlands; a conurbation driven, heart-like, by two adjacent engines: Carboniferous Black Country and New Red Birmingham.

The two combined have made this the largest city in Britain outside London – yet, uniquely among major settlements, Birmingham itself is not on a navigable river; it spreads easefully from a gentle slope in a broad sandstone plateau. Perhaps this unusual site simply made a convenient centre in the shifting sands of the New Red, but many roads had passed through the area since Roman times and it was on the London side of the Black Country. There was water from the New Red Rea, which ran where the New Red sandstone met the New Red clays; and timber from the woodlands of the New Red Forest of Arden – and, crucially, iron ore and coal a little to the west.

'*A great parte*' of this medieval town was already '*mayntayned by smithes*' in 1538 (Leland). In about 1600 Camden described a place 'echoing with the noise of anvils'. In the industrial era, the city's relatively poor transport links helped encourage an economy in which the making of small-scale metal objects – jewellery, guns, toys – long played an unusually large role. And in the end, it drew to itself the water that it lacked. The Birmingham canal, begun in 1768, connected the Triassic city to the Black Country coal; eventually a web of 200 miles of canals bored its way into and around the conurbation, making it the centre of the national canal network.

Birmingham proper embodies the centreless, shifting aspect of New Red places. In spite of heroic attempts at place-making by the local authority, its heart always feels like something stumbled on in an endless suburb. At least the Black Country hills such as the Wren's Nest render visible the landscape's rootedness in the resources of the rocks; Birmingham's amorphousness perhaps reflects its role as the place that sucks in and disperses the fruits of those resources. The pair embody the binary relationship of the two: the atriums and ventricles of the industrial-era Carboniferous/New Red synergy.

Bristol

Heading into the 'Y's mixed-up Variscan south-west, we come to Bristol, the urban expression of the region's quiet geohistorical eccentricity. Here, though the Carboniferous coalfield to the east fuelled the city's nascent industry, the visual relationship is, uniquely, between the New Red and

Carboniferous limestone. This brings upland into the city itself, making for Britain's most memorable urban mixed landscape.

Here is a place full of exceptions to the rule. Unlike its peers, Bristol was one of the most important settlements in the land even before the industrial era; whereas others powered through into the conurbations of today, Bristol's development was geohistorically strangled in mid-take-off, at once the most important settlement in the south-west and not quite a first-rank city.

The settlement was born around AD 1000, on a low New Red peninsula that separated crossing points of the rivers Avon and Frome. A circular town was laid out; after the Conquest, one of the mightiest castles in England, now effectively vanished, plugged the only land-based approach to the site.

By the twelfth century, this was England's major west-facing port, and one of its wealthiest settlements. From here were pioneered Atlantic exploration and trade, colonisation and slaving; a cultural seedbed for everything from the Reformation to Romanticism. And as it grew, so Bristol spread beyond its rivers.

The sandstone itself is most visible to the south of the Avon, where the mighty parish church of St Mary Redcliffe sits astride its eponymous New Red cliff. The proximity of sandy New Red rocks and Carboniferous coal led to a burgeoning industrial-era glass industry here (a common New Red pattern, also seen at St Helen's in Lancashire; and around Birmingham, where Chance Brothers' enormous factory made much of the Crystal Palace). In what was already a built-up area, quarrying for sand went into and under the red cliff, forming a memorable series of quarry-caves.

To the north, the sandstone climbs steeply towards Carboniferous Limestone upland. Bristol's cathedral and city hall sit on a New Red shelf overlooking the two rivers; behind them, Brandon Hill, a steep New Red knoll, embodies the city's exploratory spirit.

This was once topped by a hermitage dedicated to St Brendan, an Irish saint whose legend suggests an early exploration of the Atlantic. It is now home to a New Red Sandstone tower memorialising the sixteenth-century explorer John Cabot, who, supported by Bristol's burgesses, made the first modern-era landfall on north America.

By the eighteenth century, industrial-era expansion was climbing onto the high Carboniferous beyond. A wealthy population of plantation owners, tobacco magnates and merchants – almost all dependent on, or facilitating, slavery – draped the hillside with elegant squares and curving terraces. The visual panache of all this is a striking contrast to the dense and low-slung New Red core. Seek the hilltop – and one almost falls into the limestone gorge for which this area is named: Clifton ('the cliff village').

Clifton Gorge is so spectacular that eighteenth-century physician and antiquarian William Stukeley saw in it proof that volcanic explosions had accompanied the biblical flood (though in fact it is an ice-age creation, legend also implicates the giant Ghyston, AKA Vincent, in its making). And clustered on its edge there is an Iron Age hillfort; Ghyston Cave, whose medieval hermit might have prayed for the merchants whose fragile ships braved the rocks below; the little nineteenth-century camera obscura and observatory; and Isambard Kingdom Brunel's revolutionary, beautiful suspension bridge (from 1836). Few human attempts to defeat nature have greater visual flair. But it was a pyrrhic victory.

The gorge seals the historic quaysides of the city centre from the Bristol Channel. The hard limestone thus allowed an exceptionally well-protected port to develop inland. But the river's path over the New Red rocks was a sinuous one, and the sharp, hard limestone of the gorge meant boats had to wait for high tides to enter and depart if they were to avoid foundering, or a ripped hull.

With the industrial era came larger ships, eventually steam-powered; ironically, Bristol was at the forefront of this development, in the shape of Brunel's SS *Great Western* (1838) and *Great Britain* (1843). Upstaged by less constricted ports such as Liverpool and Glasgow, the citizens tried cheating nature by redirecting the Avon, moving the docks to Avonmouth. But ultimately the area's controlling geology was a factor in its slide from first-rank mercantile settlement to regional capital.

Bristol's stone buildings are dominated by a unique, three-way language: brittle, New Red rubble; squared blocks and flags of dusty greenish-grey Carboniferous Pennant; the crisp honey-yellow detailing of Jurassic limestones, also sourced nearby. Each structure has its own take on the resulting combinations of colour and texture; and many are as one-off as the city itself. From the fourteenth century, when the cathedral (then an abbey) was one of the most radical Gothic buildings in Europe, through eccentric warehouses such as the Granary (1871), a maverick Variscan individualism abounds.

The spirit survives in the city's modern role as a centre for alternative living and street culture; and the whole story is underpinned by the complex geohistorical relationship of Carboniferous upland and New Red lowland; the major urban expression of the complex Variscan character of the south-west.

Cardiff

Jump just 25 miles across the Severn, and you reach New Red Cardiff. This settlement has long mattered strategically: by the thirteenth century it was the largest town in Wales. But it came into its own in the industrial era, when it became the key to unlocking the landlocked Carboniferous resources of the Valleys, 15–20 miles to the north. As late as 1782, it was complained that 'we have no coal exported from this port, nor ever shall, as it would be too expensive to bring it down here from the internal part of the country'; all that was to change.

From 1794, a canal brought Merthyr iron to Cardiff, making it a major exporter of the metal. But it was John Crichton-Stuart, second marquess of Bute and overlord of much of the county, who transformed the situation. He developed the coalfields and from 1839 built docks on the River Taff, which linked the Valleys to the coast and had a harbour at its mouth near Cardiff. The railway arrived in 1841 and was soon funnelling coal and iron from each of the five Valleys to the Cardiff docks.

Export-focused trade boomed. A settlement with a little over 5,000 inhabitants in 1801 had almost 142,000 ninety years later, by which time Cardiff was the biggest exporter of coal in the world, and one of its major ports: 42 per cent of Welsh coal went overseas, compared to 11 per cent for the rest of Britain. As a result, John Patrick Crichton-Stuart, the third Marquess, was often claimed to be the richest man on the planet, and it was he who commissioned the architect William Burges to rework Cardiff castle, from 1869. The lavishly medieval zing of this place embodies the worldview of a man who was at once a feudal lord and a coal baron; it is also a hymn to the geology that was the source of his wealth.

This is a fantasy world deeply informed by the rocks. Much of the medieval curtain wall was rebuilt on its Roman base, using Carboniferous rocks that are visibly different from the Liassic older work; the joining-point is marked by a line of New Red, geology self-consciously used to indicate history. And inside, you enter a veritable lithophiliac fantasyland. The Bachelor Bedroom is decorated with paintings of Classical myths on the theme of the harnessing of the Earth's treasures, and labelled minerals from the Bute estates. One bathroom features a display of thirty-six kinds of marble, also labelled; another is lined with Triassic alabaster from nearby Penarth, with a bathtub made of marble from Rome. You could soak in a millionaire's bath, and then snuggle in bed, all while absorbing a series of geological lessons.

Cathays Park, just across the road, is a contrast to all this. The corporation had long been trying to win this site from the Butes. Success came in 1897–8; eight years later Cardiff was granted city status. In response a coordinated series of metropolitan, self-confident structures was built, using cool, hard, southern English Jurassic Portland limestone.

If it began life as a civic riposte to the feudal vision of the castle, Cathays Park became an attempt to create something that increasingly looked like a national capital; home to the National Museum of Wales and what has become the University of Wales, as well as the city council, county council and law courts. E.A. Rickards, one of its architects, even wrote a poem about its building stone: 'a tonnage of Portland stone, / shipped to a coal town as the century turned . . . / . . . unloaded in the dirt / beside the black, black coal that paid for it.' More recently, Bute's regenerated docks have been the site of a further sequence of national monuments, including the *Senedd*, or Welsh Assembly building, and the Wales Millennium Centre (2004). The latter's layered facades evoke an older, slatey Cambrian-to-Silurian Wales.

Synergistic mythospheres

Such cities make the ever-receptive New Red as powerful a repository of carboniferous culture as the Carboniferous itself. New Red Salford, not

Carboniferous Newcastle or Leeds, was the setting for Engel's studies of working-class life, and for LS Lowry's depictions of it; if half of Joy Division came from Carboniferous Macclesfield, the other half came from New Red Salford. Heathcliff may be the human embodiment of the gritstone Pennines, but he began life as a foundling in New Red Liverpool. Joseph Wright painted the carboniferous revolution at the moment of its birth – from a base in New Red Derby. Though carboniferous culture ultimately owes its birth to steam, and coal, the New Red as much as the Carboniferous is where it settled and developed.

More remarkably, the relationship seems to long predate the industrial era, and to be as alive in the imaginary of the rural New Red as the urban one. The landscape of *Gawain and the Green Knight* is as much New Red Wirral as Carboniferous Dark Peak. In a New Red/Carboniferous echo of the fourteenth-century vision of Piers Plowman (in which the 'smooth plain' below the Precambrian Malverns was the New Red Severn Valley), George Fox climbed Carboniferous Pendle Hill in 1652 and gazed west to the sea over the flatlands of New Red Lancashire, inspiring the founding of the Society of Friends (Quakers): 'From the top of this hill the Lord let me see in what places he had a great people to be gathered.' J.R.R. Tolkein's Shire may have been inspired by the New Red villages of his Warwickshire childhood (and the kingdom of Rohan loosely based on the Marches to the west); is Mordor, then, a smoking Carboniferous upland, the orcs merely hobbits transformed by a life led in factories, mines and mills?

And then there is Alan Garner. The work of this 2022 Booker Prize-nominated author is arguably more powerfully rooted in place than any other British writer, and that place is the Cheshire basin. The storied magic Garner has spun out of the landscape in which he lives – New Red Alderley Edge and its environs – short-circuits time as profoundly as any Midland crypt. Yet the nearby Carboniferous plays a fundamental role throughout: Shining Tor (*The Moon of Gomrath*), Mow Cop (*Red Shift*), the Pennine setting that dominates *Thursbitch*.

You don't have to spend long on Alderley Edge to sense its power. I was there in the deepest dusk and almost fell into some of the shadowy hollows and holes that open into the bare sandstone. Garner's *The Weirdstone of*

Brisingamen is inspired by the legend that somewhere beneath Stormy Point there is a cavern filled with treasure and sleeping men. Yet although some of the caves of the Edge may be ancient, they are mostly artificial.

Soft architectures

At the back of a garden in Nottingham, a life-size sandstone bed sits in a man-made cave. Another holds a tableau of *Daniel in the Lion's Den*, carved for a city alderman from 1856. These vernacular follies grace the gardens of the Park, an exclusive nineteenth-century estate close to the city centre.

Castle Rock rises directly above these gardens: a scarlet Sherwood Sandstone stone throne 40m high, carved by the Trent. Nottingham castle sits on top of it, a crag upon a crag. And it is riddled with more man-made hollows, including the tunnel in which Edward III caught the royal usurper Mortimer and Queen Isabella in 1330; and 'Mortimer's Hole' itself, a steep, 105m burrow that seems to have been the castle's goods entrance from the river. Many of the snugs in the Ye Olde Trip to Jerusalem, the famous ancient hostelry at the base of the cliff, are also excavated into the rock. For the stone on which the city sits is 'so soft that they easily work into it for making vaults and cellars, and yet so firm as to support the roofs' (Defoe). As early as the ninth century, Nottingham was called the 'house of caves'. An underworld of rock-carved air-raid shelters, tanneries, cool storage rooms, and even houses stretches below the Broadmarsh shopping centre: just some of the 500 or more artificial caves in this city.

All this is testament to a unique quality of the New Red Sandstone: it is generally too weak to make natural caves, but takes human reshaping easily enough that almost anyone can make a lasting impression on it. The result is a 'democratic architecture' of hollowed-out buildings, vernacular carvings and scratched graffiti.

Joseph Williamson, the 'mole of Edge Hill', is one of the most remarkable examples of this tendency. He dug a monumental labyrinth of tunnels below his Liverpool housing developments, 'vaulted passages . . . that run . . . nowhere . . . pits deep, and yawning chasms' (local historian Charles Hand). Begun in 1805 and intended as quarries, the scale of the result far exceeds its function; it may have become a philanthropic project, providing labour for the local unemployed. In Second World War Stockport, enormous subterranean air raid shelters were excavated into the sandstone cliffs; enough space for 3,000 bunk beds. In Salford, entire families inhabited cellars cut into the ground.

Not all this is urban. There are New Red Sandstone cave houses of Anglo-Saxon, medieval and eighteenth-century date at Anchor Church cave near Ingleby, not far from Repton; Redstone Rock, near Stourport; and Kinver Edge, above Stourbridge. Caynton Cave in New Red Shropshire is an elaborately carved neo-Romanesque folly. From about 1860, at Welbeck Abbey near New Red Worksop, the 5th Duke of Portland constructed an ambitious series of underground structures, including rooms up to 72m long and 890m tunnels.

And then there are the carvings. A cottage garden on the mid-Cheshire ridge sports a 4m-high sandstone elephant, complete with howdah, home-sculpted from the crumbling rock. A survey here has found heads that may be Iron Age in date and hand-carved seats used to watch Second World War dogfights: scratched sketches of passing Hurricanes are etched into them. Shallow carvings on New Red Bidston Hill, Wirral, are said by some to depict the Viking gods *Sunna* and *Mani* – Sun and Moon. The 'Sculptor's Cave' on the New Red Moray coast has Pictish carvings on its walls. In a curious Old Red/New Red connection, William Mounsey, the Victorian eccentric and adventurer who carved Persian complaints onto the Dwarfie Stane on Orkney, also fashioned inscriptions and images into the rock-faces of the New Red river Eden.

This is a rock that surrenders to the human touch; it is soft enough for anyone who wants to be able to shape it, yet tough enough to retain those traces. All this is relevant to the New Red's industrial story, which is defined by the ability of these rocks to reshape themselves, and their evaporative surrender to the desert heat.

Evaporated rocks

I've been up close and personal with Edward II. His tomb, a spiky Gothic fantasia in a dark Romanesque aisle of Gloucester cathedral, is the greatest medieval monument in Britain: and the effigy on it one of that era's most perfect works of art.

The king is a depicted as Christ-like, with flowing locks, a patrician beard, and the open eyes of the newly resurrected. His smooth body seems to emit a soft, halo-like glow. It is made of a glossy, soap-like substance which seems to hover somewhere between living flesh, exquisite corpse, and dead stone.

This is alabaster. To find it, the sculptor must have known of the best deposits of it in the land, which lie in the Midlands. Creation of the effigy meant sourcing a body-sized and flawless piece of this, and shipping it 73 miles south and west, presumably using the Severn, though it is also possible it travelled via London.

While the sculptor is anonymous, this is clearly a work of royal quality. The king had been murdered in 1327 by a party of his own barons; stories of miraculous healings flickered around his remains. It was in the interests of the young king Edward III to rehabilitate the reputation of the Crown by encouraging veneration here: nothing would do but the most shrine-like of royal tombs.

In the wake of its creation, the reputation of this material shot from Midlands specialism to national cult. Other kings and aristocrats used it for their effigies, and by the fifteenth century a minor industry was developing, manufacturing religious images called 'Nottingham alabasters', from their main place of trade.

These are extraordinary works of art, found from Iceland to Italy. And they could not exist without the subtle transformations that can take place in a familiar, white mineral, often found in deposits underground.

Salt

Salt is said to be the only geological substance that can be identified by taste alone; having once absent-mindedly reached for a Jaffa Cake and found myself taking a mouthful out of a lump of chalk, I beg to differ. But it is certainly the only rock that we eat. We would die without salt in our bodies, and it has been of huge use to humanity.

Salt enhances flavour; it also sucks moisture from materials, lowers the freezing point of water, increases electrical conductivity, has been essential to the manufacture of both acid and alkaline chemicals, especially chlorine; and makes a good surfactant (witness dishwasher salt).

But perhaps most important of all is the simple fact that for centuries salt was effectively the only way people could preserve food. This made it a politically charged material. The 1707 Act of Union, which placed England and Scotland under a single monarch, devotes a long clause to regulating its trade. The sea journeys of the Age of Empire depended on sources in strategic locations such as Cape Verde and the Bahamas. Its usages multiplied in the industrial era, a 'chemical revolution' in which salt became important in making everything from glass to disinfectant, explosives to petroleum.

Permo-Triassic salt deposits occur in various places – a former salt and gypsum mine runs below Long Meg in the New Red Eden Valley – but the most important are in the Cheshire Basin, where deep seams lie buried in the Mercia Mudstone. They were left behind when saline water evaporated rapidly in the desert sun. Their extraction is one of Britain's oldest industries, and is still active.

For centuries, the salt was accessed by evaporating the waters of briny springs. Iron Age implements used in this process have been found at Droitwich in northern Worcestershire, an important early centre, and around Middlewich and Nantwich in Cheshire. A group of Roman roads seem to converge on Middlewich, possibly known to the Romans simply as *Salinae*; by the medieval period, quite a number of important roads were known simply as 'salt street' or the 'salt way'. Salt could provide health as well as wealth: the warm, briny waters of Droitwich make it (like Leamington) a New Red spa town.

Thanks to this industry, towns such as Nantwich became wealthy mercantile centres. No fewer than thirty-nine places have names relating to the trade, and since the 'wichs' of Nant-, Middle- Left- Droit- and Northwich were all salt-trading towns, salt works in general came to be called 'wichs' too (Cheshire has a remarkably high number of geologically derived place names: 'bachs' like Sandbach, are 'beaches' of young, sandy earths sitting on top of the New Reds). Though most salt at this period came from the sea, the Cheshire salts were purer.

Near Runcorn in 1670, a failed attempt to find local coal as a fuel for brine evaporation turned into a chance discovery of rock salt. This is much purer than brine, and also needs less processing; competition from it caused significant tension between the traditional 'brine men' and the new 'rock men'.

Salt mining was dangerous, as any ingress of water could cause the salt to dissolve and the mines to collapse. While this could occur naturally, it could also result from the flushing of water underground to aid mining, or the over-extraction of the surface brine above. Salt dissolution below the ground could cause serious subsidence: some Cheshire meres, such as the linear waters near Winsford known as 'flashes', are one result.

In spite of such challenges, magnates such as the Marshalls of Northwich leased collieries and built canals to get Carboniferous coal to Cheshire (and Liverpool) for use in industrial-scale salt-processing. By 1890, 90 per cent of British salt came from the county, and the industry's consumption of coal created large areas of 'smoke and smother'.

Cheshire and the Liverpool environs were by then a centre for the chemical industries: Imperial Chemical Industries/ICI had most of its 121 British offices here. Lever Brothers used Cheshire salt in the world's first industrially produced household soap; their model town, Port Sunlight, was developed by Lord Leverhulme for his employees, and partly built with New Red from his quarries at Storeton, in the Wirral.

Such industries still make parts of northern Cheshire into that rare thing in modern Britain, an active industrial landscape; they also mean subsidence afflicts many of the area's settlements. The mine at Winsford, opened in 1844, is still active: it has more than 137 miles of tunnels, accessing seams about 25m thick: the main source in Britain of road salt, a gift of the Pangean desert that keeps our cars safe on winter days. Its 8m-high rooms are supported by pillars of the stuff, each a potential spouse for Lot.

A more recent mine removes Permian salts buried 1,100m below the surface at Boulby near Saltburn, Cleveland. It was first mined, for potash, in the 1960s: this potassium-rich material, a very effective fertiliser, is often found in salt deposits. Today extraction focuses on a salt called polyhalite, huge deposits of which were found below the potash in 2010:

the only such mine in the world. The mine also produces rock salt: 620 miles of tunnels have been excavated all told. An underground laboratory researches everything from Dark Matter to life in extreme environments.

Gypsum

As the waters evaporated in the Pangean sun, crystallising salt might bond with molecules of calcium and water. The resulting transformation into gypsum is the first link in the chain that connects common salt with the effigy of Edward II. Gypsum is a very common material, and it has historically been useful thanks to a reversal of the simple process that created it: evaporation. The largest, most dependable deposits in Britain are also those from which alabaster comes: for alabaster is merely gypsum in hardened form. They lie in a low escarpment hard by the Trent near Tutbury.

Heat gypsum and much of its burden of water evaporates. Grind the result into a powder and you can transport it. Add water again and the pasty solution gradually expands – and sets, retaining whatever shape has been imposed on it (one is effectively turning it back into gypsum). Gypsum, then, is Plaster of Paris ('gypsum' comes from the Greek for plaster). The term indicates its traditional source, for the hill of Montmartre is made of the stuff.

Gypsum has been used architecturally, not least to make plaster decorations, or, today, plasterboard and cement. Mixed with reeds, it has made a good flooring material. But its applications are broad. Though highly soluble, it resists fire and chemical attack, and so is useful for making moulds for metal. It is a good whitener: as 'silver in the woods' it whitened doorsteps in the Eden Valley; as gesso, its whitening layer underlies countless works of art; it is also a fertiliser. And it has some unexpected ramifications.

Beer

In Burton upon Trent, gypsum has leached into the local groundwater, giving the local beer a subtle mineral flavour and extending its life. The result, Pale Ale, was once the unique product of a town which developed thirty-one breweries, producing a quarter of all British beer, and included Bass, the largest brewery in the world. Comparable geologies at Tadcaster give their flavour to Samuel Smith's ales; elsewhere, beers were 'burtonised' by adding gypsum. That Pale Ale was shipped to India, and fared well over the voyage of several months, is an indication of its suitability for long-distance export. This particular blend became known as India Pale Ale, or IPA.

The most dramatic gypsum quarryscape is an unexpected and disturbing monument at Fauld, Staffordshire. Here, a nineteenth-century gypsum mine was used in the Second World War as an ammunition store, and one day in 1944, it exploded. This catastrophic event killed up to seventy people and wiped a farm of the face of the Earth. The enormous crater that resulted, 90m deep and 230m in diameter, is surrounded by barbed wire; it comes as a shock in the gentle green Midland pasturelands.

The perimeter footpath is littered by fragments of the white, dry rock that here lies close to surface of the gypsum deposits: the alabaster used to evoke the body of a martyred king.

Alabaster

Under certain conditions, gypsum can be naturally rehydrated. It then becomes alabaster. In the Midlands this occurred near the surface permafrost of the ice age, and resulted in a stone that is slightly translucent, and ivory off-white, with fine, consistent grains that are easy to carve.

The Gloucester sculptor could have marked it with a fingernail, let alone a chisel; he would have worked it with carpenter's tools, and polished and cleansed it as if it was leather or wood.

Alabaster warms quickly, and softens under heat (burnt, it makes a good, hard plaster). It quickly absorbs whatever is around it, be it candle-smoke, the oils of the human hand, or paint. It was mined around Tutbury from the Roman period onwards, and a precocious use of it can be seen in the twelfth-century doorway of the church there, where its tendency to dissolve in the Midlands rain is all too visible.

But its heyday was the fifteenth century. Over 3,000 Nottingham alabasters, with their long-fingered, high-cheekboned depictions of sacred scenes, survive. Heads of St John the Baptist, of which ninety are known, could be had pre-carved for a shilling; 150 tons a year were mined in Staffordshire. Given that fifty carved panels could be made from a single 4-ton block, that's a lot of sculpture.

After the Reformation killed the market for religious images, alabaster remained popular for tombs. Its purest deposits were worked out – only the uppermost few feet is pure white – and fashion shifted to varieties veined with a New-Red appropriate shade of salmon-pink, making it look even more like marble, while adding a blood-like quality to the rock's soapy flesh consistency; other varieties have a green tinge shivering through them. In addition to tombs, Derbyshire alabaster was being used in 1686 to make delightful 'Candle-sticks, plates and Fruit dishes'. 'Satin spar' (Selenite) from the gypsum was used in jewellery. The domed, 15m-high Marble Hall at Holkham Hall, Norfolk (1734) is made entirely of it. We are moving into the territory of building stones.

These rocks have embraced a series of contradictions. They have visibly been made of deserts, yet are associated with much that is watery; they were born in barren country, yet today support some of the greenest landscapes in Britain. They underlie many rural landscapes, yet helped create the supply lines of the industrial era, becoming the setting for some of its mightiest cities. They are notable both for a claggy historical rootedness and a responsive historical dynamism. They also sit at a fulcrum: the end-point of a great sequence of tectonic events, which gave us hard, intractable rocks – and the start of the young, easeful, giving rocks of the south-east third of our island, with its Jurassic and Cretaceous scarplands.

Lower Jurassic – Liassic group outcrops

Upper Jurassic – Limestone

Upper Jurassic – Oxfordian & Kimmeridgian or High Ground

Watling Street

Chester

R.Trent

Fosse Way

R. Severn

R. Thames

R. Exe

R. Severn

Stamford &
Burghley House

Helpston

Barnack

Peterborough

Birmingham

Felton

Coventry

Naseby

Ely

Evesham

Bredon Hill

Cleeve Hill

Cotswolds

The Rollright
Stones

Birdlip Hill

Painswick

Blenheim
Palace

Oxford

The Ridgeway

Bristol

Bath

Box

The Chilterns

Cardiff

Severn Estuary

Uffington Horse

The Mendips

North Downs

Cherhill

Brent Hill

Polden Hills

Glastonbury

Salisbury

Stoney Littleton

R. Exe

Burrow Mump

Ham Hill

Exeter

Kimmeridge

Corfe Castle

Jurassic Coast

Chesil Beach

Portland

Lulworth Cove

0   50   miles

Chapter 10

Jurassic scarplands
201–145 million years ago

Oceanic metaphors come easy in south-eastern Britain. Escarpments roll like mighty parallel waves across the landscape, 'stretching like a manifest great crest' (Leland). Ancient monuments sit like frozen surfers on the ridges that mark the wave-tops. The froth of a stony outcrop is rare: each wave seems poised at the moment before it actually breaks.

There are some higher sections to these long waves; at other times they lose their definition. And sometimes a river breaks through them and a gap is opened in the wave itself.

Bath is one such place. The Bristol Avon has cut through the hills here. A slow erosional maelstrom, it has sculpted the highest part of the ridge into scooped valleys and knolls, making for a landscape that is both bucolic and dramatic, and grand without being wild.

At the heart of this gap the river takes a bend, and a gulf in the hills opens out, its floor shelving gently into a floodplain. This spot has been known for millennia. The long wave-edge is a natural routeway: follow it, and this is where you descend to the riverside.

Nearby there is a presence that must once have been unnerving, even uncanny. I wonder how it struck its first visitors. Hidden among wildwood and scrub, it would have first been obvious by the sound – 250,000 gallons/1.1 million litres of water a day, emerging from underground and pouring into the river – and the steam: for the water comes out at a painful 113°F/45°C. And then there was the low, pervading pungency of sulphur. Draw close, and the floodplain is a boggy morass, with large pools, 'reaking like a seething pot continuously' (Leland).

Like some geohistorical whirlpool, this natural hot spring has drawn history towards itself. We know it has had a special reputation since the Iron Age, when the goddess Sul presided over it. In Roman times an important spa developed; the name of the city that was to grow around it, *Aquae Sulis* and later Bath, is clear about its *raison d'être*. Yet to walk around in, everything seems to be of a single, relatively recent, era.

In the eighteenth century, high society decamped here every summer. The city was effectively rebuilt. Controlled, genteel squares and circuses climb the hills. The only thing to suggest a more ancient origin is the sixteenth-century Gothic of the abbey church, which once owned the spring.

Bath is spectacular, but it is also one-dimensional: as if all the layers had been washed out of it. For thousands of years, the site has barely ever been abandoned (the most conspicuous silence comes after the departure of the Romans). Yet there is only one place where you can really feel this deep continuity.

A Georgian bath complex stands next to the abbey. Behind it are the battered, but substantial remains of the Roman Great Bath. The true climax of this place lies between them: an odd-shaped stone-walled pool known as the King's Bath. This is the original sacred spring, and it is visibly a patchwork of stone from Roman times onwards, with all the irregularity and oddness that implies. If Bath in general is time and geology tamed, then at the King's Bath they are rewilded; one can almost sniff that boggy, steaming clearing in the trees, and watch an entire city birthed from it.

The hot spring is not the only thing that pulls this landscape together. From Roman pediments to the buildings of the modern spa, everything here is of the same warm, honey-coloured, fine-grained limestone. And all this stone comes from the surrounding slopes.

The spring is a geological phenomenon, too. Rain that falls on the Carboniferous Limestone of the Mendips descends 1.6–2.7 miles below the ground, following a long Variscan curve until it returns upwards, 18 miles away and thousands of years later, having been heated and suffused with minerals.

Bath is a great harmony of geology, history, architecture and landscape, rooted in the gifts of the Earth. We have visited other places with something of this quality, but perhaps Bath's only equal is Edinburgh. They make a fine pair: one a place of mountains, visibly the creation of plate tectonics and glacial carving; the other a great dip, its verdant rocks made in and eroded by water. And if Edinburgh's Carboniferous sandstone is a very Scottish (and northern English) rock, Bath's Jurassic limestone is oh-so-English. Indeed this rock and its variants in England's 'stone belt' – the long outcrop of mid-Jurassic rocks that includes Bath – are the Jurassic era's great contribution to the geohistorical story.

Bath exemplifies much about the rocks of this period. Their English focus, their fine building stones – many of them freestones – and also the character of the landscapes they form, and the genteel England that makes places like the Cotswolds so popular. River-carved gaps in escarpments make obvious sites for settlements: Bath is one, Lincoln another.

This is the landscape of the scarplands. The escarpments are its leading edges: they seem to advance across the landscape, engulfing the softer rocks at their foot. Explore the wave-top and find a drystone-walled pastureland that slopes into a gradual descent known as a 'dipslope'. Eventually the slope flattens into a broad, clay vale, interrupted only by the wavelets of occasional hills, and shoal-like clusterings of towns and villages. Beyond, the next stone breaker – at Bath this is the Cretaceous chalk – awaits.

Scarpland geologies

The rocks of the scarplands are the result of a seaward shift in our story which began in the late Triassic, and replaces the freshwater-and-desert rocks of the New Red with seawater-deposited Liassic ones. Such waters will dominate the next 137 million years or so, as we move through two successive geological periods: the Jurassic and the Cretaceous.

These ingresses of the sea are partly caused by the break-up of Pangea. This is an epochal development, for pieces of that supercontinent became land-masses that are still with us. At the other end of the planet, the south Atlantic has begun to open. The distant echoes of such events created fault-systems and opened basins into which these waters might move.

For now, we are in an island-studded sea between major land masses, and have reached the latitude of the Mediterranean. Reptiles are the dominant life-forms: ichthyosaurs in the warm waters of the seas; ammonites without number; great land monsters. Human reactions to their traces will form an intriguing twist to our story.

The landforms of the era make human history a series of clear proposals. Each is a linear, elongated stone throne. This wave edge can almost seem engaged in geological surveillance of the clay vale below. Hillforts slobber on ridge-edges, intervisible for miles on end on the mid-Jurassic limestone between Bredon Hill and Painswick, Gloucestershire; or the Cretaceous chalk between Uffington and Cherhill, Wiltshire. Such scarps played a strategic role in the outcome of the battles of Towton (1461) and Naseby (1645), and in the modern era their level, well-drained, fault-free rocks have made the scarp-tops particularly popular for airfields and military bases: 'a giant aircraft carrier anchored off northwest Europe' one expert called this concentration (which also extends onto the younger rocks of East Anglia). The stop-lines planned to hold back the Wehrmacht often run with the scarpland ridges.

The escarpments are also a kind of road: the track that follows the Jurassic ridge to Bath, today the A46, is one such 'ridgeway'. The modern Ridgeway National Trail, here running along the Cretaceous chalk scarp, is another. The history of such routes is hard to pin down, and they can shift significantly, but the Romans did much to fix them into the landscape. Ermine Street, one of this island's great historic arteries, follows the Lincolnshire scarp for much of its length; in 1066, when Harold Godwinson and his army rode from New Red Stamford Bridge to Cretaceous Hastings, or when Edward I built Eleanor Crosses along the route of his wife's funeral cortege from Lincoln to Westminster in the 1290s, a substantial part of their journey followed this ridge.

As they drive their way across the landscape, the scarps make very visible the westish- to north-westish-facing exposure of most Jurassic and Cretaceous rocks. This is a new, and very marked, grain to the British landscape: I call it the 'Atlantic Grain'.

Limestone and Chalk

The limestone and the chalk are the dominant formations of their respective periods, and they created the most important scarps. They are akin in other ways, too. The Jurassic limestone is different in character to the dense material we have grown used to: its constituent particles are quite visible, and it does not make sink-holes or cave systems. All this is also true of the chalk; this rock is essentially a variety of limestone.

Partly because they absorb water so readily, these landscapes are scored by valleys that are either dry, or followed by a stream that is too tiny to have carved such a path – the rest of the water simply sinks in. There is something inexplicable about such valleys, a strangeness that helps rescue some limestone and chalk places from an oblivion of prettiness. Each is a ghostly but special placelet of its own; if there is a stream it will run swift and clear, and villages will drink from it in a sheltered chain that is delectable to follow: try the Dunt in Jurassic Gloucestershire, or the aptly named Chalke in Cretaceous Wiltshire. Place names distinguish 'deans', long, gentle, narrow valleys, more common on the dipslope, from 'coombes', which are shorter, steeper, more bowl-like, and most common on the scarp.

Like all limestones, these rocks make grassland uplands; but these are never especially high, and their relatively benign environment and thin, grain-friendly soils, easily cleared of scrub, made them an early centre for agriculture.

But ultimately the clay vales were better places to settle, and the tops became pasturelands, preserving traces of an ancient past that is largely invisible below; they remain open in feel, with few settlements. The many '-ham' place names indicate a settlement in an isolated place. Though today they are dominated by agri-industrial fields, the Cotswolds were once open heath, full of 'high wild hills and rough uneven ways' as Northumberland puts it in Shakespeare's *Richard II*; it was once so easy to get lost on Lincoln Edge that in 1751 the Dunston pillar, a unique inland lighthouse, was built there.

As grain fields, their products helped feed the Roman empire. As pastures they provided particularly good-quality wool, making them engines of prosperity. Yet the younger cover is where almost all the 'deserted medieval villages' of England lie: quietly haunting places of shallow earthworks, perhaps with a lonely church standing in the middle of fields.

The clay vales have a somewhat symbiotic relationship with the scarplands, not least because these relatively featureless landscapes give the limestone and chalk heights a drama that far exceeds their actual elevation. Like the marly plains of the Triassic they are dense with settlement, and while some places are very fertile – the Liassic Vale of Evesham is famous for its fruit – in others woodland is common. A tract of royal forest centered on the heavy Oxford clays ran from the Wash to Dorset. Much of this is farmland today.

Where it reaches the scarp-foot, the impervious clay is topped by porous limestone and chalk, and the water that falls on the wolds and downs above suddenly springs out. Strings of villages follow this 'springline': the roads that connect them, such as the B4507/Ickneild way between Wanborough, Wiltshire and Wantage, Oxfordshire, make a geohistorical join-the-dots. Parishes run in linear strips from scarp-foot to scarp-top, giving each community a share in the wet clay country, the steep scarp-edge, and the dry tops: a human 'grain' of boundaries running at right angles to the geological one made by the scarps themselves.

All in all, these stones should not be underestimated. The Jurassic limestone holds the greatest concentration of first-rate freestones in Britain; and while chalk and limestone may sound rather alike, in fact the landscape often simply called 'the chalk' has one of the most distinctive geohistorical characters in this book. Not for nothing were these two rock-types given specific names very early. The Germanic *lim* and *cealc* describe their key qualities from a human's point of view: sources of lime/calcium, useful as both mortar and fertiliser; the latter word is also freighted with implications of softness, whiteness, and usefulness for marking things. This chalk will dominate the story of the Cretaceous.

Jurassic landscapes

The arrangement of the Jurassic rocks is relatively simple. There are a handful in Scotland and, as with the Triassic, they have often attracted human attention. Parts of Skye, Raasay and Mull benefit from their fertile soils, if compromised by heavy rain, poor drainage and interrupting volcanic rock; they have also yielded building stones and iron ores. Other exposures are smaller.

The Jurassic outcrop proper then starts in North Yorkshire, from where it runs continuously to the Dorset coast – a 300-mile strip running north-east to south-west across the country, in places over 70 miles wide, along which the Jurassic's geohistorical themes repeat and rebound.

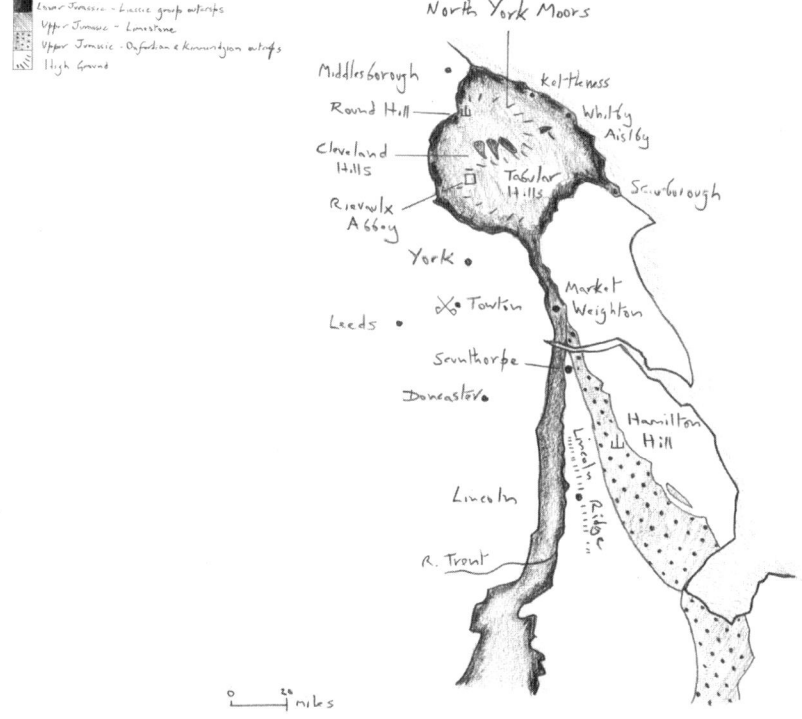

Within this, the main contrast is between the rocks of the North York Moors and the rest. Laid down in an ever-changing coastal and riverine environment in the 'Cleveland Basin', the moors are almost a mini-Pennines. Like that range they make high, bare-formed hills ('brows') capped by a hard, grainy (mid-Jurassic) sandstone, and are rich in resources. The Cleveland ('cliff-land') hills are their much-indented northern scarp: here, at Round Hill, Urra Moor (454m) in the north-west is the highest ground made by the Jurassic, and indeed the entire younger cover. The Hambleton hills form the western scarp; the southern edge, the flat-topped Tabular Hills, fall to the Vale of Pickering, a flatland of Jurassic clay. On their eastern side the North Sea cuts clean across them, making high cliffs.

The change to the 'classic Jurassic' starts after we pass a buried group of hard ancient rocks known as the Market Weighton High. From here southwards a series of formations spread out like skeins of wool, widening and becoming more emphatic after they pass beneath the Humber and enter Lincolnshire.

From west to east and from oldest to youngest, these rocks start with lowland vales of early Jurassic or Liassic rocks: clays and mudstones, with hills of Blue Lias limestone, they are the products of changing environments, and often rich in organic remains. Then, in the middle of the period, the scarp- and dipslope-forming mid-Jurassic limestones are the detritus of a warm, shallow sea. The waters deepen in the late Jurassic, creating the Oxford and Kimmeridge clays. Reefs in their calm, spreading vales have left their traces as occasional hills of 'Corallian' limestone; the later clays are rich in carbon. The clay-dominated story spreads on into the Cretaceous, the chalk scarp of which is the next incoming wave.

But the mid-Jurassic limestones are the defining entity. Bath is set in them. The Lincoln Edge and the Cotswolds are where their scarp is most emphatic, though their highest point (Cleeve Hill, Gloucestershire), is fully 124m lower than that of the North York Moors. Between the two, in an area centered on Northamptonshire, a coast drew nearer and iron became concentrated in the rocks: here the scarp loses its definition and a curious and motley range of chocolate-brown rocks known as ironstones dominate. As we head south of Bath the Cotswold heights fall away and things become Variscanly varied, especially as one nears the Dorset coast. Here the grain of the geology does a dog-leg and starts to run east–west, creating a spectacular mixed landscape of hidden valleys that often run parallel to the sea. I call this east–west tendency the 'Alpine Grain'.

The features that make this coast so entrancing are often the result of this new grain: Lulworth Cove is a perfect O, albeit open to one side, where the sea has eroded two east–west 'Alpine' arms of rock. The cliffs from Devon to Hampshire trace the story of the rocks from the Carboniferous to the Quaternary, but the Dorset stretch – the 'Jurassic coast' – is their centrepiece. One could explore this territory, and then Shropshire, and finally jump north to Assynt, and tell the entire story of the British rocks while immersing oneself in what are arguably this island's three finest mixed landscapes.

The sequence of relatively varied early Jurassic Liassic rocks, mid-Jurassic harder limestones, and late Jurassic clays holds true throughout. Within this, the dominant geohistorical story is of building materials, especially the (mostly) mid-Jurassic limestones. Their most important quarries were clustered where stone quality was high and water transport accessible: around Stamford in Lincolnshire; in northern Oxfordshire; around Bath; and in various smaller pockets of the south-west. Portland and Bath stone are so famous that almost everyone is aware of them; but Ancaster in Lincolnshire, Barnack, Clipsham and Ketton near Stamford, Taynton in Oxfordshire, and Ham Hill and Purbeck in the south-west are among further names that get the pulses of any stone-lover racing.

But they are not the only geohistorical aspects of these rocks. The North York Moors are home to the most considerable range of resources in the younger cover: iron, jet, alum. There is more iron in the ironstones of Northamptonshire, and the youngest Jurassic clays are significant for their fossil fuels. And the whole escarpment-wave formed by the mid-Jurassic rocks plays an intriguing role as a kind of historical snagging line in the younger cover: like Bath, its greatest city, it almost seems to suck geohistorical energies into itself. It is, after all, a mighty thing in the gentle context of the British south-east, seen coming for miles across the landscape's ocean, a wave in the wake of which much is subtly changed.

The 'Jurassic divide'

Nowhere in the country does landscape mimic sea-edge more vividly than at places like Birdlip Hill in Gloucestershire. Gazing out over oceanic expanses of inner England, it is not hard to believe that this scarp-edge might be a kind of geohistorical dam, holding back a store of historical forces.

But a wave is a moving thing, its limits ever-shifting. In general the younger cover marks the wealthiest portion of Britain, and arguably the area with the greatest density of settlement over time. Yet within this generalisation, the scarps work as snagging-points for history's flow. And the mid-Jurassic scarp is the most substantial of all. A whole host of historical tendencies which start to emerge as we hit the Permo-Triassic can seem to gather most thickly around it, and then put down their deepest roots as we move beyond its ridge and into the country that lies to the south and east of it: the fuzzy-edged geohistorical boundary of the mid-Jurassic wave.

This ridge plays a vital role in distributing the water that hits southern Britain: the Thames rises on its dipslope; its scarp separates that river from both the Severn and the Trent.

As we hit the Neolithic, it lies at the centre of a family of ambitious 'Cotswold-Severn' long barrows. That at Stoney Littleton in Somerset has an enormous Jurassic ammonite fossil at its entrance, like some totemic creature of stone.

Typically for the Jurassic divide, this phenomenon bleeds into a wider area: though about 140 examples sit on the Cotswolds, the remaining sixty run from Carboniferous/Devonian Gower to Cretaceous Wiltshire. Likewise, all but a handful of the sixty-six or more known causewayed enclosures in Britain lie to the south and east of the scarp. And by the late Iron Age, almost all the cultures that had started to produce coins and build proto-towns (*oppida*) also lay in this portion of the younger cover, which is also the part of Britain that draws closest to the continent.

But the theme really comes into its own in the Roman period. Here the 'Jurassic Divide' snaps into linear definition in the form of the Fosse Way. Straightness aside, this is an ordinary-looking country road: yet it remains the best route from parts of southern England to the East Midlands and the North: many research trips for this book began with a bleary-eyed dawn drive along it.

For a period of time in the AD 40s, this road lined the boundary of Rome itself, helping defend the south-east of Britain while providing supply lines to the north and west. Eventually, Roman villas clustered with special density on the dipslope to its west, suggesting both a zone of grain production and an atmosphere of quiet agrarian wealth.

Right through the medieval period the Fosse remained the only major route in England to follow the camber of the rocks rather than fan out from London. Not always a classic ridgeway, it moves between the edges of the Liassic and the mid-Jurassic rocks, and can drift down onto the Triassic – but it always runs parallel to the mid-Jurassic scarp-edge.

In the early medieval period the ridge formed an edgeland along which incoming and British cultures, and, later, competing Anglo-Saxon kingdoms, rubbed against each other: the lands of the Hwicce and those of Wessex, for example. Other patterns are more unexpected.

The ridge seems to become a kind of 'naughty step' beyond which 'bad' medieval kings could be buried with suitable dignity, if suitably isolated from the traditional royal mausoleums of Winchester, Westminster and Windsor. So the burial places of King John, Edward II and Richard III – Worcester, Gloucester and Leicester respectively – lie west of it; all other monarchs buried in England lie to the east. From this perspective, this New Red-dominated country becomes a kind of edgeland, not *quite* 'one of us' from the point of view of the south-eastern, Jurassic-and-later geohistorical elite.

Industrial-era enclosure created a distinction between 'ancient' and 'planned' countryside in the world of the younger cover. The latter zone is where freshly enclosed land is focused, and while it bleeds onto the central Triassic and parts of the Cretaceous, it is centered broadly on the Jurassic. John Clare, the nature poet, grieved over how 'Inclosure came and every path was stopt / Each tyrant fix'd his sign where paths were found' in his mid-Jurassic village of Helpston, the open fields of which were enclosed between 1809 and 1820.

James Hawes, from whom I have taken the phrase 'Jurassic divide', has published a series of maps which illustrate further such patterns. As I look at them, the impression strengthens of a scarp that holds back great stores of power and privilege: the most wealthy counties in medieval England; the greatest strongholds of nineteenth-century Anglicanism; the majority of Conservative constituencies at various dates. As ever, looked at more closely, the division is first detectable in Permo-Triassic areas, but it is after the scarp that it reaches its greatest intensity.

No wonder that the scarp plays an important role in the psycho-geography of modern England; for many, the 'North' jokingly begins at the pass through low Jurassic hills in Northamptonshire known as Watford Gap. Through this runs Watling Street/the A5, the Grand Union canal, the mainline from Euston, and the M1 – routes that embody the funnelling of wealth, power and people between north and south (but usually in the southerly direction) that is such a theme of English history.

All in all, a south-east English sense of comfortable superiority, it seems, is both very old, and to a significant extent, bordered by this ridge.

Industry

Not that the North is a backwater. I approached Whitby on the stillest, clearest evening imaginable: the North Sea was a glass mirror, the hilltop abbey a dark crystal ruin. The cliffs slumped happily away below me, a steep and stripey array of layered rocks. It was hard to imagine this place as a centre of industry, let alone a boom town whose industry was gloom.

The town falls down the shoulders of these cliffs until it hits the Esk, which runs from the Cleveland Hills. The North York Moors are full of such sudden valleys, formed where rivers have cut through their hard mid-Jurassic sandstone capping and exposed the softer, more varied Liassic rocks below.

Such places are hidden until you stumble into them, but generous and fertile within; like the dry valleys of the Cotswolds on some wild steroid.

Flagged paths known as 'trods' connect high ground to market towns. The liassic valleys are lined by drystone walls that stop where the hard upper sandstones begin, and in them the many resources of the region are accessible.

Where, as here, these valleys hit the coast, they make openings known as 'wykes'. The slumped grandeur of the cliffscape, its instability caused by the varied layers of the Liassic rocks, reminded me of the western part of the Dorset coast, a world of landslips, and cliffs from which fossils almost seem to want to break free. The connection had good cause, for that stretch of the 'Jurassic coast' is also Liassic.

These rocks are the detritus of a coast drained by mighty rivers, its shore thick with decaying trees. And they are jammed with resources; seventeenth- and eighteenth-century Whitby grew rich on one of these: alum. It developed a shipbuilding industry to service that trade, importing coal to fuel alum-processing works. It also became a major distribution centre for coal itself: 30 per cent of north-eastern coal came through here.

Alum is partly derived from iron. It was important for its ability to fix dyes to woollen textiles. For a long time it was mostly imported; the sources around Whitby were discovered in about 1608. The complex processing involved has been described as the 'first chemical industry': the works at Kettleness have made a desert of that headland.

Later, Whitby fell into decline. The harbour was too small for nineteenth-century ships; the demand for alum fell away. The local industrial story had in any case by then moved into the Cleveland Hills in pursuit of iron.

This iron has long been won from the valleys of the North York Moors. Rievaulx Abbey, Eskdale, was one important pre-industrial centre. But it was industrial-era mining, plus the demand created by the Bessemer process, that transformed the industry: 21 per cent of British iron was of Jurassic origin in 1860; 93 per cent in 1937 – and most of this came from Cleveland.

Whitby was now a sideshow compared to Teeside, connected by rail to the mines, and at the core of a Jurassic/Triassic/Carboniferous reprise of the classic Triassic/Carboniferous synergy. Situated between the Carboniferous coal of County Durham and the Jurassic iron ore of the North York Moors, and with access to the sea via the New Red mouth of the Tees, New Red (and Magnesian Limestone) settlements like Sunderland and Middlesbrough became important industrial centres.

Sunderland's great shipworks were just one result. Middlesbrough, which sits on the New Red/Lias border, went from little more than a farm to a settlement 91,000 strong in the eighty years after its foundation in the 1820s. The Middlesbrough Transporter Bridge dominates the town like a great metal beast; it was forged here by Dorman Long, who also made the Tyne Bridge at Newcastle, and Sydney Harbour Bridge in Australia: the products of a powerful whirlpool of Carboniferous energy, Triassic transport routes and Jurassic metal ores.

But you won't find shops in Whitby specialising in local iron, or alum-mordanted wool. There are, however, any number of chances to purchase things crafted from a stone so black it seems to absorb light.

This is jet. It originated as monkey puzzle-like trees, decaying slowly in brackish, oxygen-free swamps (it is thus a kind of coal, thin seams of which were also mined on the North York Moors). It can be shaped and polished; its alluring waxy sheen is potentially reflective enough to be used as a mirror. It often gives off static electricity, which may have given it supernatural associations in early times.

Jet jewellery is known as early as the Bronze Age, and the products of Roman jet workshops in York/*Eboracum* have been found as far afield as Germany. Sourced on the shores and cliff around Whitby, production has been centred on the town since at least the eighteenth century. Frighteningly, labourers were winched down these cliffs in baskets, a practice known as 'dessing', in order to access their shallow fragile drift mines. But jet is just one of several geohistorical qualities that gather around Whitby like swathes of dry ice. To explore this aspect of this remarkable dense place, we need to go back to the start of its story.

Whitby Gothic

Grand, shattered, dark and right by the cliff-edge, it is hard to imagine a ruin more apparently designed to grace the cover of an albumful of dirgey riffs than Whitby Abbey. Yet this is a site of huge significance.

At once defensible, eremitic and well connected, it was perfect for early Christians, and a monastic community was founded there by St Hilda.

She was an important figure in early English Christianity, and also the focus of a wonderful geo-cultural story: the land is struck by a plague of snakes, and miraculously Hilda solves the problem by turning them to stone. Remarkably, the same legend crops up again 250 miles south-west along the Jurassic, at Keynsham in Somerset, where another prominent holy woman, St Keyne, enacted the same miracle.

Such stories are surely a response to the many 'stones in form of serpents folded and wreathed up' (Fiennes) found in the Jurassic limestone: fossilized ammonites. The *Hildoceras* variety is named after Hilda.

Destroyed by the Vikings and later refounded, by the thirteenth century the site of Hilda's monastery was centred on a clifftop church of cathedral-like proportions. This became the blackened sandstone ruin of today after the dissolution of the monasteries; the wild drama of its setting, combined with tales of local shipwrecks, inspired Bram Stoker to set *Dracula* in Whitby.

The medieval Gothic church thus helped inspire a work of Victorian Gothic horror, even as Victorian mourning culture transformed Whitby's economy. Queen Victoria wore black following the death of her husband Albert, but permitted herself jet jewellery. The idea caught on and soon, the Jurassic forests of the North York Moors winked a sepulchral ebony gleam from the breasts of the grieving wives of Britain, and the Whitby jet industry was employing around 1,500 people. Remembering Hilda, Victorian visitors also came away with 'snakestones' – ammonites carved with serpents' heads. The fossil even features on the town's coat of arms.

More Jurassic industry

The North York Moors are not the only place where the Jurassic rocks have held industrial resources. The shallow headland at Brora, Sutherland, is the period's northernmost exposure; it has been home to a coal mine, a mill to process wool from the nearby uplands, a stone quarry, and the most important brickworks in the Highlands. I even glimpsed an oddly-out-of-place-looking terrace of brick houses.

Brora is basically an outcrop of rocks which continue under the North Sea bed, which is the focus of most Jurassic industry today. The late Jurassic Kimmeridge clay is perhaps the most important source-rock for oil in Britain, especially in the northern North Sea.

This aspect of the rich, black material comes onshore at Kimmeridge itself. Around this bay on Dorset's Purbeck coast, the shaley rocks are so oil-rich they can burn below the ground. Small black discs of the material were traditionally known as 'Kimmeridge money' and attributed to some lost race. Like the jet further north, the shale was worked into Iron Age and Roman-era jewellery; it was also used as a fuel. Today, a single 'nodding donkey' is the main visible sign of the industry, though the largest onshore oil operation in the UK is located nearby.

There is more iron in the south, too. Though the Northamptonshire ironstone does not contain more than about 30 per cent iron, and is difficult to smelt effectively, its ores have been exploited since the Iron Age, and the 'Bessemer boom' gave it new prominence in the industrial era. Towns such as Scunthorpe, Lincolnshire and Corby, Northamptonshire, only exist as a result; Jurassic industrial settlements in very un-industrial country.

But the main industry of the mid-Jurassic rocks is wool. The sheep of the Cotswolds in particular had a special reputation. Here, there were seams of soft Fuller's Earth (also found in the Cretaceous Greensand, especially in the Weald). This material originated as ash-falls from volcanoes probably located where the North Sea is now, subtly altered on the Jurassic ocean floor. Among other applications, its detergent properties help remove oil and grease from dirty raw wool.

By the seventeenth century, the Cotswolds were becoming a centre of early industry. Where fast-flowing rivers tumbled out of scarpland gaps, places such as Stroud, Gloucestershire and Frome, Somerset (called by Defoe a 'little Manchester'), became home to important mills. Carboniferous settings only upstaged them when steam power gave the advantage to areas with proximity to coal.

Such towns share certain qualities in common with Bath. Buildings, many funded by wool wealth, cling to hills and valley-sides with picturesque abandon; all are built of a single, fine stone. But wool wealth has long funded great architecture: medieval 'wool churches' such as Fairford and Northleach are justly famous.

This is a vision of the architecture of industriousness unsullied by the dourness that would overtake their Carboniferous peers, and it has bequeathed a great harmony of geology and landscape. There is a sense in which all the mid-Jurassic is a single dense place, often built on wool wealth, and every village an outcrop of some small local quarry. Human economy, architecture and geology speak as one. Yet the intersection of building materials and landscapes is a major theme of all phases of the Jurassic.

Building stones, building landscapes

Scarborough does not leap out as an equal to Bath or Oxford. But this slightly faded resort on the edge of the North York Moors is also a place of Jurassic spectacle, with its castle on a high knoll and its handsome sandstone buildings. Here, on the side of a wyke that has been dressed up as a pleasure garden, is one of the most remarkable geohistorical structures I know.

The cliffs of the castle promontory were first analysed by William Smith, the 'father of English geology'. Having begun his career among the Jurassic rocks of Oxfordshire and Somerset, he came to the moors as land surveyor for local magnate Sir John Johnstone, and helped the Scarborough Philosophical Society establish the elegant, circular Rotunda Museum (1829).

Within this domed building, Smith's rock collection was displayed in stratigraphical order; his nephew, also a prominent geologist, added a painted geological cross-section through the North York Moors coast. The rotunda is made of North York Moors sandstone from Johnstone's estates: a softly brown, hard-wearing rock that was popular in itself. Much of Whitby and Covent Garden Market in London are made from such sandstones, here sourced at Aislaby, and used to build water-resistant piers and quays as far afield as Tangier, Morocco. They are very like those of the Carboniferous Pennines, and the Rotunda Museum's square base is a later addition made of the latter rock: visibly weathering differently to the rotunda, it gives this appealing building a stratigraphic quality.

One of the most striking examples in Britain of a 'feedback loop' between geology and architecture, the museum is a temple to the replacement of myth by geology, of stone heroes by cross-sections, of churches by museums, and of preaching by 'interpretation'.

Here, then, we are on the sandstone of the North York Moors. But it is the limestones, especially those of the mid-Jurassic, for which the period is most famous.

As if in proof of that, en route to Iona I made a long diversion down a single-tracked road to the beach at Carsaig on the Ross of Mull. Ammonites without number feasted together on the rocks of this tree-lined bay, the limestones of which supplied what was probably the only true freestone in the entire western Highlands.

In England, the Blue Lias limestone has also been used for building. That from Hornton on the Oxfordshire/Warwickshire border is prized by sculptors. Easily overlooked, these limestones make memorable hills, their profile 'quirky, tumbled, often abrupt' (Alec Clifton-Taylor); the Howardians, which seal the Vale of Pickering from the New Red vale of York; Edge Hill, Warwickshire, a verdant inselberg of inner England. But in Somerset they are the key to an entire geohistorical landscape.

Liassic: Somerset Levels

Wetlands have two things in common: a site that barely drains at all, and the large quantities of peat that result. In Britain, Jurassic clays underlie several of these flat, bleak, spacious places, but on the surface one is rarely aware of the local rocks – unless you are in the Somerset Levels.

Here, outcrops of Blue Lias make sudden, island-like hills among the waterlogged expanses of late Triassic and Liassic clay. They must have had a powerful presence in earlier times, when the landscape was flooded; although many low gravelly rises often marked by -ney and -zoy place names, created low islets in the wetland, the lias hills are in a different category. They also mean that, uniquely among wetlands, the Levels produce their own building stone.

These elements in combination give the area its compelling character. Brent Knolls looms like a great Liassic monster over the M5, rising from the former swamp that surrounds it. A hillfort circuits its peak; its foot, where pervious limestone hits impervious clay, is ringed by springs and thus by villages, as if drinking from the flanks of some great stone animal. The whole thing is only there, legend tells us, because the devil was persuaded to dump a load of earth on the ground.

Explore further, and find buildings of 'dusky blue' Lias (Leland), visibly lined with the 'layers' from which its name derives. Some hills have a special presence; the Poldens are a long, spiny Liassic wrinkle that makes a natural routeway, followed by the Roman-origin A39. Burrow Mump is a diminished Brentor or St Michael's Mount. There is a further example of the sudden-hill-and-St-Michael's-church syndrome here, and it draws you wherever it is glimpsed: Glastonbury.

The Isle of Avalon, for millennia almost literally an island, is mostly a low presence, rising above the drained wetland. But rising from it is the electrifying, pimple-like prominence of Glastonbury Tor, with the tower of St Michael's church a scintillating vertical accent at the very peak.

St Michael's was one of various churches and chapels on the isle, all of them outposts of the great church that nestled on its gentle western slope: Glastonbury Abbey. Unlike the more ordinary buildings of the Levels, the abbey church was built of mid-Jurassic freestone from Doulting, the quarries of which it owned. The far south-west has a way of producing such high-quality pockets of Jurassic freestone: Ham Hill is another, as is Dundry, near Bristol.

Glastonbury abbey was the focus of more major medieval cults and myths than any site in Britain. St Patrick, King Arthur and Joseph of Arimathea, to name but three, were believed to lie there. It was also one of the wealthiest and most powerful institutions in the land. It claimed a uniquely early, semi-miraculous foundation ('not built by hands'); and it owned and controlled the Levels almost as a separate fiefdom. Only the tower of St Michael's survives; the abbey is a magnificent ruin. In 1539, as part of the dissolution of this monastery, the last abbot was hanged, drawn and quartered on the top of the tor.

The disappearance of the region's defining corporation left behind a kind of spiritual and geographical vacuum, as if this was some great single-industry town in which the prayer-factory had closed. The vacuum was not filled for about 300 years, when an entirely new group of cults began to relocate the spiritual focus of the Isle from the low-lying abbey site to the eye-grabbing sacral stone throne that is the tor, and its associated iron-rich spring.

In a spiritually charged mythospheric unconformity, Glastonbury is now a Haight-Ashbury of rural western England, and a testament to the power of a series of Liassic landforms – the wetland, the isle, the tor – which have proved irresistible over centuries, perhaps even millennia.

We have jumped from Scarborough to Mull to Somerset, skirting around the most famous Jurassic rocks. It is already clear that the Jurassic has a way of generating remarkable combinations of landscape, history, geology and building stone, revealing a series of versions of England: enquiring, industrious, innovative, mystical. Before we turn to the 'superstar' limestones there is one other source of building material to visit, and it is on another flatland: the anonymous plain of late Jurassic clay that stretches across much of counties such as Bedfordshire.

Late Jurassic brick-clay

Material for making brick has been dug from these Oxford clays for centuries; indeed Jurassic clays in general still produce about a third of UK brick-clay. Around 1880, however, near the village of Fletton not far from Peterborough, it was discovered that the lower levels of the clay were unusually rich in carbon.

This was the 'clay that burns'. Its production consumed significantly less fuel than normal (indeed one did not necessarily need coal at all, just coal dust or 'smudge'). It was also uniform in consistency, very plastic, and neither lime nor water needed adding to it before firing.

The resulting products were to become the brick equivalent of Welsh slate. In a handful of locations, of which Fletton was the most important, a major industry developed. In many places – especially London – the products of the 'London Brick Company' replaced the myriad textures and variations of bricks made from local clays. Close to major north/south transport lines, the Fletton brickworks became the largest in the world. As recently as the 1970s, they produced over 40 per cent of UK bricks.

The landscape has largely vanished, apart from water-filled brick pits. But when I was a child the procession of thirty-two chimneys that marked the kilns was one of the landmarks of any journey north; a monumental gathering of tall, red-brown verticals rising from the horizontal, grey claylands. Three survive: reminders of the great era of extraction and processing, and the ways in which Jurassic geology has shaped human architecture.

The mid-Jurassic limestones

All this is a prelude to the story that brings us back to where we began: the fine-grained, yellow-to-white, mostly mid-Jurassic limestones of Bath and elsewhere.

To see what all the fuss was about, I visited the mason Sam MacArthur in his traditional, open-sided shed, commonly known as a 'lodge'. Picking up a chisel and bashing away like the least practical person on the planet that I am, I was amazed to find the rock falling away as easily as if it was a rather dry lump of cheese. Stonemasonry is an exacting craft, one it takes years to master, but it only took an hour or two for this total beginner to rough out a rather cack-handed green man. One can see why these rocks have been so favoured.

The rock was beautiful, too. Jurassic limestone can be very even-toned, but this piece shifted in shade from soft Cheddar to hard honey over a square foot or two. Other such rocks can be quiet lemon or tawny white: the gentle oxidisation of small but varying quantities of iron in particles that spent 11 million years drifting to the Jurassic sea floor. And while most of the older British limestones are so densely textured it is hard to see their individual grains, these rocks are often visibly made of millions of little spherical nodules.

These are 'ooids'. They are made of particles of calcium carbonate derived from the skeletons of sea-creatures; and look like roe – indeed the name comes from the Ancient Greek for egg. Each particle, shifting around in undersea currents, acquired further layers, until it became a little ball, 2mm in diameter at most. The rocks can also be visibly a glut of fragments of bone and shell: Ham Hill, Somerset, the remnant of a reef that now forms a sudden, hillfort-ringed eminence, is jammed with lumps of sea creatures' bone.

These rocks depended on animal life for their very existence. Without them, the great historic buildings of south-east Britain – from Norwich Cathedral to Buckingham Palace – would not exist in their current form. In parts of the Cotswolds, every structure is built out of them, the stones – to quote J.B. Priestley – 'faintly warm and luminous, as if they knew the trick of keeping the lost sunlight of centuries glimmering about them'. Manor houses feature steep roof-lines, dormers and prominent gables, often topped by little balls. Poised and gentle-toned, village after village glows with smug Jurassic perfection.

Even the roofs are local. Jurassic stone-slate roofs can be particularly delicious, their stones delicately textured with the lichens that love this calcium-rich rock, and reducing in size as they approach the gable. Large, heavy 'cussems' are at the bottom, small 'farewells' at the top.

Their main quarries lay near the villages of Collyweston near Stamford, and Stonesfield in Oxfordshire. Formed as frost separated the bedding planes of the layers nearest the surface, some 'presents' were lifted straight from the ground without the need for quarrying. Nevertheless, by the seventeenth century mines over 10m deep were being dug. Often, alarmingly, workers waited for the roof of a given section to 'talk' – make clicking sounds, indicating imminent collapse – before removing any supports, withdrawing and then returning to remove the fallen slabs.

Work was carried out in autumn and winter, and those stones not already split by nature were stacked in the open air, covered, and watered daily like fissile plants, waiting for a heavy frost. In Oxfordshire, when such frosts came, church-bells were rung so every able-bodied man could get to work splitting the rocks.

There are some significant variants to the mid-Jurassic rocks. They include the ironstones of Northamptonshire: extraordinary-looking things, their colour varying from strong chocolate brown to orange. Buildings like Stoke Park, Stoke Bruerne (1635), use ironstone and more typical Jurassic limestone to make striking combinations of yellow and brown; where this is applied throughout entire villages, the buildings can be almost painfully stripey. One moves 'past walls of broken biscuit, golden gloss / Porridge or crumbling shortbread or burnt scone/Puma, mouldy elephant, Persian lamb' (Louis MacNeice). These rocks can as easily be Liassic as mid-Jurassic; indeed the landscape itself here is mixed, the long, mazy Liassic valleys working their way deep into mid-Jurassic country.

There is variety, too in the far south-west. As one approaches Dorset, grains of Variscan and Alpine and rocks of many periods interweave to create places of disarming beauty. Among them can be found various famous stones that are not mid-Jurassic: Ham Hill has recently been placed at the end of the Liassic; Portland stretches into the late Jurassic; Purbeck continues on from it and into the earliest Cretaceous. All share much of the character of the mid-Jurassic rocks, and can be considered a piece with them.

The use of such limestones starts early. The frost-shattered layers near the surface were used in Severn/Cotswold long barrows and stone circles such as Rollright. The Romans transported Ham Hill and Purbeck at least 160 miles to the grand Temple of Claudius at Colchester/*Camulodunum* – and to London.

Walk out of Cannon Street station in the City of London, and in a wall of an office building almost opposite is set the Jurassic 'London Stone'. There is something primeval about this pale lump. First mentioned in the Anglo-Saxon period, William Blake thought it had been a setting for Druidic sacrifices. Archaeologists suggest it was associated with the Roman governor's palace.

The mid-Jurassic limestone is the only rock in Britain that demonstrably sustained a quarrying industry, as opposed to occasional one-off delves, in the Anglo-Saxon period. The products of Barnack near Stamford, Taynton in Oxfordshire, and Bath were being exported 50–60 miles from source at this time. At Barnack we know there was a distinction between *wercstan* and *walstan*: freestone and wall-building/ dimension stone. At the Anglo-Saxon church of St Laurence in Bradford-upon-Avon, Wiltshire, one can see the marks left by stonemasons to indicate how many pieces each had carved, and thus should be paid for, suggesting a well-organised craft.

Many of England's greatest medieval churches are built of mid-Jurassic limestone. A distribution map of those with spires clusters all along the stone belt; near-miraculous structures such as Lincoln cathedral are built of the very rocks below them.

This is a building of stupendous grandeur, a visual power-grab, utterly dominating Lincoln Edge and the surrounding flat Liassic/Triassic lowland. It shares its ridge-edge location, initially the site of the forum of Roman *Lindum Colonia*, with the Norman castle, an architectural 'nice policeman' and 'nasty policeman' if ever there was one. Its (now lost, lead-and-timber) fourteenth-century spire made it for a time the highest man-made structure in the world, an oolitic vision of Heavenly power, adding an artificial 159m to the 65m escarpment.

There are many signs of rivers being straightened and canals built partly to transport these superlative stones. Those of the Stamford area may have moved along the Roman-origin Car Dyke; Lincoln stone may have reached the New Red Trent valley along the equally ancient Fossydyke. And along the east coast, such relatively distant outcrops of mid-Jurassic rock have reshaped the architecture of an entire region.

East Anglia lacks good building stones; yet it arguably possesses the most extensive collection of top-flight medieval churches and castles in the land. Their most important structural or carved elements are invariably made of mid-Jurassic limestone, almost all of it floated across the Fens from the Stamford area (or even along the coast from Caen, Normandy, where the stones are very similar; in Kent, Marquise stone from Pas-de-Calais, is also seen). The ashlar walls of Norwich Castle, Ely Cathedral and many other structures are made of them.

All this has created the remarkable quarry landscape at Barnack, Stamford, known as the Hills and Holes. I've almost become lost wandering this extensive area of tight rises and hollows, quarries so long abandoned they have developed a thin covering of calcareous soil.

The result is a miniature, man-made limestone grassland, rich in orchids, wild flowers and butterflies, like some enormous crazy golf course gone beautifully to seed. Among the dozens of great medieval buildings lifted from here is the abbey (now cathedral) at Peterborough, which owned the quarry.

But perhaps the most extraordinary mid-Jurassic quarry landscapes lie in the south-west, where in Dorset, certain stones on the Isle of Purbeck became the focus of a near-obsessive medieval lithophilia.

Purbeck

Though completely attached to the rest of the country by dry land, one can see why this headland in eastern Dorset is called an 'isle'. Approached across a marshy lowland, and hidden behind a wall-like east–west Alpine Grain ridge of Cretaceous chalk, it can feel like some secret club known only to the *cognoscenti*. If so, the bouncer on the door is the terrifying medieval hulk of Corfe Castle, which blocks the only gap in the ridge. A dark grey stone-trading town clusters below it.

Once one has entered this land apart, everything is built of the local limestones; often, in the case of drystone walls, quarry-waste. Drift mines sit on steep coasts, sometimes marked by little slag-heaps known as 'riddings', or the settings for the timber donkey-wheels which hauled out the quarried rock.

In the Oxford clay here there are 'septaria', round calcium-rich nodules containing brown and grey patterns which can be cut in half and polished, making beautiful decorative features. But the 'star turn' is a thin band of polishable limestone.

This Purbeck 'marble' is a product of a mixed environment of marsh and saline lagoon. It is rammed with fossils of the freshwater mollusc *Viviparus carinifer*. Pale cross-sections of their shells make curly, whiteish bone-like patterns in a dark matt-blue matrix. Purbeck can be polished to a fine glow (and sometimes rendered almost black through the use of pig fat).

Known since the Roman period, twelfth- and thirteenth-century architects developed an infatuation with this rock, which 'flashes with glint upon glint', and 'can hold people's minds in suspense', as Henry of Avranches put it in the 1220s. A Carboniferous Limestone from Tournai, Belgium, was first used to create such effects, and other English sources – including Jurassic stones from Alwalton near Peterborough, and Somerset Blue Lias – were to also become popular. But only that of Purbeck became an industry of national significance.

Its 'marblers' still meet annually in Corfe town hall. They play a traditional game of football in the town's streets afterwards. Effigies and architectural elements could be ordered from their shops around St Paul's churchyard in London, the results shipped far and wide. The monument to one thirteenth-century archbishop of York, Walter de Gray, appears to have had a bishop rather than an archbishop's effigy delivered in error, but no one has ever returned it.

Most memorable are the great pipe-like shafts of dark, glossy Purbeck to be seen draped over cathedrals, from Salisbury to Durham, like some heavenly scaffolding. Lincoln has over 1,000, and at Exeter the columns display subtly calibrated shades of varying glossiness and warmth. Even after this craze died down, Purbeck remained a go-to rock for church fittings, tombs, grave-slabs and the settings of brasses. Pieces of the Isle of Purbeck can thus be seen in thousands of parish churches across the land, commemorative monuments set in a glimmering cemetery of late Jurassic/early Cretaceous life-forms, death on death.

There are active quarries on Purbeck, but I wanted to find the remains of their medieval predecessors. In the shallow Alpine-Grain valley of the Swanbrook, I found myself following a delicious chain of pool-filled former 'quarrs' overlooked by stands of trees. The setting jumped vertiginously from one to another: caravan park, country cottage, farm, junkyard-like graveyard of sea containers. This was a rough rural place, yet from here had been wrested a literal attempt to use rock to evoke the glittering stones of Heaven. I kept hoping to see an abandoned stiff-leaf capital or praying knight poking from a pool or emerging from a wall, abandoned Excaliburs. Perhaps they lie sleeping.

The marble beds are only about 45–60cm deep, so pieces are often relatively flat, and structurally weak if upended to make columns. But laid parallel to its grain, the rock is hard-wearing; indeed, Purbeck stone generally was popular for paving right into the modern era.

Flagstones from the isle were exported in large numbers from Swanage, especially to London. The town was eccentrically enriched by John Mowlem and his nephew George Burt, 'King of Swanage', from whom the construction company Mowlems is descended. They brought bits of the capital back as ballast: the Wellington Clock Tower at Peveril

Point was designed for London Bridge; and the entire facade of London's Mercer's Hall is now the frontage of the local town hall, a metropolitan swagger of broken pediments and caryatids, like some Edwardian swell down from town.

It was such Renaissance taste that brought the mid-Jurassic limestones into even greater favour. The crisp detailing and unwavering tone of the best rocks was in harmony with contemporary taste, as can be seen at such palatial houses as Blenheim (Taynton stone); Burghley and Audley End (Ketton, from near Stamford). It is now that, thanks to a certain inherent elegance, the sources at Bath and Portland had their day in the sun.

Bath

The good stone lies up to 30m deep in the hills around Bath: tiny crystallised shell-fragments between the ooids help absorb moisture, making the best varieties especially strong. Its bedding planes dip to the east, and as demand for it spread, quarrying moved away from its centre around Combe Down above the city, and towards Box and Corsham. It also descended underground, where the best beds had benefited from frost-free years of compression, and agricultural land was not compromised by being quarried.

Almost invisible on the surface, these quarry-mines are among the most extraordinary artificial caverns in Britain. 'The cathedral', a hole 30m deep, 58m long and 9m wide, was one of the sights of the Box/Corsham area.

It was the eighteenth-century rebuilding of the city which catapulted Bath stone to national prominence, and it was inspired by a unique vision of an ancient England. Its primary architects, John Wood the Elder, and his son, Wood the Younger, were convinced that the Druid civilisation of the Iron Age had been the equal of that of the Classical world. For them, structures such as the Royal Crescent were Classical evocations of the stone circles of ancient Britain. Lay a plan of the Royal Crescent and The Circus over one of the nearby stone circles at Stanton Drew, and one is clearly modelled on the other.

But it was Ralph Allen who promoted the stone itself. He purchased and leased quarries on Combe Down, and built an innovative tramway to transport their products downhill. His town-centre base, extended in 1727, and his mansion on the hill, Prior Park (c.1733), seem to have been designed to show off the qualities of the material, even as he helped finance local development.

The Kennet & Avon canal, begun in 1794, brought the stone in reach of London, and gave prominence to quarries close to its route. Both the canal company and, later, the Great Western Railway, used Bath stone for their buildings, creating ribbons of structures made of the material between London and the West Country. The tunnel through the scarp at Box (the longest railway tunnel in the world when built in 1841), revealed new supplies of a source first said to have been discovered by St Aldhelm over a thousand years earlier.

But this stone has spread far and wide. With access to the Thames and the Severn alike, honey-coloured limestones from the Bath area are everywhere, from Ireland to London, from Cape Town City Hall to Union Station, Washington DC. In the late nineteenth century there were forty-seven separate quarries; and an estimated 60 miles of tunnels and tramways to move the stone around.

These quarries, really mines, have had a remarkable afterlife. In the Second World War, some were reused as bunkers for ammunition, or even factories. Aircraft engines were made below the Corsham countryside. From 1961, one became a potential seat of government in the event of a nuclear attack, with space for 4,000 civil servants as well as the Cabinet, and 10 miles of corridors that could be navigated by electronic buggies.

Surface subsidence has been an issue, and as a result much of this artificial underground world has been filled with enough stone and foamed concrete to cover a football pitch to a depth of nearly 90m. So for vivid quarry landscapes, we have to go back to Dorset.

Portland

Perhaps the Isle of Portland holds the greatest Jurassic stone of all. It also embodies a kind of Englishness. The story is one of a well-mannered exterior that sheaths the potential for violence.

Every time I approach the isle it seems aloof. This great wedge-shaped mass can only be reached across the fragile pebbly umbilical cord that is Chesil Beach. Once entered, this is a little limestone universe, its short stern scarp turning its back to the rest of Britain, its south-facing dipslope shelving towards the sea (and thus providing a suitable site for a port). There are even, in typical scarpland fashion, settlements following the springline: Fortuneswell and Clearwell.

This rock has been cut into, hollowed out, removed in a manner matched by few other places. Even untouched parts of it, such as stretches of sea-carved cliff, have a crispness comparable to the facades of imperial London, which are largely made of bits of the isle. It's not a beautiful place, but it is a compelling one.

Usage of the stone starts in the prehistoric period, with tools of Portland chert and querns of Portland limestone. Yet when one sees how many buildings over the last 300 years came to be made of or clad with this rock, it is amazing there is anything left of the isle at all; and much of what has not been removed has been used to make its buildings.

The Isle of Portland is an outpost of the state, in Crown hands since at least the eleventh century. The harbour was once a major Naval base; there is a castle built by Henry VIII; the Verne Citadel (1860) is a former fort, now a prison, whose defences tunnel deep into the rock. A forbidding-looking Young Offender's Institution overlooks the sea. Many of those imprisoned on the island were sent to work in the quarries: the 'felon-quarried stone' (A.E. Housman). Among all this architectural coercion sits the handsome eighteenth-century church of St George, surrounded by the tombs of quarry workers and next to the Tout Quarry Sculpture Park.

A karst-like landscape of clefts and gorges has been dug here in pursuit of the stone. More recently, an array of sculptors have been commissioned to respond to and carve the quarryscape. I came to Antony Gormley's *Still Falling* (1983): the simple outline of a human figure, diving through Jurassic seas, his body visibly crossing the layers of the rock.

This is a good place to look closely at this calcium-carbonate-rich stone. It is almost white in colour, and very fine-grained. Its close, unchanging texture gives it a certain cold impersonality; it is also strong. Bath stone cannot bear half the weight that Portland can. Diving down through its layers, one first reaches the famous Roach: hard, durable and water-resistant, its texture delightfully pitted thanks to the many shelly fossils it contains. Then comes the magnificent Whit, very pale, crisp and easily carved; and below it, the Base, arguably as fine, if a little less durable.

The heyday of Portland stone starts in London, and with England's great seventeenth-century progenitors of English Renaissance architecture, Inigo Jones and Sir Christopher Wren. The stone complemented the air of elegantly rational authority beloved of these designers; it was also resistant enough to withstand the onslaught of coal pollution. Fuelled by James I of England/James VI of Scotland's desire to create a capital fitting for a newly united Britain, the resulting buildings are dominated by the requirements of the British state.

Jones used Portland on the Queen's House at Greenwich (1616), and in a major pre-Fire upgrading of Old St Paul's Cathedral. Port facilities were built on the isle, and Henry Farley, variously described as a stone importer and a legal clerk, gave poetic voice to the material itself: 'In Earth's wide womb, as in our nat'rall bed / We have been hid, conceal'd, and covered… / We were discover'd, and to London sent', being 'in all things firm and sound / Fairer and greater than elsewhere are found.'

Portland's subsequent takeover of London architecture was kick-started by the Fire of London – and by a curious Carboniferous/Jurassic synergy. Coal pollution had partly driven the desire for such a freestone; now a tax on it helped pay for Wren's post-Fire rebuilding of the city. It was used to build the present St Paul's Cathedral, fifty-one new parish churches, the Monument, the Royal Exchange and more. The cathedral alone consumed 50,332 tons between 1674 and 1700: a relative sliver of the million tons eventually used by Wren. By the 1700s Defoe could call it 'our best and whitest freestone', from which 'the public edifices in the city of London, are chiefly built'.

Yet this cool, white stone would only get more popular. Major eighteenth-century buildings that employ it include St Martin's-in-the-Fields, the west front of Westminster Abbey (1734); the Admiralty building (1723), Horse Guards (1750), and Somerset House (1776). By the 1790s over 30–40,000 tons were being shipped annually. Many Georgian towns, such as Brighton and Cheltenham, covered brick buildings with white stucco so as to imitate its effects.

Such materials are a reminder that limestone is important in the making of cement. The eighteenth-century rediscovery of 'hydraulic' cements, capable of setting under water, was vital to industrial-era building; stuccos and artificial limestones could create more refined effects, not least in Georgian and Victorian London.

Portland's reputation strengthened yet further as London became the centre of a global empire. The isle's population grew by 75 per cent in the first half of the nineteenth century; over one hundred quarries are known. Steam-powered railways and traction engines helped move the stone to the port. There is barely a street in the capital in which there are no Portland buildings, and almost all the great offices of state, culture and empire are built of it: the British Museum (1823), National Gallery (1833), Foreign Office (1863), Royal Courts of Justice (1871), Admiralty Arch (1913), South Africa House (1935), and many more. It was used for the Cenotaph (1920), and most Commonwealth War Graves in England. Portland had become a kind of lithic embodiment of English imperial prowess: a WASP building material.

Its use outside London underlines this. From the eighteenth century, Portland was much employed in Dublin, then a British possession: a source of controversy, especially as imprisoned Irish nationalists were among those forced to extract this 'English convict stone'. Belfast City Hall is also made of it. Cold, civic and powerful, it is used throughout Cathays Park in Cardiff, that early attempt to give the city a look befitting a nation's capital. In Liverpool and Manchester, two cities particularly keen to look London in the eye, it dominates the great buildings on the waterfront and the monumental central library, respectively. Across the country, banks (Stafford) and city halls (Leeds) employ it.

It is not hard to see how these rocks have acquired the patina of a very powerful, but also very civilised and very English, kind of privilege. As if to confirm that, it is rarely seen north of the border (there are a handful of buildings in Glasgow and Edinburgh).

The furthest north I have seen Portland stone is the tomb of the explorer Dr John Rae in Kirkwall Cathedral, Orkney; but it was exported for the British Memorial Garden built after the 9/11 attacks in New York, the United Nations headquarters in that city, and many of the stones that mark the Mason-Dixon line. The relocation of the Portland St Mary Aldermanbury to Missouri and London Bridge to Arizona has placed further man-made erratics from the isle on 'the other side of the pond'. There are Portland stone buildings in Japan, Kuwait, and several European countries. Portland was declared the first Global Heritage Stone Resource in 2013, and has the unique claim among stones of having been mentioned eighty-eight times in Parliament. One local resident, it is said, told his MP that demand for the stone increased whenever the Conservatives came to power.

There are other Jurassic Englands. On Purbeck, where the stone has been used to evoke an experience of Heaven, aesthetic ambition is matched with eccentricity. Mad mystical mythospherical fantasies have been spun at Liassic Glastonbury. Bath's genteel terraces mask a vision of the ancient past. And at Oxford, intellect replaces authority – and fantasy, too has been spun from within the city's parade of limestone buildings.

Oxford

A series of fantasy, parallel Englands have been coined here: Wonderland (Lewis Carroll was a Don at Christ Church college), Middle-earth (J.R.R. Tolkein, Pembroke), Narnia (C.S. Lewis, Magdalen). In Philip Pullman's *His Dark Materials*, these include a version of Oxford itself. T.S. Eliot hated his time in the city, but it is striking that three of his *Four Quartets*, each of which is at once deeply rooted in, and leaps free of, a specific place, are set on the English Jurassic.

Oxford is a city in which buildings and landscape alike embody the range of the Jurassic succession. It sits on the late Jurassic Oxford clays, in a bowl of woody, discontinuous Corallian hills, at a point where the flooding, meandering waters that drain the mid-Jurassic dipslope coalesce into the Isis/Thames, facilitating stone transport. Here the river could be forded even by oxen (hence the name).

The city's building stones range across the period, from Liassic Hornton to early Cretaceous Purbeck. At its heart, from St Mary's church to the Bodleian, the university has created one of the most extraordinary sequences of buildings in Britain. Running in date from the medieval to the modern, each is impressive, and individual, and none dominates the others.

One can almost date Oxford buildings by their source materials: the oldest, such as the Anglo-Saxon tower of St Michael Northgate, use the local Corallian ragstone: the remains of coral and shell fossils, textured like solidified sponge, hard to shape but very strong. It was used for centuries as a rough building stone, and its quarries at Headington and Wheatley supplied the ashlar seen in medieval colleges such as Magdalen (1474).

Freestone work at this time is usually in mid-Jurassic stones from the Burford/Taynton area. From the seventeenth century, as these quarries become worked out, Headington began to be used as a freestone, too: the Radcliffe Camera (1737) is mostly of Headington and Taynton. But the former rock does not last well; as transport networks improved, so Bath replaced it as the go-to material. The Ashmolean (1841) has a delightful Jurassic colour combination: yellowy Bath stone from Box; pale Portland. The Gothic revival saw some return to local sources, though the dominant material from the late nineteenth-century on was Clipsham stone from near Stamford, often in combination with a (sometimes polishable) local mid Jurassic 'Forest Marble', sourced at Bladon, as at Rhodes House (1929).

One can ignore chronology, and simply enjoy moving through this great sequence of privileged enclosures and monuments. Their subtly various Jurassic shades and textures ultimately boil down to the balance of fossil and iron contained within each stone-type. Cheshire-cheese white Portland has less iron; watery tangerine Taynton more. Corallian is pitted with great lumps of coral reef; Clipsham is delicately textured by millions of tiny shells, which slowly stand proud of the surface as the softer matrix around them erodes. If Bath has a single, mid-Jurassic texture, Oxford has a variety, an individuality, not only in its buildings but in its stone-sources; an important element in what Philip Pullman has called a very human city.

In the University Museum (1855–60), the city has one of the most memorable works of 'geological architecture' in Britain: enclosing the cathedral-like iron-and-glass spectacle of its main hall is a stone quadrangle, enriched by thirty columns, each in a different British decorative stone. There is everything here from the glistening greys of Aberdeenshire granite to the softly suffused red of the New Red sandstone.

The scheme was planned by John Phillips, first Keeper of the museum: a celebration of the beauty that geology can give to buildings, in a city that displays the rich and subtle virtues of the British Jurassic. The oceans of this period bequeathed us an extraordinary series of places, in each of which geology, its extraction, and its rearrangement into buildings has presented a series of visions of what England has been, and might be.

The Jurassic rocks have included our last true superstar building stones. There are many distinctive rocks, landscapes, building materials and geohistorical stories to come – but none have quite shaped the built identity of the island in a way that matches those we have now visited.

The earliest of these superstar stones – Snowdonian slate and Aberdeenshire granite – were by-products of the tectonic birth of this island's rocks. The others – Carboniferous sandstones, Permian Magnesian limestone and Permo-Triassic sandstones – seem to occupy a 'golden zone' in which sediments lay below the ground long enough to mature and compress into freestones. Now, with the remarkable Jurassic rocks, the sequence is coming to an end.

As our story moves on through further layers that mantle south-east Britain, the stones get younger and, as a general average, softer. They may not be as willing to be precisely shaped as those that preceded them, but they are even more responsive to the hand of human history.

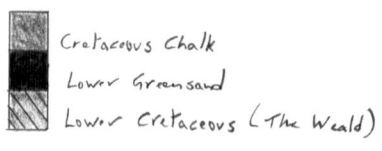

Cretaceous Chalk
Lower Greensand
Lower Cretaceous (The Weald)

Yorkshire Wolds
Stonehenge
The Weald

Hunstanton Cliffs
Peddlar Way
Brancaster
Kings Lynn
Castle Acre Priory
Norwich
Grimes Graves &
Brandon
Dorchester on Thames
Ely
Bury St Edmunds
R. Severn
Uffington
Totternhoe
Aylesbury
Cambridge
Royston Cave
Ipswich
Avebury/Silbury Hill
Oxford
Colchester
R. Thames
The Chilterns
Cardiff
Vale of
Pewsey
Swindon
Bristol
Bath
Marlborough
Gosham
London
Richborough
Adam's Grave
Surrey Hills
Kent Downs
Canterbury
Penpits
Salisbury Plain
Dover
Wellington
Monument
High Weald
South
Downs
Battle
Cerne
Abbas
Portsmouth
The Solent
Brighton
Ashdown Forest
Maiden Castle
Stonehenge

0   20
|————| miles

Chapter 11

Cretaceous scarplands
145–66 million years ago

No matter how long or short the research trip, the roads that take me home funnel towards a low Wiltshire escarpment. It's as I climb this scarp that I truly start to feel as if I am back. And at the top of the rise, the flatlands behind me fall away – and suddenly one might as well be on the Moon.

A green, light-filled space. A close-cropped smoothness to the hills. Copses sitting on ridge-edges like neat little toys. A curious, tense, old-but-man-made ripple to many surfaces, as if the past itself is a muscle waiting to burst out. Where erosion cuts down into the thin soil, the rock below is a blazing white: as it should be – because it is effectively made of bone.

This is the chalk, the remarkable rock which dominates the story of the Cretaceous (indeed *creta* is Latin for chalk). The landscapes it forms embody an exquisite balance between human activity and the qualities of the rock itself. If such a relationship can, through the happenstances of many thousands of years, produce something equivalent to a work of art, it is here on the chalk that this has happened.

But the chalk only appears about halfway through the Cretaceous. Several distinctive phases of geological changes preceded it. All these phases are united by comparable watery narratives to those that shaped the Jurassic.

Just as with that earlier period, our patch of the planet lies in an area of ocean punctuated by islands, set between continental land-masses. But in the course of the Cretaceous much of the dry land is submerged. Meanwhile, the world is gradually becoming more familiar. We are roughly on the longitude now occupied by Spain. Tectonic events remain off-screen, but entities we can call 'America' and 'Africa', and perhaps even 'Europe', are emerging from the gradual disintegration of Pangea. Much of the crust around Britain is subsiding, and forming basins that attract sediment. Dinosaurs continue to stalk the land and swim in the oceans.

Cretaceous landscapes

Most of the Cretaceous rocks lie parallel to and just east of those of the Jurassic, and they too make a great sloping series of stripes, in this case about 260 miles long north to south. As with the Jurassic, the rocks get generally younger as one moves from west to east. One can even compare the alternation of clays and harder rocks that characterise both periods; and the fact that each becomes dominated midway through by a single, distinctive, consistent, scarp-forming limestone: the mid-Jurassic limestone, the Cretaceous chalk. For chalk is a limestone, just one that has so many distinct qualities – whiteness, softness, purity (it can be up to 98 per cent calcium carbonate) that it has acquired a name of its own.

In a north–south overview, the Cretaceous begins at the Yorkshire Wolds, which rise immediately south of the late Jurassic clays of the Vale of Pickering. From here the rocks sweep south and slightly east through Lincolnshire, and then pass under the Wash to Norfolk, even as they begin to curve west. By now they lie over 30 miles wide east to west. Soon they are heading almost due south-west, running through the Chilterns and across much of Wiltshire towards Dorset, where they touch the coast in several places; we've seen some early Cretaceous rocks on the Isle of Purbeck.

Throughout this great sweep, narrow strips of early Cretaceous rocks – the gault (and other) clays, the sandstone known as greensand – lie to the west and a wide, younger strip of chalk lies to the east. The leading edge of this latter rock often forms an emphatic scarp: its highest point is probably Walbury Hill in Berkshire (297m); over 30m lower than the mid-Jurassic Cotswolds.

All this runs with the same camber as the Jurassic rocks. But in England's south-east, there is a further major Cretaceous area, and it runs west–east. Long chalky limbs reach from Hampshire to the Kent and Sussex coasts; the scarp-edged North and South Downs, which put their white enclosing arms around a unique area of Cretaceous high ground: the Weald.

In this south-eastern zone, the east–west Alpine Grain is more marked than anywhere else in Britain. We first glimpsed this story in Dorset; in Kent, Surrey and Sussex it defines the landscape as surely as the Variscan Grain does that of Cornwall and the Caledonian one, Scotland. This country is a Cretaceous world apart.

The Wealden rocks

The dry, sandy rocks of the Weald have a crumbling, earthbound character. The soils are thin and acidic and nutrients drain away. Tree-roots descend into soft rock above sudden streams; there are occasional crags and boulders. 'Weald' has the same origin as 'wold': a wooded area. 'Wild' may be a related term.

The complex ridges and valleys here run with the Alpine Grain, their sides broken up into small enclosures. A thick swathe of woodland covers almost a quarter of the country, and there is much heath, too. Villages are widely scattered, lanes deep, towns few.

These 'Wealden rocks' date from early in the Cretaceous. They were mostly laid down in a basin that had a freshwater, or brackish, environment. Great braided river-systems and mudflats washed over the land; even the climate was wet. The varying deposits of these ever-shifting rivers have left in their wake rocks of varying hardness, with a dominant tone of soft, green-tinged brown. But shades and textures vary, the colourways of the bed of a great, lost river-system.

There is something subterranean, almost submerged, about the resulting territory. And though the porous sandstones that define it are unique, it is part of their power that they are shut off: surrounded and moated by the clay, greensand and chalk that are generic to Cretaceous Britain.

All these rocks were laid down flat, one on top of the other; but in the Tertiary period — millions of years later – they were hit by a subtle but powerful tectonic ramrod pushing from the south, flexing them along the Alpine Grain. The layers were bent upwards, creating a great upturned bowl, longer east–west than north–south, its surface — which may have been over 3,300ft above the present ground level – made of the youngest formation, the chalk.

Even as it rose, erosion got to work on the great chalky dome, and over time it was stripped away, exposing the rock beneath, each older than the other, each eroding according to its own specific character. What had been nested like an onion was now more like the layered curve of a great vulva, with the Wealden rocks at its heart.

The North and South Downs form rims on either side, an enclosing rampart of remnant chalk. The greensand makes hilly, wooded scarps that run parallel to these downs, and in the Surrey Hills out-top them, reaching 294m at Leith Hill. The chalk and greensand (sometimes with a valley of gault clay) look inwards, where the Weald itself can be divided into the clay-dominated Low Weald and the sandstone-dominated High Weald.

This entire assemblage has been cut across by the English Channel (indeed the rocks continue beyond, forming France's Bas Boulonnais). As a result, the white cliffs of Dover are a cut across the North Downs; east of Hastings, Fairlight cliff is a section through the Weald; and at Beachy Head we are gazing at the interior of the South Downs: a cross-section of the Cretaceous – and it includes the only serious cliffs between the Humber and Hampshire.

This region is a particularly emphatic example of that common geological phenomenon, the anticline: the entire structure, taking in both sides of the Channel, is known as the Weald-Artois Anticline. And perhaps the key to its Wealden heartland is that it has been (to use a geological term) exhumed, as layers of covering rock have been stripped away.

It often feels as if the Wealden rocks can never forget that their constituent grains cemented under suffocating layers of younger material;

as if they cannot quite lose the sense that a much greater upland once rose high above them, of which the flanking downland walls are the remnants. It is as if one is deep underneath something, in a place that should not be exposed; Kipling, who lived here, wrote of its 'wooded, dim, blue goodness'.

A quiet wealth seems locked into the landscape, detectable in a thousand cosy retirement cottages nestling down back-lanes, and the prosperously suburban quality of some of the towns. The area's literary associations are with a wildness that is childlike, cosy and unthreatening: *Winnie-the-Pooh* is set in Ashdown Forest; Kipling's children's book *Puck of Pook's Hill* is also set here; the video for the Beatle's *Strawberry Fields Forever*, that evocation of childhood memory, was shot at Knole, on the greensand just south of Sevenoaks.

Before the railway brought London so close, this country was a sparsely inhabited area of real poverty. Cobbett called Ashdown Forest 'a villainously ugly spot'; Fiennes describes 'blind dark lanes' and 'steep hills'. The place names speak of the '-leighs' associated with clearings in woodland; the '-dens' of wooded vales. Little woods are known as 'shaws', sudden dips and clefts or 'ghylls'/'gills'. The region still manages to be 'other' enough to sustain a unique ballgame: stoolball. A little like cricket, but with differently shaped bats and wickets.

Iron is the principal resource in these rocks. It explains their brownness; enriches the waters of Tunbridge Wells, a spa since 1606; and has left behind a unique landscape of industry. The industry's demand for wood as fuel (and for shipbuilding) meant that woodland was managed, and ultimately preserved when in other places it disappeared. But water was also required, to power the bellows and hammers recorded in place names such as Abinger Hammer, and to cool fresh-forged implements: and this is the cause of the industry's principal legacy to the modern landscape.

Wealden industry

I parked in a lay-by and took a path past a timber-and-brick cottage. Small isolated clusters of cottages often mark the sites of former ironworks: this one seemed almost to be melting into its own tweeness. This was the kind of heavily managed landscape that makes you feel like you are trespassing even when you aren't, but the map said there was a right of way, so I persevered. Descending into a steepish and earthy valley, I stumbled on my first 'hammer pond'.

At first it was the elemental peace that struck me. Then I noticed the unusual shape of this still, small, woodland lake: a long, thin tail; a straight, wide front. Made by damming a typical stream-fed Wealden valley with local clay, it was the entirely artificial product of the Wealden iron industry. Forty such survive, of 180 or so known to have existed. One, at Abinger, Surrey, is now used to grow watercress; another, at Chithurst, West Sussex, is ringed by the meditation path of the nearby Buddhist monastery.

For centuries such valleys were filled with the sound and smell of forges and foundries. Local timber, slowly burned, could be turned into charcoal, a dense store of carbon. This was used to smelt the local iron. Under the Romans, and again in the early modern period, the Weald was the most important iron-making area in Britain.

This ore is mainly found as nodules; though variable in quality it is exceptionally low in sulphur and reasonably well placed for transport to London, or across the Channel. The local clays and sandstones could be used to build heat-resistant furnaces and forges. Wealden iron was being traded into Europe as early as 100 BC; over twenty Iron Age production sites are known, and 113 Roman-era ones. Roman roads in the area were sometimes surfaced with the resulting slag, and linked the Weald to ports on the south coast.

Wealden iron was only exploited to a limited extent by the Anglo-Saxons. But later in the medieval period huge quantities of nails, horseshoes, arrowheads and other products were made here. Migrations of European ironworkers and their know-how brought what were probably the first blast furnaces in Britain here in the 1490s, and transformed the industry. About 9,000 tons of iron were produced annually in the 1590s, and cannons of Wealden iron were used against the Spanish Armada.

Defoe describes the area's 'abundance of waste and wild grounds . . . forests, and woods', in which 'cauldrons, chimney-backs, furnaces, retorts, boiling pots . . . iron cannon, bomb shells, stink-pots, hand-grenades and cannon ball' were made 'in infinite quantity'. But in the industrial era, thanks to Abraham Darby's innovations, the focus of iron-founding moved closer to sources of coal. The last blast furnace closed in 1827.

Glassmaking is another Wealden industry, centred around Chiddingfold in Surrey. Here the main attraction was Wealden wood, used as fuel; and ash, a key ingredient for glass-making; but the local sand was also crucial. The iron in these sands causes the greenish tinge often seen in old glass. Of medieval origin, the industry again moved towards coal-producing areas, a process hastened by a seventeenth-century ban on the use of wood for fuel in glassworks.

But Wealden iron is the main industrial story of the Cretaceous, and the period's building stones are also focused in this early part of the period.

Wealden and early Cretaceous building stones

There is no denying the charm of Wealden towns like Horsham. The sandstones have the texture of crumbled soft brown sugar; the other main building materials are brick and tile, fired from local clay, and oak, from local woods. The buildings are at once varied in texture and rooted in the locale. In some places one even sees gravestones and other features made of Wealden iron.

In the late medieval period a whole vernacular building-type developed here: the handsome 'Wealden style' timber-framed house, its side-wings symmetrically flanking a central, inset entrance bay. Timber buildings might be protected from the elements by weatherboarding; by the wooden tiling known as 'shingling'; and from the seventeenth century by clay 'hanging' or 'weather' tiles, which gave walls a layered effect, like an architectural pangolin. Wealden clays were also an important source of bricks, the subtle shades of which are lavishly praised by Alec Clifton-Taylor.

The buildings of Midhurst, West Sussex, can have a curiously pernickety feel, which is odd, given the generous sunset-yellow of the building stone. The reason is the widespread use of galletting, in which small pieces of stone – dark flint and fractured local rocks (and in some places even slag from iron-making) are pressed in long lines into the mortar. Invented as a way of breaking up the large amounts of mortar required when the local stones are hard to shape, this can become a decorative technique in its own right. Like weatherboarding, there is more of it in the Weald than anywhere else. The furthest north I have seen it is the Black Isle in Ross and Cromarty.

Horsham flagstones and Sussex Marble, both sourced in the Low Weald, are perhaps the most celebrated Wealden stones. The former rock is often lined with the ripple-marks of early Cretaceous beaches: split to a stone-slate or slab, it is 'so durable that it never wears out' (Defoe). One of the only stones suitable for this use east of the Cotswolds, it can be seen everywhere from the floors of Roman villas to the roofs of Wealden houses.

Sussex Marble or 'winklestone' is a polishable limestone with a lavish sheen of deep blue-grey; it is as jammed with the remnants of the *Paludina* snail as Purbeck Marble was of the *Viviparus*. Their squirming white calcite make the rock fragile: it can fall apart when exposed to the elements. Sourced in Bethersden, Petworth and elsewhere, its poddy patterns and shiny textures are seen in paving, or are used to add a precious lustre to interiors. The thirteenth-century archbishop's throne in Canterbury cathedral is made of it.

More ordinary Wealden sandstones are rarely of very high quality; this is less true of the greensand that succeeds them. Kentish ragstone is a hard, durable limestone, known to the Romans and good for walling; Reigate stone a pale, sandy freestone. Both were very popular in London: the former can be seen at the Tower of London and the latter, though it does not last well, at Westminster Abbey. As with the Permian Magnesian Limestone, these stones gave the capital a taste for white, crisp materials long before Portland took over.

There are many greensand-era building stones outside the south-east; the gault clay and its peers are likewise used for brick-making in many places. Witchert is an earth-based material unique to parts of Buckinghamshire. The prehistoric quern quarry at Pen Pits in Somerset features 200,000 pits distributed over 17 acres/7ha (and the products of those at Lodsworth, West Sussex, were exported as far as the Midlands). East Anglia's main native building stone other than flint, the carstone, is the colour of a rusty shed. More unusually, greensand sometimes contains 'Coprolites': poo-like lumps (sadly, not literal 'dino dung') found in Cambridgeshire, Buckinghamshire and Bedfordshire. Rich in fertilising phosphates, they were the focus of a brief but intense nineteenth-century 'gold' rush. Such rocks sit between the Wealden rocks and the chalk in the Cretaceous sequence.

Greensand and clay

As it passes from clay to chalk, my journey home briefly passes over a strip of greensand. This territory is only a few hundred yards wide, yet it comes on like a mini-Weald: streams, thatched cottages; brown gorgelets eating into the Earth. It and the gault and other clays can be found across Cretaceous Britain; their outcrop is long, but narrow.

Such rocks had their origin on the seafloor that developed as the freshwater Wealden environment disappeared. The world was heating up, partly thanks to volcanic events accompanying the splitting up of Pangea, and as the ice caps melted the sea levels rose. Submerged, the differences between basins faded. When the coast drew close, rivers deposited heavier sands, and organic detritus which caused the fawn-green mineral glauconite to develop. This is the greensand. Further out to sea the particles were finer, creating blue-grey gault clay. None of these rocks lie more than 9 miles wide, east to west — yet their sequence of flattish claylands and low greensand hills flows like a slim rock river along much of the Cretaceous outcrop.

Greensand also seems to encourage microscopic attention: the eighteenth- and nineteenth-century authors Richard Jefferies and Gilbert White, just north of Swindon and in Selbourne, Hampshire, respectively, wrote exceptionally loving, intimate accounts of the natural history of their greensand homelands. And it is true that some of these landscapes have a real presence.

The Surrey Hills 'resemble the bubbles upon the top of the water of a pot which is violently boiling' (Cobbett); their height caused by a capping of tough greensand-era chert and carstone. The Blackdown Hills in Somerset make a sudden woody line, dominated by the great obelisk of the Wellington Monument. It has been said that the greensand-era

'Red Chalk' of Norfolk makes the cliffs at Hunstanton look a little like a Victoria Sponge. Greensand-era 'hassock' makes the earths which dominate the Kentish orchards and hop fields, the conoid oast houses of the latter their architectural expression. Cretaceous rocks thus provided the setting for the annual summer migrations of generations of nineteenth- and twentieth-century east Londoners and Travellers, for whom the hop-picking season was a summer 'holiday'.

Moving towards the chalk

Everywhere in the greensand and gault clay, one is aware of the incoming chalk. The resulting combination is the signature mixed landscape of the Cretaceous. One example, south of Oxford, is a particularly compelling, dense place.

Here the Thames, only newly a serious river, slugs its way through late Jurassic and gault clays. A mighty series of Neolithic ritual complexes – now mostly invisible – once lay along these banks, and at Dorchester, the Romans founded a settlement which, under the Anglo-Saxons, became the first seat of the bishopric serving Wessex.

A potential major seat of power, but a complex later story included the relocation of the cathedral to Lincoln, and today the 'town' – really a large village – feels like it has been fading gradually since at least the eleventh century. The cathedral was replaced by an abbey church that remains one of Britain's oddest buildings, at once barn-like and packed with artistic and architectural intrigue.

Not far away lie the earthwork remains of the town's Roman walls, and a massive Iron Age earthwork that seals off the junction of Thames and Thame. Here, the river cuts into a greensand scarp, hiding from view the landscape's climax.

The low but haunting Sinodun hills are chalk outliers capped by Iron Age hillforts; wrecked islets from which you can overlook the quiet, flood-soaked drama of the whole area; a landscape so rich it almost drowns under the weight of its own history. It is easy to understand why they were a lifelong touchstone for the artist Paul Nash.

Over 40 miles to the south-west, another low greensand scarp greets anyone approaching the Vale of Pewsey from the claylands to the west. It is climbed by the Caen Hill flight of seventeen locks (1810), an engineering miracle that made possible the connection by canal of the east-flowing Kennet with the west-flowing Avon.

At the top of the hill one reaches Devizes, one of Britain's most rewarding historic towns. Sitting literally at 'the divide' – the meaning of this place name – of chalk, greensand and clay, not far beyond it one comes to Potterne, and plunges deep into the greensand itself.

This is a secret country of soft, fructile gulleys; holloways sensed before they are seen; 'with trees growing on the rocks, or apparently out of them' (Cobbett). Timber goes the colour of stone, and stone the colour of moss and fern. Roots reach calligraphically down the sides of rooty gorges, distinguished from the crumbling rock more by form than by texture.

The church here sits on a lip of the greensand scarp, and its Anglo-Saxon font is inscribed with words from Psalm 42:1 (here freely translated): 'As the deer pants for running water, so my soul is thirsty for you, oh God.' Perhaps a millennium old, they seem to capture much of the spirit of greensand places.

Behind Potterne and Devizes stretches the Vale of Pewsey proper: a tongue-shaped valley of rich, quiet farmland that makes its way deep into the surrounding chalk. As one of the most obvious east–west corridors through the Cretaceous rocks, the Kennet & Avon Canal and the main line from Paddington to Penzance make use of it. The M4 was originally going to head this way too, before it was directed to the Jurassic clays around Swindon.

Like the Weald, the rocks of the vale have been 'exhumed'. Erosion, eating along an Alpine-Grain faultline, has removed a mantle of chalk that once ran continuous from the Marlborough Downs to Salisbury Plain. The scarps of these two blocks of strange, white stone line the Vale, green-and-white waves caught in the middle of a bid to re-cover the land between them.

The Chalk

A long farm track leads from one side of the Vale into the voluminous arms of Tan Hill. This chalk hilltop, just inches below being the highest

Cretaceous Chalk
Lower Greensand
Lower Cretaceous (The Weald)

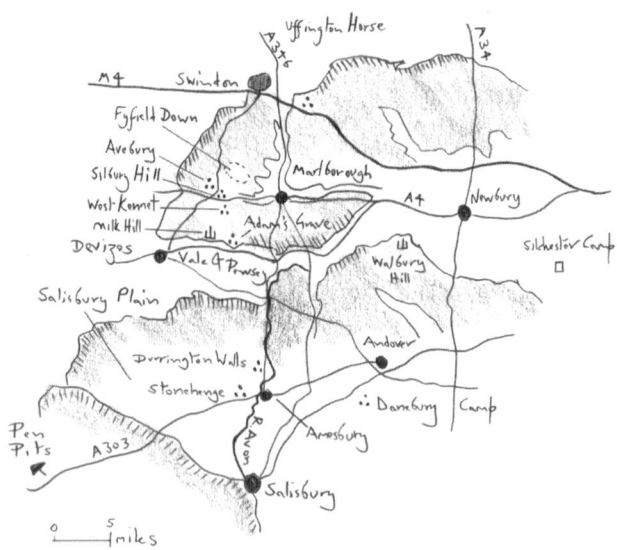

point in Wiltshire (Milk Hill, next door, is at 295m a little higher), is one of the best chalkland landscapes I know – which for me almost makes it a match for Suilven.

A hammerhead promontory reaches into the Vale, hillforts sitting like earthen saucers on its knolls. Rybury, the largest, has turned its small, round hilltop into a battered and layered place. Here an Iron Age enclosure sits right on top of a Neolithic one; the pits of undated quarries, presumably for flint, litter the interior.

Looking down from here, enormous barns float where the hill's flanks flatten out; an old droving route grooves its massive slope. One is aware of great spaces, curving gulfs in which starlings murmurate spectacularly.

Yet as with so many apparently significant peaks, the top of Tan Hill itself is archaeologically relatively bare, which hasn't stopped some suggesting that this is the sacred mountain in the lee of which Avebury was built. In recent centuries, the large and rowdy gathering known as Tan Hill Fair was held up here.

Beyond the peak, the dipslope opens out. Muscular chalk ridges slope into a great broad bowl drained by the River Kennet, the conoid form of Silbury Hill a regal presence in the distance. The way down is blocked by the serpent-like Wansdyke, a great earthwork perhaps built to separate post-Roman kingdoms. Cross it and explore, and each dry valley becomes a unique world apart. I call this 'dipsloping'; it takes one far from the more obvious spectacles of the scarp-edge into places more intimate with the subtleties of the chalk.

It is where this rock's slopes are steep that it most consistently remains unploughed, and its ability to make visible the layering of human activity comes to the fore. The fields shift from arable monoculture to grassland rich as deep velvet, infinitely full and infinitely soft. The surface ripples and shifts with the patterns of long-vanished activities: from the simple early modern geometries of stock pen and dew pond, to the mighty earth-sculptings of prehistory. All in a landscape that in spite of all this human shaping feels untouched and open.

Not far from Tan Hill, one can visit a scarp stepped with lynchets: a colossal staircase made by medieval ploughing. Or one can walk to Oxonmere, a dew pond hollowed out and lined with clay so as to provide liquid in this waterless landscape. It is mentioned in a boundary charter of AD 825, and is still functioning.

This geohistorical sensitivity lies at the heart of what makes the chalk special. The Carboniferous rocks may have had a greater historical import; the mid-Jurassic limestones put a more profound stamp on the nation's buildings – but there is something about this rock that strikes a unique balance between the natural and the man-made, charging it with the presence of the creatures who have lived upon it. Perhaps this is because the stone itself has an animal aspect, somehow suffusing it with hints of sentience.

Chalk origins

We've visited several limestones, and seen how the calcium carbonate they contain mostly originated as parts of living creatures. The Jurassic rocks in particular can be visibly stuffed with such remains. But with the chalk, the sense that this is a rocky remnant of life itself finds a new gear.

For chalk is dominated by countless billions of minute, circular plates of calcite, effectively tiny scales, which formed the outer casing of a jelly-like single-celled creature, the coccolithophore. These tiny body-parts are called 'coccoliths'.

Each coccolith is only a few thousandths of a millimetre across. For millions of years, these microscopic skeletal elements precipitated slowly through ocean waters up to 300m deep. It could take a century for a millimetre of new ocean floor to be laid down, churned only by slow, deep-water currents. Hundreds of metres were eventually deposited. It is hard to imagine how many such individual fragments this means.

This book is interested in the relationship between rock and one particular animal – us – and here is a rock that visibly sits somewhere between the geological and the biological. With our thin cover of living skin and supporting framework of bone, we have much in common with chalk hills. Perhaps their organic origin is also why the curvaceous lines of chalk landscapes can almost be erotic.

Chalk is also soft. You can crumble it in your hands. Only occasionally is it much use as a building stone (only two major freestones have been quarried from all those hundreds of miles of outcrop). It began forming from about 99 Ma, in the mid-/late Cretaceous, during a rising of the waters which covered about 80 per cent of the planet. All of Britain was engulfed, except perhaps the very highest parts of Scotland and Wales.

Almost everywhere, the chalk is white; it covers perhaps 13–14 per cent of Britain, and stretches on east as far as the Aral Sea. I have been told that some of the groundwater in the chalklands of Champagne originates in those of England; if that is the case, then something of the *terroir* of this fabled French beverage derives from English rain. Yet in Britain, chalk is also a very English stone; it is the first major phase of our story not to be present in Scotland or Wales at any level one could call a landscape.

The whiteness of this rock can be almost blinding – the canons of the twelfth-century cathedral at Old Sarum complained that the chalk motte of the adjacent castle gave them headaches. Centuries later, soot had to be used to disguise chalkland RAF runways from the Luftwaffe. Having spent many happy hours mountain-biking on chalk tracks, I can understand: the reflected light can be bright, hard, and painful on the eyes.

Consistency is a quality of the chalk. Even more than the mid-Jurassic limestone, it looks much alike wherever it is found, and it forms even longer escarpments. One could travel from Flamborough Head in Yorkshire to the Dorset coast mostly following these road-like landforms, give or take a boat trip across the Wash; from Cambridgeshire onwards the escarpment runs for over 100 miles, its hilly lip of stone unbroken except by a few river-mouths. This must make it the longest ridge in Britain, and within it the rocks change very little.

Simplicity and strangeness

All in all, the chalk is at once not really like any other rock, and a kind of purification or summation of characteristics we've seen in other limestones. This is a material that strikes a delicious balance between simplicity and strangeness.

Even hills like Tan Hill do not quite do as other hills do: they seem smoother, their curves more gradual. Here there are no caves, crags, or drystone structures. This white, soft material can barely feel like 'stone' at all; and water sinks into it like a sponge, leaving only occasional rivers: 'bournes' that often vanish altogether in the summer months (I have found twenty-one settlements in England with 'winterbourne/borne' in their name; all but one are on the chalk).

So this is dry country, and any explorer who associates valleys with streams can come away baffled. Sudden sharp grooves and scoops can seem unrelated to any visible, or even likely, water-flow, and attract a number of the chalk's stone heroes: the Devil scooped out the almost insanely sudden and steep Devil's Dyke, north of Brighton; the great sculpted combe known as the Manger was the feeding-trough of the White Horse of Uffington, Oxfordshire.

These landforms are partly a result of freeze-and-thaw in the deep permafrost which gripped the chalk during the Ice Age, but their distinctive form is also a result of the corporeal smoothness and curvy drama that is chalk's way of being eroded. And if this is true of the chalk's natural face, it is equally true of what is left behind when people mound and work it. Just as its hills look oddly alive, its earthworks look oddly geological; a retention of form that sits somewhere between the natural and the artificial.

When the rivers flow, they are exceptionally clean and clear. The Test valley in Hampshire seems lined with industries that are drawn to these qualities: a paper mill for banknotes, two former silk mills, a gin distillery; it is thanks to that river's smooth-flowing, weed-free quality that the rabbits who eventually find refuge on the chalk ridge of Watership Down are able, in Richard Adams's novel, to effect a successful escape from their pursuers.

Villages string the bournes, making the landscape 'most beautifully intersected, and cut though by the course of diverse pleasant and profitable rivers . . . with innumerable pleasant towns, villages and houses' (Defoe). The regularity of these settlements, like the metronomic spacing of the hillforts on the ridges, is a reflection of the simplicity of the landform itself. On the South Downs, the rivers Arun, Adur, Ouse and Cuckmere cut through the scarp every dozen miles or so. The Normans placed castles like corks in the neck of each of these valleys — Arundel, Bramber, Lewes — and thus controlled access to the south coast. The regularity and clarity of such landforms can make the chalkland seem like a template for geohistorical Place, the $E = mc^2$ from which a billion variants might be coined.

Very white and very sheer, where chalk cliffs do occur they can seem exceptionally fresh, sharp and bright. And in other situations where crag, cliff and tor might form, chalk instead makes grass-covered slopes of gravity-defying steepness: one such, on Tan Hill's western flank, is the steepest slope I know that has not simply become an exposure of bare rock. Experience tells us that anything this sheer should be hard, bare and rocky: yet it is like walking over a pool table set at an impossible angle. Instead of good crag, chalk gives good curve.

Walking over these softly reducing hills, it is easy to believe they are depleting themselves grain by tiny grain as the climate works them over. It is said the South Downs are reducing by 35cm a year. All rocks, of course, are being eroded and reduced, but the chalk does not hide the process by putting up craggy fists.

There is also a liquidity about these sediments of a lost sea floor: John Aubrey, a seventeenth-century philosopher and writer, described Salisbury Plain as 'the greatest remains that I can hear of the smooth primitive world when it lay all under water'. Others have likened the downs to galleons in sail, or great beached whales. Many world's ocean floors today are made of a grey-white sludge, which after millions of years of compression could become new chalklands.

Perhaps these slow, subaqueous curves help explain the bewildering distortions of scale one experiences when dipsloping through chalk country. Behind Tan Hill, the next field can look an ocean away, and the hillslopes beyond undulate into infinity, yet ten minutes later they have passed. It can feel like taking weightless leaps on the pathways of another planet. Yet it's not even clear that these downs should really qualify as upland. Seemingly vast, they are not really particularly big or high. They sit in a distinctive zone of their own, at once full of the swift, free energy of the steppe – and utterly safe. There is indeed something park-like about chalkland's soft drama. Cobbett said the chalk valleys are to the downs, 'what ah-ahs [sic] are, in parks'.

Of all the hill country in this book, this is the only one from which our commentators from the past did not recoil; Defoe called downland 'fruitful and pleasant' and 'delightful'; Cobbett, 'delicious'. We even have a special word for it: the 'up' land we call a down. This is a world of subtle contradiction: chalk downs have been tamed, yet have a wild freedom to them; geologically young, they are covered in ancient marks. Neither big nor small, neither tame nor wild, they are both old and new.

All in all, if the Precambrian of north-west Scotland is the geology that most profoundly embodies the natural forces that shaped this book, then the English chalk is a subtle testament to the interaction of those forces with human beings. For my money these are the two truly world-beating landscapes of Britain.

Chalk landscapes

There are subtle variations within this basically unchanging rock. Partly because ice-age glaciation hit harder there, the northern chalk is harder than that of the south; it also contains fewer flints. The rock-type as a whole can be divided into the Lower Chalk, greyish and more impervious because it contains more clay; and the Middle and Upper Chalk (today grouped into a single formation), purer, whiter, more flinty, and dominating the downland. Throughout, though, it is almost always possible to see that this is a grainy material; the most obvious things that look like bedding planes are the horizontal seams of flint.

This upper/lower distinction is a crucial element in the landscapes of the chalk. Often there is a change of angle between the two; sometimes there are even two scarps, separated by a plateau. The moonscape that opens out on my homeward journey is a downland of Upper Chalk, but it is only revealed after one has climbed a scarp of Lower Chalk and greensand. Often the highest country is where the two scarps come together, as if the landscape itself had caught a really good wave: chalk 'mountains' such as Uffington and Cherhill, Wiltshire, are Upper/Middle Chalk scarps sitting directly on top of Lower Chalk ones.

But there are other chalk landscapes. The ice age left a layer of flint-studded clay on top of many chalklands, a layer that is more marked the further north one goes. Such places are covered in beechwoods: the difference between the tree-covered Chilterns and the bare Marlborough Downs. The beeches around High Wycombe generated a furniture industry in that town. This 'wooded downland' is criss-crossed by many rights of way, and dotted with isolated farms and woods. Historically important areas of forest, such as Savernake, Wiltshire, sit on it. The bare chalk, by contrast, is open and empty; the few paths provide droving routes, and often follow the ridges.

And then there is an easily overlooked chalk lowland. In Cambridgeshire, the chalk scarp can be little more than a barely noticed rise. Yet the country of the chalk, here often covered with glacial earth, continues east for nigh on 30 miles into East Anglia, with significant implications for that region's geohistory. Large parts of Hampshire and Hertfordshire are like this, too: near-featureless, rolling like a gentle ocean, with plough-snapping nodules of flint everywhere in huge fields.

Salisbury Plain is unique, 150 square miles of almost landmark-free chalkland, too elevated to count as lowland, too flat to be a 'down':

Britain's steppe. This is the largest area of unimproved chalkland in north-west Europe — because it is also Britain's largest army training area, and has thus lain unploughed for much of the twentieth century. Of the 'unimproved' chalk in Britain, 40 per cent lies here, where Wordsworth noted the 'strange marks of mighty arms of former days'. There are places here where the earthwork outline of a Roman-British village street is perfectly legible, and ancient pottery fragments lie scattered on the ground not far from tank-tracks and craters.

Chalkland towns, meanwhile, have a contradictory quality rather typical of the poetics of the chalk. While the landscape itself richly evokes great depths of human presence, and there is nothing historically young about these settlements, places like Marlborough in Wiltshire, and Dorchester in Dorset, can feel lightly placed, fragile, almost temporary.

This is even true of Salisbury, that planted city of the thirteenth century, down the streets of which chalkland streams were canalised into 'pleasant little rivulets ... to wash and cleanse them' (Lieutenant Hammond, 1635). Perhaps this is a side effect of the building materials that dominate their historic cores: oak, brick, tile-hung walls, piles of flint bound together only by mortar. The grander buildings are often of Jurassic freestones, which had to be hauled there. The result is a certain sense of impermanence: as if the towns, like the downs, are on the verge of being removed by the erosive force of history.

Chalkland geohistories

As will already be clear, human history is written into the chalk. The story starts early, for the thin soils of the Downs were easy to clear of their low-level scrub; and the white rock is jammed with potential tools, in the form of flints.

Take a step back and follow the chalk scarps, and their arms – south from Yorkshire, north from Dorset, and west from the North and South Downs – converge octopus-like on Wiltshire, metropolis of the chalk. The county is famously the site of such monuments as Avebury and Stonehenge: perhaps its Neolithic prominence was a side effect of its location at the centre of these natural routes.

Ridgeways and roads

Old roads seem particularly vivid in chalkland landscapes. As you approache a scarp-edge, you can often see the rise striated with deep, intertwining grooves, wrinkle-like holloways at once fresh and ancient in feel, created by centuries of feet, wheels and hooves making their way up and down the slope.

The ridgeways that follow the scarps themselves can be hazy entities archaeologically, but the route-like nature of the landform is unmistakable. The very earliest humans may have followed the ridges of the North and South Downs from northern France to Kent (for a long time there was a land-bridge between the two).

One ancient path, the Peddar's Way, seems to connect the low-lying country of the East Anglian coast and the Norfolk flint mines with the 'infrastructure' of chalk ridges: is it Neolithic in origin? Roman (in its present form) Watling Street follows the lower edge of the North Downs chalk dipslope; one of the medieval pilgrim routes to Canterbury follows much of its ridge.

As ever, lines of hills make borders as well as routes. The southern escarpment of the Marlborough Downs is followed not only by the ridgetop Wansdyke but also, 2,000 years later and in the vale below, by a line of Second World War defences. Several Cretaceous vales were used as such 'stoplines', blocking the progress of a Third Reich invasion from the south coast. The landform suggests its own possibilities, which lie in wait until history takes a course that activates them.

Avebury and Stonehenge

As for Avebury, its great chalk bank is some 4,000 years old; the district in which it sits contains a yet older Neolithic landscape: causewayed enclosures on hilltops, long barrows on gentle slopes. The people who created such sites knew the lie of the land intimately. Perhaps they too went dipsloping.

Avebury seems to me almost like a great abstracted ideogram of the downland, its henge a circular scarp, its ditch a dipslope dry valley, the four openings in it as regularly spaced as river-mouths. The comparison is stronger because, while most scarplands are linear rather than circular, the Marlborough Downs are bounded by scarps and valleys on all sides. Originally Avebury was anything but natural in feel: it was a great geometric land-sculpture, its ditches and banks sheer and blazing white with exposed chalk.

Silbury Hill, not far away, is a giant ritual mound closely related to the place where a winterbourne stream becomes a year-round river, the Kennet. In spite of its floodplain setting — the ditches around it fill with water in winter, like a true winterbourne — its peak sits at just the right height to ensure it can be glimpsed as one approaches along the Kennet.

Silbury's likeness to geology is more than skin-deep. Effectively a cairn 39m high, it was built in stages over several generations, making its upturned bowl a kind of human anticline. In an archaeological version of the hunt for coal or ore, miners from the Bristol coalfields were employed in 1776 to dig into it in search of the treasure buried within (there was none).

By the beginning of the second millennium BC, although Avebury remained a place of power, it had ceased to be actively used. Over three hundred round barrows cluster on the surrounding hills, honorific flotillas of UFOs circulating a great mothership. Today the A4361 runs through two of the Neolithic gateways in the henge, and a village half-occupies the earthwork, its church and manor house visibly structures with complex, layered histories. The combination makes this one of the greatest dense places in Britain.

The area around Stonehenge, too, is littered with round barrows. This monument is famous for its 'stones of wonderful size, erected in the manner of doors' (Henry of Huntingdon, c.1130). There is a lithophilia in its stone choices, and topophilia is latent in its design. Aligned with the axis of the solstices, Stonehenge is approached along a processional path from the river Avon. In both respects it is presaged by a series of long, low, natural ridges and gullies in the chalk itself. Created by glaciation, they must have seemed to be the creation of some solstice-honouring ancestral spirit.

Even the great ring of ritual pits surrounding Durrington Walls near Stonehenge, discovered in 2020, appear to be an artificial expansion from a handful of pits of glacial origin. Pits of uncertain function – their contents often so distinctive and carefully arranged that they are unlikely to be rubbish dumps or storage sites – are an easily overlooked type of monument. While these are Neolithic, such pits were particularly common in the Iron Age. It seems a particular charge has often been associated with the placing of objects below the ground, returning them to geology: a mine or quarry in reverse.

Moving on

The downs remained an important focus of settlement and farming for thousands of years after the Neolithic. The edges of Bronze Age fields are perfectly visible as one crosses Fyfield Down in Wiltshire, and Iron Age hillforts are everywhere in the chalklands, but after that, settlement moves to the valleys, and the traces of human life become less dramatic. The chomping of a million ovine teeth — more calcium – prevented the scrub from growing back, giving the downland its soft cover of grass, and leaving visible the remains of the past. The sheep were only there because they were useful to people, so this is a human intervention.

The Anglo-Saxon kingdom of Wessex had its heartlands on the chalk, and its capital at chalkland Winchester – a city so long-settled that the walls of its houses are visibly made of chunks of lost buildings. Perhaps the city's quiet self-assurance reflects its long history as an important place. Its surrounding hillforts suggest it has been a major centre since early times. From here, Alfred the Great laid out a series of defensive burghs to hold his kingdom against the Viking threat; an impressive and early sequence of planned towns, and a harbinger of its medieval achievements. In the late eleventh century, its cathedral was one of the largest roofed structures on the planet.

But perhaps the most artistic chalkland geo-phenomenon of all was to flourish in the early modern period; fittingly, it connects the Bronze Age with the Enlightenment.

White horses and follies

A sinuously abstracted steed 111m long gallops west along the scarp-edge at Uffington, Berkshire, as if chasing the setting sun along the scarp.

Reproduced on everything from T-shirts to album covers, it is arguably the best-known work of art to have survived from British prehistory.

This piece of landscape art is the product of a brilliant geo-artistic idea: because the chalk is white, and covered by a consistent, sheep-cropped green, all one has to do to create an eye-catching image is to cut sections of the grass and shallow soil away and a white 'drawing' can be created. Ensure one does this on a scarp and the image becomes widely visible: an engraving in the landscape itself.

The Uffington white horse may have been cut as early as the second millennium BC. The very fact that it has survived is almost as remarkable as the elegance of its conception. Such figures need constant maintenance or the skin of grass re-covers them. Regular 'scourings' are recorded from the seventeenth century; similar interventions must have occurred every few decades, perhaps with longer gaps, for up to four millennia – the springline village of Uffington, the local settlement, has been there for less than half that time.

Though almost all subsequent figures are also on the chalk, they are not exclusively equine. The giddily priapic 55m giant that dominates the chalk hillside above Cerne Abbas, Dorset, is Anglo-Saxon in origin (that this visibly engorged presence lies adjacent to what was long the site of a major monastery makes me proud to British). The eighteenth-century white horse at Westbury, Wiltshire, may have had an Anglo-Saxon predecessor. The 62m Long Man at Wilmington, East Sussex, apparently holding Norwegian walking poles, was created in the seventeenth century. There are other images of uncertain date not on the chalk, including lost giants on Clifton Down, Bristol, and Plymouth Hoe.

Yet it is the chalk and the white horses that dominate. Of at least twenty-three known, nineteen are on the chalk (the furthest from the formation is in Aberdeenshire), and over half date from the eighteenth and nineteenth centuries: the heyday (hayday?) of the genre. Most are on the Marlborough Downs, where Uffington must be their ultimate grand-mare; indeed, there was once one on Tan Hill. Perhaps they evoke a certain pride in a landscape then being revealed as a major prehistoric centre by figures such as John Aubrey and William Stukeley.

Perhaps, too, they reflect the fact that the chalk is great riding country, today host to training stables at Newmarket and Lambourn, and racetracks at Epsom and Brighton. Another development of this period also reflects the chase: the planting of geometrical stands of trees, providing cover for game while breaking up the landscape. Enjoyably, these downs are also the homeland of a more recent form of landscape art or rural graffiti, one that requires both large arable fields and smooth-sided slopes: crop circles.

The chalk plays a role in some of the more obviously designed landscapes of the period. Soft and easily removed, it has in several places been used to create artificial folly-caves. This is presaged at Royston Cave, a bottle-shaped man-made cavern descending 7.7m underground just a few yards from the Hertfordshire intersection of Ermine Street and the Icknield Way. On its walls, elaborate if untutored carvings, most of them of medieval religious subjects, are worked into the soft rock; the cave has been claimed as everything from a cold store that acquired religious significance to an omphalos, a geomantic navel, to England as a whole.

At West Wycombe in Buckinghamshire, Sir Francis Dashwood transformed a chalk quarry into a man-made subterranean landscape in 1750–52. Behind a Gothic flint facade, a maze of chalk tunnels leads to such curiosities as a domical 'Great Hall' and faked-up 'River Styx', running directly below his hilltop church and mausoleum. A certain extravagant mischievousness is afoot in this 'folly cave'; the spirit, perhaps, of the Hellfire club, Dashwood's society 'of worthy, jolly fellows, happy disciples of Venus and Bacchus', which met on his nearby estate.

The art of the chalk hill figure is by no means dead: from 1916 a series of regimental badges were cut at Fovant, Wiltshire, and since then nine further chalkland figures have been created, ranging from a kiwi to an aeroplane, and including white horses in Wiltshire and Kent cut to mark the year 2000. Copies overseas include a giant facsimile of the Uffington original, running across a desert ridge near Chihuahua, Mexico.

The chalk today

Today, the chalklands can be a grim bellwether for some of the negative aspects of modern agricultural practice. As recently as the 1940s, much downland remained open, unfenced, unimproved grassland, in some places unploughed for 2,500 years: infinitely full, infinitely soft; possessed of a certain Mongolian wildness, yet with the patterns of long-vanished earthworks visibly shifting like veins beneath their skin.

But after the Second World War almost everything that could be reached by powered vehicles was ploughed and much of it given over to arable. In 1990 just 4 per cent of a total of 3.3 million acres/1.3 million ha of chalkland survived unploughed. The big fields and long fences help accentuate the slow curves of the land, but their grain-filled expanses and nettle-lined fringes gives them an industrial edge. One can theoretically restore the grassland habitat, but once the archaeology that is such a fundamental part of its identity is flattened, it is gone forever.

The chalk has both the openness and fluidity of open grassland and the layered, lived-in quality of an ancient building; it shows its age, yet wears it lightly. Many of the places in it are so dense that we forget that hundreds, even thousands of years separate the creation of each of the monuments that comprise them. They are in effect layered gatherings of unconformity, archaeological and geological at one and the same time. Yet they also make punctuation marks in this flowing landform. Humanity and nature in symbiotic partnership, making places: geohistorical poetry.

Chalkland industries and building stones

The chalkland's geohistorical power is all the more remarkable given its relative lack of those essential glues of 'geology' to 'human history': mineral deposits and building materials.

Like all limestones, chalk has been used to generate lime for building, industry and agriculture. And it is perhaps the best mark-maker of all rocks: used to make white paint, and leaving a clear line on any darkish surface, as the countless people who were taught their lessons using sticks of it can testify.

Rare industrial uses include one of the few Scottish Cretaceous rocks, a silica-pure sandstone at Morvern, Highlands, which has been extracted for use in high-precision lenses; and a soft, brown coal, mined at Cobham in Kent. There are Cretaceous reservoirs of oil and gas in the North Sea.

The chalk is also the setting for the unexpected coal-mining country of eastern Kent. As early as the 1850s geologists had argued that Carboniferous deposits might lie buried between those of western Britain and northern Europe. In 1890, Carboniferous deposits of coal were found over 245m below the surface. The main quarries were at Betteshanger, Chislet, Snowdown and Tilmanstone; the resulting migration of northern miners to this rural south-eastern setting caused significant social tension.

As at West Wycombe, chalk quarries might become mines. Those at Lavant in West Sussex were in use as early as the Roman period. There are many such excavations beneath Norwich, some up to 4m high: a bus fell into one in 1988.

The material extracted here is usually too soft and porous to be a first-rate building material; it also tends to disintegrate when used externally. But the 'chalk rock' or clunch of the Lower Chalk can quite often be seen on barns and cottages. When ashlared it has a white-edged precision, and is often seen in combination with flint or brick.

Ashbourne House, on the Berkshire/Wiltshire border, is a rare example of an ambitious building made of this material, but perhaps the most extensive use of it can be seen on the hard chalk of the Yorkshire Wolds. The stark seventeenth-century lighthouse at Flamborough is only the most striking of the many chalk buildings of the area. Several local Neolithic children have been found buried with toy-sized carved chalk drums which vie with the stone balls of Aberdeenshire as among the oldest finely carved stones in Britain.

Though clunch freestones are rare, the best can take beautiful carving. There are a cluster in the Cambridgeshire/Bedfordshire/Hertfordshire region, where perhaps the most famous quarry was at Totternhoe: some of the horizontal mines or adits were 200m long. The clunch-carved fourteenth-century Lady Chapel in Ely cathedral has one of the most breathtaking sculpted interiors in England; as if the walls themselves had come to organic life.

The other major chalk freestone is at Beer, near the south Devon coast: almost the south-westernmost outcrop of Cretaceous rocks in the land. Like Totternhoe, this rock has been known since Roman times. Roman, medieval and later phases of the 4–5m-high quarry caves can still be identified: enormous spaces, supported by mighty, column-like stays of unquarried rock. Much of the best carved work at Exeter Cathedral is of this fine, white material, which was also exported as far as Kent and Westminster.

The chalkland mythosphere

Standing on Tan Hill, a great *dramatis personae* hovers invisibly over the landscape. Wansdyke is dedicated to the god Woden; Silbury was legendarily the burial place of King Sil. The name of the hill itself is a contraction of 'St Ann': so this matriarch of Wiltshire hills is named for God's granny.

On Walker's Hill, a couple of miles away, there is the long barrow known as Adam's Grave, previously also belonging to Woden (*Wodnesbeorg*). I love the way this name-change records the historical shift from pagan to Christian, and find Adam's Grave a particularly poetic coining. What more appropriate an occupant of this primal building-type than the first man? Various traditions connect this figure to the Earth itself: 'Adam' is Hebrew for 'formed from the ground', just as the 'hu' in human and humus, soil, have the same Latin root.

The chalk, it seems, has let culture sink into it as easily as liquid. Has any other rock entered the language in so many ways? People talk of 'chalk and cheese' without any knowledge that the saying is an elegant contraction of Wiltshire's dual geological identity: Jurassic clays dominate the dairy-producing pastures of the north-western third of the county, chalk downland the rest. For Aubrey, the inhabitants of the claylands were 'slow and dull, heavy of spirit . . . melancholy, contemplative and malicious', whereas those of the chalk where strong, fit and hard-working.

And while we have seen many place names that evoke the colour of a rock – and chalkland examples include White Waltham, Berkshire and Whitcomb, Dorset – those that name the rock-type itself have been rarer. Yet we have Broad Chalke, Wiltshire; Chalgrave, Bedfordshire; Chalk, Kent, and at least thirty-two others.

While many geologies have inspired great writing, rarely has this addressed the rock itself. Yet authors from G.K. Chesteron to H.J. Massingham have written specifically on chalkland landscapes. The painter Paul Nash was besotted with the crypto-geometrical forms of chalk hills and earthworks, as seen in his *Equivalents of the Megaliths* (1935). His contemporary, Eric Ravilious, made the chalk his special subject matter, and perhaps comes closer than any artist to capturing its essence in works such as *Chalk Paths* (also 1935).

In the mid-1820s Samuel Palmer relocated to Shoreham in Kent, a village that nestles in a narrow gap in the North Downs. There, he and a small group of artists inspired by William Blake created some of the most numinous evocations of landscape in British art.

Place is everywhere in Blake, but it is either a parallel, mystical London or a generic countryside of spires and wooded hills. Yet the chalk may lurk even here. *Jerusalem* was written in the lee of the South Downs, and what other land is both 'green and pleasant' while also having 'mountains green'?

More recently, the chalkland mythosphere has taken a darker turn: Graham Greene's 'Kick these hills and they bleed white' (*24 Hours in Metroland*); the edgy associations evoked by singers such as Natasha Khan ('The Haunted Man') and P.J. Harvey ('White Chalk'). Perhaps this has something to do with the chalkland Armageddon that was the Western Front. Which brings us to one of the most difficult aspects of the chalkland mythosphere: its association with English identity itself.

At Dover, the sea has cut across the South Downs like a knife. Here, above the most defensible and historically important of the Channel ports, is Dover castle. We are at the English Channel's narrowest point and the white cliffs near Calais are perfectly visible. On this stone throne, Dover castle embodies every defensive phase of English history, from the remains of a Roman lighthouse to elaborate responses to the Napoleonic and Nazi threats.

According to tradition, Britain itself was first named because of such cliffs, for the name 'Albion' is derived from the Latin *albus* or white. For millennia, these white cliffs have been the visual signature of our island. More recently, this association has acquired an unspoken but distinct English tinge. Perhaps this is because the rock of which the cliffs are formed has no meaningful presence in Scotland or Wales; perhaps it is because the colour chimes with the white-and-red of St George's cross; unfortunate associations relating to race and to blood might be followed from here.

But before chalk becomes a lightning rod for jingoism or worse, it is worth remembering that its vast outcrop makes it the most European of rocks, and that places like Dover tell a story of migration as well as of defence. 'There'll be bluebirds over...' sang Vera Lynn; 'I can't seem to find my way...' responded Jimmy Cliff. Many modern migrants might agree.

We are edging close to one of the chalk's most significant historical themes; but first we should turn to two unusual rock-types with which the chalk is intimately associated. Here again, we are in unique territory, for both — unlike the chalk itself — have a significant role to play in the geohistory of Britain: yet neither forms a landscape. They are flint and sarsen.

Flint

Flint is easy to find. These dense, dark, glassy nodules lie littered in chalkland fields. Their contribution to the human story has been fundamental.

This material is chalk's opposite: it is made of silica rather than calcium ('silica' derives from the Latin for flint); it is hard and brittle rather than soft and crumbly; and its shades of fawn-grey to black stand in contrast to the chalk's intense white.

The silica of which it is made originated in the skeletons of the sponges and other creatures that lived in the warm Cretaceous seas. Gradually buried on the sea floor, this was transformed by the changing chemistry of its surroundings and compressed under pressure into a kind of quartz.

The flint gathered in horizontal seams ('tabular' flint) and in the burrow-systems dug by worms and other creatures, where it came to be shaped like moulds of their globular interiors. Such nodules can look like some sculptural love child of Henry Moore and Salvador Dalí. Each is a cast of what was once some creature's home.

Often enclosed in a thin white skin of lime, this distinctive rock is both as hard as diamond and very brittle. Struck at the right angle it shatters easily, leaving a sharp fracture line that is surprisingly effective as a knife, and yet hard enough to use as a hammer. A superficially convincing example, made in about twenty minutes under the tutorship of Dr James Dilley, sits on one of my bookshelves. A craftsman more skilled at this 'knapping' can turn a piece of flint into a beautifully crafted tool, one that also has an ebony glow.

Flint can only be said to form a landscape on certain beaches, such as the 18-mile-long bank linking the Isle of Portland to the Dorset mainland known as Chesil Beach. Here wave action has sorted the flints and cherts so that they are larger at the Portland end than the Abbotsbury one. Rounded by the waves, flints gathered here in the Iron Age were hoarded as slingshot ammunition at nearby Maiden Castle. Locations such as Loe Bar, Cornwall, far from modern sources of flint, are smaller-scale equivalents (Our Variscan stone hero John Tregeagle is said to have formed it when he dropped a sack of sand). Everywhere else, flint is merely one element in a wider landscape.

There are incredible quantities of it around. The chalk in which it grew is its primary home – it is particularly common in the Upper Chalk. But its great hardness means that when the chalk has been removed by erosion, the flint that was in it was left behind, effectively pre-quarried and ready for use.

This makes it a geological gift from the Cretaceous to the rest of Britain. It is especially common in the young Tertiary and Quaternary country that succeeds the chalk, which occupies Britain's southernmost and easternmost edges, and extends below the North Sea. Other places it can be found include valley-heads in the Midlands, the paths of former rivers, and on estuaries and coasts as far north as Orkney, where pieces were washed up from a Cretaceous outcrop on the sea floor 10–20 miles to the east.

This ubiquitous rock has been the go-to material for stone tool-making since the Palaeolithic, and it was as fundamental to the great cultural expansion of the Neolithic as was coal to the industrial revolution – the first 'black stuff', as David Miles puts it. More than any other single material, it facilitated the first true attempts to shape the landscape – cutting down trees, moving stones, and changing forever the visual balance between us and our environment.

Other rock-types may have provided posher tools, but flint was useful and ubiquitous: a geological B&Q. It was widely traded, though that of the Yorkshire Wolds is relatively poor in quality and scarce, tools sourced there have been found across northern England. Most of this material was simply picked up on the surface, or from cliffs. But not all.

A third of the thirty-three known Neolithic mining sites in Britain are for flint. A ridge of glacial gravel at Den of Boddam, Buchan, is the only major inland source in northern Britain. Far to the south, Cissbury, West Sussex, may be where the story of mining in Britain begins.

This impressive chalk hill elbows its way into a gap in the South Downs like a drunken bouncer in a nightclub. It is said to be a spoil-heap from Satan's excavation of Devil's Dyke, 8 miles away. From it you can survey much of the chalk country and the coast. The largest Iron Age hillfort in Sussex grips its upper flanks, but one end is pock-marked by some 270 craters, as if the ground had been peppered with acne.

Once, these were open pores in the landscape, some several dozen yards wide. From the base of each, galleries just large enough to crawl in extended. Sometimes the miners stopped to carve fragile images of animals into the soft rock. Originating in about 4000 BC, each is today host to a sudden thicket, the mines affecting the way plants grow 6,000 years after they were dug.

Cissbury is the most important of several sites hereabouts, sites that between them may have been the source of most of the flint tools of south-eastern Britain. They were not the scene of constant, day in, day out, labour: activity went on episodically, over long periods of time. Nevertheless, as Nicholas Crane points out, they were also for some time the largest artificial structures in the land.

At Grimes Graves, Norfolk – the graves of *grim*, broadly dated around 2500 BC – a specific layer of flint, the floorstone, was deemed important; to reach it miners had to dig through 9–13m of chalk, passing several other flint layers as they went. They then tunnelled along the top of the seam, using antler picks to separate and lift each piece. This suggests a sophisticated apprehension of the subtly varying qualities of particular flint beds, as well as a canny proto-geological understanding of where they might be found.

There is every sign that these locations held a symbolic, or at least prestige, dimension. Good flint is easily found near to several of the South Downs sites without climbing the scarp: the mines themselves seem positioned to crest dramatically when viewed from below. We got a comparable sense at Ordovician Pike O'Stickle, the only industrial monument of the era to match Cissbury and Grime's Graves in scale.

Ritual deposits have been found below the ground at both Grimes Graves and Cissbury; carved chalk objects, deposited stone tools, bones. Perhaps these artificial, underground places were felt to breach 'the transition between the layers of the cosmos', as David Miles puts it: the sky, the earth, the underworld.

Gunflint

Flint's ongoing story is dominated by its use as a building material. But there was also an industry knapping flints for use in striking the sparks that ignited gunpowder. This gunflint industry came to be focused around Brandon in Suffolk, thanks to the approval given to its flints by the Board of Ordnance. Towards the end of the Napoleonic wars, over a million flints a month were being produced by 160 workers here. Not all were for guns: strike-a-lights made of flint were supplied to soldiers fighting in the Boer war, and were depended on by explorers.

Claiming continuity with the Neolithic miners, whose mines at Grime's Graves 3 miles away they reopened, the knappers also made fake prehistoric arrowheads and other items. Their own mines or 'burrows' could be up to 9m deep, formed of undercutting steps, a technique winningly called 'bubberhutching on the sosh'. The (considerable) waste they generated went into local buildings: Brandon railway station is one.

As gun technology changed, the industry contracted, but managed to survive thanks to a worldwide export market, for example from historic weapons enthusiasts; the last workshop closed in 1996.

Flint buildings

English flint architecture is unique in Europe; and it shows a remarkable sensitivity to the qualities of this remarkable material: coloured like something precious, available in small pieces, easy to knap but impossible to carve. As early as the Iron Age, Danebury camp in Hampshire was approached along a 46m flint-lined drystone corridor. But flint is not suited to drystone, and Roman mortar provided the key to its potential for making rough, strong walls.

Thus was born a way of building that has been used in flint country ever since. Wooden boards are erected and flints poured between them, along with large amounts of mortar, the lime for which was itself derived from the chalk. Let the mortar set and remove the planking and you have a wall, its noduley surface instantly recognisable, if prone to disintegration should the mortar decay.

Roman walls of this type survive up to 7m high, often with distinctive horizons of stabilising tiles, at such places as Silchester and Porchester in Hampshire, and Richborough in Kent; they have outlived Rome by almost 1,700 years.

In the medieval period, flint gave rise to some unique structures. This is not a material given to the construction of sharp, clean corners, and in medieval East Anglia many church towers were round rather than square: 165 are known, of which the vast majority are in Norfolk.

It was in this county that a remarkable flint-based form of architectural art was invented. In many areas where flint was ubiquitous and good limestone had to be imported, limestone ashlar might be alternated with stretches of knapped flint; sometimes the two were placed in chequerboard patterns.

East Anglian 'flushwork' takes the idea further by placing the flints inside limestone frames, which could be cut to just about any shape. This delicious combination of pale, crisp, smooth freestone and dark, shiny, knapped flint was used to make inscriptions, complex Gothic patterns, and other devices, as seen in the fourteenth-century St Ethelbert's Gate in Norwich, or fifteenth-century Long Melford church in Suffolk.

Even where an East Anglian building looks to have been made of limestone ashlar, it actually depends on flint. The walls of its great abbeys and cathedrals have outer skins of Jurassic Barnack: but between them lie countless Cretaceous flints embedded in rough mortar. At the dissolution of the monasteries such churches became an unintended, but equally unique, architectural genre: the flint ruin.

The expensive, imported limestone that clothed once-grand buildings such as Castle Acre Priory and Bury St Edmunds Abbey was stripped away for reuse, leaving exposed the flint-and-mortar mix within. These great rotten flint fingers make some of the most visceral ruins in Britain, their Jurassic skin flayed away to reveal the rough Cretaceous body beneath, architecture visibly eroded by politics.

Architecture is geological: rocks are piled up in a kind of human orogeny, and then time, or neglect, or history, erodes and rearranges them, creating stratigraphies and unconformities within structures, as well as, as here, landscapes of ruin. Shorn of its caldera and eroded to its subterranean roots, Ben Nevis no longer looks like a volcano; its Jurassic facing robbed and its flints eaten at by East Anglian rain, Bury St Edmunds Abbey no longer looks like a church.

As brick became common, flint building grew rarer; but it was revived in the eighteenth century, when its weird shape, eye-catching colour and relative cheapness made it popular, not only for decorating follies and grottoes, but as a kind of flint ashlar. Laboriously cubed flints about 10cm square were used to build entire walls, each piece 'headed so curiously that it looks like glass and shines with the sun's reflection' (Celia Fiennes). In East Anglia, the technique is called 'Suffolk Diamonds'; it is also found on the south coast. Such flints may be placed in simple patterns within walls made of brick or stone.

Often, one can tell the source of the flint in a building by looking closely at it. Field flint, plucked from the surface, looks weathered; its benefit is its size — individual pieces a foot or two across are not unknown. Quarried flint is much fresher and crisper. Flint from beaches makes greyish pebbles, often marked by the wave-driven battering of one against another. Flint from river gravels is larger – pieces can be up to 15cm across. Both of these types are useful for being regular in size and simple in form, making good cobbles. Today flint is still used, for gravel, and in the ceramics industry.

Chert is very close to flint, but more associated with limestone than with chalk, and not always Cretaceous: Carboniferous and Jurassic cherts are known. Its homeland is on the borders of Devon, Somerset and Dorset, where it is of Upper Greensand age and often a 'milky brown' (Alec Clifton-Taylor). There are squared chert buildings in Chard, Somerset; and Pennine chert of Carboniferous age was a popular source of prehistoric flint tools in the Midlands.

Sarsen

There is no stone with quite the presence of sarsen. Its preternatural density and inscrutability is almost an energy in its own right. I understand it when I see visitors to Avebury embracing the great lumps of it that stand there.

Palpably unlike the country rock on which it lies, these large, flattish, brown boulders demand a response. The name reflects this: it may derive from *sar stan*, a difficult or troublesome stone; or 'saracen', a non-Christian foreigner – at once powerful and 'other'. Sarsens can have a creature-like quality, especially when seen at dusk: their other local name, 'grey wethers', comes from the Wiltshire for 'sheep'. Speaking as one who has tried to instal shelves into a sarsen wall, it is also almost insanely hard.

Sarsen is not Cretaceous. It was born in the Tertiary period, perhaps during a period of intense global heating around 55 Ma. Silica dissolved in fresh water became mixed with the silica-rich sand on the river bed, cementing its grains together hard: 'silcrete'. Perhaps it was the heat that made this process very fast: sarsens are often punctured by the root-holes of plants that were growing in it as it cemented. Softer areas eventually eroded away, leaving boulders behind.

Other Tertiary boulders include conglomerates known as Puddingstones, jammed with chunks of flint and found mostly in Hertfordshire; and 'heathstone', a term perhaps especially applied when iron has made the rock very brown. Despite their origin, the vast majority lie on Cretaceous rocks: from Suffolk to Dorset, with major concentrations on the North and South Downs, the Chilterns, and (especially) the Marlborough Downs. There are significant numbers on adjacent younger rocks, too.

Partly because their distribution was always patchy, and partly because they have often been pushed aside to make fields or broken up for use in buildings and roads, sarsens are frequently encountered as one-off boulders or a group of boulders, sitting on the edge of a field. Yet there are places where these rocks lie as close together as clitter.

One such is Fyfield Down, on the chalk of the Marlborough Downs. This small but magical tract is the best surviving 'Sarsen landscape'. Some of the rocks are enormous; others seem to work their way like little herds down hillsides, to cluster in dry valleys, following the general tide of moisture in the chalk, even though no flowing water is visible, reflecting the effect of cycles of freeze and thaw.

Such rocks attract speculation. Stukeley thought they must have been flung to the surface from below the ground, under the sudden impact of some great centrifugal force; the only event that could have caused this, he reasoned, was that of the planet itself, 'when its rotation was first impress'd', at the moment of creation.

The puddingstones, so visibly made up of smaller rocks that they look like lithicized fruitcake, were also called 'Growing Stones', because they were believed to grow in the fields; 'Breeding Stones', because their constituent lumps were believed to be baby rocks; and as 'Hag stones', they were used to ward off evil. There are many stories in which they move under their own volition.

Sarsen lithophilia

The sarsens and their peers are the last in our litany of stones that lie around in separate pieces, and which are thus perfect for the use of early monument-makers: such as the Devonian rocks of Orkney and the granite clitter of Dartmoor.

This makes it a go-to building material in long barrows and stone circles from Kent to Dorset. It is a mark of their ubiquity in the Wiltshire landscape that, when John Aubrey discovered Avebury in 1649, the area around it was so dense with the things that many believed the entire district was some shattered prehistoric city, the place 'where the giants fought with huge stones against the gods'. Surely, poet and collector Iolo Morganwg said in 1777, Fyfield Down was 'the grand seat of the Druids before the Roman invasion'.

Aubrey's discovery was an act of discernment, separating the monumental landscape from the natural one; as sarsens also made field boundaries within the henge itself, and many of its great standing stones had fallen or been buried, this was an achievement in itself. Re-erected, we can see the rocks there are arranged in alternating longer and squatter stones, with particularly enormous monoliths marking entrances and key foci. Yet each rock is also an abstract presence in its own right.

Even more remarkably, fifty-two of an original eighty or so sarsens, the tallest 9m high, form the trilothons of Stonehenge. Amid all the glamour of the much smaller Ordovician bluestones and their journey from Wales, it is easy to overlook the fact that the transportation of such rocks as much as 18 miles across rolling country, including descending at least one steep scarp and climbing the slope from the Avon, is a jaw-dropping achievement in itself.

These colossal stones were then shaped using sarsen hammers, giving this rock the honour of being one of the first stones to be 'dressed' as part of the building process: the primordial parent of every ashlar wall in this book.

Stonehenge is thus an agglomeration of three stone-types: smaller but carefully curated bluestones; the monumental sarsens; and the single piece of Old Red which is the Altar Stone. Each of these stone-types was favoured by Neolithic monument-makers, whether in Orkney, or Pembrokeshire, or the south-east; their gathering here is all the more compelling for the vast gulf of geological time that separates the truly ancient Ordovician from the almost-yesterday Tertiary.[*]

---

[*] Orkney has now been ruled out as the origin for the Altar Stone as of September 2024 – the hunt for the source continues: https://www.theguardian.com/uk-news/article/2024/sep/05/stonehenge-tale-gets-weirder-as-orkney-is-ruled-out-as-altar-stone-origin?

Sarsen and its variants were later widely used for querns, and again became building stones in historic times. They had the advantages of being exceptionally tough, and positioned in areas where there were few other good rocks – and the disadvantage of being exceptionally hard to break up.

Traditionally, fires were lit at the intended splitting-point of a rock, cold water poured over it, and the rock struck hard. The resulting rubble was good for wall-building, and its compact, subtly varying, grey-brown toughness can be seen in various parts of south-east England; squared off, sarsen also made excellent cobble and setts.

From the nineteenth century the use of powered tools made both 'quarrying' and shaping easier. Hundreds of stones were removed from the landscape, leaving the natural sarsen spreads in relatively inaccessible locations. The largest structure of such rock in Britain is surely Windsor Castle, much of which, including its colossal retaining walls, is faced with ashlared local and Chiltern heathstone.

Synergy

Flint is the chalk's gift to the Tertiary and Quaternary rocks that came after it; sarsen is what that more recent era gave back to the chalk. Clearly, the Cretaceous and the rocks that succeeded it are interconnected.

In fact, this geohistorical interrelationship is almost as richly symbiotic as that between the Carboniferous and the Permo-Triassic: and here one simple geographical fact dominates. The part of Britain nearest to Europe is also the part dominated by the rocks of these periods. They have thus been the setting for much of the relationship between the British island and its continental neighbour.

These are the gateway rocks, the portals and thresholds across which history has moved; the venue for the traumatic and vital balancing act between connection and isolation which characterises the story of Britain's relationship with the continental mainland.

Here it helps greatly that rocks younger than the chalk in general form flat, accessible coasts with many harbours and river-mouths, country that is easy to penetrate but also hard to settle, with wide stretches of mudflats and marshes; and that the first dry, stable country beyond the mud (and, indeed, any serious cliffs on the coast itself) is usually Cretaceous – Wealden rocks, greensand, but mostly chalk. These rocks thus form a kind of geological 'hard standing'. Not only that, but the entire sequence meant that much of the country that stretched behind the coast was fertile and lacked major physical barriers.

So from Yorkshire to Dorset, the cliffs, beaches and mudflats of the British coast make a series of geological gateways mostly formed from combinations of harder Cretaceous rocks, and softer, mostly younger, muds. The historic ports of Portsmouth and Southampton may depend for their existence on the young soft-rock estuary of the Solent; but they are both guarded to the north by a ridge of older chalk. The Cinque ports, those medieval gateways to Europe, are all either on chalk (or, in the case of Hastings and Rye, the Wealden rocks), or depend on proximity to it. The Medway estuary opens through the younger rocks, but its historic centre of power at Rochester and great naval base at Chatham are both on the chalk. The theme can be followed north to East Anglia, where crucial European *entrepôts* from Ipswich to King's Lynn are on soft, damp clays, but in immediate proximity to harder, drier Cretaceous country.

Nowhere is this more evident than in the far south-east, where the chalky lips of the Wealden vulva push the British coast just 20 miles from the European one, and the North and South Downs form natural routes running inland from it.

It was because of the hardness of the chalk relative to the younger rocks that this area was the last part of Britain to be severed from the Continent. From the Neolithic onwards we can watch invaders, migrants, cultures and ideas coming and going across the resulting strait, using these rocks as geographical stepping stones, 'reconstructing the land-bridge to Europe out of culture', as Nicholas Crane puts it; and as he points out, it must have helped incomers that the rocks they found beyond the coast, with all their implications for landforms and resources, were very comparable to those they left behind — because they were geologically a single entity.

Mining itself was seeded into the British landscape at its south-east corner, for the flint mines of the South Downs are the direct successors of earlier ones in Europe. Later, it has been argued that the name of the chalk island of Thanet, at Kent's eastern corner, is Phoenician: a sign of its significance as a base for these first-millennium-BC eastern-Mediterranean traders. The first British-made coins, Iron Age objects which clearly mimic those of Rome, are found in Kent; according to Caesar, the people there were 'by far the most civilised' of all the Britons.

It is in Britain's furthest south-east that the landscape becomes most densely charged with our theme. We have already visited the chalk redoubt of Dover, today a major point of migration-related tension; but anyone who glimpses that town's white ramparts from the sea and then moves along the coast looking for easy anchorage will reach mudflats and estuaries on younger rocks. The best locations of all will offer an easy landfall there, but with the dry, stable security offered by harder rocks, usually chalk, immediately to hand.

The strait known as the Wantsum Channel was just such a location: a navigable, young-rock passage between the chalk of the North Downs and that of Thanet. Having silted up in the medieval period, it is today a drained wetland, lightly draped in farms and ribbon development.

One site here is particularly remarkable, though here the harder rocks on which it stands are Tertiary. In AD 43 Claudius's invading army made landfall at the Wantsum's southern mouth, selecting a spot where the mudflats were backed by a little knoll. This was soon made into a permanent place of entry to Britannia, proudly marked by a 25m-tall triumphal arch. The massive platform on which it stood is still there: on its surface there are fragments of the over 390 tons of Carrara marble carried across the sea from Italy.

Thus was born *Rutupiae*/Richborough, a thriving port which survived over 200 years. But as Rome's authority contracted, the triumphal arch was incinerated and its building materials used to help enclose the site with walls of flint and Roman brick. Richborough had become one of the forts of the 'Saxon shore'.

These defended coastal settlements line the south-eastern British coast; from *Branodunum*/Brancaster, Norfolk, to *Portus Adurni*/

Porchester, Hampshire, many are located in settings that combine chalk and softer rock. 1,500 years later, the eighty-two Martello towers that lined the coast of Kent and Sussex, and subsequently East Anglia, from 1805, and the Royal Military Canal, on the Kent/Sussex border, both Napoleonic defences, have a very comparable geohistorical footprint.

It was on the Wantsum, too – here at Ebbsfleet – that Julius Caesar may have landed, as well as the first Anglo-Saxons; and Gregory the Great's Christian mission to the incipient English. The latter group were asked by the Anglo-Saxon king of Kent to wait on chalky Thanet before they were invited to the ruined chalkland Roman town that became Canterbury.

Other such stories extend the pattern. The Normans, coming from further west, made landfall in Cretaceous Sussex rather than Kent; but Duke William's fleet landed on the Weald clay of Pevensey Bay, while his army won its battle with King Harold on the harder Wealden sandstones at Battle. The Vikings' Scandinavian origin gave their initial attacks a northern geographical focus, yet the Cretaceous and younger rocks of the Kent coast were the setting for their fateful turn from plunderers to invaders. Viking armies first overwintered in Britain in the mid-ninth century; the venues were Thanet (chalk) and Sheppey (younger rocks).

Today, it is through the Kentish chalk, specifically the relatively hard and impervious Lower Chalk, that the Channel Tunnel reunites Britain and the Continent. Two tunnels each over 31 miles long have been pushed below the surface, necessitating the removal of 173 million cubic feet/4.9 million cubic metres of white rock, some of which was used to create new land below Shakespeare Cliff, near Dover. One of the first stations on the British side has been name Ebbsfleet.

This narrative has replayed many times, as continental forces, institutions and ideas have made their way across the Channel, drawing the island of Britain into their orbit, and then retracted. The chalk-and-younger-rocks coast becomes a kind of geological cipher for everything from the Catholic church to the EU; from the Napoleonic and Nazi threats to Protestantism.

* * *

All in all, it is one of the great themes of this island that its south-eastern corner is at once close enough to the 'Continent' for influences to leap across it — and far enough away for bridging the gap to be a logistical challenge. The British side has thus long oscillated between insularity and connectedness. As a result, the Straits of Dover have probably been the focus of more geohistorical political tension than any other single place in the entire island. Perhaps the Iapetus Suture is the nearest competitor: the two are geohistorical faultlines in our island's story; and in origin they sit at opposite extremes of it. For the story of our physical breach with Europe is just one of the climactic events revealed in the Tertiary and Quaternary rocks of our final chapter.

Doggerland (7,000 BCE)

Upper Cretaceous (Chalk)

Lower Cretaceous (Clay)

Quaternary (Alluvium

Igneous

Igneous - eroded volcano

Igneous intrusions

Igneous volcano & Lava flows

St Kilda

Trotternish
Macleod's Table
Sgùrr Alasdair
Borreraig Long House
Black Cuillin
Rum
A830
Ben Nevis
Fort William
Staffa & Fingal's Cave
Oban
Raschoille
Loch Bà
Dunnad
Glasgow
Ayr
Arran
Goat Fell

Elgin

Aberdeen

Highland Boundary Fault

St Andrews

Berwick on Tweed

Edinburgh

Southern Upland Fault

0   30
| | Miles

Chapter 12

Tertiary and Quaternary fire, ice, people
66 million years ago–present

I

From fire to ice

I'm walking along the Suffolk coast. The landscape falls into a repeated sequence that, as I walk, takes on an almost dreamlike aspect. Stretches of marsh that seem to be sinking into the North Sea alternate with low, pine-topped cliffs that are more like pebble-studded piles of sandy earth than anything made of rock. To one side, the waves; to the other, a stratigraphic layer-cake of tan, ochre and earth known as 'crag'.

As I pass Dunwich, the cliffs have dropped dry-looking lumps of a deep-baked red onto the shingle. These are the brick fragments of a town once large enough to have contained at least eight parish churches. Up above, a solitary headstone a few feet from the cliff-edge is all that remains of that of All Saints'. Everything else been swallowed up.

Dunwich has come and gone. The crag on which it stood is the remnant, not of some lost ocean on some alien continent, but of the floor of the North Sea itself: its edges have shifted, but the sea is still there. It is now destroying the very cliffs that it created, which draw back from its onslaught like a geological wave.

The processes that have dominated this book are visibly under way here. The rocks have not yet cemented into anything hard; one gets the sense it would not take much for them to be removed entirely. And there are places where they contain traces of human activity that are older than the rocks themselves. In the crag, geological and human history – the two time-lines of this book – overlap.

Can we pinpoint when and where this happened? As of 2013, the answer is at Happisburgh, about 50 miles to the north of Dunwich, and about 800,000 years ago.

The scene is also one of walking. A group of five people are moving along what was then a river estuary and is today a village on the North Sea coast. Probably Homo Antecessor, they left fifty or so footprints (and a tool of black, glassy flint) in the sandy mud.

These were the oldest human footprints outside Africa. They have since succumbed to erosion as surely as every mountain in this book. The houses on the Happisburgh cliffs are following in their wake.

If there is a moment when the story of the rocks and the story of people overlap, then this is it. At the same time, a landscape we are familiar with is snapping into focus, in a remarkable sequence of events dominated by fire, ice and the activities of human beings.

Fire

Late in the Cretaceous, the waters that birthed the chalk started to recede. Plateaulands of this white former sea floor were revealed, extending over much of our Britain-to-be. They surrounded the Scottish Highlands, and may have covered Snowdonia altogether.

I couldn't resist the thought of chalk in Scotland; it just seemed so profoundly associated with the far south. So I pushed my way up a rocky gully on the island of Mull, and there it was, white and crumbly at the back of a burn – one of the few outcrops to prove the chalk indeed once extended here. For a moment Mull and Wiltshire were one.

The exposure was small, and above it the rocks steepened to a cliff made of a very different rock which, because it sat on top of the chalk, seemed certain to be younger than it: this was material dating from the Tertiary, which succeeds the Cretaceous (the term is widely used to cover two periods, the Paleogene and the Neogene).

These rocks were solidified lavas. Their presence is a sign that plate tectonics are about to come dramatically centre-stage, as the disintegration of Pangea comes to affect the rocks of Britain.

From about 60 Ma, the north Atlantic began to open. With the crust under tension, a major series of volcanic events took place.

The Atlantic Grain

The resulting rocks form some of Scotland's most famous mountainscapes. As if running parallel to a zip-line in the crust, they run generally north–south, with exposures from St Kilda, through Antrim in Northern Ireland to the Bristol Channel. And they dominate the Inner Hebrides.

They are the result of a great welling-up or 'plume' of magma below the crust. A side effect of the opening of the Atlantic, this bowed the Earth's surface upwards to the north and west of Britain – perhaps by as much as 1¼ miles.

As well as creating remarkable suites of igneous rocks in the far north–west, the magma plume had a profound impact on patterns of erosion across Britain. The effect is rather is if one had taken a tray full of sand, lifted it at one top left/north-western corner, and then gently agitated it from that angle. Material is removed most completely here, and is left most deeply piled up at the bottom left/south-east.

So softer rocks such as chalk were expunged from the north and west – except where, as on my gully at Mull, the new lava flows covered and preserved them. This exposed the older, harder rocks beneath, which were also rising: potential mountains. The softer rocks were left at their deepest in the south and east, the 'leading edge' of the removal of each of these layers of younger cover an emerging escarpment; so were born the scarplands.

A single grain unites volcanic mountains and scarplands alike. Spreading from an epicentre to the north and west, it runs mostly north–

south, before swinging south-west. This is the Atlantic Grain, and it is the root cause of the arrangement of old, hard rocks in the north and west and soft, young ones in the south and east that is such a defining feature of our island. Though like the other grains it is tectonic in origin, unlike them it is caused by seafloor spreading rather than continental collision; by stretching out rather than squashing up.

A letter from America

It's not hard to find a country and western band playing in a Highland bar, or a square dance at a Scottish ceilidh. Indeed, from pop music to populism, it can sometimes seem as if we are culturally and politically positioned in the mid-Atlantic, as much a part of America as of Europe.

Bizarrely, this very modern truth is prefigured by geology: the line along which the Atlantic split its way through the Precambrian-to-Silurian rocks; rocks that, remarkably, happen to record the conjoining of two ancient continents (Laurentia and Avalonia), and the disappearance of an ocean (Iapetus) 400 million years ago. Now the remnants of the Caledonides, a single mountain range 4,600 miles long caused by those events, were separated by the Atlantic. The Appalachians and the Grampians were once one and the same; the Old Red Sandstone can be found gathered at the feet of both.

Some extraordinary geohistorical quirks are side effects of this remarkable fact. The colonisation of the Americas by Europeans is one of the most significant events in recent world history; yet any migrant from highland Britain to the American east coast was moving between territories that had once been united, and which in some cases shared an environmental likeness.

As a result, Cape Breton island, Canada, shares with the Isle of Lewis both Precambrian gneiss and Gaelic-speaking inhabitants. When the Pilgrim Fathers landed at Cape Cod, they were standing on a portion of land that is separated from the rest of America by the Iapetus Suture as invisibly-yet-fundamentally as England is from Scotland.

The British Isles are, in a sense, offshore monuments to the splitting of Pangea, lying between two entities that were once one; and somehow – like the rocks themselves – spiritually located further into the Atlantic than a map would suggest. The political and cultural consequences are enormous.

The Alpine Grain

Our era sees continental collision as well as extension. Africa was moving towards Europe, and in the course of the Tertiary the compressive power of this bowed and concertinaed the crust along an east–west axis. The Mediterranean basin is one resulting downswing; the Alps its upward equivalent.

Britain was far from the centre of these events, but their outer edges created the Alpine Grain so visible in the far south-east: just as the mountains of North America and those of Scotland share a geological DNA, so the hills of the Weald are in a sense distant foothills of the snow-capped peaks of central Europe.

As the Weald was raised upwards, the surrounding country flexed downwards. Basins formed, today the setting for the Thames and the Solent, and the London and Portsmouth/Southampton conurbations: the last major cities in this book.

These rivers drain into the North Sea and the English Channel, the waters of which fill further basins which formed or deepened during the Tertiary. By the end of the period a prescient geologist (had one been around) might have noted that, were sea levels to be sufficiently high and the Weald/Artois anticline severed, Britain was a potential island.

Emerging landforms

Landforms are starting to develop that still survive. Indeed – in spite of the age of the rocks of which they are made – it is unlikely there is a hill or valley in Britain that is older in origin than the end of the Cretaceous. The rocks are old: the landforms they make, relatively young: this is a fresh world, emerging after the deluge, the creation of a specific compact between climate, erosion and the ever-twisting crust.

As the crust tilted and the younger cover was eroded away, the detritus was washed into surrounding basins, where it started to form the 'younger rocks' mentioned in the last chapter, drained by an emerging pattern of rivers that were also the dim prefigurement of those which flow today.

Usually the rivers of the era sketch in a drainage pattern rather than being literally the 'same' river that is still there. Often, they cut their way down through layers now lost, their modern paths only fully comprehensible when one factors in a lie of the land that no longer exists: the lost dome of chalk that covered the Weald, for example.

But in the far south, the Solent, Hampshire, Avon and Kennet have been establishing their current paths since the early Tertiary. They may be the oldest rivers in Britain; in the case of the Kennet and the Avon, overlooked by some of our oldest man-made landscapes. Likewise, many of the peaks of our highest hills level off at a single level, or sometimes a 'staircase' of levels. The higher points of Bodmin Moor, for example, sit at around 260m. They mark the surface of early Tertiary plateaux that have eroded into the mountains and valleys that surround us.

This story was hastened in the mid-Tertiary by a long period of exceptional heat and humidity, which weakened many rocks and hastened their erosion; unusual rocks such as the sarsen were one by-product.

The Tertiary is a turning point for life as well as landscape; 75 per cent of the creatures on the planet, from the ammonites to the giant reptiles, became extinct at the end of the Cretaceous, largely thanks to a meteorite impact in the Yucatán area of Mexico. The takeover of the mammals was one result. Primates emerged – at this stage not particularly like us in appearance – and were evolving into apes as the Alps were building.

By the time the crag was forming, Britain was part of a large peninsula or headland of the main European land-mass. The North Sea basin was a mighty, rolling plain that archaeologists call Doggerland. In Africa, the Homo genus of ape was emerging, while in Britain creatures that still exist – elephants, horses – were running around on a land surface that was a kind of rough-out for that we inhabit today. But now an event took place that was so dramatic it marks a new period, the Quaternary, from 2.58 Ma: the coming of the ice.

Ice

I climbed to Bleaberry Tarn, high above Buttermere in the Lakes. This little rounded lake occupied a scoop-like opening high in the valleyside:

a broad, curved, sudden feature typical of those carved by ice. It is the elevated location of this one that marks it out. Known as a 'corrie', it was formed by a nub of ice that gathered above the glacier that once filled the main valley.

The surface of this great river of solidified, slow-moving, sharp-toothed water would once have stretched out not far below me; I can almost hear it creaking as it gouges the valley into a vast, smooth-sided, U-shaped trough. This was a landform that mere water would never have created: 'overdeepened', water pools in it, forming just one of the many lakes which make the region so memorable.

I was standing almost at the junction of the rock-types from which this landscape is carved; and I could see how each had responded in its own way to the pressure of the ice. The slopes opposite me were relatively smooth; they were made of the sedimentary material of the northern Lakes, anciently dredged from the floor of Iapetus. Above me, however, the ground had responded very differently. These were the Ordovician volcanics (and, here granites) of the central lakes, rough with crags and cliffs.

Such hard rocks would always tend to make high ground. With erosion-resistant volcanic material at its centre, and sedimentary rocks around its edge, by the end of the Tertiary the region had probably already eroded into a domical upland. One would expect rivers to run radially from this high centre. But without the ice the peaks would not be so craggy, the valleys not remotely as spacious and deep, and there would be no lakes in them. So no 'Lake District' – and thus no Wordsworth, no Wainwright, no Scafell or Pike O'Stickle. The ice, in short, acted in concert with the rocks to create this famous landscape.

All this is testament to the brute, inexorable power of this material; to the sheer weight and grind of it as it bears down on everything in its path. Valleys are deepened, rivers are diverted, rocks shattered. It is erosion on steroids.

Phases of glaciation – and there were many – might last up to 100,000 years, each separated by an 'inter-glacial' period of thaw. As each wave tends to scour away the traces of its predecessor, two are particularly crucial for understanding the landscape as it has come down to us: the

Anglian, of 423,000–478,000 years ago, which reached further south than any other; and the Devensian, 11,800–116,000 years ago, which is the most recent. Much of what we see around us is the cumulative result, as seen from the point of view of the post-Devensian interglacial in which we live.

There is nowhere on this island that has not to some extent been affected. Combined with a Tertiary 'prep', the ice helped bring out the various grains that govern the landscape. The Great Glen may follow a scar-line of Caledonian-era origin, a line of weakness waiting for some powerful force to excavate it; but in its current form, that force is the ice.

Carving things up

To repeat an old pattern, the ice was deepest up in the north and west, and its impact on the rocks there particularly intense. Below the central Scottish ice-cap entire block-like massifs were severed one from another, creating crucial paths through the Highland landscape: Glencoe is one such; another is followed by the A830/Road to the Isles.

A little further south, the ice was forced along the bounding, Caledonian-era escarpments of the Scottish Midland Valley as if they were mighty river-banks. This frozen river shaped any nubs of hard igneous rocks it encountered parallel to its direction of flow. The rocks became stone thrones, often with a sloping tail of rock and earth in their lee.

This, surely, is why Edinburgh follows the Caledonian Grain, even though its rocks post-date the Caledonian events. A rough icy magic has transferred the Caledonian axis of the valley to Edinburgh's Castle Rock, Royal Mile and Nor' Loch. Far from being a taciturn and craggy Scottish icon, the city is a geomorphological over-exaggeration, a drama queen among urban landforms.

Many striking natural forms – Arthur's Seat here is an example – have come to be associated with stone heroes; figures whose supernatural size and power shaped the landscape. It now seems all are at least partly attributable to glacial processes. Perhaps the giants of legend are the ice itself.

The effects of freeze-and-thaw were almost as influential as the ice itself – especially when glaciers were in retreat, or in areas beyond their reach. In these conditions, water made its way into fissures and faults, and, when the temperature dropped, expanded within them until they shattered; it slipped off permafrost as off a frozen slide, carrying with it abrasive lumps of frost-shattered rock.

It is this that shaped the crags above me at Bleaberry Tarn. The high plateau here was once entirely covered by ice, but it was later freeze-and-thaw that 'finished off' its work, sculpting glacially scoured rocks into the gnarly, muscular upland so beloved by walkers. The scree that drapes its way down the valley-sides was created by similar processes, but after the glacier had finally melted.

The process often removed or loosened rocks, especially where ice worked its way into bedding planes. Many of the stones beloved of Neolithic monument-makers were made available in this way. On the moors of the south-west, beyond the reach of any glacier, freeze-and-thaw created the tors and clitter fields that became a great open-air quarry for cairns, stone rows and stone circles.

In parts of Britain some such rocks are 'erratics', lumps of stone that had fallen from the frostbound heights onto a glacier's surface, and were carried along with it. When the glacier melted, they were deposited onto the surface below. Some of them piggybacked for hundreds of miles before being dropped.

Erratics often sit by themselves, each a geological surprise, a potential landmark. 'Thunder stones' of Lake District granite mark parish boundaries in the Yorkshire dales. The Thurgarlstone in East Ayrshire has attracted a range of folk beliefs.

From rock to earth

From Holderness to Caithness, Norfolk to the Vale of York, lowland landscapes in northern Britain have a broad 'big country' roll that extends on regardless of the nature of the rocks beneath. These are the glacial earths mentioned so often in this book. More properly called 'boulder clay' or 'till', they are made from the vast amounts of sediment churned up by the glaciers. Such material covers at least 30 per cent of the British land surface.

Glacial earths are often clayey, and studded with erratics. They can make sudden hills and ridges, many of which are 'moraines', piles of rocks and earth that were pushed by glaciers, and left mounded up when they retreated. Meltwater flow generated egg-shaped hills, 'drumlins' that run in swarms with the flow of the water itself: the grids of streets that mark Edinburgh New Town and the centre of Glasgow march over them.

Such earth was a quarry in itself. Crushed shells and lumps of limestone embedded in it have been useful for fertiliser, harling and building. Pieces of flint made stone tools. Igneous and metamorphic boulders became roadstone and aggregate. Clay was used to make brick.

Even more significantly, the glacial earths have been fundamental to the creation of fertile soil in parts of the far north. There are places in the Highlands where it is hard to see how human life could have been sustained without them.

The intractable gneiss of the Western Isles is a case in point. Here, vast numbers of sea creatures froze to death during glaciations. They fell to the ocean floor, where they made loose, shelly deposits which, once the post-glacial thaw came, were deposited onto the shore by the tides. This calcium-rich sand attracted marram grass, which helped hold it in place: the result is known as the machair ('flat field by the sea').

Fertilised with kelp and dung, machair can be remarkable productive. More than any other factor, it may explain the relative density of population on these challenging coasts; a density that goes back deep in historical time, making this young material rich in archaeological deposits. A Norse longhouse at Bòrnais, South Uist, contained pieces of imported green Greek porphyry, a stone also used in Hagia Sophia in far-off Istanbul.

Only a few thousand years old, the machair sits on top of some of the most primeval, hard and ancient rocks on the planet. Fragile and vulnerable, it and the glacial earths are our first of a range of post-glacial materials that are not quite rock at all. Materials so young that their geological story is profoundly interleaved with the human one.

The ice also redirected rivers. Our walkers at Happisburgh were 15 miles inland, exploring a great estuary in which two major rivers had come together as they made their way towards the Doggerland coast. One has been called the Bytham river by geologists: it was to be expunged entirely by the Anglian ice. Its path is detectable today as a slither of pebbles across the face of East Anglia. Many of these had originated in the Midlands, allowing us to trace its course.

The other was the Thames. The upper part of that river has run east from the Jurassic scarp since early in the Tertiary; but at some point long after our Happisburgh group had passed away, the lower part shifted dramatically south. Then the Anglian ice came, and pushed it south again onto its present path through the London Basin. Thus was born the site of the British capital.

In short, the ghosts of the glaciers are everywhere. It can begin to feel as if they have only just departed the landscape, leaving it a geomorphological Marie Celeste. A frozen crew have abandoned the ship: they have only just gone out of the door. They might even return.

Old and new

None of these Tertiary and Quaternary processes has come to an end. The Atlantic is still opening (Iceland marks the location of the magma plume today), the Alps are still rising (hence the earthquake-prone nature of several Mediterranean countries), our patch of crust, roughly on the latitude of France at the start of the Tertiary, continues its stately and primordial motion. The next wave of glaciation could be only a few thousand years away (though tens of thousands is more likely). The landscape flows on, and in a few million years the Britain of today will look oddly out of focus as ocean, climate and crust continue their ceaseless dance.

The landscape we inhabit is also rather atypical. The only other glaciation on the scale of the Quaternary took place some 580 million years ago, in the late Precambrian: that's half a billion years without U-shaped valleys or glacial earths. And no other animal has reconfigured the land in the way that human beings have.

All this serves to put into perspective the fragility of the 6,000 or so interglacial years in which we humans have visibly shaped the landscape. One wonders how history would have developed had the magma plume been in a comparable location to the south and east, or the glaciations not occurred: would those arriving at our island be greeted by the Grampians of Kent and Essex? Would we travel north to admire the downland, grainfields and sun-soaked, bustling metropolises of Assynt?

Throughout the period between the shrinking of the oceans and the coming of the ice, suites of new rocks formed: sedimentary in the far south and east – the 'younger rocks' – and igneous in the north and west, where the opening of the Atlantic created this island's youngest mountains, and most vivid volcanic landscapes.

New igneous rocks: the Inner Hebrides

Parts of Mull look as if some race of inconsolable giants had attempted to carve steps into the side of every hill – only to give up, turn around and dig a downward flight on the other side. The 'treads' of these stair-like hills make tempting walking routes, until one realises they do nothing but make an overgrown contour around any given eminence, and that attempts to go up or down only leave one faced by a series of short but sheer cliffs.

These stepped landforms are known as 'traps' from the Swedish trappa, 'step'. They are the remains of lava fields that pulsed their way across the landscape in layers 4–8m high, each pushed over the top of its predecessor.

The artificial-looking result has generated its own mythosphere. MacLeod's Tables/Healabhal Mhòr and Bheag are two near-circular, flat-topped eminences on the island of Skye. They are said to have been miraculously flattened so as to provide a bed and a table for St Columba after he was refused hospitality by a local chief.

As one approaches them, the surface of the trap cliffs can look almost corrugated, and in some cases the basalts have cooled into geometrically perfect hexagonal columns that look strikingly architectonic. The island of Staffa ('stave'), on the west side of Mull, was called by Keats 'the cathedral of the sea' for its facade-like arrangement of shafts, its vault-like capping of less 'shaped' rocks, and its great portal, Fingal's Cave. It famously inspired Mendelsohn's Hebrides Overture (1833), and probably acquired its name in honour of James Macpherson's poetic confection of Gaelic lore, Fingal (1761).

There are also rocks that formed below the Earth. One, 'gabbro', makes the jagged mountainscape of Skye's Black Cuillin. Granites make Arran's Goat Fell and, far to the south, Lundy Island. And in places, and to a greater extent than older volcanic rocks, the very form of the volcanoes that stood high above these rocks can just about be detected.

I walked the edge of Mull's Loch Bà, enjoying the great circus of rocky hills that rose around me. Superficially, this country looked much like that elsewhere in the 'mainstream' Highlands, but threaded through the rocks of central Mull is the story of three successive calderas of the great 'Mull Volcano'. At Ardnamurchan on the nearby mainland the village of Achnaha visibly sits within amphitheatres of rock 5 miles wide, hardened circles of rock that formed the edge of an underground magma chamber.

And then there is the former volcanic plug known as Ailsa Craig, a 340m-high hemispherical lump off the Ayrshire coast. People have found the rocks of this island useful in some unusual ways.

Igneous resources

Ailsa Craig makes an elemental, almost threatening presence when seen from the coast. It is made almost entirely of a dense 'microgranite', flecked with tiny coloured specks.

The exceptional consistency, reliability, smoothness and resistance to impact of this rock, combined with its low thermal conductivity, has made it the unique source of Olympic-standard curling stones. Dependent on granite and ice, curling is a game that could only have been invented in the far north. The microgranite has also been used as an ornamental building and paving stone, as have the Tertiary granites of Skye and Lundy.

It is not the only resource found in these rocks. Walk along the beaches of Arran, and your way is interrupted by dozens of groyne-like fingers of hard, blind, dark rock: exposures of subterranean veins of magma known as 'dykes'.

Such 'dyke swarms' moved out with mind-boggling energy from the Tertiary volcanoes, pushing through the rocks they encountered. They were a source of a natural glass known as pitchstone, much valued for the making of prehistoric tools; as was bloodstone, a dark green, red-flecked igneous rock from Rum.

Later, the dykes were quarried for roadstone. The Cleveland dyke in the North York Moors has in places been hollowed into a trench up to 25ft deep. It makes an unerring straight line about 65–100ft wide, pointing directly at its point of origin in the Mull Volcano, 300 miles to the north-west – a reminder of the protean power unleashed when continents split.

More mythospheres

Take a series of low-lying rocks of many eras, many of them sedimentary. Add a covering (and some intrusions) of magma, and leave to cool. Leave to erode for 60 million years or so, and then apply a glacial grinding and shattering. Settle the waters of the ocean around the resulting mountains, and serve.

This is the geological recipe for the landscape of the Inner Hebrides. It results in spectacular mountain tracts; but also, where the underlying rocks are still exposed – Caledonian-era limestone Lismore, Permian southern Arran, the Jurassic parts of Skye and Raasay – relative fertility. In some places, for example the island of Muck, the basalts themselves have weathered into good soils. The ever-present sea makes communication easy, and acts as a spectacular foil to the young, sharp mountains.

As a result, the geohistory of the Scottish west coast is as dependent on the young rocks of the Inner Hebrides as it is on those of Caledonian origin. Entities such as the kingdom of Dál Riata, or the Lords of the Isles, used the many islands here as stepping-stones of power and influence. The Tertiary and Jurassic Trotternish/Tròndairnis peninsula in northern Skye contains Scotland's chief majority-Gaelic areas outside the Precambrian Outer Hebrides.

Today, one only has to witness coachloads of tourists making their way to Skye to know how powerful the sheer magnetism of such landscapes can be. Many come to see the Trotternish ridge: the most Tolkienesque scenery in Britain.

Here, a spiny cliff of Tertiary gabbro overlooks a Jurassic plain that slopes towards the sea: a classic Inner Hebridean combination. With hard igneous material sitting directly on top of much softer rocks, the ridge is inherently unstable: the unforgettable 37m basalt pinnacle known as the Needle has detached itself from the cliff and may one day collapse entirely.

A unique combination of rocks thus defines these beautiful islands. Their story could not be more different to that of the sedimentary material that, far to the south and east, began forming at around the same time.

New sedimentary rocks: the south and east

The Thames and Solent basins

'Ugly country . . . flat as a pancake . . . a nasty stony dirt upon a bed of gravel . . . bad in soil and villainous in look', said William Cobbett of the fields between Kensington and Egham; and it is true that the young rocks of the Thames and Solent basins are among the dullest in this book. Yet they have been a major gateway to Europe, and are the setting for major conurbations. The key to this is the softness of the rocks and the landscapes they form, and their connectedness to the sea; qualities they share with the yet younger rocks of East Anglia.

Today, the Solent basin covers a long stretch of the south coast, and reaches as far inland as Salisbury; while that of the Thames dominates Essex, London and parts of north Kent, narrowing inland into Berkshire. But they originated as a single basin, the downwarp to the upwarp of the Weald: erosion has removed much of it, leaving hard rocks such as the sarsen behind, as many lying on the chalk as on the Tertiary rocks.

These basins are today dominated by the wide, easy, open mouths of the rivers that drain them; the rocks over which they run were deposited in pulses throughout the first two-thirds of the Tertiary (that is, the Palaeogene), by rivers, estuaries and seas that foreshadow those of today.

Apart from one-offs such as the sarsen, or sudden rusty concretions of ironstone, these rocks are soft: dense clays; gravelly, sandy, ill-cemented sediments. A boring succession that can be divided into about ten layers.

And the oldest are in the Thames basin, where deposition ceased about 10 million years earlier than in its sibling to the south.

The Thames estuary is a haunted world of cracked mudflats and slinking waterways that eat into the London Clay. Forming early in the Tertiary, this material is the detritus of a warm, shallow, estuary-watered 'North Sea'. The dominant 'rock' of the Thames basin, it throws a dense, deep blue-grey blanket over much of Essex and London. At Bradwell-juxta-Mare, Essex, the remains of a Roman fort, an Anglo-Saxon chapel, and a recently decommissioned nuclear power station stand side by side: dense places such as this have an almost brutal melancholia to them; a quality we will see again as the rocks become ever younger and ever more impermanent, and landscapes increasingly artificial.

This is all the bleak eastern overture to London, long the major port in Britain as well as its capital. Southampton, on the Solent, with its 'very fair road for great ships' (Leland), has likewise provided a major haven since medieval times; Portsmouth, too, has early roots, and by the late seventeenth century was the main base of the English Navy. There are major naval centres at Chatham and Greenwich, too.

Indeed, the power of the state is a major focus of the landscapes of the younger rocks. Colchester/Camulodunom on the London Clay preceded London as a capital of Roman Britannia; Windsor is almost as significant as Westminster as a royal seat. Here, in an inland example of the Cretaceous/younger rocks synergy, the castle sits on a stone throne of chalk surrounded by London Clay.

The nearby Bagshot Sands can stand in for the more pebbly and unconsolidated Tertiary rocks. Poor at retaining water, they have become a confusing territory of heathy woodland suddenly interrupted by anonymous suburban high streets and gated oligarchical villas. Hampstead Heath, London, is of comparable vintage.

Heavy clay and sandy soils attract wood and heath, and much of both Hampshire and Essex were once forest. Villages can be scattered affairs: Epping Forest, on the London Clay, remains a true woodland, in spite of proximity to the capital; Hampshire's New Forest, its mid-Tertiary Barton Group clays and sands generating both bog and heath, was carved out of thirty-six heathy parishes in 1079. The forest is managed by a medieval system of rights exercised by its resident Commoners and Verderers. Though the underlying geology is Tertiary, there is much Quaternary and post-glacial-era material here of comparable character; a statement true throughout the country of the younger rocks.

The beaches south of here are part of a delightful coast, in which crumbly cliffs are broken by sudden gullies known as 'chines', and low islands and headlands provide safe harbours. One such is Hengistbury Head, at Dorset's eastern extreme. This is a sandy, hook-shaped promontory of the mid-Tertiary Brackleshome Beds, its cliffs, woodland and heath a foil to ice-cream stands and beach huts. The hook reaches across the mouth of the Hampshire Avon, creating a sheltered harbour, and below the holiday sugar-coating it remains a memorably dense place.

Leave the car park and walk towards the cliffs; the way is blocked by a massive earthen dyke. On the nearby shoreline, great dark brown lumps of rock seem to collapse onto the beach. These 'doggers' are boulders of ironstone, once – as with many one-off rocks – believed to be thunderbolts.

This was already a long-inhabited site when, in the Iron Age, the proximity of ore, a harbour, and woodland for fuel led to the development of an important industrial and trading centre. A hardstanding was built; smithies worked the ore; silver and lead from Cornwall and/or the Mendips were traded. The dyke was built to defend the head.

Fast-forward to the nineteenth century and the doggers of Hengistbury are being quarried once again. All told, human beings have removed about a third of the headland, leaving a cliff which looks entirely natural but which in its current form is only about 200 years old. The final twist in our story is drawing increasingly close: a 'cultural Anthropocene', in which 'natural' landforms turn out to be radically artificial.

East Anglia

Before we reach these youngest places of all, we come to our last landscape-forming rock: the crag. This dominates the eastern third of East Anglia, and it begins to develop in the Neogene, right at the end of the Tertiary: fully 20–25 million years after the rocks of the Thames and Solent basins come to an end.

This great unconformity, which covers the Miocene subdivision of the late Tertiary/Neogene, is perhaps the most significant gap in the British rock record. Among the few outcrops of this era, a series of undergrowth-filled pits near St Agnes, Cornwall, mark the quarries for 'candle clay' used by miners to fix candles to the walls of tin mines. The clays of the Brassington Formation in the Peak District have been quarried to make fire-resistant bricks.

After that, we come to the crag; a material that takes us right through the Quaternary. Indeed, alongside limestone (and thus mostly Carboniferous) caves, whose interiors were protected from the ice, most of what we know about our most ancient forebears come from these rocks, and other equally young deposits in the south-east.

East Anglian geohistories and mythospheres

For churchcrawlers like me, East Anglia is the Happy Hunting Ground. Mazes of tiny lanes link hamlets with eccentric names; gentle vales lead to equally gentle rises. Just as it seems you will never see another town, a lonely and grandly magnificent church rears up.

In summer these places can almost seem to glow with the collected love of centuries; but in winter a beautiful, compelling sadness seems to emanate from the very earth, and concentrate itself within. Open the door, and everything is white, and bare, and invisible presences invisibly shift. These places were built for acts of congregation, yet I am always disappointed not to be alone in them.

The walls of East Anglian churches are peppery with the hard silica gleam of flint. By and large this is the only local building stone, the gift from the Cretaceous to the younger rocks, left in the landscape by the ice: a relationship that is the key to the region.

Architecturally, much here is unique: round towers and flushwork are examples. Secular buildings can be a riot of half-timbering, and in Suffolk the oak may be hidden beneath 'pargetting', a kind of decorative plasterwork. Brick structures often have stepped gables sucked from the Low Countries by the same osmosis that brought limestone here from Northamptonshire, Lincolnshire and Normandy.

Chalk dominates the western part of this great hip of land, the crag the eastern one; Anglian-era glacial earths up to 75m deep cover everything. Norwich, the regional capital, lies on the chalk/crag boundary; one of the major metropolises of medieval England, it is now a self-sufficient, historic place on the way to nowhere: a description that could be applied to the entire region.

There are subtly varied sub-regions within this. The grand, spacious roll of the western chalk plateau is effectively a downland flattened by the ice. To the east, the crag underlies a low-set world of soft earthy hills and gentle valleys into which estuaries throw gentle watery fingers. But it is only on the coast, at places like Dunwich – or Aldeburgh, or Southwold – that the crag really exerts its character independent of the mantling earths. The low, pine-topped cliffs and marshy estuaries are known as the 'sandlings'; the word 'crag' itself comes from a local dialect term for shelly sand.

The glacial earths contain both calcareous and sandy materials, so in many places their influence interweaves. In Thetford forest, wood grows on the sandier earths, with the chalkier ones more likely to be grassy clearings. Fittingly, as such material is arguably the uniting feature in this landscape, the highest ground is a 9-mile long moraine, Norfolk's 105m Cromer Ridge.

Such differences divide up the region geohistorically. The Fens, a great post glacial sump sitting on impervious Jurassic clay, separate East Anglia from central England; the forests of the London Clay were long a barrier between it and the south. The heathlands of Thetford forest and the flooded Brecklands help form an east–west barrier across the middle.

The result is a north–south divide within the region that is detectable as early as the Iron Age, when the Iceni inhabited the area to the north, and the Trinovantes that to the south. The Anglo-Saxon kingdom of the East Angles was divided into 'north folk' and 'south folk', a distinction still present in the names of the two counties that most emphatically constitute East Anglia.

Ways around such physical barriers were strategically significant. The area around Cambridge was an important corridor running south

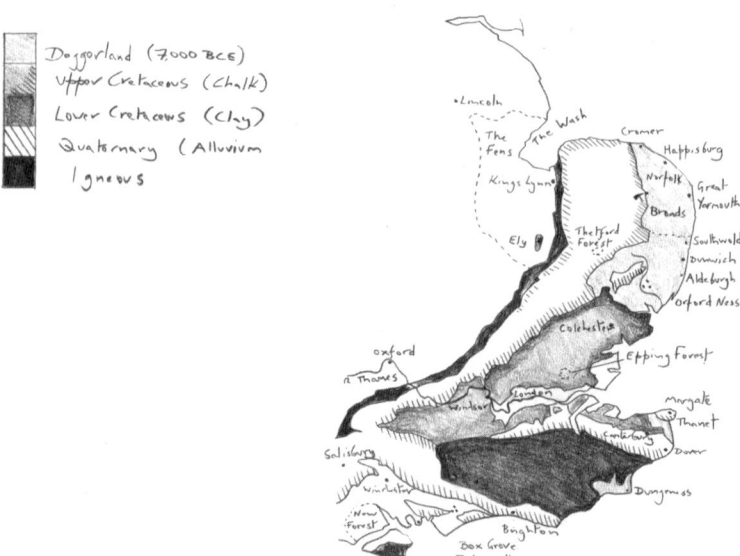

of the Fens, linking the English/Mercian 'mainland' to the East Anglian interior. The Icknield Way here was blocked by an aggressive series of post-Roman dykes; and Cambridge itself was a major trading centre.

Nonetheless, East Anglia can feel like a region which has been swept across by incoming cultures with such ease that each has rendered its predecessor superficially invisible. When the North Sea barely existed, early people walked here across Doggerland. The fen-edges were richly settled in the Bronze Age. But one rarely sees early monuments above the ground.

The Anglo-Saxon kingdom of the East Angles presents the most substantial exceptions. At the royal cemetery of Sutton Hoo, Suffolk, burial mounds scatter a ridge of crag that rises steep above the Deben estuary. The ship burials found within these mounds are a testament to the brilliance of the era. The many 'ham' place names suggest villages developed on sites hemmed in by water or the edge of woodland.

All this is a preamble to the medieval period, when trade in wool and herring, and proximity to the European mainland, made East Anglia one of the most prosperous regions in the land: ports such as King's Lynn and Felixstowe had an economic footprint that extended to Iceland and the Baltic. The region's magnificent churches are the result. If New Red's oldest and most defining voice was Mercian, then this world of chalk/ crag and glacial earth speaks Middle English.

In the industrial era, the great estates of north Norfolk were a kind of agricultural Coalbrookdale, the focus for experiments by figures such as Viscount 'Turnip' Townshend of Raynham Hall and Earl Thomas Coke of Holkham Hall, who promoted 'marling' to improve the productivity of their lands. They dug through the thin, sandy glacial earths, found chalky clays below, and spread them over the topsoil so as to improve its texture and reduced its acidity. This 'marl' could also be profitably exported. Proud modernised farms with enormous barns were built; large, regular, hedge-lined fields came to dominate the landscape.

The big skies and gentle contours of this country created a flourishing place-inspired artistic movement in the early nineteenth century, embodied in the work of the Norwich School of Artists. They are a reminder that many great landscape painters have been drawn to the younger rocks. Constable's Dedham Vale is on the London Clay of the Suffolk/Essex border; the spacious light that drew Turner to Margate is as much a creature of the Tertiary north Kent coast as of the chalk of Thanet.

Elsewhere, proximity to Europe makes defence as visibly a theme as it was on some of the scarplands. Several World War II stoplines for Nazi invasion run across East Anglia, leaving strings of decaying pillboxes in their wake. Major USAF and RAF bases – Lakenheath, Mildenhall – take advantage of the level, well-drained country. Ports such as Great Yarmouth have become major terminals for the pipes which bring to shore the gas and oil reserves of the North Sea. Enormous wind farms raise their solemn revolving heads from the shallow seabed, as if seeking mechanical expiation for our reliance on fossil fuels.

Soft, young building stones and resources

With their sandy deposits, and vast quantities of clay, these young rocks have been a rich source of aggregate – and are the heartland of brick, whether baked from Tertiary or Quaternary clays, or from even younger, post-glacial materials such as the wind-blown, silica-rich 'brick-earth', and riverside alluvium. Just under a quarter of the clay extracted in the UK today is Tertiary or Quaternary, and in the 1930s at least, 17 per cent of it was post-glacial.

It is in the Suffolk and Essex heartlands of London Clay and crag that this technology came back to life in the twelfth century, after a long post-Roman absence; the technique had come from the Low Countries. It is on post-Devensian clay round the Humber that brickmaking first became a serious industry: as early as the fourteenth-century the city walls of Hull alone consumed about 4.7 million local bricks.

Brick and cement works lined the Thames and Medway estuaries, too. 'London stock', a distinctive, yellow brick typically made of brick-earth mixed with chalk, and ash from the city's fireplaces, became the signature building material of the capital from the Great Fire onwards. It was praised for harmonising well with Classical tastes, and even resisting the comparable, but more repetitive, Jurassic clays of Fletton.

In Scotland, clayey glacial earth, freed of the rocks that studded it, played a vital role in supplying an industry that grew from an estimated 15.25 million bricks a year in 1802 to 47.75 million by 1840, exporting as far afield as Russia and Australia.

Some such materials were more unusual. There are various fine ball or 'pipe' clays, notably on the site of a vanished Tertiary lake near Bovey Tracey, Devon. Filled with kaolin from the rotted granite of Dartmoor, and lined by sequoia trees that decayed into a kind of coal, the deposits here bequeathed a serious ceramics industry. Around Bournemouth, there is copperas, green crystals of ferrous sulphate, used as a dye.

Harder materials – the sarsen, the doggers of Hengistbury – are more likely to appear as nodules embedded in softer rocks than as entire layers of stone. Ferricretes are rough, dark nodules rich in iron, and make an unusual building stone in Essex and parts of north Kent. Here, too can be found septaria, clayey limestone lumps in the London Clay, used to help build the great Roman victory arch at Colchester/Camulodunum, and later exploited for stucco and cement.

And then there are the youngest freestones in Britain. The most significant is the mid-Tertiary 'Quarr' or 'Featherbed' limestone quarried on the Isle of Wight, known to the Romans, and rediscovered in Anglo-

Saxon times. It is seen in many older buildings in Hampshire and West Sussex, especially Winchester and Chichester; one variety was used as a stone-slate. Younger still – just 150,000 years old – but much poorer in quality, 'sandrock', made from calcium-carbonate-cemented sand, was used around its sources on the north Cornwall coast.

Thus comes to an end a story of British freestone that began with a couple of examples among the old, hard rocks of the Cambrian, and peaked in the 'Goldilocks zone' that ran from the Carboniferous through to the Jurassic.

II
After the ice: people

My visit to Dunwich came at the end of a memorable week. Just eight days earlier, my wife and I had made our way to Amsterdam for a gig by one of our daughters, who is a singer. It turned out to be in a shabby-chic bar that stood almost alone a couple of miles down the North Sea coast from the resort of Zandvoort-aan-Zee.

The sun was low over the steely ocean, brightly backlighting the stylish crowd who'd come to this Instagrammable little event. Before the gig began, I climbed the cliff against which the bar sat.

This was really just a solid sort of dune: a dense sandy mound bound into place by thick, sharp grasses. Behind it stretched a dunescape that looked as if it might slip below the rising waters as easily as a cocktail slips down on a sunny day. I sat on top and watched the sun spread its sinking liquid glow across the broad ocean.

The journey home was somewhat convoluted. We made it to the station, overnighted in Amsterdam, Eurostar to St Pancras International, Circle line to Paddington, First Great Western to Swindon, and finally to our car.

It was pure coincidence that meant I had to be in Suffolk the following weekend. My business took me as far east as Framlingham, but under the circumstances I couldn't resist pushing on to the coast to look back at where I'd been a week earlier.

So there I was at Dunwich. As if inside some geological mirror, I sat on top of another flimsy hill, the light now failing behind rather than in front of me, and looked back at myself. Six hundred miles or more of travelling, just to cross a gap that if someone would build a bridge would be about 120 miles.

The journey from Holland to Suffolk wasn't always a roundabout one. For the best part of a million years, people have pad-pad-padded straight across Doggerland. Our distant ancestors at Happisburgh had been unshod, yet there they were, on the edge of the great estuary that flowed onto Doggerland; pad-pad-pad – the impression of toe, bridge and ankle repeating itself in the forming crag-era mud.

Our feet connect us to the Earth. Their imprint is at once our most ubiquitous and most intimate geological impression. At Wells cathedral there is a staircase of Jurassic limestone into which the feet of processing churchmen over 800 years have worn a rippling series of waves, an oddly immediate evocation of this absent congregation. The footprint used for kingmaking at Dunnadd will be visible for millennia on its Precambrian knoll.

Thousands of years of glacial silence separate each pulse of human presence: millennia during which no one walked these ice-bound paths. Yet in most interglacials, here they were again, and as they passed through the landscape they left in the forming crag and other Quaternary deposits the traces of subtle but significant evolutionary leaps.

People like the Homo heidelbergensis are glimpsed butchering a horse on a Quaternary shelf in Boxgrove, West Sussex, 500,000 years ago, and had perhaps knapped a flint from West Tofts, Norfolk, to deliberately display the perfect fossil trapped within. Or the Neanderthals of around 100,000 years later, who used ochre to colour things, and whose flint scatters show how they organised the manufacture and transport of stone tools with a previously unmatched sophistication.

Homo sapiens first appear in Britain about 40,000 years ago, just before the Devensian. We vanish with the ice, return as it thaws about 14–15,000 years ago, and then disappear for another millennium or two during an intense late-Devensian 'cold snap' known as the Younger Dryas. We have already met them in such limestone caves as Paviland, Creswell Crags and Aveline's Hole.

We have only been living here continuously for about 11–12,000 years, by which time agriculture and architecture were emerging in the Middle East, and the improved stone-working skills that mark the Mesolithic, and then the Neolithic, are around the corner.

The whole human story has waxed and waned with the climate. When the ice came: no people. When it went, there we were again: enquiring, exploring, spreading out across the planet. And every one of us travelling by foot. It's even been speculated that the rapidity of human evolution was caused by the dramatic environmental adaptions caused by the ice ages.

An island emerges

Even 11,000 years ago you could still walk here. But not for long. The melting ice raised sea levels. The east coast was sinking; partly because the effects of the magma plume were still in play, but also because of another ice-related phenomenon.

As the ice melted, the crust rose like a mattress suddenly relieved of some great burden; a process most dramatic where it had been thickest and thus heaviest, in the far north-west. Some parts of western Scotland may have risen a full 120m, a development so dramatic that to the south and east, the coast was tipped even further into decline. Britain is still lifting, at less than 1mm a year its 'highland' north and west, and sinking at its 'lowland' south and east at under 1.5mm.

Ireland probably became disconnected from Britain relatively early, during the rapid sea-level rises that took place at the end of the Devensian (perhaps 40m in 4,000 years). Initially the Irish Sea was narrow and shoals and islets eased contact across the straits to the south, creating strong cultural connections between southern Ireland and the British south-west during the Neolithic.

But as the waters deepened and the sea broadened, it was the physical proximity of north-east Ireland to south-west Scotland that became the geohistorical focus. Here, population movements and politics have been deeply intertwined. The early medieval Scotti of Ireland created a kingdom on the British west coast. The flow went in the other direction later, especially after James VI/I's Protestant settlement of Ulster, a key element in the origin of the Troubles.

Developments in the sinking south and east of Britain are even more epochal. A gradually submerging Doggerland finally disappeared about 7–8,000 years ago. A major tsunami (or series of tsunamis) known as the Storegga Slide may have hastened this; Mesolithic communities were swept away, and a dark line of ripped peat on the eastern Scottish coast left behind.

One might have expected the Weald-Artois anticline to have formed a more formidable barrier, and for millions of years this had been case – but this Cretaceous ridge between England and France had long been breached; and again the ice was the chief cause.

The first severing of this umbilical connection between Britain and Europe was dramatic indeed. A great ice-impounded lake developed in the southern North Sea during the Anglian glaciation; eventually it forced its way through the ridge like an overtopped dam. The combined waters of the Thames, Rhine and Seine, all of which had flowed across Doggerland, plummeted down the Channel Basin, further eroding the emerging coast; a second ice-bound lake and catastrophic collapse occurred about 125,000 years ago. These are some of the most catastrophic inundations the world has ever known, their traces still detectable as deep troughs on the floor of the Channel.

It was erosion and climate, sea levels and tectonics, that severed Europe from Britain; and though it had been prefigured in all kinds of ways, that event only occurred for good about 8,000 years ago. The white cliffs of Dover, the geohistorical focus of our fraught relationship with the rest of Europe, are thus in their present form a very young entity. Indeed they are still receding at a rate of about 20–30cm a year.

Bouncing back

Crustal rebound, or 'isostatic uplift', has shaped the human landscape in all kinds of ways, especially in the north. The Clyde originally flowed east towards Berwick-upon-Tweed, but the rebounding crust diverted it, leaving behind the riverless corridor known as the Biggar Gap. This is one of the few east–west routes in the Southern Uplands, its importance marked by a line of prehistoric monuments and defensive buildings. The river's new west-running path created the site of Glasgow; comparable stories could be told in many other places.

The pace of rebound was balanced against rising sea levels, and in many places the coast was cut into steps. Each is a former beach-line – and a potential setting for a settlement, or a road. Seaside caves were left high and dry: one such, Raschoille in mid-Argyll, was by the sea when Mesolithic people used it for fish-curing and the processing of shellfish; by the Neolithic it was well above the waves, and became a burial place. On the east coast, broad 'raised beaches' form the sites of Aberdeen, Kirkcaldy, Leith, Elgin and many other towns and cities.

These raised beaches are coast-hugging, linear landscapes, their sand dunes riddled with tight, reed-lined hollows. The Scots for them is 'links', and they have given birth to a global sport.

Golf was being played on the proto-fairways and bunkers of the links at Musselburgh by 1672 (and on the site of the present course by 1774); St Andrews is recorded early, too. Every golf course on the planet, from Tokyo to Buenos Aires, is the tidied-up ghost of a specific aspect of the post-glacial geology of Scotland, and the Scots term for that landscape has migrated round the world with it.

Building materials and resources

Remarkably, some rocks have formed since the end of the Devensian. To see the hardest – and it is brittle as toffee, and as crumbly as damp wood when soaked – I made my way to Southstone Rock, Worcestershire, on a particularly cold, damp February day. This craggy rock looms up like some great soggy eyebrow in a tree-covered valley near the Teme: a stream of fresh water pours over it.

This rock is no more than 6,000 years old, and it is growing still. It is made of calcite that dissolved in underground water, only to harden again as the water emerged into the air. In this case the source was a buried and ancient layer of late Silurian/early Devonian limestone.

Known as tufa, this material is not uncommon around limestone springs. 'Full of holes and pores' (Leland), it is both strong and light, and was beloved of the builders of medieval cathedral vaults. Shaped into decent ashlar, it gives a distinctive pumice texture to the walls of many local buildings.

A comparable process makes thin calcite layers on the walls of caves, where it could grow into stalactites and stalagmites. At Creswell Crags such layers lie on top of prehistoric art, helping establish its early date. At the Petrifying Well in the Carboniferous Limestone at Matlock, and Mother Shipton's Cave in the Magnesian Limestone at Knaresborough, man-made objects have been suspended so that they too can fossilize.

Erratics in the glacial earths have been an important source of cobbles and, sometimes, a rough building material. In Holderness, East Yorkshire, field boundaries, walls, and sometimes entire buildings are made of these shining rounded rocks of many colours, textures and origins, from fragments of the Whin Sill to chunks of Scandinavia.

The rocks were freed up when the farmland was cleared for ploughing; or gathered on the beaches, hastening coastal erosion. Sometimes they are set in herringbone pattern, a glossy colourful zigzag composed of material which encodes the paths of lost ice sheets.

We are increasingly exploring materials which are younger and less solid than standing man-made structures. And as we do so, we come to a group of landscapes in which the dominant voice is not so much the geology, but human activity itself.

In such places, which are mostly on the gently tilting south and east side of Britain, geology and history are peculiarly inseparable. They make figurative basins, gathering points for man-made sediments that form a potential new geological age: the Anthropocene.

A cultural Anthropocene

Are we entering a new geological period, a phase of the Quaternary defined by the impact of human activity on the geological record itself? The concept has only been in wide circulation since the year 2000. For geologists, the new period needs to be capable of precise definition, and to have left a clear man-made signature in the rocks. Candidates include the fossil-fuel boom of the industrial revolution, which affected the amount of carbon and methane in the atmosphere; and the nuclear explosions of 1945, which left radioactive elements in their wake. Unquestionably, it is since the industrial revolution that the scale of our use of earth materials has increased dramatically – and since the mid-twentieth century it has beggared belief: a phenomenon known as the Great Acceleration. So that is a further candidate.

From the less exacting perspective of geohistory, however, the key moment comes much earlier. The landscape has been changed in a profound and unprecedented way by human beings: and that story starts with the Neolithic. The lithophilia that gave us tools from the tops of Cumbrian mountains, and extraordinary monuments from Brodgar to Bodmin Moor, is when this cultural Anthropocene begins.

The impact on the landscape goes far beyond monument-making: the improved stone tools of the period made possible the first major reduction in tree-cover. As well as transforming the appearance of many places, the sediment released measurably changed the slopes on the sides of river-valleys, and may have increased the pace with which peat was forming.

But it is with the industrial era that change gathers force, making modern cities the ultimate 'Anthropocene places': landscapes in which one is more aware of the work of human beings than the underlying landform or geology. Places one can live and never consider the natural environment, other than to gripe about the weather between home and Tube. And nowhere in Britain is this truer than in London: 670 square miles of the planet, covered by houses and tarmac, tunnelled into by utilities and transport, artificially landscaped even in its green parts. The city's buildings weigh down the underlying geology by almost 6 billion tons, all of it ultimately won from the Earth.

London

At one point in the 1980s I worked as a bicycle courier, based in an upstairs office just off the Gray's Inn Road. It's a calling that brings with it a significantly enhanced awareness of when one is going uphill.

Pedalling my way sweatily from Whitechapel to the West End and back, with a pager on my belt and a large, heavy bag balanced across my back, the whole shape of central London worked itself into my soul.

A dip came at the same point in each of the parallel, mansion block-lined streets of Mayfair: this was the diminutive valley of the River Tyburn, the culverted waters of which went on to form the lakes in St James's Park. The waters of this unremarkable stream went on to help fix the site of Westminster, the seat of political power in Britain.

Today, I imagine many of the owners of flats in those mansion blocks are Saudi, or Russian, or Chinese. But London has long been a place in which people put down deep roots quickly. My mother's family were Unitarians who had roots in Dorset before they settled in Edgware. My father's were Ashkenazi Jews who at the turn of the twentieth century fled to the East End following persecution in eastern Europe (and also ended up in Edgware). Both parents were Londoners to their core. As surely are more people of more varied origin than almost anywhere else.

Even now, my Devon-based adolescence and adult years in Wiltshire have not dimmed the sneaky sense that to be surrounded by fields is to be on holiday. I still get off the train in Paddington and feel I am back in my manor. As a child, it seemed clear that to be British was to be urban, of mixed heritage, non-religious by conviction and Lefty by inclination. Perhaps it is; though to my surprise Wiltshire was full of Tory Anglicans of Anglo-Saxon origin who thought the same thing. Some of them are actually very nice.

The rocks of the city share something of the youthful, mobile, open quality of London's people. Its centre is defined by the young path of a river, and the young, low gravelly deposits left as its course has shifted. Unrelated to resources such as coal or metal ore, this site is quite unlike that of Britain's other major modern-era cities (the Portsmouth/ Southampton conurbation being the exception that proves the rule). Lacking decent building stones, it has sucked man-made erratics into itself in precocious waves of geohistorical migration.

Though no longer the largest city in the world (as it was in the era of industry and empire), London remains Britain's only settlement of truly global significance. And it has long been the most important urban phenomenon on this island. It has been unequivocally the capital of England, and later of the United Kingdom, since the twelfth century; and before that, as Londinium, it was the capital of Roman Britannia.

And London is also our final great mixed landscape, its geohistorical story combining the Tertiary, the Quaternary, and a human voice so loud it almost drowns out the geological one. Until we look more closely.

A platform of Silurian and Devonian rocks lies buried 300m below the surface of the metropolis. It helped make this part of Britain an island for much of the era of the younger cover, and prevented it bowing upwards with the Weald when the Alps were building. It is a reassuring thought, given how many much weight humans have placed on the earth here, that something so solid lies deep beneath the soft rocks of London.

On top of these buried rocks lies an Alpine-Grain basin, its young rocks cupped between the North Downs and Chilterns, chalk hills that effectively delimit the edges of Greater London. Though most of London's water comes from the Thames, the groundwater they contain has helped sustain dense human settlement.

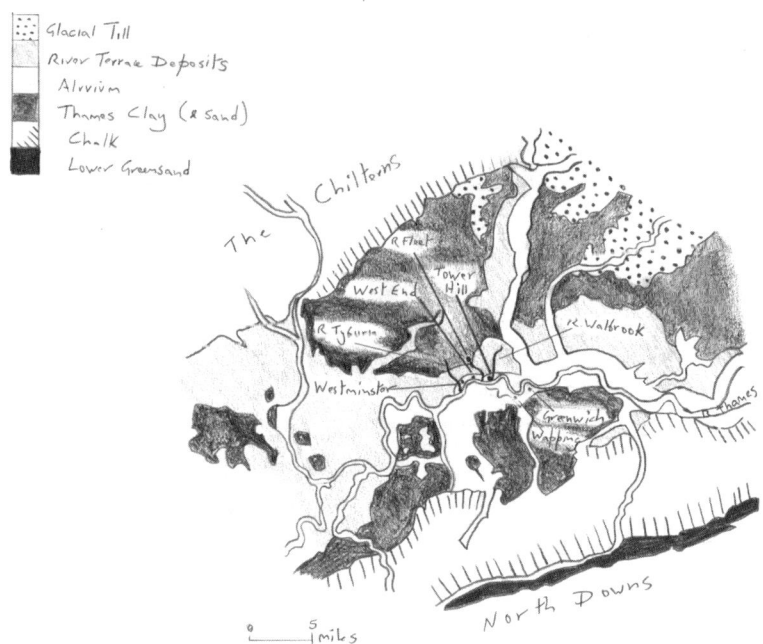

Low heights topped by pebbly Tertiary and Quaternary materials line this bowl. These, from Hampstead to Norwood, roughly enclose 'inner London', the area that had been built over by about 1900. These discontinuous ridges have been stone thrones for statements of Imperial prowess: Alexandra Palace, the Crystal Palace.

Between these rises lies a great bowl dominated by London Clay. So with its layers of Cretaceous, Tertiary and Quaternary rocks getting younger as one moves inwards, this is a great syncline: and down the middle of its central axis runs the Thames, shaping deposits and creating further ones: it is the settlement's defining entity.

The river generates a litany of associations Londoners will recognise without a second thought: posh west (posh because the water was cleaner upstream), poor east, intellectual north, taxis that refuse to take you south. North/south-running tributaries such as the Tyburn and the Effra drain the high ground to either side, helping further define and subdivide the landscape. London's historic core – the City, Westminster and the West End – clings to its banks.

This landform has a natural openness. The London basin forms an easy corridor for anyone approaching Britain, whether from Doggerland or, later, the North Sea. It has been speculated (not without dispute) that the 'Lon' part of the city's name is Bronze Age or earlier, perhaps indicating the unfordable lower section of a waterway. If so, it joins a tiny group of British place names of such antiquity, of which only one other, Winchester, is today a settlement rather than a natural feature.

The river has left sandy deposits on top of the clay: low rises which formed the city's earliest settlement sites. Freshwater streams sprung out where the permeable Thames-dropped sands met the impermeable clay beneath.

Pushing my way up Ludgate Hill on my bike, I am moving off the London Clay and up a rise made of Thames-dropped material around 50,000 years old. The ground flattens out, and then after St Paul's descends slightly before rising again to Cornhill, site of the Bank of England.

These two low, young rises, positioned by the river's easternmost fordable point – which became the site of London Bridge – are divided by a freshwater stream: the Walbrook. The Romans placed a settlement here, and threw a wall around it (and the much subtler Tower Hill), creating the framework for an entity that, despite an early medieval period of near-abandonment, is still guided by the line of this wall: the City, one of the great centres of global capitalism.

The City has an Anthropocene geology of its own: a layer of sedimentary detritus 3–5m deep made entirely by human beings. Coal and ash dominate the lower parts of this, but – and this brings home the scale of the Great Acceleration – $^2/_5$ of it has appeared since 1945, and is mainly concrete and plastic.

Cycling on east, I come to Aldgate; the name marks a gateway in the absent wall, and almost immediately some of the most valuable land on the planet gives way to a scuzzy and multi-racial world in which real deprivation lurks. The lost wall is like an economic forcefield, and its route is ultimately generated by the low sandy hills and their intervening stream. At Tower Hill a chunk of it survives next to the entrance to the Tube: Cretaceous Kentish ragstone and tile, presumably from young local clays.

Westminster is a separate settlement of Anglo-Saxon origin. It sits on Thorney Island, another riverside gravel platform, brought into prominence in the eleventh century with the establishment there of a royal palace and burial church.

A road soon linked it and London and a suburb grew along Whitehall, the Strand and Fleet Street, from the seventeenth century spreading onto nearby Thames-carved terraces. Thus was born the West End, the capital's modern retail and entertainment centre. Trafalgar Square sits on the lip of one such terrace; Oxford Street follows the edge of another. With power in the west, commerce in the east, and leisure between them, all human life has zoned itself on top of those young, gravelly terraces. 'When a man is tired of London, he is tired of life' (Samuel Johnson).

Throughout, many roads are of Roman, Anglo-Saxon or medieval origin, or follow old field boundaries and paths. But the architecture largely postdates the 1666 Great Fire, after which it became illegal to build in timber, hastening the creation of a city of brick and limestone. A city reconfiguring itself for a new England; expanding into the world, proudly Anglican, British as well as English.

By this point, royal and commercial docks were changing villages like Deptford and Greenwich into maritime centres. Rivers such as the Fleet were being gradually culverted over. The fuel supplied by London Clay forests had been exhausted, and the city became a precocious market for the Carboniferous coal of the English north-east and the Firth of Forth. The resulting pollution meant that as early as 1661, John Evelyn, writer and courtier, could describe London as a 'hellish and dismal cloud of sea-coal'; and in living memory the city was simply known as 'the Smoke'.

But coal was only one of the city's invading stones. Portland was beginning its takeover of the capital's architecture; Aberdeen granite and York flagstone would follow. The geological absence that is London's site was turning it into a great repository of man-made erratics.

With pavements made by chunks of Pennine Yorkshire, lined by setts carved from bits of Caledonian-era Aberdeenshire, and the Cambrian slates of Snowdonia on the roofs above, a hard and ancient Britain is brought deep into the city's gentle, young geological heart. But there is barely a street in which at least one building is not clad in a mid-Jurassic limestone, especially Portland, or red Permian sandstones from Locharbriggs and elsewhere, and countless bricks from the Jurassic clays of Bedfordshire are ubiquitous.

My courier's gear rendered me suitably invisible, and on a couple of occasions I took the opportunity to explore. The deserted staircases that accompany each lift-shaft combined the thrill of the trespasser with the adventurousness of the mountaineer. Once I emerged onto the roof of one of the Edwardian blocks that line Regent Street, enriched with little domes that give them an imperial flourish when viewed from below. I wondered if anyone would notice if I took up residence in one, coming and going like any other courier. On another occasion I caused a major alert by locking myself out on the roof of an office block near the Temple.

London has only recently become a setting for very tall buildings, and one of the reasons is that London Clay is prone to sequences of expansion and shrinkage. Foundations here have had to be forbiddingly deep. The NatWest tower ('Building 42'), in 1981 the first truly tall building in the City, had to reach over 47m below the ground to steady itself on the sands that sit below the London Clay. More recently, underground concrete rafts from which deep piles descend have been developed: an imitation bedrock that has enabled a cluster of meretricious architectural cheese-graters and gherkins to grow. For some reason it seems to be important that London look like New York, Dubai or Shanghai, rather than itself.

Even as the centre took its modern form, the city expanded exponentially, engulfing former villages until the London Clay bowl became filled by a great constructed sediment of brick, concrete and humanity. Yet each of these former centres retains a clear identity, giving a sense of place to what might otherwise be an amorphous spread. Even when one is unaware of the Anglo-Saxon origins of Hackney, Chelsea or Camberwell, or the waterways and rises which help explain their locations, one can sense these places are deeply rooted.

All depend on rapid transport to the centre. Here, at least north of the river (the sands to the south are much more of a challenge), the London Clay has been an advantage, for its deep, consistent, soft and impermeable nature is well suited to tunnelling. One can still travel from Wapping to Rotherhithe along the world's first artificial corridor under a major river, completed in 1843. The London Tube, from 1863, is the grandparent of every metro in the world. These were tunnels on the scale of a major mine, but designed for transport rather extraction; the nature of the clay through which they bored helping make them possible.

To this day, some of my favourite London rides involve following the paths of the lost rivers that moved through, and created, the landscape on which the city stands. The Fleet has a proper valley, cutting along the foot of Ludgate hill. There is something reassuringly organic about the curving, gentle, watery course this route takes as it continues north up Faringdon Street, through Holborn ('the stream in a hollow') and on to King's Cross, Camden Town and Hampstead.

The area between King's Cross and Camden is one of my favourite urban sequences, best taken at high gear, with brain and muscles pumping. Plunge between the cathedral Gothic of St Pancras and the 1850s brick geometry of King's Cross. Shoot past some of the earliest social housing in the country, perhaps glimpsing a spectacular series of iron gasometers. Cut left and then right down Pancras Road, past a row of Gothic-arched warehouses. Soon I reach the point where an Art Deco housing estate rises on one side of the road – and opposite is the sacred slice-of-early Middlesex that is Old St Pancras churchyard, palpably still sitting on a gently sloping riverbank. The absent river separates the two; I can almost feel the water flow beneath my wheels.

St Pancras station (1868), I discover, is a none-too-subtle advertisement for the lithic resources accessed by the Midland Railway Company, which had standing arrangements for the transport of the building's Scottish and Cumbrian granites; the lines of which passed its sources of Triassic Mansfield Red limestone, Ancaster and Ketton Jurassic limestone, and Cambrian Swithland slate; and all of it set among millions of bricks made from marly New Red Nottinghamshire clays.

Such hidden messages are everywhere. The capital's war memorials often use material from the country commemorated, such as the 2,600-million-year-old Laguna Verde from Jerramungup on the Australian monument at Hyde Park Corner. A concrete replica of the rune-carved Jelling Stone sits outside the Danish church in Regent's Park: a spirited Viking interruption to the gentility of the Georgian terraces. A sarsen block from near Avebury sits quietly in Gordon Square Gardens, marking the 75th anniversary of the founding of the Institute of Archaeology.

In contrast to the Fleet, the little valley of the Walbrook is best taken at a walk. Londinium's main source of fresh water, it is today deeply buried – yet the gentle trough it carved can just about be followed from Mansion House to the banks of the Thames. On one side of the lost stream, you pass Wren's exquisite St Stephen Walbrook; just beyond, on the other bank and far below the present land-surface, lie the remains of a Roman riverside temple to Mithras, which can be visited via the Bloomberg London building. Finally, a rusty stepladder leads down to a low beach, where a little rivulet still gurgles out of a grille and potters into the Thames: and nature, and geology, reveal their controlling hand. Remove the granite and concrete embankments which entomb them and the City returns to sandy islets set in floodplain mudflats, separated by a stream.

London's mythosphere is almost too vast to contemplate. How much music, or fiction, or art has taken the capital as its subject? In recent times Iain Sinclair and Peter Ackroyd alike have virtually built careers inspired by the city's psychogeography. But the Cretaceous/younger rocks symbiosis is a surprisingly constant theme. Chaucer's tellers of Canterbury Tales move from a Tertiary/Quaternary capital to a Cretaceous cathedral city. Dickens's overwhelming focus is on London, but the sole area he returns to outside the city is Cretaceous/Tertiary Rochester and Chatham. It can sometimes feel as if a significant part of London's mythosphere has been outsourced to the coast.

England is a beach

Beaches are the soft edges to our island. Landscapes which vanish and reappear twice daily as the moon pulls the waters over the surface of the planet. Geologically short-lived and very young – all have formed since the last glaciation – they are the most reliably temporary of worlds, all the more alluring for being covered by the only common rock that could be described as comfy to lie down on.

They play a unique role in the British psyche. The foreshore, as the inter-tidal zone is known legally, exists in a kind of limbo, theoretically as much in the hands of the Crown or a private landlord as anywhere else, yet culturally assumed to be beyond ownership: an inherently public space.

From the eighteenth-century sea-bathing craze onwards, beaches have been places where people tested the limits of convention. An entirely new kind of settlement, the seaside resort, developed beside them – especially after steam brought mass transport. These can be city-sized settlements with no reason to exist other than the allure of the coast: single-industry towns which manufacture leisure.

Before the industrial era 'Brighthelmston', positioned alongside a chalkland dry valley, was a small fishing town; it has transmogrified into Brighton. Bournemouth was a 'barren and uncultivated heath' before in the late eighteenth/early nineteenth century it was laid out along a Tertiary chine. Each has an umbilical relationship with population centres at London and Portsmouth/Southampton, just as Blackpool and Lytham St Anne's do with industrial Lancashire, and Ayr or Largs with Glasgow: a beach within reach of a day trip.

From the Art Deco Morecambe Hotel to Brighton's Regency squares, the seafronts of such towns feature architectural cliffs, often coloured white, as if the chalk cliffs of the south-east had become a national signature for 'coast'. Promenades and piers seek to defy the tides by moving the beach out over the sea while preserving (and monetising) its freedoms.

We abandon the niceties of life as it is led on more fixed geologies; on beaches public undressing is acceptable to an extent that would be scandalous anywhere else. They have been a crucible for the ways in which the modern British have explored pleasure and abandon, from Pierrot troupes, to Mods and Rockers, to raves.

Yet it is hard to think of a more melancholy settlement than the out-of-season or out-of-favour resort. The temporary nature of the sea-edge seems to bleed onto the silent streets; and some are genuinely the 'last in/first out' of British landscapes. Fairbourne, Gwynedd, sits on a marshy floodplain which may only have been dry land for a few hundred years. It was laid out as a holiday resort in 1895; in 2013 it became one of the first places in Britain to be earmarked for 'managed retreat' because of rising sea levels.

There is something of the memento mori about these places, a quality that will become ever more vivid as we moved to our final, most Anthropocenically sensitive and temporary landscapes.

Lost places

Here, on Cardigan Bay, a lost country lies below the sea. This great lowland, drowned from about 4000 BC in the post-Devensian thaw, preserves the visible traces of trees and footprints from its time as dry land: walk along the mudflats at Borth, Ceredigion, at low tide and the tree stumps stick out as if they had just been felled.

Such features gave rise to the legend of Cantre'r Gwaelod, the 'lowland hundred': causeway-like banks known as sarnau run into the ocean. Actually moraines, they were interpreted as lost field boundaries; a pile of rocks out at sea, a ruined palace. Comparable stories are replicated for Lyonesse, between Cornwall and the Scilly Isles; and along the North Wales coast. The Scillies were once a single island; a prehistoric stone row, built to overlook what was presumably its central bowl, runs down the beach on the island of St Martin's, as if running into the sea for a paddle.

For a few years I was slightly in love with the quiet melancholy of the little town of Winchelsea in East Sussex, which retains a mayor and corporation in spite of being smaller than some villages. Here everything seems to have been disintegrating with quiet and geologically inevitable gentility since the fourteenth century. Just getting there involves departing the train at a halt that feels like it is about to sink back into the gurgling marsh.

The original town, Old Winchelsea, was located on a shingle bank on what was then the Channel coast. By the late thirteenth century the rising sea was rendering it uninhabitable, even as it was turning the foot of a nearby outcrop of Wealden sandstone into a potential port. In 1283 a new town was laid out on the hilltop above. It became one of the busiest trading ports in England – until the harbour silted up, reversing the process which created it. Winchelsea's magnificent church of St Thomas stands half ruined, most of its grid of streets undeveloped: a 'poor skeleton', John Wesley called it in the 1790s.

As Anthropocene places in which nature has played the most powerful hand, such sites stand in contrast to London. But there are rural locations that are as artificial as Trafalgar Square. Often, as one passes a Scottish loch, a craggy, tree-covered islet rises just offshore, a little geomorphological hedgehog and a spiky foil to the high surrounding hills. Many of these are 'crannogs', islands created by piling material – timber, but also stone and peat – into the water to create a defensible site for a timber roundhouse, and (often) linked to dry land by a causeway. Appearing in earnest from the early Iron Age, some were still the sites of homes (and even castles), as recently as the seventeenth century: tiny artificial dense places.

In addition to protection, these sites must have offered rich resources: even under siege there would be no shortage of fresh water or fish. Nearby peat would have provided fuel, and this material, like glacial earth and machair as much soil as rock, is the defining feature of our major wetlands.

Marsh and fen

With its vast regular fields, straight-as-die waterways, and marching pylons, the Fenland of East Anglia is as engineered as a great city, as defined by straight lines and right angles as a tower block. Isolated brick farmhouses and tiny hamlets struggle to keep their heads above water; the skies are vast, and the weather comes towards you as slowly as the traffic crawls along roads whose tarmac twists with the drying of the peat beneath. Distinctions between land and air blur as clouds settle their rainy burdens from vast skies.

The towns here feel temporary, and often seem deserted. Enormous fields fill supermarkets with their produce, exacerbating the 'Fen blow', the stripping of topsoil by the wind. If the churches of East Anglia proper contain a silent and sacred melancholy, here in the Fens it intensifies into tragedy. The grandeur and grief embodied by structures like West Walton, Gedney and Terrington St Clement almost make you want to weep. At once slumped and magnificent, it is as if the building is doing you a noble favour by not disintegrating back into the impermanent earth.

Cities aside, such drained wetlands are Britain's ultimate Anthropocene landscapes, and the key to them is peat: a dense gathering of waterlogged plant material that gathers in a setting where drainage slows almost to a halt, and little rots. Given a few million years of compression peat would eventually become coal; it is a greater store of carbon globally even than the rainforests.

Peat covers great tracts of upland Britain – no less than 9.4 per cent of this island's land surface, almost a hundred times more than is covered by cities. This dense, black, rooty stuff can lie in bogs 6–7m deep. It is also young, and temporary: tide-marks left by former layers of it can be seen on the stone circle at Callanish/Calanais on Lewis, a man-made structure that has outlasted the rise and fall of the surrounding soil.

In most such places, the peat is palpably an expression of the impermeable, acidic rocks on which it gathers. The dark, gullied peat of the Pennines is to the gritstone beneath what the inscrutably tortured

Moinian rocks are to Sutherland's Flow Country. Here, in Europe's largest peatland, distant, gradual peaks rise from a dark, formless, yet compelling world.

But it is clay, scoured flat by the ice, that underlies our greatest wetlands; clay so deeply buried that the peat defines the landscape rather than the rock below. Here, early inhabitants were terrified by the 'immense marshes, now a black pool of water, now foul running streams' with 'many islands, and reeds, and hillocks, and thickets, and . . . manifold windings wide and long', in which, according to his medieval *Life*, the eighth-century Fenland hermit St Guthlac went to live.

Such country presented unique challenges to settlers, but was also rich in resources. Before the industrial era, peat was far more significant than coal as a source of carbon-derived heat. It is easily cut, and dried, and divided into turves, resulting in a transportable and sweet-smelling fuel. Many Scottish crofting communities retain the right to cut it. Wetlands are also profitable sources of fish, eels and wildfowl. And when drained, they can become extremely fertile.

Twice since the end of the Devensian, the Firth of Forth in the Carboniferous of the Midland Valley has stretched 25 miles further inland than at present. The great bog that developed here was as strategic as it was treacherous; Stirling, on its Variscan volcanic stone throne, its vital guardian: royal seat, crossing-point, port. In 1314, the wetland assisted in the defeat of the English army, forced into a corner by the Bannock Burn.

But in the eighteenth century the region was drained, reclaimed, and converted into the rich arable country of today, celebrated for its hay production. The work was partly done by people relocated in the Clearances. Flanders Moss, one of the largest raised bogs in Britain, reminds the visitor of what once was.

Such large-scale drainage was often an industrial-era project. An exception is the Broads, where medieval turbaries quarried the peat that runs up the valleys around Yarmouth. The diggings flooded and became forty to fifty small, interconnected lakes. Most of those who enjoy a boating holiday here probably imagine they are entirely natural.

And so we come to the Fens. The great sea-gulf whose remnant is the Wash once reached inland almost to Cambridge – about 84 miles.

Here the ice age formed a vast, shallow, flat bowl in the soft, impervious Jurassic clay: the 'sink of no less than 13 counties' (Defoe), it gradually filled with vast quantities of plant detritus.

This wetland was long a vital waterway. Boats from Europe and the east coast could unload at King's Lynn or Wisbech, or come inland as far as Cambridge or Peterborough. And it has been an Achilles heel in the strategic body politic of England, bringing an ever-changing maze of islets and meres close to centres of wealth and power: 'a most dangerous place in case any sedition should arise', as Henry III put it.

There are really two Fenlands: marshland, up near the Wash, is dominated by saline waters, and pale, sea-deposited silt. The tides dropped banks of shingle and silt, making natural areas of drier land. These could be extended by pushing reclamation inland towards the freshwater Fen or ever-further into the Wash: the tide-lines of the latter process are visible as successive strings of settlements to this day.

Try and find the coast here and things start to feel as if they are stretching out forever, like one of those dreams in which you never quite reach your goal. Finally, the sea wall rises above vast agri-industrial fields, and brown mudflats stretch beyond. The island of Outer Trial Bank is a perfect circle: it was created in the 1970s to assess the feasibility of turning part of the Wash into a freshwater reservoir.

This country was vulnerable to sudden catastrophe if an exceptional storm or tide overwhelmed the sea-bank. Boards in West Walton church record 'the Violence of the Sea' that 'broke in and overwhelmed all Marshland' in 1613 and 1671.

The pay-off was wealth. In addition to fertile soil, marshland had access to both freshwater and saltwater resources: eels and fish, sedges and salt, wildfowl and mammals. The part in Lincolnshire was the richest area in Domesday England, explaining the enormous medieval churches.

Large, barrow-like mounds near to the sea wall are the detritus of a salt industry which could be found in many parts of sea-edge Britain, especially where peat (or on the Firth of Forth sea-coal) was close by for use as fuel. Of 1,195 salterns mentioned in Domesday, most are in Lincolnshire, Norfolk, Kent and Sussex.

Inland, peat and freshwater influences replace silt and saline ones. Here we are in the true Fen, a country in which reclamation was a greater challenge. Any stretch of peat fen successfully drained immediately began to dry out, and shrink, and flood once more. Failures, or 'drownings', were common. The meandering wetland needed special skills to live in: the locals moved around on stilts, or in shallow boats known as 'skerries'. Settlements stood on 'roddons': subtly raised banks of earth that marked the paths of dried-out streams or 'lodes'; or on the occasional island.

The most important of these formed a great southern archipelago, dominated by the Isle of Ely, a 'stone throne' of Cretaceous Greensand barely 28m high within a causeway's reach of the Cambridgeshire 'coast'. Serious rebellions – of insurgent Anglo-Saxons against the Normans, in 1071; of nobles against King John in 1216, and against Henry III in the 1250s – used the Isle as a base: it is said the Norman army floated across the marsh on inflated pig-bladders, only to lose the most diehard rebels, Hereward the Wake and his followers, in the snaking wetlands.

St Etheldreda, a seventh-century princess of East Anglia, fled from her Northumbrian husband and founded a monastery on the Isle. A cathedral since the twelfth century, this church ruled the Fen much as Glastonbury dominated the Somerset Levels. Such monastic houses played an active role in digging dykes and draining the bog. Even today, the great church expresses its dominance over the natural landscape, its bristling beauty at once terrifying and imperious.

Industrial-scale pumping and earthworking were the only permanent, large-scale solutions. We met the seventeenth-century Dutchman Cornelius Vermuyden at Cromford, Derbyshire – his first major project was the draining of part of the great wetland around the head of the Humber. The success of the project led to him being knighted in 1629, 'in recognition of the skill and energy that he had displayed in adding to large a tract to the cultivable lands of England'.

Now he turned his attention to the Fens, his 'numerous company of lusty, sweaty, stout, sweating pioneers . . . digging, delving, casting up and quartering . . . to gain ground and to make that large continent of vast, foggy, miry, rotten and unfruitful soil, useful fruitful and beneficial', as Lieutenant Hammond put it in 1635.

Hundreds of thousands of acres of dry land were created, and rivers such as the Ouse redirected along clay-lined dykes, their waters alarmingly flowing higher than surrounding fields. To keep the new land drained, 700 windmill-powered pumps were built, replaced by eighteen steam engines in the 1850s. This is the single greatest man-made transformation of the landscape in British history.

In stray survivors of meres such as that at Whittlesea, once 6 miles across and now vanished, one can encounter a pre-drainage Fen. Holme Fen is one such: a place of dense birch woodland and silent, still stands of water that whisper of what the landscape was like before human beings found it. And in the middle of this natural reserve, there stands an iron post.

Height above sea level has been a rough index of landscape character since the beginning of our story. Taken in chronological order, the Caledonian events created the highest points, with Ben Nevis reaching 1,345m; the Carboniferous tops out at Cross Fell: 893m; and the younger cover's highest point, on the North York Moors, rises to 454m. The igneous Tertiary makes 992m at Sgùrr Alasdair on Skye; but the sedimentary south-east of the same era can only manage 150m or so (north London); and the Quaternary Cromer Ridge 105m. As the height of the rocks decreases, so the landscape shifts from mountain and moor to suburb and farmland.

So it is fitting that here, close to the youngest, most artificial countryside in Britain, we are 2.7m below sea level. The Holme Post marks the spot; when it was erected in the 1850s, only its pyramidal top poked out above the peaty earth – 4 metres of it have appeared since. That is how far the peat has shrunk, and the land surface fallen.

Temporary places

There are places that are more fragile and geohistorically sensitive still. Spits and headlands of sand and glacial earth; places at once uncomfortably young and profoundly haunting.

Such places continue to be made and destroyed by washing tides and passing currents. The boundary of sea and land here is fluid and very recent. They are at once embodiments of the coming crises of the Anthropocene – and impermanent as a dream.

Often these landscapes were made by a combination of wind direction and tidal currents, pushing mobile geologies of sand and shingle along the coast and leaving them piled up in new configurations. They can feel wild, yet turn out to be profoundly implicated in human history.

In Kent, Dungeness is a great triangular shingle-bank that intrudes 5 miles into the Channel, dragging Romney Marsh behind it. The nudging tide has pushed this enormous, flat-topped mound of rocks east over the centuries; in another 150 years it may have disappeared altogether.

Shut off from the 'mainland' by Saxon shore defences, the Napoleonic-era Royal Military Canal, and Second World War defensive lines, the whole area has been described as the 'fifth continent' for its air of otherness.

The place is dominated by an enormous nuclear power station, positioned where it can drink the cooling waters of the Channel. A cathedral to twentieth-century energy needs, its frightening and arcane mysteries help keep civilisation afloat even as the power it contains could destroy it. Perhaps people once said something similar of York Minster, or Avebury henge.

The power station dwarfs the little wooden bungalows and brick houses, yet even here, the garden of Prospect Cottage manages quietly to hold its own. Here, the film-maker and artist Derek Jarman turned the flotsam and jetsam of the shingle into a singular and perfect little garden. The flora that flourishes in this salty desert is complemented by the queer forms of flint, carefully selected pieces of which form miniature stone circles and other geometrical arrangements. There is no garden fence: this is an unbounded creation.

This man-made place is as rooted in the fragile geology of Dungeness as Bath is in the Jurassic or Aberdeen the Caledonian; and, thanks to the politics and identity of its creator, it has a special claim to be a man-made landscape, tiny though it is, that celebrates LGBTQIA+ identities.

In contrast, Orford Ness, Suffolk, embodies conflict. Over 800 years, natural forces have added 12m a year to this shingle bank, which now runs as a long, narrow neck of dry land fully 9 miles south from Orford itself.

The Ness was acquired by the then War Office in 1913, and among its now-abandoned buildings are the structures in which radar was developed, bombs and rockets tested, and from 1960 the Pagodas built:

six colossal concrete bunkers that were used to test components of nuclear bombs; they give the landscape an air of frozen apocalypse. A veritable museum of modern humanity's most destructive tendencies.

And finally, there is Spurn. This landscape of 'unfenced existence' (Philip Larkin) is shaped like the curling, skeletal finger of some geohistorical witch, or the neck and head of a giant snake. It droops south for some 3.5 miles from Holderness into the Humber estuary. Often, it is just a few dozen yards across.

This mound of wind-and-wave-deposited sand and shingle, all on a bed of glacial earths, sits in a kind of depositional stand-off between the currents of the East Yorkshire coast and those of the Humber, intensely responsive to their changing patterns of flow.

Spurn was long believed to disintegrate and rebuild itself a few yards west every few centuries, leaving in its wake a litany of lost places whose names are recorded as far back as the seventh century. The port of Ravenspurn/Ravensur Odd stood here: founded in the mid-1230s, it was lost just over a hundred years later, meaning Shakespeare's Henry IV had to land 'upon the naked shore' of Spurn in 1399.

It now seems that while Spurn's neck is moving west with the Holderness coast, which is disappearing at a rate of 2 metres a year, its head, which in places rises as much as 10m above the waves, is more stable; and the whole landform has an unexpected capacity for self-regeneration. It also responds like a fine-tuned geohistorical string to human activity.

Vermuyden's draining of the Humber wetlands; the quarrying of cobbles and gravels from the Holderness coast; the construction and abandonment of sea defences: all these have measurably affected the form of this fragile place. And there are plenty of signs of humanity among the sands and grasses: there has been a lighthouse here since the fifteenth century; there are First World War defensive structures, and a lifeboat station.

Spurn is strangely compelling on the map, and a few years ago I tried to make the headland on the same day that I was due to give a lecture in Hull. The distances involved got the better of me and I arrived at the Kilnsea car park with much less time than I'd hoped for.

I mounted my folding bicycle in a strong headwind, and pushed south along the tarmac strip which sat so unconvincingly on the flimsy surface.

The strangely tentative nature of this place, the urgency of the situation (I could not be late for my own lecture, nor be covered in post-Devensian mud) and the physical effort combined to induce a kind of reverie.

In my head, the landscapes of England coalesced into patterns. Forget such millions-of-years-long niceties as the Silurian and Jurassic, or Laurentia and Pangea; throughout our story, certain rock types have generated certain landforms, in terms stimulating certain histories. The remnants of volcanoes have become stone thrones and mountaintops. Sheaved and upended sedimentary rocks have become bare and open uplands. More gentle sedimentary country has been intensely farmed and settled. Tectonic forces and erosion have worked in concert to create the rhythms of inlets, valleys and rivers which directed the paths of people. Rotting vegetation – coal, peat, even some iron deposits – seemed to be as significant as metal ores in the seeding of the rocks with resources. Certain combinations of lithology and frost-action lent themselves to the creation of everything from stone circles to drystone walls. Geology was history's puppetmaster.

What, I wondered, will happen, over geological time, to the geo-historical achievements in this book? At worst, our Anthropocene manipulations of the environment will destroy civilisation itself; but at best, they are a kind of communal work of art, a testament to our brave, destructive, creative tenure of this particular piece of continental crust.

Yet in comparison to the planet, everything we have made is as young and fragile as Spurn. It will sooner or later be lost to the forces that engulf all places. Whatever intelligent species are to come will not find it difficult to work out that a rapid transformation of the climate took place in the twentieth and twenty-first centuries; but it may only be able to guess at our achievements.

I imagined the sarsens of Wiltshire's stone circles buried under sedimentary layers unknown, until they became flat subterranean lenses of hard sandstone which might just remain arranged in circles. Cathedrals and country houses collapsing into unexpected gatherings of limestone and sandstone, the metals and sands that comprise their fixtures, roofs and windows migrating into nearby fault-systems:

their architectural design would be utterly lost, but their geological footprint would be unmistakable.

Entire cities could be consumed in this way, creating dense geological burdens of concrete, steel and plastic. And what of our roads, those linear webs of crushed Precambrian hardcore, held in a matrix of Carboniferous oil? The two might separate out, but still form buried, linear erratics, presumably placed within proximity of each other, and running in a fragile network through layers of rock yet to form.

As my mind spun on, the tarmac gave out. The road to the headland was breached in 2013, and chunks of black tarmac lay at angles as they disintegrated into the eroding claws of the sea. A 500m-long breach in the neck of the spit appeared, but Spurn had regenerated within a year. Traces of road and sea defences were left behind, crumbling back into the simple routes and piles, paths and cairns, with which this book began. Man-made sediments on the shore of a rising North Sea, pregnant with geologies to come, and places unimagined.

My eyes were caught by a distinctive pebble: a rounded thing, shaped like a dumbbell. It was deep red at each end, but its narrow neck was a kind of matt shade of cream. New Red Sandstone, washed down the Humber from the Midlands? Or some ancient, far-from-home conglomerate, dropped on the Holderness coast by a vanished glacier?

I picked it up, and studied it. The wide, red ends of the 'rock' were brick; the narrow, whiteish centre, mortar. Clay, baked in a kiln; limestone, crushed, burnt and mixed with sand and water. Portions of two red bricks so eroded by the waves that their rectilinear forms had become curved ones. The pale neck that linked them was narrower than the rest because of the relative softness of the mortar that bonded them together. This was a man-made object, made of the materials of the earth; abandoned, it had been reshaped by the same processes which have affected every landscape in this book.

This was a kind of human geology, a stone-like object, sourced from the earth, made by human beings, and transformed by erosion. It seemed at once the end and the beginning of landscape itself.

Acknowledgements

I would like to thank so many people. Above all, to my friends Ben Tarring of the *Observer* and Suke Wolton of St Cross College, Oxford, for being willing to read the whole manuscript through and comment on it; Professor Priscilla Grew of Lincoln College, Nebraska, and Professor Cornelius Gillen of Edinburgh University, for reading through the text from the perspective of professional geologists. I am hugely grateful to all for their time, patience and insights.

For assistance and advice, the librarians of the Geological Society of London, the Royal Society of Antiquaries of London; and Historic England, Swindon; Graeme Kirkham and Peter Herring for Bodmin moor; Samuel MacArthur for guiding my chisel over a lump of Bath Stone; James Dilley (www.ancientcraft.co.uk) for showing me copper smelting and flint knapping, Hugh Torrens; Andreas Campomar and Claire Chesser of Constable, for near-infinite patience; Simon Taylor of the University of Glasgow for information on Gaelic place-names; Margaret Wood for queries on Anglesey; Jonathon Wright on Clearwell caves (www.clearwellcaves.com); Adam Welfare for extra thoughts on recumbent stone circles; Ann Davies for telling me about the Landsker line; Anne F Harris for showing me her work on alabaster; the author of the BGS Mendips website. Prof Jane Geddes, University of Aberdeen, for correspondence RE Pictish symbol stones, and Nigel Ruckley, for general discussion of building stones of Scotland. Katy Whitaker kindly read my passage on sarsens. Phil Smith, author of *Living In The Magical Mode*, helped me to remember to drift. Various members of staff at the BGS, especially Luis Albornoz-Parra and Clive Auton, for helping me with the geology of the Caithness flags; Andy Farrant of the BGS; Patrick Cashman of the RSPB for talking to me about archaeology and nature on the chalk; Sarah Singleton. May Liu Cannon for the maths; Ann Liu Cannon for the songs; all my family for the company. Jamie Wright, David Cannon for deserted medieval villages.

Local guides were particularly helpful at Beer Quarry Caves (www.beerquarrycaves.co.uk), Cardiff Castle (www.cardiffcastle.com), Salford Lads Club (www.salfordladsclub.org.uk) and Llandudno Great Orme ancient copper mine (www.greatormemines.info). Members of the Facebook groups: Prehistoric Explorers Club, Prehistoric Society, Church Crawlers Anonymous, Churchcrawling. Welsh place names and Scottish place names provided ideas, information and 'watercooler moments' in a lonely calling. I particularly want to thank people I feel I know well but have never (or barely) met, such as Sean Bredin, Peter Slinger, Edmund Harris, Colin Smith, and Richard William Parker. Also to my dear friends Tony Lidington and Emma Potter, Simon Pascoe and Caitlin Easterby, James O. Davies, Robert Adams, Danny O'Donoghue and Rupert and Izzy Bound for good conversations and joint explorations.

David and Jez Dolan Martin twice put me up in Manchester. Gary and Georgina Bridgens offered a warm welcome and a private tour of Barrow-in-Furness; Esther Roberts and family gave me a welcome overnight on the Gwynedd coast. Many members of the Arts Society provided overnight accommodation associated with lectures, unwittingly facilitating explorations the day before or after; I'd particularly like to thank Lisa and Ian Henderson in Staffordshire and my host in Kendal for extended stays. Another kind host let me stay on in an Airbnb in Edinburgh when she heard I was an author; Marie Clausen and Chris Traynor generously let me overnight at their holiday accommodation in the Wye Valley. Wendy and Philip Wilby gave me a memorable night in a windmill on the Magnesian limestone edge; David McOmish and

Carenza Lewis provided two nights in Lincoln. Celia and Al Smith twice put me up in Forres, Morayshire; I'm especially grateful to Celia for driving me around the Black Isle and the Moray Firth. Various YHA managers found me an empty dorm when they saw I was a) knackered and b) carrying an office on my back while pushing a folding bike. David Cannon was great company on a trip to Kent.

To the thousands of geologists on whose research I have depended.

I should also thank the life-saving services, not to mention occasional plugs, WiFi and caffeine, provided by cafes everywhere, from ubiquitous Costa and Caffe Nero to happenstance facilities in various parts of the Highlands to independent cafes in Bristol, London, Lindisfarne and Edinburgh. And latterly, Dr Sarah Lowndes and Mr Merv Rees saved my life, as has my beloved Liu Hong.

Afterword

For most of our thirty-one years of marriage, you were journeying. Sometimes I was with you. Like that trip you took me across Britain, in your mother's car, when we first started dating. We were still two distinct, separate entities then, so I paid for the petrol. From Land's End to Butt of Lewis, you drove; you knew the land well, I could see that, especially religious buildings, and you were happiest taking me to a dark, secluded spot, sometimes to steal a kiss, but more often to point out a gargoyle, a ballflower, a graffiti mischievously left by a stonemason in far gone times . . . I realised, even then, that there would always be a third presence in our relationship – a special place.

Perhaps the seed for this book was planted even then?

With the publication of *Cathedral*, your identity as a writer was firmly established, as was your preferred state of being: journeying, alone. You were a restless soul and research trips for subsequent books took you across continents and oceans. But then, three girls and two more books later, the wanderlust was somehow sated. You grew fonder of home, and cycling all over the Downs near us.

I asked you: 'What next?'

'A book on stones, here in Britain.'

'Why stones?'

'I cannot explain, but you will see. It will be like nothing you've read before.'

So you started journeying again, alone; but unlike before, you were always in touch, and I could hear the pull of home in your voice, even as you relished the solitude of being on the road. Since presenting *How to Build a Cathedral*, you frequently gave lectures and led tours, and you combined these with researching for this book. The tours took you up and down the country, sometimes abroad. Ever the performer, you fondly called these your 'gigs'. From time to time, I joined you, occasionally the children, too. We were thrilled to gain access to inaccessible places: inside Stone Henge at dusk, when the tourists were gone; on the rooftop of Bristol Cathedral admiring the skylines of the magnificent city . . .

It was an exhausting, but fun and fulfilled life. You wrote to your heart's content, you met amazing people, and felt lucky. 'I have a vocation,' you said, 'and it's to do with places; with communicating, enthusing, analysing – in short – extollagising – about the nature of "old places", and what makes them tick.'

But the universe, apparently, had other plans. To your utter frustration, your body slowed you down. You were once again home bound. In the last few years I have enjoyed writing side by side with you, our eccentric Labradoodle by our feet. Right until the last day, even on the specially adapted hospice bed, you kept on writing, drawing, journeying in your head when your feet could no longer carry you.

Journeying as means and end.

You have reached the end. And leave us with this book.

I've read the draft twice now. I am no geologist, and English is not even my mother-tongue. So what I conclude, to the best of my ability, is this:

This book is a love poem.

Your love for me, for the girls, for your family and friends is embedded in this landscape. You love this land like no other. You love it through trying to understand it – so thoroughly, that to read it is to want to love it ourselves, as you so ardently do.

You write in such a way that time becomes both irrelevant and of the utmost importance.

You write it so that rocks have distinctive personalities. Precambrian rocks, 'at once very hard and very soft,' 'have a long mind'; clays 'have an unexpected intimacy about them'; Old Red Sandstones, 'the colour of blood' – representing grief – 'are suffused with a precious cosmopolitanism'. Portland stone 'embodies a kind of Englishness'; chalk, 'effectively made of bone', 'strikes a unique balance between the natural and the man-made, charging it with the presence of the creatures who have lived upon it'. And finally, 'There is no stone with quite the presence of a sarsen. Its preternatural density and inscrutability is almost an energy in its own right.'

You write in such a way that I feel as if I am in a Shakespearean play, that even as I cannot always grasp the fast moving plot, I am taken by the voice, which I trust and will follow anywhere, knowing instinctively that I will be rewarded with a good story. I was going to skip the chapter on flint and you got me hooked with one sentence – 'love child of Henry Moore and Salvador Dali'.

How can I not read on?

If we ever need a messenger to other species, to aliens on another planet, can you please be that person? Articulate, enthusiastic, considerate, and oh so good looking, you will be the perfect spokesperson to explain how our land and its people are formed.

As human beings, you believe we are 'brief bursts of Carbon-based energy', 'more substantial than cloud, less so than stone,' and that 'death is where people have always been most inevitably and profoundly connected to geology, reduced to dust, interred within the bones of the Earth, becoming a part of the place'.

You have now become part of the place, this place.

The same place where I will be with you again: cheek to cheek, bone to bone, rock to rock.

Here in the Marlborough Downs, we shall be chalk together.

Liu Hong

Like all unfinished works of art, this book owes its final completion to so many. In additional to Jon's original acknowledgement I should like to add my own heartfelt gratitude to the following:

Thank you, Little, Brown, for going ahead with the publication of the book. Thank you, Andreas Campomar, for being instrumental in commissioning the book and for keeping faith in Jon; thank you, Holly Blood, for your sympathetic and inspired editing.

Thank you, Simon Pascoe, for finishing the maps where Jon left out within tight deadlines and with painstaking care; thank you, Professor Cornelius Gillen for kindly stepping in at very short notice to approve the accuracy of the maps.

Thank you, James Davies, for your timely help with finalising the photographs and to ensure that the ones chosen for publication are of professional quality.

Thank you, Isabella Bound, for your endless patience and valuable advice on designs and layout.

And finally, thank you, Robbie Adams, for your ongoing support, friendship and words of wisdom.

Index